Anthropological Papers
Museum of Anthropology, University of Michigan
Number 97

I0378896

Culture Change in a Bedouin Tribe

The *'arab* al-Ḥğerāt, Lower Galilee, A.D. 1790–1977

by

Rohn Eloul

Ann Arbor, Michigan
2010

©2010 by the Regents of the University of Michigan
The Museum of Anthropology
All rights reserved

Printed in the United States of America
ISBN 978-0-915703-73-9

Cover design by Katherine Clahassey

The University of Michigan Museum of Anthropology currently publishes two monograph series, Anthropological Papers and Memoirs, as well as an electronic series in CD-ROM form. For a complete catalog, write to Museum of Anthropology Publications, University of Michigan, 4013 Museums Building, 1109 Geddes Avenue, Ann Arbor, MI 48109-1079, or see www.lsa.umich.edu/umma/publications.

Library of Congress Cataloging-in-Publication Data

Eloul, Rohn, 1945–
Culture change in a Bedouin tribe : the ‘arab al-Hgerat, Lower Galilee, A.D. 1790–1977 / by Rohn Eloul.
p. cm. -- (Anthropological papers ; no. 97)
Includes bibliographical references and index.
ISBN 978-0-915703-73-9 (alk. paper)
1. Bedouins--Israel--Galilee. 2. Hujayrat (Arab tribe) 3. Palestinian Arabs--Israel--Galilee. I. Title.
DS113.75.E48 2010
305.892'7205694509034--dc22
2010038107

The paper used in this publication meets the requirements of the ANSI Standard Z39.48-1984 (Permanence of Paper)

Front Cover: The author in front of tent, Bīr al-Maksūr, 1976.

Back Cover: Bīr al-Maksūr from the cemetery on the Mzyreh, 2009.

"The Study of Change . . .

is the study of survival."

Edward T. Hall
(1959:90)

Contents

List of Tables *viii*
List of Illustrations *ix*
List of Abbreviations *x*
Acknowledgments *xii*

Part I: Introduction and Background

Chapter 1. Introduction *3*

Chapter 2. Geographical and Historical Background *9*

Part II: The Ottoman Period (ca. 1790–1917)

Chapter 3. The Ottoman Period at Tel al-Šummām (ca. 1790–1870) *19*
- The Story of the Ḥğerāt's Origins *19*
- The Yearly Round at Tel al-Šummām *20*
- Ḥğeri Internal Organization *23*
- In Retrospect *26*

Chapter 4. The Ottoman Period at al-Ẓahara (ca. 1870–1917) *27*
- The Traditional Account of the Move to the Ẓahara *27*
- The Ẓahara *28*
- The Yearly Round in the Ẓahara *30*
- Regional Dynamics *31*
- Ḥğeri Land Acquisition *33*
- Ḥğeri House Construction *34*
- Ḥğeri Economics *35*
- Ḥğeri Demographic and Marriage Patterns *36*
- In Retrospect *40*

Part III: The British Mandate Period (ca. 1917–1947)

Chapter 5. The British Mandate Period (ca. 1917–1947) *43*
Some Historical Notes on the Rise of Palestinian Nationalism *43*
The Establishment of the Mukhtarship *45*
Ḥğeri Entry to Police Service *48*
Ḥğeri Population Count in the Early 1920s *50*
Land Registration and Economic Development in Palestine *51*
Ḥğeri Relations with Ṣafūriyeh *52*
The Purchase of the Lands of Bīr al-Maksūr *53*
The Beginnings of Ḥğeri Market Orientation *55*
The Ḥğerāt and the 1936–1939 Arab Rebellion *56*
The Yearly Round in the Ẓahara and Bīr al-Maksūr *59*
Ḥğeri Demographic Patterns during the Mandate Period *63*
Ḥğeri Marriage Patterns during the Mandate Period *64*
In Retrospect *67*

Part IV: The Israeli Period (1947–1977)

Chapter 6. The Military Government Era (1947–1966) *75*
The 1948 War and Its Aftermath *75*
The Early Years *78*
The Rise to Power of *ulād* Ḍiyab al-Ibrāhīm *81*
The Rise of Muḥammad al-Ḥsēn to Power *83*
Changes in the Ẓahara *85*
The Moving of the Tribal Center to Bīr al-Maksūr *89*

Chapter 7. Ḥğeri Economics *95*
Overview *95*
Wage Labor *100*
The Agricultural Sector *111*
The Herding Sector *123*
Characteristics of Ḥğeri Economic Adaptation *131*

Chapter 8. Bīr al-Maksūr *141*
Overview *141*
The Development of Bīr al-Maksūr *146*
Private Enterprise in the Village *149*
Maksurean Population Dynamics *152*

The Social Dimensions of the Village *162*
House Construction and Use *163*
Habitational Space Use *166*
Formal Education in Bīr al-Maksūr *169*
Education and Other Change Promoters *173*
Intergenerational Tensions as Agents of Culture Change *179*
The Marriage Pattern of Generations VII and VIII *188*

Chapter 9. Ḥğeri Politics *201*
The Segmentary Foundation of the Ḥğeri Judicial and Political Structure *201*
The Traditional Leadership: The *ḥatyariyyeh* *207*
The New Leadership: The Mukhtarship *216*
The 1977 National Elections *246*

Part V: Conclusions

Chapter 10. Epilogue *271*

Chapter 11. Conclusions *277*

Appendices

Appendix A. Patrilateral Genealogy of the *'arab* al-Ḥğerāt *286*
Appendix B. Estimated Land/Population Ratios *290*
Appendix C. Israel: Consumer Price Index (1948–1977) *291*
Appendix D. The 1975 Inventory of Store No. 1 *292*
Appendix E. Comparative Inventories of Stores Nos. 2 and 4 in 1975 *293*
Appendix F. The Population of Bīr al-Maksūr in 1961, 1972, and 1977 *295*
Appendix G. A Short History of the Sedentarization of the Bedouin in Israel *296*
Appendix H. Citizens' Complaint *299*
Appendix I. Minority Relations in Israel *300*
Appendix J. The *ṣulḥa* Agreement of Masarwah and Yūnis *302*
Appendix K. The Land Problem in the Negev *303*
Appendix L. Election Practices in the Arab Sector *304*

References *307*
Index *325*

Tables

1. Number of adult males of each subunit from Generation III to Generation V, *23*
2. The marriage pattern of Generation V by major categories, *37*
3. The marriage pattern of the fifth generation by lineage, *39*
4. Frequency of inter-tribal marriages of Generation V by lineage, *39*
5. Probabilities for having one wife or more among the Ḥğerāt of Generation VI, *49*
6. Average number of children among the Ḥğerāt of Generation VI, *49*
7. The temporal distribution of Generation VI marriages, *65*
8. The marriage pattern of Generation VI compared with that of Generation V, *65*
9. Comparison of generational distance of endogamous marriages, *65*
10. The marriages of Generation VI by lineage, *68*
11. Comparison of direction of marriages among the three lineages of the Ḥğerāt, *67*
12. Comparison between marriage patterns of Generations V and VI by lineage, *68*
13. Ḥğeri age structure, 1959 and 1964, *87*
14. The 1961 distribution of Ḥğeri population in its core settlements, *101*
15. Age distribution of Ḥğeris in the security forces in 1977 by branch, *106*
16. Distribution of the Ḥğeri active labor force by age group, *112*
17. Distribution of the Ḥğeri active labor force by lineage, *113*
18. Population of Bīr al-Maksūr by age and sex in 1961, 1972, and 1977, *153*
19. Comparative distribution of Maksurean family size, 1961 and 1977, *158*
20. Comparative household size distribution in 1961, 1972, and 1977, *161*
21. The educational level reached by Ḥğeris born 1940–1964, *170*
22. Differences among Ḥğeri sublineages in educational levels, *175*
23. Comparison of the marriage patterns of Generations IV–VIII, *189*
24. Marriage pattern of Generations VII and VIII by lineage affiliation, *193*
25. Marriage pattern summary, *195*
26. Arab sector support for *MaPaI* and its successors, *238*
27. Israeli Arab membership in *MaQI*, *238*
28. Israeli Arab membership in *RaQaH*, *238*
29. Vote for *RaQaH* in the Arab sector, *238*
30. Parliamentary election results of the *‘arab* al-Ḥğerāt, 1951–1977, by lineage, *249*
31. Comparative voting participation of the Ḥğerāt, the Arab sector, and the national average 1949-1977, *305*

Illustrations

Maps

1. Ḥĝeri settlements and camps, *7*
2. The Galilee, *10*
3. The Galilee in the late eighteenth century, *21*
4. The Galilee in the late nineteenth century, *29*
5. The Galilee during the Mandate Period, *47*
6. The Ẓahara in 1968, *86*
7. The Galilee in the 1970s, *90*

Figures

1. The genealogical and sociopolitical structure of the *'arab* al-Ḥĝerāt, *8*
2. Traditional house construction, *35*
3a. The master plan of Bīr al-Maksūr, *144*
3b. Aerial view of Bīr al-Maksūr in 1975, *145*
3c. Bīr al-Maksūr in 1976, *146*
4. The population structure of Bīr al-Maksūr, *154*
5. Frequency distribution of family sizes (1961 and 1977), *159*
6. A schematic development of a house, *165*
7. The "core" Council, *208*
8. The mukhtarship, *232*
9. Aerial view of Bīr al-Maksūr council area, 2007, *274*
10. Bīr al-Maksūr in 2009, *275*

List of Abbreviations

ABL: Arabic Bedouin List
B-Z Exchange: Brother-Sister Exchange
BAAA: Bureau of the Advisor on Arab Affairs
CBS: Central Bureau of Statistics
CPI: Consumer Price Index
DaSh: Democratic Movement for Change
DMP: Domestic Mode of Production
F: Father
FB: Father's Brother
FBD/S: Father's Brother's Daughter/Son
FZ: Father's Sister
G.: Generation
G.B. Col.: Great Britain. Colonial Office
G.B. Col. R.: Great Britain. Colonial Office, Report
G.B. Com.: Great Britain. Commission on Palestine
G.B. Naval: Great Britain. Admiralty—Naval Intelligence
G.B. Par.: Great Britain. Parliament
G.B. Pls.: Great Britain. Palestine Royal Commission
HH: Household
ID: Identity (Card)
IDA: Israel Defense Army (*TzaHaL*)
IEC: Israel Electric Corporation
I£: Israeli *Lirôt* (sing. *Lirah*)
ILA: Israel Land Administration
Isr. CBS: Israel. Central Bureau of Statistics
Isr. CBS Abs.: Israel. Central Bureau of Statistics, Statistical Abstracts
Isr. IGE: Israel. Inspector General of Elections
Isr. Laws: Israel. Laws of the State of Israel
Isr. MI: Israel. Ministry of Information
Isr. Survey: Israel. Survey of Israel
JNF: Jewish National Fund
E£: Egyptian Pounds
MafDaL: National Religious Party
MaPaI: Israel Workers Party
MaPaM: United Workers Party
MaQI: Communist Party of Israel
MBD: Mother's Brother's Daughter

MG: Military Government
MK: Member of Knesset
MB: Mother's Brother
MBr: Minorities' Brigade
MU: Minorities' Unit
NA: Not Available/Applicable
NCO: Non-commissioned Officer
NRA: Nature Reserves Authority
NSBC: Northern Supreme Bedouin Committee
OETA: Occupied Enemy Territory Administration
PD: Progress and Development List
PEF: Palestine Exploration Fund
PJCA: Palestine Jewish Colonization Association
PLO: Palestine Liberation Organization
P£: Palestinian Pounds
Pls. Gov.: Palestine. Government of Palestine
Pls. Survey: Palestine. Survey of Palestine
PRA: Palestine Rescue Army
RaFI: Israel Workers List
RaQaH: New Communist List
SSBC: Southern Supreme Bedouin Committee
UAL: United Arab List

Acknowledgments

The ideas and data forming the basis of this book were originally researched, gathered, and formed as part of the requirements for a Ph.D. in Anthropology at the University of Michigan in 1982. In the original work, "Culture Change in a Bedouin Tribe: An Ethnographic History of the *'arab* al-Ḥğerāt, Lower Galilee, Israel ca. A.D. 1790–1977," I experimented with ways to represent in writing several interdependent layers of cultural complexity: individual, tribe, state, and world. To re-work the original document for publication as a book at that time would have required the motivation of an academic appointment in anthropology, which, at that period, was not in my stars. It was Henry T. Wright III, archaeologist extraordinaire and old friend, who persuaded me to re-conceive the document and some subsequent research now, for its own sake. That this book is available, therefore, owes a debt of gratitude to Henry. I would like to thank my wife Meg who helped edit the original text and continued to provided support and encouragement in recent times while I was wandering around the house wondering which parts to keep, which to discard, and how to shape the new work. I will always owe a great deal to the remarkable people I acknowledged in my dissertation including Giora Zaïd and Oded Yanai (who were not mentioned before in order to protect their identity) and always, above all, to the *'arab* al-Ḥğerāt whose generosity with their time, insight, hospitality, and friendship enriched my life and made my study not only possible but meaningful. I also owe deep gratitude to Jill Rheinheimer, who edited this volume with humor, efficiency, and exactitude, catching my many mistakes, and to Kay Clahassey, who designed the eye-catching cover.

Finally, any remaining mistake, oversight, or error is naturally my own.

PART I

Introduction and Background

— I —

Introduction

This monograph details the ethnographic history (ca. A.D. 1790 to 1977) of the *'arab* al-Ḥğerāt, a bedouin tribe in the Lower Galilee, Israel, and approaches culture change as a continuous dynamic and interactive set of processes. Although the analysis of change has been of general interest to me, this study's emphasis on process arose from the character of the field data. Thus, an initial interest in the effects of sedentarization on a previously short-range nomadic tribe expanded when data from the field convinced me that to adequately understand these effects, they must be set in the tribe's historical context and within its sociopolitical environment, and, further, that the history must be analyzed and presented as a process rather than as a two-dimensional backdrop to the ethnographic present.

Originally, my idea was to look at the effects of sedentarization as a two-part case study of culture change, the first part being the impact of changing economy on the sociopolitical and ideological organization of a previously semi-nomadic pastoral tribe, and the second being that tribe's political adaptation to state control. I chose Israel as the site of study because it best met my requirements in several ways. First, sedentarization had been going on in the Ottoman province (*vilāyet*) of Beirut/Palestine/Israel for over half a century so its effects were not new and could be observed with some confidence. Second, and connectedly, the various regimes that controlled the area during the twentieth century were able to maintain a situation in which sedentarization was the most viable alternative available to many of the local tribes.

The Ḥğerāt seemed attractive and singular on several counts. They owned a relatively large tract of communally owned (*muša'*) registered land plus several registered private landholdings. They had been involved with house construction since the turn of the twentieth century. And unlike most bedouin tribes in Israel, they were not heavily traumatized by the 1948 War—they had only four members in refugee camps (two women who followed their non-Ḥğeri husbands and two young men who ran away after 1950) and by 1975, two of these (a widow and one of the men) were back in the tribe—nor did they lose their communal land. Consequently, the process of their sedentarization was uninterrupted. Moreover, their *muḫtār* (village headman), who oversaw the post-1949 continuity of Ḥğeri development, had risen from a tribal to a regional leader, thereby providing a case study for the operation of a "power-broker" and of a patron. The Ḥğerāt were thus a thriving society that provided a good case study for investigating culture change as an uninterrupted adaptation; through the study of the Ḥğerāt, one could hope to isolate a few of the major mechanisms that are associated with this process, and shed light on other topics of theoretical interest (such as ethnicity, patronage, cultural brokership, and the like).

During the fieldwork period (August 1975–July 1977), I established my base at the house of the *muḫtār* (who preferred living in his tent) in Bīr al-Maksūr (the tribe's main settlement) and was adopted by the families of two of his brothers, who cared for me as one of their own. After a period of adjustment, during which I studied the village, I ranged to the other settlements and camps of the Ḥğerāt in my quest for data. Throughout this period, I found myself a welcomed member or guest (depending on the degree of my acceptance) in every Ḥğeri quarter, and most Ḥğeris were cooperative and willing informants. For them, the importance of my work lay in its historical aspect—preserving their factual heritage, which was being gradually forgotten. It was clear to me, too, that although at the time the Ḥğerāt were the largest and most important of the tribes in the region, they had risen to this status within the memory of their middle-aged members. I thus realized that to describe the Ḥğerāt in the ethnographic present would, from the Ḥğeri point of view, deprive them of their history and their adaptive achievement, while from the ethnological perspective, it would provide a static display of a dynamic social reality.

In addition to the historical dimension, I became aware of the high degree of interaction that has existed between the tribe and its sociopolitical environment throughout its history, and which has affected the fortunes of the Ḥğerāt as a society. The importance of this aspect of the data increased proportionally as my attempts to understand and explain the *'arab* al-Ḥğerāt at different periods of its evolution progressed. I was led, therefore, to partially portray and explain the larger milieus within which the tribe has lived in different times. Although these forays might seem to lie outside the domain of orthodox ethnographic description, I believe that without them, it would be difficult to demonstrate that the adaptation of the Ḥğerāt to their environment has been an interactive rather than a passive process.

It was thus that the idea of writing an ethnographic history began to take shape. The maturity of this idea, however, came only after my return from the field to Ann Arbor. It occurred to me that since what I was dealing with was change, it would be only appropriate to adopt a form that would correspond to the content—that is, an ethnographic history. Second, I found that in order to project the complexity of an adapting, or viable, system such as a human society, while describing the causes for change in its existence, I needed to provided a very detailed account of its past. My decision to provide these details in a high-content description was governed by two additional reasons. First, I have tried to immerse the reader in the complexity of the phenomena on a somewhat experiential basis. That is, whereas applying critical judgment to each set of details proves informative, absorbing several such sets will hopefully blur the detail of each and leave just an image of what it is like to operate in the milieu within which the Ḥğerāt operate. Second, my own theoretical bias might be described as "social cybernetics" of the Stafford Beer variety (e.g., 1972, 1974, 1975). As such, I see these details as a necessary item if one is interested in a working model of the *'arab* al-Ḥğerāt.

Structurally, following my perception of human societies as multidimensional viable systems, this monograph portrays Ḥğeri history and adaptation as a multi-stranded time-related "braid." The "braid" is organized so that now one "strand" (e.g., regional competition) generates more change, thus propelling the "braid" in one direction, and then another "strand" (e.g., land acquisition) takes over as the major effector, thereby modifying the original direction. I then take advantage of such major change generating dimensions to discuss the traditional ethnological categories (e.g., economics, politics) and descriptions. Nonetheless, I would like the reader to perceive these traditional categories as time-related dimensions of Ḥğeri culture and not as independent entities that govern Ḥğeri structure. To provide a complete sense of the interrelatedness of these various "strands" or dimensions, I have tried whenever possible to point to secondary sources and targets of change that were related to the instance in question.

The result of this approach was to divide the work according to the major periods in the life of the *'arab* al-Ḥğerāt. Thus, Chapter 2 provides a historical background of the region that traces the development of some of the more important processes in the Galilee that affected the Ḥğerāt's evolution. Chapters 3 through 9 present the four major time divisions of the work:

(1) Ottoman Period at Tel al-Šummām (Tel Šem): ca. 1790–ca. 1870
(2) Ottoman Period at al-Ẓahara (Yodfāt): ca. 1870–1917
(3) British Mandate Period: 1917–1947
(4) Israeli Period: 1947–1977

Chapter 10 (Epilogue) summarizes changes that have occurred since 1977, and Chapter 11 (Conclusions) summarizes the broad changes in the life of the Ḥğerāt and provides a discussion of culture change and its mechanisms.

Within this time framework, the narrative alternates between detailed historical accounts of specific developments and more general ethnographic descriptions of Ḥğeri lifestyles and customs. Change generating events are thus woven into the traditional milieu of Ḥğeri life. Although this approach may cause uneven reading, I hope it will help portray Ḥğeri life in the various periods more accurately.

In transliteration I followed the DIN 31635 standard. In recording names, sayings, and other items in Arabic, I followed the Ḥğeri dialect whenever it differed from standard Arabic. Thus, for example, the Ḥğerāt replace *q* with *g*—as in *ḥagg* (law) instead of *ḥaqq* and *gahawah* (coffee) instead of *qahawah*—and often replace the *k* with <u>ch</u> (a hard *ch* like in /<u>ch</u>air/) and say *dab<u>ch</u>ah* (a dance) instead of *dabkah* or ask *kif ḥali<u>ch</u>?* (how are you? [feminine form]) instead of *kif ḥalik?* (although they pronounce *kif ḥalak?* in the masculine form). Similarly, they often convert /__ah/ and /i/ to /__eh/ and /e/ and although the standard written form of their name is *al-ḥuğeyrāt*, they pronounce it *al-ḥğerāt* and *ḥğeri*, and so I recorded it. Finally, although the common English rendition of /*'arab*/ is /Arab/, to the Ḥğerāt there is a big difference between these two forms: *'arab* = bedouin while "Arab" is a term that appeared only post-World War I during the drive for nation states in the region and includes peasants and city dwellers as well. Hence, I preserved the bedouin designation in their name and refer to them as the *'arab* al-Ḥğerāt.

Throughout the work I have quoted informants who spoke Arabic, Hebrew, or both. I took the liberty of translating their statements into English and provided the transliterated phrase only when it was a saying or an expression whose ethnolinguistic flavor would have lost some in the translation. I hope I did them justice. I also translated many of the Hebrew literary sources quoted in this work and, hence, unless accredited, the translation was done by me, and I am responsible for any errors.

In order to avoid the inexact usage of ethnological terms such as "maximal," "major," "minor," and "minimal lineages" (Evans-Prichard 1940:6) because their basic unit—the minimal lineage—is "three to six, generally four to five, steps in ascent from the present day" (Evans-Prichard 1940:199), I use the number of recognized generations to the apical ancestor at the last day of my fieldwork (July 29, 1977). Thus, "Generation IV" (or "G. IV") refers to the fourth generation from the tribe's founder.

Since government institutions, personnel, and their publications usually carry long names or titles whose repeated use would have been cumbersome and wasteful, I used abbreviations (and acronyms in the case of the Israeli political parties) whenever possible. Save for reference sources that always appear in their abbreviated form, after the first mention of a title or a name I added its abbreviation (or acronym) in parentheses and thereafter used the abbreviation rather than the full name. A listing of these abbreviations and acronyms can be found in the List of Abbreviations.

Finally, since the ethnographic history of the Ḥğerāt "begins at the beginning" (that is, in the last quarter of the eighteenth century when the founding fathers of the tribe arrived in the area), a few introductory notes are warranted to provide the reader with a frame of reference to facilitate following the story of their evolution. These notes predominantly describe the Ḥğerāt as they were in 1977.

In the traditional anthropological parlance, the Ḥğerāt are a patrilineal, patrilocal, Sunni Moslem bedouin tribe employing bifurcate collateral kinship terminology and segmentary lineage sociopolitical organization. Their history extends over a period of about two hundred years during which they shifted the tribal center three times and transformed from semi-nomadic sheep, goat, and cattle herders to sedentarized households involved in mixed agriculture, herding, and wage labor. Their first center was established toward the end of the eighteenth century by their founding fathers who constituted some three to five households near Tel al-Šummām (Tel Šem in Hebrew), where they remained until the Ottoman authorities tightened their control over the area. They moved, then, about 1870, to the Ẓahara, a mountainous and relatively inaccessible area. From there they spread to their present settlements, the larger of which, Bīr al-Maksūr, became their new tribal center during the 1960s.

By 1977, they were the largest and most influential bedouin tribe in the Galilee and numbered some 3400 individuals. These resided in three tribal settlements (Bīr al-Maksūr, al-Mikmān, and al-Ḏmeydeh); in two subdivisions (one of the nearby town of Shfar'am [Šfā'amr in Arabic] and the other of the nearby village of 'Uzeyr); in three permanent

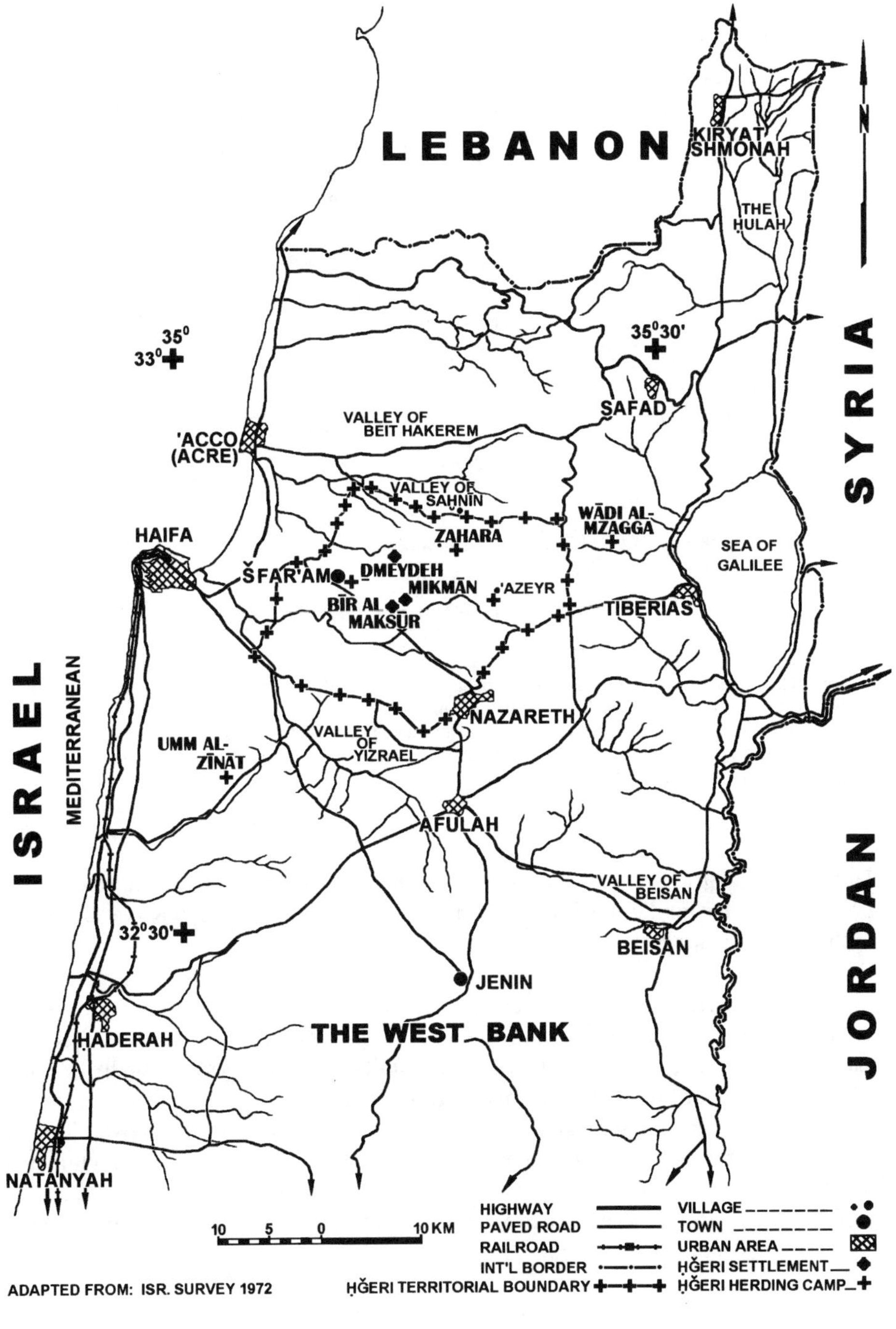

Map 1. Ḥğeri settlements and camps.

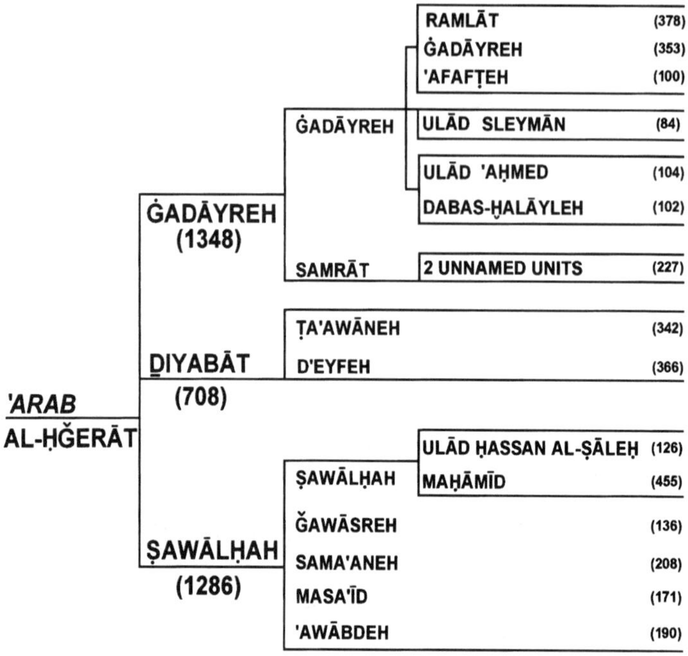

Figure 1. The genealogical and sociopolitical structure of the *'arab* al-Ḥğerāt. The figures in parentheses refer to the total number of persons in each tribal subunit in June 1977 and are based on a household census. It should be noted, however, that several single families were not enumerated and that due to fecundity and the duration of the census taking, some babies were not counted. The numbers quoted, thus, somewhat underrepresent the actual tribe's population size at that date.

herding camps (in al-Ẓahara, *wādi* al-Mzagga, and Umm al-Zīnāt); and as isolated households all over the northern half of Israel, from Haderah in the south to Kiryat Shmonah in the north (see Map 1).

Genealogically and sociopolitically, the Ḥğerāt are divided into three major lineages, or *ḥama'il* (sing. *ḥamūleh*): the Ġadāyreh, who lead the tribe; the Ḏiyabāt, who are allied with the former; and the Ṣawālḥah, who are in segmentary opposition to the first two. Each of these is subdivided into smaller named units that may be further subdivided into subunits, which may or may not be named (see Figure 1).

Finally, the Ḥğerāt have valued their unity and common concerns above all other interests. It is precisely this sentiment, a consequence of their segmentary structure and ideology, that has underwritten their ability to rise to their present regional status and is, therefore, important to remember. Most other aspects of their culture have been changing as if obeying Heraclitus' dictum:

> Upon those who step into the same rivers
> different and ever different waters flow down.

— 2 —

Geographical and Historical Background

The Lower Galilee, where the *'arab* al-Ḥğerāt has lived since the arrival of this tribe's founding fathers, is a region of valleys and ridges. Its borders are the Mediterranean Coastal Plain in the west; the Jordan Rift Valley to the east; the southern edge of the Valley of Yizra'el in the south; and the northern edge of the Valley of Beit ha-Kerem in the north (see Map 2). North of the Valley of Beit ha-Kerem lies the Upper Galilee, a mountainous region about 600 m higher than the Lower Galilee. The Lower Galilee, together with the Coastal Plain and the Jordan Valley, encompasses more than 2000 km^2. The average height of the mountains of this region is about 500 m above sea level, and the highest summit (Mt. Kamon) reaches 598 m. The valleys between the mountain ridges accentuate their relative height and degree of steepness. Thus, for example, Mt. 'Atzmon (547.8 m) rises almost 400 m above the floor of the Valley of Beit Netofah within a distance of 1.2 km; although not the highest peak in its range, it has been described as "the most conspicuous point on this range" (Conder and Kitchner 1881:262).

Historically, only one major road traversed the Lower Galilee: the northeast extension of the *Via Maris*. This ancient road comes from the Sharon through Naḥal 'Iron (*wādi 'ara*) eastward along the Valley of Yizra'el, turns northward in the Jordan Valley, and turns again northeast toward Damascus. The two other roads of regional importance were the Acre-Safad and the Acre-Nazareth roads. The former passed through the Valley of Beit ha-Kerem (*sahel beyt kārem*) and delineated the northern boundary of the region. The latter passed through the Valley of Beit Netofah (*sahel baṭṭūf*) and had a southward extension that connected Shfar'am (Šfā'amr) to Acre and Nazareth. The layout of the regional roads left the area between the Valley of Beit Netofah and the Valley of Beit ha-Kerem in relative isolation, and removed from direct administrative control, in spite of its proximity to Acre and Nazareth. By 1917 the northeast extension of the *Via Maris*, with

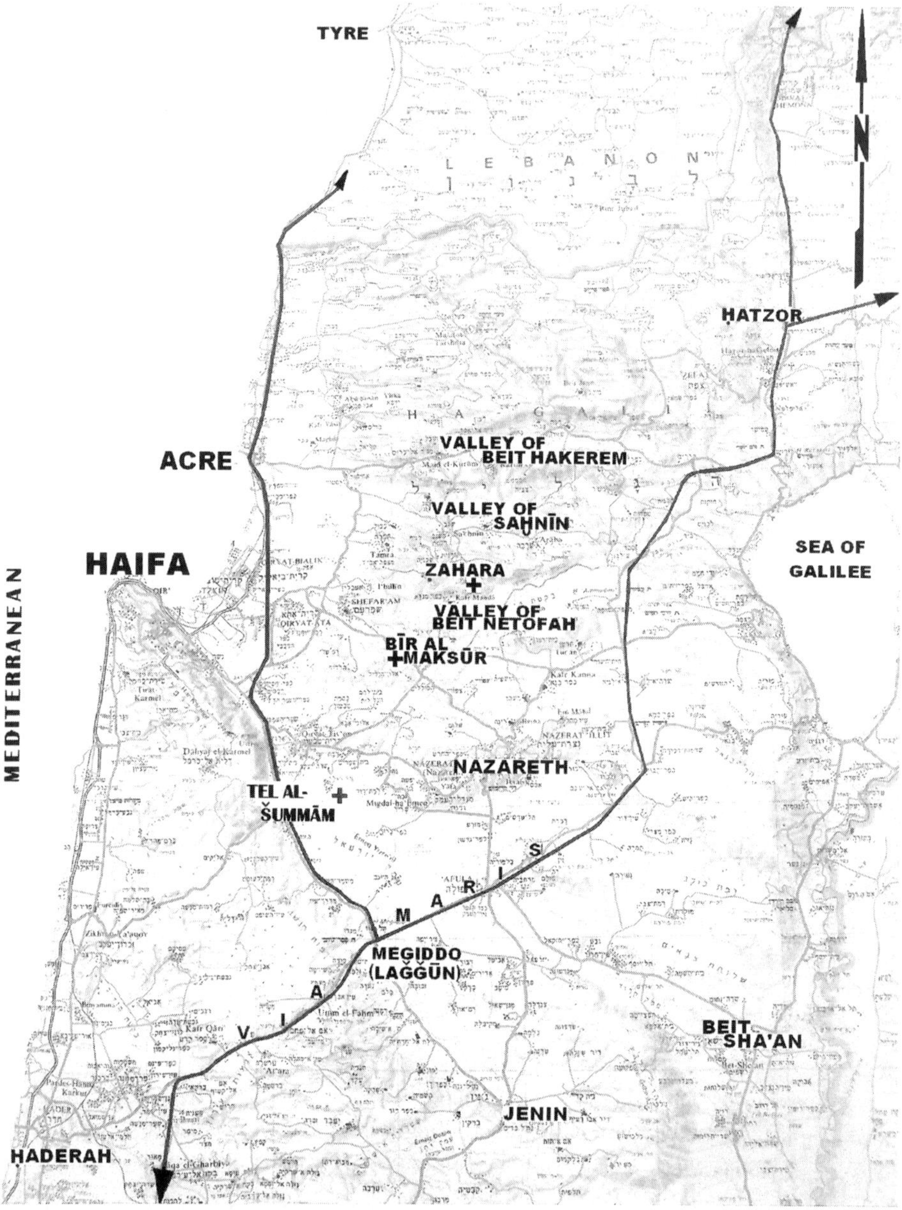

ADAPTED FROM: ISR. SURVEY 1972

Map 2. The Galilee.

some modifications, was paved and passable all year round, connecting Haifa, Nazareth, and Tiberias. In the vicinity of this road passed the western extension of the Damascus-Hejaz railroad tracks, completed in 1905 (Sawwaf 1938:315–16), and connecting Haifa with Hamma in Syria. The Acre-Nazareth road was still a dirt road passable only during the dry season. In the early 1930s, the Mandate Government paved the Acre-Safad as well as the Beisan-Tiberias-Metullah roads. Yet, no paved road passed between the Acre-Nazareth and the Acre-Safad roads, so that the Yotvat mountain range, where most of the Ḥǧerāt lived at the time, remained in relative isolation (see Map 2).

Prior to and during the nineteenth century, several factors that would impact the evolution and adaptation of the Ḥǧerāt could already be discerned. First and foremost among these was the presence of bedouin in the Galilee. Other factors include the decline in rural population density, which enabled the Galilean bedouin tribes to acquire agricultural land; the development of the Galilean pluralistic society with its concurrent factionalism, rivalries, and animosities (creating a dependence on higher level administration to buffer and keep them apart as well as providing a fertile field for mediators); and increasingly tightened administrative control from the end of the Ottoman Period through the British Mandate Period to the present.

The Lower Galilee, and especially the alluvial soils of its valleys' bottom-lands, is a fertile region that can support a dense population. To do so, however, the region has to be administered by a stable, strong political authority that encourages dense rural population and keeps the pastoral bedouin tribes from encroaching on the cultivated land. The interest of the Byzantine emperors in the Holy Land and the defense requirements of the Empire provided an impetus for such authority. Consequently, Palestine's total population in the Byzantine Period was estimated at several million people (Sharon 1976:15). The replacement of the Byzantine administration by the Umayyad administration in Damascus had little effect on the region. However, the Abbasid transfer of their capital from Damascus to Baghdad in A.D. 763 "lessen[ed] the interest and weakened the influence of the central imperial government in the Mediterranean provinces" (Lewis 1970:177). With reduced administrative efficacy in Palestine, the rural population began to decline. Lack of interest in maintaining waterworks and the absence of more than a minimal military force in an area that was no longer a border province enabled the bedouin tribes east of the Jordan to invade the agricultural west, thereby accelerating the deterioration of the rural areas. Bedouin penetration of western Palestine peaked in the eleventh century when smaller tribes were pushed northward due to the mass migration of the Banū Hilāl and Banū Sulaym westward via the Negev, Sinai, and Lower Egypt to North Africa (Sharon 1976:24–25). As the bedouin gained increasingly freer access to western Palestine, the sedentary population density declined and agriculturalists retreated into the mountainous regions of the country, ceasing to cultivate those lands that were "beyond a daily reach of the mother village" (Amiran 1953:72). In addition to the bedouin and administrative mismanagement, several natural disasters such as earthquakes, droughts, and epidemics destroyed the urban centers and reduced the population even further. This process was then aggravated by emigration to centers of trade and political power outside the province (Sharon 1976:25–26). A measure of the decline of the sedentary population in the province can be appreciated by comparing the estimated population size during the Byzantine Period (see above) with that of the first Ottoman tax register (*daftar-i mufaṣṣal* of 932 A.H. or 1525/26 A.D.) from the sixteenth century. According to the register, there were only "some 45–50,000 households, probably about 300,000 souls" in Palestine (Lewis 1954:475; see also Hütteroth and Abdulfatah 1977:43).

The Ottomans, who took control of Palestine in A.D. 1516, did little, if anything, to improve the administrative management of the province and did not succeed in containing the bedouin during the first 350 years of their rule of the country. Being occupied in Europe and the eastern provinces of their empire, they could spare neither the army needed to control the bedouin nor the resources needed to manage *vilāyet* of Bayrūt (as the country west of Jordan became known). In fact, the opposite was the rule. They tried to change the status quo in their provinces' internal affairs as little as possible so long as the Imperial Court (or "the Sublime Porte") in Istanbul was recognized as the supreme authority in the empire (cf. Finn 1878[I]:220). In accordance with this policy, Süleymān I (*al-qanūni*, the lawgiver) established a Civil Code (*qānūnnāme*) for each province separately rather than for the empire as a whole (Ma'oz 1969:20). In line with its policy of minimal intervention, the Porte also attempted to prevent its appointed provincial governors from gaining too much local support, which might enable them to revolt and form independent political entities (cf. Volney 1798[II]:228–29). To do so, the Porte employed a method of rapid succession of these governors who were thus prevented from entrenching in their provinces, but which, at the same time, was "a sure sign of slackening authority" (Lewis 1970:177). For example, during the first 180 years of Ottoman rule in Syria and Palestine, 133 governors manned the post in Damascus and only 33 of them served for two years or more in that capacity (Ma'oz 1969:13).

In addition to its political advantages, the rapid turnover of governors provided the Porte with substantial income because each of these officials bought his administrative post. The practice, however, aggravated the lot of the peasantry as each governor in his turn attempted both to reimburse himself for the price of the office and to increase his personal fortune by levying taxes and bribes on the local population as rapidly as he could (cf. Volney 1798[II]:226). The effect of these gubernatorial efforts was the continuous decline in rural population. The changes in the Ottoman taxation policies from feudal to tax farming in the seventeenth and eighteenth centuries (Ma'oz 1969:18–19; Baer 1971:11–13; Cohen and Lewis 1978:43–44) did not change this demographic trend. On the contrary, the decline in rural population density continued, as peasants preferred to abandon their land rather than pay one-half to two-thirds of their crops in taxes (Ma'oz 1969:18–19).

A second aspect of the Ottoman minimal intervention policy was the use of "divide and rule," both among the centrally appointed officials (Ma'oz 1969:30; Cohen 1973:54) and among strong local leaders, be they bedouin, Druze, or indigenous landowners (e.g., Volney 1798[II]:60; Finn 1878[I]:219–28). Due to the inability of the Porte to control either the mountainous regions, where the Druze and strong landowning families resided, or the desert territories, where the bedouin held sway, local leaders were often appointed as "*sanğaq bey*," that is, district governors (Ma'oz 1969:30; Sharon 1975:24–26), and were played against each other to keep them from becoming too independent (Abir 1975:285; e.g., Finn 1878[I]:296). Nevertheless, the more talented among these local leaders were often able to create de facto independent political entities and to give only nominal recognition, at best, to the supremacy of the Porte. It was primarily during the reign of such local leaders or dynasties—such as the Ṭurabāy of *sanǧaq* of *laǧǧūn* (Sharon 1975:26–30), Faḥr al-Din II of Mt. Lebanon (Gichon 1969:78–79), and Ẓāhir al-ʿUmar of the Galilee (Volney 1798[II]:57–85; Heyd 1942; Cohen 1973:7–19, 30–53, 83–92)—that the regions under their rule experienced some degree of civil order and economic prosperity. These short periods, however, were far from tranquil because each of these leaders had to defend his domain against contenders backed by the Porte. As a result, devastation of the countryside and a general decline of the rural population—so well documented in the travelogues of eighteenth- and nineteenth-century travelers such as Volney (1798), Badia y Leblich (1816), Buckingham (1821), and Burckhardt (1822)—continued, resulting in the emergence of uncultivated vacant areas between the contracting lands of the villages, which allowed for the infiltration of small bedouin tribes into these lacunae. The major effects of the Ottoman method of "divide and rule" were to maintain the country in a state of turmoil and to intensify traditional rivalries, create new ones, and emphasize distrust and political competition between local factions.

The first signs of change appeared with the conquest and occupation of Palestine and southern Syria by Ibrāhīm Pasha, son of Egypt's independent governor Muḥammad ʿAli, between 1831 and 1840. With the help of a large army estimated between some 35,000 (G.B. Naval 1920:168) and 60,000–90,000 troops (Maʿoz 1968:13), Ibrāhīm Pasha had an early success in pacifying much of the country. In particular, he succeeded in controlling and collecting taxes from the small bedouin tribes in the area (Maʿoz 1968:14). He also attempted to introduce modern agricultural techniques, similar to those introduced by Muḥammad ʿAli in Egypt, in order to encourage the cultivation of cash crops (especially cotton) for export purposes. He was not very successful in this endeavor, facing stiff local opposition that arose in response to his efficient taxation and conscription policies (Maʿoz 1968:16–17). Nevertheless, some interest in export production remained in the country after his withdrawal in 1840.

When the Porte regained control of southern Syria and Palestine in 1840, it attempted to implement the reforms of Sulṭan Abdulmajid that were decreed in the end of 1839 to preserve the integrity of the empire, which was threatened by the independent behavior of Muḥammad ʿAli. In order to curb Muḥammad ʿAli's aspirations, the Porte sought the support of the Western Christian powers. Consequently, the reforms included granting equality to non-Moslem residents of the Empire, particularly Christians, as well as reorganizing the Imperial administration and army, and establishing a policy for the control of the bedouin and similarly semiautonomous peoples. Ibrāhīm Pasha's retreat to Egypt, the antagonism that the endowment of equality to the non-Moslems aroused, and the revenue loss caused by some of the reforms brought these progressive efforts to a halt in 1841 (Maʿoz 1968:21–25; Horwitz 1957:501).

In 1856, however, Abdulmajid reinstituted the reforms in order to rally Western support against the Russian Empire—the Ottomans' foe in the Crimean War (1854–1856). The

Western Powers, especially England, were able thus to apply direct pressure and demand the equalization of the status of non-Moslems (Finn 1878[I]:223–24). While the reforms were slow to gain momentum, they nevertheless had two major effects on the Galilean population. The first was the increased control over the bedouin tribes, with a consequent gradual increase in rural population densities. The second (resulting from granting equality to the Christians) was the strong antagonism between Moslems and Christians, culminating in the 1860 massacre of Christians in Damascus—but which prepared the way for a pluralism based on equal access and hence competition for the favors of the administration, be it the British Mandate Government or its successor, the State of Israel.

The Ottoman policy toward the bedouin included several strategies: (a) using one tribe to contain the behavior of another; (b) forming and deploying a new army (the *Ardu* of Arabistan) to punish rebellious tribes; (c) fortifying and settling the desert fringe areas with peasants, particularly with Circassians (Caucasians) who were accomplished warriors, and (d) attempting to make the smaller bedouin tribes sedentary (Ma'oz 1968:48, 129–48; Ma'oz 1969:56; Smith 1975:93; Amiran 1953:253–54). None of these strategies was new in Ottoman administrative history; nonetheless, the systematic approach and the intense execution that the Porte adopted were quite novel. Success in implementing this policy was gradual, and only toward the end of the nineteenth and beginning of the twentieth centuries began to be apparent. Meanwhile, however, the larger bedouin tribes of trans-Jordan continued to raid western Palestine (e.g., Conder 1889a:295), and the Galilee was ruled, for all practical purposes, by 'Aqīl Aga of the Hanādi tribe until his death in 1870.

'Aqīl Aga's rule can serve as a good example of the state of affairs in the Galilee during the mid-nineteenth century (Ma'oz 1968:138–40; Ma'oz 1969:55; Sharon 1964:88–93). 'Aqīl was a descendant of the Hanādi tribe, the majority of whom arrived from Egypt in 1831 as part of Ibrāhīm Pasha's army and were used to control other bedouin tribes. Members of the tribe continued to arrive with their families during the next half century, and some served in 'Aḥmed al-Ğazzar Pasha's army when he became governor of *sanğaq* of 'Akā (Acre) in 1775. 'Aqīl rose to prominence as the head of the irregular cavalry in northern Palestine under Ibrāhīm Pasha. Later, he turned against Ibrāhīm Pasha, and when the Ottoman returned, he entered their service. He remained off and on in Ottoman employ until his death. When he became too strong—in the assessment of Ottoman officials—he would be dismissed; once dismissed, he would join a bedouin tribe in revolt and incite them to raid the Galilee (e.g., the Banū Saḫr in the mid-1840s), or incite a revolt himself (e.g., in 1854), at which point the administration would enlist him again. In short, "he threatened the government with the Bedouin and the Bedouin with the government" (Ma'oz 1968:140).

During 'Aqīl's reign, the Galilee was kept in relative peace and order. He took *ḫawa* (tribute, protection fees) from the peasants, but unlike tribes and leaders before him, he efficiently defended them from bedouin raids. Similarly, he protected local religious minorities, particularly the Christians during the riots of the 1850s and especially after the Damascus massacre of 1860 (Ma'oz 1968:139, 230; Sharon 1964:92). 'Aqīl's independence illustrates local variability in the success of the Ottoman policy to control the bedouin during the second half of the nineteenth century. The effects of this policy were nonetheless cumulative and by the beginning of the twentieth century, they facilitated the institution of "*pax britannica*," to use Amiran's (1953:255) term, during the British Mandate Period (1917–1948).

'Aqīl's benevolence toward the Christians points to another change. Regardless of whether it was a political tactic designed to reinforce his position vis-à-vis the Ottoman authorities (cf. Sharon 1964:93), or whether it was an integral part of his general policy of maintaining peace and order in his domain (the disruption of which might indicate weakness on his part), it points to the ever-increasing influence that the Christian Powers were exerting on the Porte in general, and in Palestine in particular. Growing Western influence at the Porte enabled the Western consuls to extend protection not only to local native communities and visitors, tourists, pilgrims, and scientists, but also to agricultural settlers such as the German Templars who arrived in 1869 and, after 1882, the first Jewish colonists (Smith 1975:93; Assaf 1967:9).

While the new cultivation methods introduced by these European agriculturalists were not adopted by the Arab rural population to any measurable degree (cf. Baer 1975:498), the country was drawn into some agricultural production for export. These exports, primarily cereals, lowered the nutritional standards of the rural population (Avitsur 1975:487) and induced the richer landowners and tax farmers to increase the collection of revenues. Between overtaxation, the bedouin, and natural disasters such as droughts, many peasants had to obtain loans at exorbitant rates in order to meet their expenses—loans that they could not repay. The peasant was thus left with two options: either to abandon the land, or to become a tenant on his own land and continue to cultivate it for a powerful landowner in return for relative security (Ma'oz 1968:161–62; Ma'oz 1969:56–57). As a result, the rich landowners grew richer while independent peasantry declined.

The process of increasing disparity between landowners and peasants was reinforced by the Ottoman Land Code of 1858, which required the registration of land in the owner's name. Many peasants did not register their land in order to avoid the taxation and conscription that resulted from land ownership; others did not register because they could not afford the registration fees. Similarly, many villages did not register their communal land (*muša'*) because the Land Code did not recognize collective ownership. Alternately, they would register the *muša'* in the name of a respected individual (Baer 1971:55). In that manner, "the basis for collective ownership of village lands (*muša'*) was being undermined, as this institution was becoming progressively more fictitious" (Avitsur 1975:494). At the same time, members of the important families in the region registered title in their names to land from which they had formerly only collected taxes (Porath 1971:11). Between them and the landless peasants, a new middle class of landowners was emerging. This middle peasantry was made up of successful peasants who could preserve their independence and buy out other peasants, and who were often those in whose name the *muša'* was registered.

The concentration of land in the hands of a few facilitated large-scale acquisition of land and the establishment of Jewish and Templar agricultural settlements, which paved the way for Jewish mass immigration. It also helped the smaller bedouin tribes to buy land when they no longer could acquire it by force, due to the increase in governmental control.

PART II

The Ottoman Period

(ca. 1790–1917)

— 3 —

The Ottoman Period at Tel al-Šummām

(ca. 1790–1870)

The Story of the Ḥğerāt's Origins

The Ḥğerāt trace their origin to the *'arab* al-Ḥağarah—a 300-tent section of the Bani 'Amr in 1925 (Oppenheim 1939:344)—from the Laǧa' in the Ḥūrān, Syria. According to tradition, their present number descended from two brothers, Baḥar and Sulṭan, who were banished for seven years from that tribe. Accompanied by their father, they moved west of the Jordan River, never to return. The reasons for their banishment are no longer remembered but are assumed to have been the result of some transgression of the Tribal Code (*ganūn al-'aša'īr*) that had to do either with the killing of a lineage member or with an affair with a wife or daughter of such a kinsman.

The "official" version relates that the two brothers and their dependents were nomads in Marğ ibn 'Amr (Valley of Jezreel) for several years. They finally established a permanent base in Tel al-Šummām (Tel Šem), 4.5 km southeast of the village of *šeyḫ* Abreyk (Ḥorvot Beit Še'arim) in the northwest section of that valley (see Map 3). These events can be estimated to have taken place toward the end of the eighteenth century (Eloul 1982:39, note 5).

Despite the apparent coherence of this account, the Ḥğerāt have more than one traditional version of their history, and at times neither the "official" nor the alternate versions adequately explain events in the tribe's history. In fact, most Ḥğeris know very little about their origins, and the amount and consistency of such knowledge is directly related to age. The version quoted above can be considered the "official" version, for this is the version of the elders of the Ġadāyreh lineage as recounted by the elder who was considered "the knowledgeable one" and who, accompanied by a friend, went to the Ḥūrān in the 1920s to corroborate the story with the Ḥağarah. The elders of the Ṣawālḥah have neither a unified version nor a knowledgeable elder. When I asked them for historical-genealogical details, they sent me to the elders of the Ġadāyreh. Besides the "official" version, one account, whose source was in the D'eyfeh, is of particular interest. According to this version, the three were not father and sons, but were brothers—Baḥar, who fathered the Ġadāyreh; Sulṭan, who fathered the Ṣawālḥah; and Ḏiyab, who fathered the Ḏiyabāt (to which the D'eyfeh belong)—and one of them was killed by the men of 'Aḥmed al-Ǧazzar (the butcher), the governor of *sanǧaq* of 'Akā (Acre) from 1776 to 1804. This last version is supported by a calculation of the generational depth of each of the current three lineages of the Ḥǧerāt separately (see Appendix A). It is also highly possible that the two brothers were accompanied by other close relatives (for example, first cousins) who, with the former, comprised a herding camp, and that one of them later became incorporated as a "father."

Similarly, the elders did not remember the specific cause for the exile, and were unable to ascertain the father's name on their trip to the Ḥūrān in the 1920s. They were, nevertheless, insistent on two points: (a) the two brothers were banished and (b) they were accompanied by their father, although his name is no longer remembered. It is notable that, as of the mid-1970s, the assumed offenses were the current transgressions that were punishable by banishment and, hence, could be a rationalization of the reasons for exile. Another possible explanation of the missing details is that the brothers were not exiled but left because of a quarrel or the threat of blood revenge in the same way others have left their lineage and tribe and attached themselves to the Ḥǧerāt more recently. If so, the reason for arguing exile over choice or escape could very well be an attempt to project a positive image. Quarrelsomeness, short temper, and fear are not respected qualities of the ideal bedouin character. Violence and the seduction of women, on the other hand, are accepted in the younger men as part of having "hot blood"—a desirable quality in the young. (For a similar story about the origin of the *'arab* al-'Adwān of Trans-Jordan, see Conder 1889a:291.)

The routines of life around Tel al-Šummām are no longer remembered. Nor, for that matter, are other stories about the founding fathers. Despite the paucity of detail in the traditional account, many general life patterns of the tribe as well as the origin of some of its current ideological and organizational characteristics can be reconstructed in order to gain a diachronic understanding of the adaptation and evolution of the *'arab* al-Ḥǧerāt.

The Yearly Round at Tel al-Šummām

Tel al-Šummām is an archaeological mound (cf. Conder and Kitchner 1881:353) located near the center of the northwest half of the Valley of Jezreel. The Tel was not far from the course of the Kishon River (*nahār al muquṭṭa'*) and its swamps (Conder and Kitchner 1881:265–66). It is very likely that the Kishon served as a partial barrier between the incipient tribe and the users of the Meggido (*laǧǧūn*)-Acre section of the *Via Maris*, specifically the army. Conder, for example, writes about his experience at the very beginning of the rainy season: "we crossed the Kishon and found by experience how treacherous are the banks of this apparently insignificant stream" (1878[I]:131). It is hard to ascertain today whether the Tel was also isolated on its northern and eastern sides at the close of the eighteenth century.

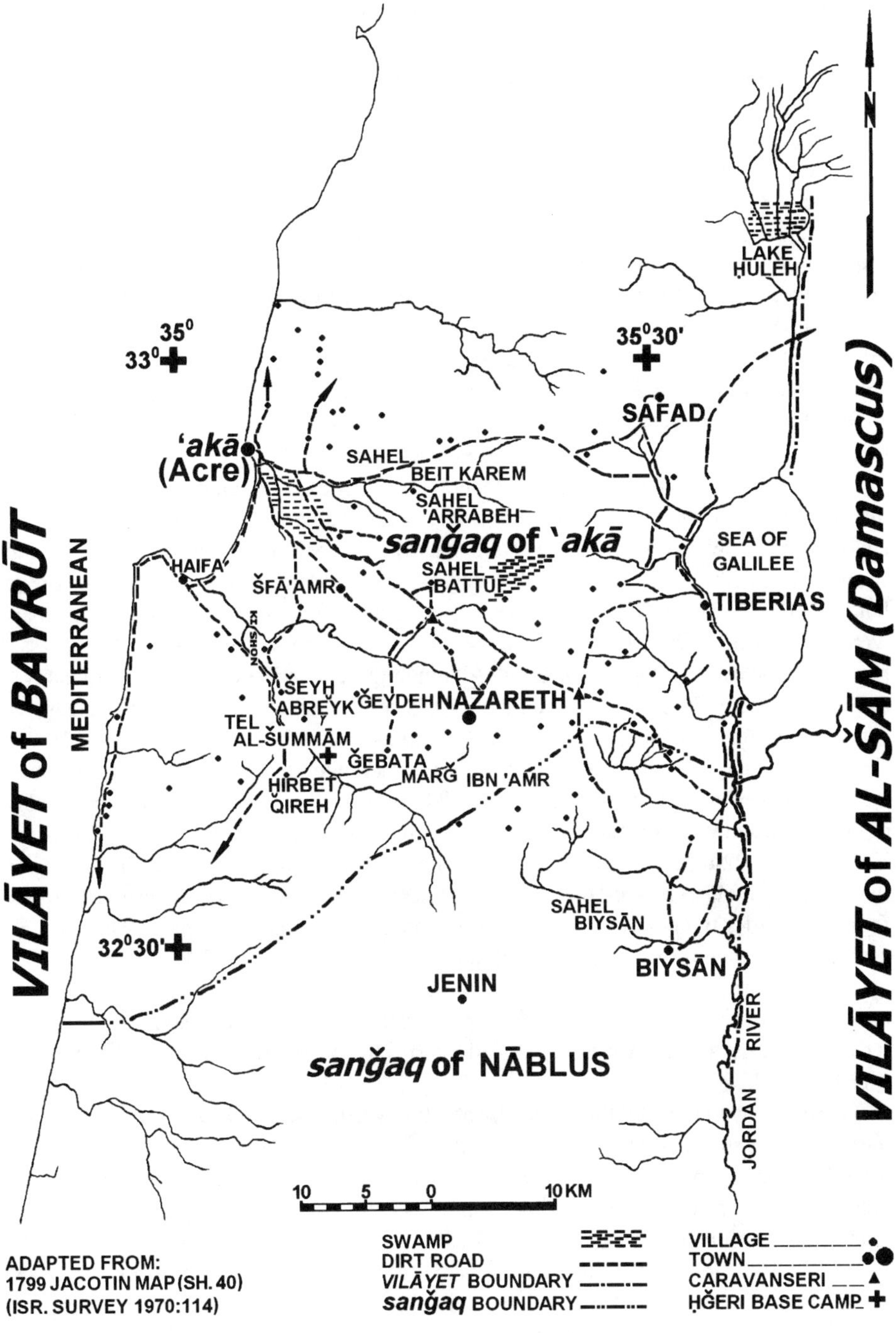

Map 3. The Galilee in the late eighteenth century.

Nevertheless, it seems to have provided a large measure of isolation for the developing tribe while being located in a well-watered, if swampy, fertile land. It thus answered the primary needs of the founding fathers at that time: maintaining their safety and independent existence.

The perennial water supply of the Kishon and its feeder spring, the highly fertile land of the Valley of Jezreel, and the proximity (about 5 km) of the Shfar'am Hills with their 40-mi^2 forest (Volney 1798[II]:140; Badia y Leblich 1816:252; Buckingham 1821:89; Conder and Kitchner 1881:252) of Tabor oak (*Querous ithaburensis*)-*Styrax officinalis* association and palatable annual grasses (Zohary 1962:94–96) provided for the needs of the Ḥğeri herds nearby. Like other small tribal fragments that filtered into the relatively deserted areas, the Ḥğerāt were surrounded by the older surviving villages (cf. Golani 1966:5; Sharon 1964:10). The modus vivendi that developed facilitated the transfer of ideas, customs, and technological information primarily from the sedentary population to the bedouin, and provided harvested land (sometimes preharvested fields) for pasture. Finally, the reference in Ḥğeri tradition to *owning* Tel al-Šummām suggests usufruct claims derived from some land cultivation, similar to other small tribes in the area (e.g., Conder and Kitchner 1882:74).

The Ḥğerāt, thus, present the same general character as other small tribal fragments at that time period in the Galilee and there is reason to assume that their life routines, herds, and migratory cycle were similar as well. Their herds are likely to have been small and composed of goats and sheep with a few cattle and some donkeys and camels as beasts of burden. These animals were of the stock common throughout the Middle East. The goats were of the black *ma'aze ğabalī* breed, the sheep usually the fat-tailed white *'awāsi* (Awassi) breed, and the cattle of the *baladi* breed. Although these breeds are not highly productive, and in the nineteenth century were diminutive in size (Conder 1878[II]:262), they are hardy and well adapted to the local climate, water, vegetation, and disease (cf. Hirsch 1933).

Most probably, the tribe spent the summer in the valley feeding the herds on stubble, either in their own fields or in those of the *fellāḥīn* (as well as invading unharvested fields of the latter), and keeping them near the water of the Kishon (e.g., Abramson 1937:212–13; Fleisher 1937:220–21). From the end of summer through fall they moved their herds to the Shfar'am Hills to pasture on undergrowth as well as on the trees themselves. About four weeks after the beginning of the rainy season in October/November, the dropping season commenced, marking the beginning of the third major division of the herding cycle—the spring. During the dropping season, the tribe probably used the caves and rock shelters that abound in the hills to protect the newborn lambs and kids from the weather. Finally, around April, they would return to the valley (e.g. Ashkenazi 1957:151; Fleisher 1937:220–21).

Due to the short range of this cycle, variability—whether in the whole or in its basic elements (namely time and/or location)—could be easily accommodated. Therefore, whether the Ḥğerāt began some cereal cultivation when they arrived at the Tel or whether they adopted the practice later, this activity could have been incorporated into the herding regime without many problems.

An additional resource in those days was the collection of wild edible plants by women and hunting by the men in an area teeming with different species of wild fowl, gazelles, rabbits, porcupine, and other edible animals (cf. Volney 1798[II]:140; Conder 1878[I]:163; also

G.B. Naval 1920:507). These activities provided much of the plant minerals and vitamins and some of the animal protein in their diet and did not interfere with the herding regime at all.

Ḥğeri Internal Organization

The three to five households that formed the original Ḥğeri camp did not allow for much organizational complexity. Nor was such complexity necessary a hundred years later when their camp numbered some thirty households. In general, consultations were open to all adult male members, although the final word was always that of the elders, one of which served as their leader and the spokesman for their lineage as a unit. As time passed and the lineage developed into a tribe, the Ḥğerāt increasingly exhibited a segmentary structure. Nevertheless, a very slow rate of growth enabled them to maintain and entrench the unity and cooperation that characterized their original camp, and which had made survival possible in a hostile environment in spite of their small numbers.

Another factor that helped maintain unity and favored consensus over coercion in decision-making was the relative interfamilial demographic balance in the number of males each subunit had, as Table 1 suggests. Since the Ṭa'awāneh have been traditionally more closely allied with the Ġadāyreh than with their sibling sublineage, the D'eyfeh (for instance, their marriage pattern from Generation V on, as discussed below), the latter most probably served as the balance that prevented one subunit's domination over the other two, if such balancing was necessary.

The emphasis on unity, cooperation, and negotiated solutions of conflicts reflected also on the male/female relations in the tribe. Ḥğeri females appear to have been freer than their *fellāḥīn* counterparts. First, it seems that the bedouin allowed their women more independence as long as they did not dishonor their families (e.g., cf. Conder 1878[II]:283; Abramson 1937:212–13 and Fleisher 1937:221–22 for the Turkoman of the Sharon; Mohsen 1967 for Awlad 'Ali of the Egyptian Western Desert; Dickson 1910:364 for Kurdish nomads in Kurdistan; Nelson 1973 for a general discussion). Second, when the labor force was small, women occasionally had to assume roles outside the usual sphere of women's roles (for example, coffee preparation or even as a proxy for the host until a male could be summoned). Third, while the period at Tel al-Šummām is all but forgotten, during the following period at the

Table 1. The number of adult males of each subunit from Generation III to Generation V (cases).

Generation	Ġadāyreh	Ṭa'awāneh	D'eyfeh	Ṣawālḥah
III	6	1	3	7
IV	10	4	7	17
V	26	13	18	39

Ẓahara, women were involved as proxies for their husbands in hospitality, ceremonial coffee preparation, and, covertly, in the political sphere. It is likely that such was the situation earlier.

Two major strategies can be discerned in Ḥğeri response to their sociopolitical environment: increasing their demographic weight, and employing aggressive and uncompromising responses to challenges from other groups in the area. Three tactics were used to bolster their number: absorbing new members, formal alliances, and inter-tribal marriage alliances.

Absorption was—and is—an extension of the bedouin tradition of hospitality. The Ḥğerāt simply received and helped individuals or small families that came to live with them. Often these individuals were given Ḥğeri wives and within three or four generations were absorbed into the tribe's genealogy as well. Such policy of absorption was not unique to the Ḥğerāt and was, in fact, quite common among both small and larger tribes (e.g., Shmueli 1970:31–33 for the Ta'amrah and 'Ubaydiyah of the Desert of Judea; Ashkenazi 1957:37; in regard to the general question of the purity of agnatic ideology, see Sahlins 1965). In the case of the Ḥğerāt, this practice is not only well documented in the tribe's genealogy but is still (as of the mid-1970s) practiced, although due to the shallow time depth, such individuals or small families have not yet been incorporated into the genealogy. As an example of genealogical absorption, consider the following: the founding father of the Ṭa'awāneh was allegedly a *mahabūl* (crazy, retarded) who moved from camp to camp and worked with the women. One day two elders, one from the Ġadāyreh and the other from the D'eyfeh, saw him. The former, in jest, told the latter "*hada ibn 'amak*" ("This is your Father's Brother's Son [FBS]"). The D'eyfi took Ḏiyab *al-mahabūl* and gave him his sister for a wife. Ḏiyab sired one son and died. When the son became of age, his mother went to her brother and told him, "you gave me to the *mahabūl*, now give your daughter to his son," and from this union rose the Ṭa'awāneh, who together with the D'eyfeh formed the third maximal lineage of the tribe—the Ḏiyabāt. (The catch in this story is that the two elders belonged to the fourth generation while the *mahabūl* belonged to the second, unless, originally, the /*al*/ in his name is not the article—i.e., *the* crazy—as it is today but the possessive—i.e., *of* [the] crazy—as is used in proper names and which will assign him to the third generation.)

The second tactic used to increase the tribe's fighting strength was a formal alliance of the type known as "eat and put in blood" (Ashkenazi 1957:111–12). Like absorption, this tactic is not unique to the Ḥğerāt and is known from other small tribes as far south as the Sinai, although its specific descriptive name may vary (e.g., cf. Bailey and Peled 1975:19). About the middle of the nineteenth century, the Ḥğerāt made such an alliance with the *'arab* al-Ka'abīyeh, who had splintered from *'arab* al-Ka'abneh of the Hebron area and moved into the southern part of the Valley of Yizra'el near Ḫirbet Qireh (Ashkenazi 1938:249). During the 1890s, the Ṭababšeh lineage (around which rallied the *'arab* al-Ḥelf) joined, and the alliance became tri-tribal. According to this arrangement (which replaces the *ḫams*, the five generations co-liable group, common in the Negev), the partners to the alliance share in pursuing blood revenge and share in collecting and distributing blood compensation. The alliance between these three partners was cemented by some exchange of wives, and the Ka'abīyeh are now claimed to be genealogically related to the Ḥğerāt.[1]

The third method used to reduce the danger of their small number was the exchange of women, without a formal alliance, with other small tribes in their vicinity. No data exist for the marriages of the first two generations for which 3 and 6 named males respectively are remembered. For Generation III (ca. 1820–1844), 14 named males and 2 marriages are remembered: one with a female of another small tribe and the other the marriage of the above-mentioned son of the *mahabūl* with his Mother's Brother's Daughter (MBD). Thirty-eight males and 8 females were named for Generation IV (of the third quarter and the first half of the fourth quarter of the nineteenth century) at around the time of their move to the Ẓahara. Of these males, one was killed before marriage and 4 had 2 wives each. Thus, a total of 41 marriages involving Ḥğeri males were made. In 8 cases, the wife's identity or affiliation (that is, whether she was of the Ḥğerāt or not) is no longer remembered, leaving 33 remembered marriages involving male tribesmembers. Fifteen of these were intra-tribal marriages, that is, with female members of the tribe, which include 7 of the above named females. One marriage was a Father's Brother's Daughter/Son (FBD/FBS) union and the other 14 were either between families that are now sublineages or between the three lineages. The other 18 marriages involving males and a female were made with members of twelve other small tribes in the area. Thus, of the 34 (33 males and 1 female) marriages remembered, 52.9% of them were made with members of other tribes.

This figure is probably a very conservative estimate of the Ḥğerāt inter-tribal marriages due to the underrepresentation of female members who married out and are no longer remembered. When the adult sex ratio of Generation VII (ca. 1920–1944) is calculated, there are .951 females for every 1.00 males. For Generation VIII (ca. 1945–1969), the ratio is .929 females per 1.00 males. Although these ratios are tentative, inasmuch as all three generations still reproduce, they suggest that even if a ratio as low as .900 females per 1.00 males is assumed, a figure of 33 males will assume 30 (29.7) females providing for all 15 intra-Ḥğerāt marriages, leaving 15 females who can be assumed to have married inter-tribally, raising the overall percentage of inter-tribal marriages to 68.8% as compared with 31.2% intra-tribal marriages.

Finally, by adopting aggressive, uncompromising behavior in their dealings with other sociopolitical entities, the Ḥğerāt could ward off all but the most powerful opponents. Such a policy would have been advantageous in the ever-present regional competition, would fit the ideals of honor and independence that are so central to bedouin culture and behavior, and would accommodate the claim of the Ḥğerāt, and especially their leading lineage, for having "hot blood" and for having been "robbers and hoodlums."

Although today the Ḥğerāt maintain that they have never paid or received *ḫawa*, it is likely that they were coerced into payment of taxes to 'Aḥmed al-Ğazzar (cf. Cohen 1973:104–11) as neither their numbers nor their degree of mobility would have enabled them to oppose him. Paying taxes throughout that period, however, was dependent on the authorities' ability to collect them, which fluctuated greatly (e.g., Ma'oz 1968:8–9, 14); hence, this symbol of submission was more an occasional event than the routine. Consequently, the amount of outside interference in Ḥğeri affairs was minimal and sporadic throughout most of their residence in the environs of Tel al-Šummām.

In Retrospect

The period spent at Tel al-Šummām was thus a formative one during which the general direction of the evolution of the Ḥğerāt was set. To wit: rather than assimilate into another larger and stronger tribe, they set themselves as the focus for rallying small tribes into a competitive political entity. The choice of the Tel as their main camp was in line with this policy for it provided them with the necessary relative isolation, which enabled them to run their lives largely without interference. It must be remembered that the Ḥğerāt were a very small, if growing and economically self-sufficient, lineage trying to survive in a relatively hostile region. The avoidance of excessive contact with the more dominant local elements, such as larger and stronger tribes, villages, or the authorities, was a fundamental requirement.

Note

1. An early version given to me regarding the origin of the Ḥğerāt was as follows: a man was exiled from the Ḥağarah of the Lağa'. He became *ṭanīb* (cf. Aref 1937:131–34; Ashkenazi 1938:78–80; Ashkenazi 1957:119–20) or protègè among the Banū Saḫr in Šbekah, Trans-Jordan, where he married one of their daughters and had children. Later, he moved to the environs of Hebron and from him sprang the *'arab* al-Ka'abneh, who still reside there (also, cf. Oppenheim 1943:238 and 1943:78). Many years later the Ka'abīyeh splintered from the Ka'abneh and moved to the Valley of Yizra'el and from them came the two brothers Baḥar and Sulṭan who gave rise to the Ḥğerāt.

— 4 —

The Ottoman Period at al-Ẓahara
(ca. 1870–1917)

The Traditional Account of the Move to the Ẓahara

Of the several versions of when and why the elders decided to move from Tel al-Šummām to al-Ẓahara, the following is the most widely accepted "official" version. According to this account, when the Ottoman authorities demanded that the Ḥğerāt register title to the land of the Tel—in order to tax and conscript them—the Ḥğeri elders avoided the Ottoman intention by traveling to Beirut, and they "sold the land to Sursuk," a rich Greek Orthodox banking family (cf. *New York Times*, April 18, 1897). Thereafter, the whole tribe migrated to the Ẓahara (a section of the Yotvat mountain range). According to tradition, this event took place under the leadership of the grandparents of the mid-1970s elders, or sometime between 1865 and 1889.

This "official" version seems to be a reorganization of the elements in order to adjust history to the tribe's status in the mid-1970s. As mentioned previously (see Chapter 2), in 1856 Sulṭan Abdulmajid reinstituted his reforms to gain the support of the Western Powers in the Crimean War. This reform program included the Ottoman Land Code and the decree of the Land Registration Law, which were enacted in 1274/1275 A.H. (A.D. 1858). Land registries, and hence attempts to enforce the law, were open only when the Porte gained more control in the country, between 1867 and 1873 (G.B. Col. 1937:39). When land registration became a fact and the Porte needed money, the Sursuk (or Sursock) family bought the *'iltizām* (tax farming) concession to the area, which included Tel al-Šummām and Sheikh Abreik, where they placed an agent to represent them (Conder and Kitchner 1881:356; Baer 1971:55–56; Oliphant 1976:53). These changes brought the authorities all too close to the semi-isolated Ḥğerāt, and it is probable that Sursuk demanded rent fees, convincing the elders to move. It is thus likely that between 'Aqīl Aga's death in 1870 and the decline of the *'arab* al-Hanādi and the 1872 visit of Conder and Kitchner to the area east of Šfā'amr (1881:335) the Ḥğerāt, who by then numbered some forty to fifty households, had established a new base camp in the Ẓahara.

The Ẓahara

The Ẓahara occupies a section from about the center to the western edge of the Yotvat mountain range (see Map 4), and to the 1875 eye presented "deep valleys and rugged ridges clothed with brushwood" (Conder 1889b:102). Its southern boundary is Mt. 'Atzmon (*ğabel Daydabe*) and the Valley of Beit Netofah (*sahel baṭṭūf*), with an access path through Naḥal Yodfāt (*wādi* Ğfāt) at Ḫirbet Kana. Although the valley itself was cultivated and by April its western half was "a sheet of emerald green, as the young crop extended before us" (Oliphant 1976:155), its eastern half remained a swamp until July (Conder 1878[II]:178) and a year-round segment of this swamp blocked easy access to the path at Ḫirbet Kana (cf. Conder 1889b:96). In the west the Ẓahara bordered the lands of the village of Kawkab Abū al-Hejā'. These lands insulated the Ḥğeri territory from the other possible easy access through *wādi* I'billin in the southwest. The northern border followed the 450-m elevation line, with a drop of about 150 m within 0.5 km into the Valley of Saḫnīn. The eastern boundary ran through the dense trees and brushwood vegetation of the mountain range (Conder and Kitchner 1881:312). The Ẓahara territory therefore provided isolation, seclusion, and relative protection for the Ḥğerāt. At the same time, located about 20 km (aerial distance) east of Acre, about 10.5 km northeast of Šfā'amr, and about 15 km northwest of Nazareth, it offered ready access to these urban and administrative centers.

In addition to security the Ẓahara provided ample pasturage, firewood, and space. The botanical structure of the vegetation at the time was a mature *Querus calliprinos-Pistacia palaestina* association (Zohary 1962:97–102), characteristic of the Mediterranean vegetation zone. This community, which demands relatively low winter temperatures (Zohary 1962:97–102), thrives above the 300-m elevation line (Zohary 1957:181) and includes palatable perennial grasses (such as *Dactylis glomerata*, *Phalaris bulbosa*, *Hordeum bulbosum*, and *Oryzopsis holciformis*) and many annuals—all of which make for good pasturage (Zohary 1962:99, 215). Below the 300-m elevation line, and especially on the western slopes of the range, the dominant form was a carob-lentisk (*Ceratonia siliqua-Pistacia lentiscus*) alliance with its perennial and annual grasses, which also provide for good pasture (Zohary 1962:102–3).

Finally, although no natural sources of water are to be found in the range itself, the area of the Ẓahara includes Ḫirbet Ğfāt—the ruins of Josephus Flavius' first-century A.D. fortress Yodfāt (or Yodefet), with its ancient and newer cisterns, some of which "still hold water" in July (Conder and Kitchner 1881:312). The nearby Valleys of Beit Netofah and Saḫnīn, as well as the hills west of the former, offered pasture; the wells, cisterns, and pond near the villages provided water. It was an almost ideal location for a small tribe in search of a secluded territory.

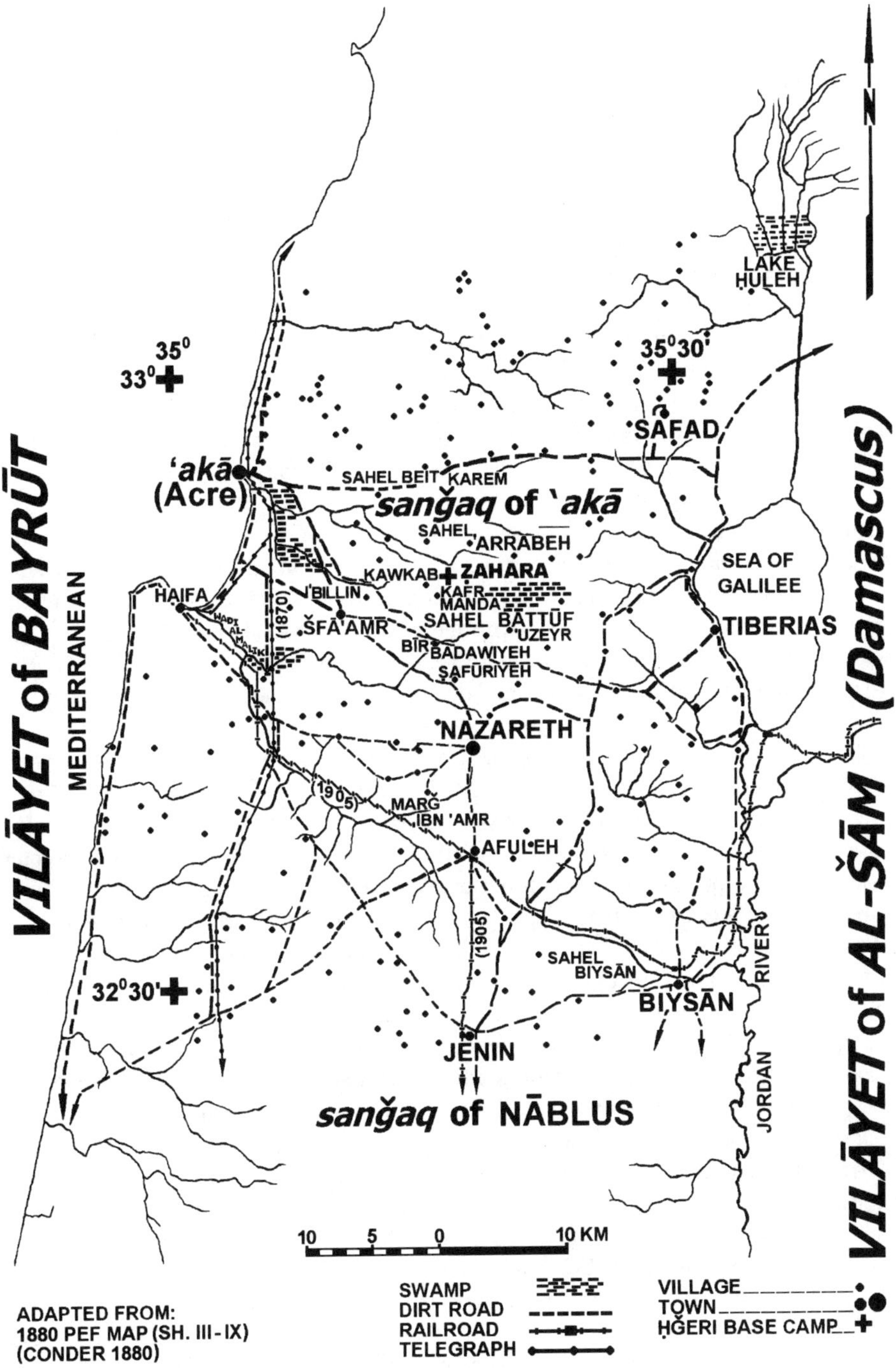

Map 4. The Galilee in the late nineteenth century.

The Yearly Round in the Ẓahara

The yearly cycle of the Ḥǧerāt rapidly fell into a routine. They wintered in the Ẓahara, taking advantage of the area's caves to protect their goats from the cold and wet weather (see also Hirsch 1933:58). The cattle and sheep were kept outside among the trees, as they could withstand the climate better, while kids and lambs were kept in the tents. During March (the beginning of spring) they would pasture the herds around the Ẓahara and down into the foothills of the Valley of Saḫnīn to the north and the edges of the Valley of Beit Netofah to the south. The herds would leave the Ẓahara every morning and be back in the evening. By April fresh pasture in these locales grew scarcer and it became necessary to move further away. It was then that the tents were moved to the hills west of the Valley of Beit Netofah, where lush pasture was to be found until mid-May. These three months—March, April and May—were, as one informant said, "the months of plenty," for there was pasture, water, milk, *laban* (yogurt), *labne* (drained yogurt cheese), *ǧibneh* (cheese), *samneh* (clarified butter), and fat lambs and kids. April and May were thus the months of weddings.

In June the camp would break up and smaller groups of two to five households would disperse in the Valley of Beit Netofah and into *wādi* al-Malik (*naḥal tzipporī*), once the *'arab* al-Hanādi began their trek eastward (Conder 1880: sheet V; Conder and Kitchner 1881:355; Schumacher 1887:186; Oppenheim 1943:32; Ashkenazi 1938:245). They would pasture their herds on dried natural vegetation, on the stubble of the winter grain crops, or on fields that had to be deserted due to heavy infestation by weeds. Sometimes they would use the cover of night to invade fields of the *fellāḥīn* before harvest.

As summer wore on, water became an increasingly greater problem because "the water supply of the hill district north of *wādi* al-Malik is derived almost entirely from wells and cisterns near the villages, the only springs and those not very large being 'ayūn al-Kawkab to the southeast of the village of that name" (G.B. Naval 1920:538). Some could procure water from the rapidly drying open ponds or ancient cisterns without payment, especially if they camped away from the villages. Others would buy water by the handbreadth (or *šibr*—the variable measure between the tip of the thumb and the tip of the little finger of an outstretched hand) from the wells of Kafr Manda, Bīr al-Badawiyyeh, B'eyneh, and Rummāneh. Those with smaller herds could return to the Ẓahara for there was still enough pasture, and water could be found in the old cisterns of Ḫirbet Ǧfāt and Ḫirbet Kana. These owners, however, soon found out that sheep do not thrive in the Ẓahara (e.g., cf. G.B. Naval 1920:509), and slowly all those who remained year around in that area shifted to herds of goats and cattle only.

After the first rains, in September and October, when the new grass sprouted rapidly and the parched brown land became lush green, the Ḥǧerāt and their herds would start back toward the Ẓahara. If the rainy season was slow to follow, they would have to haul water on pack animals from Kafr Manda and Bīr al-Badawiyyeh to water their herds.

During the first decade or so after their arrival at the Yotvat range, all the Ḥǧerāt camped together in the Ẓahara and would return there for the winter. As their sense of relative security became more established and the plight of the sheep became apparent, some segments of the tribe remained in their spring and summering areas, thereby relieving the emerging herd and population pressures on the resources of the Ẓahara. Thus, toward the end of the 1880s the households of the D'eyfeh who camped in *wādi* I'billin in and around al-Ḏmeydeh, some 4.5 km to the southwest of the Ẓahara at the western foot of the Daydabeh, made this place their base camp. They were followed by *ulād* 'Aḥmed, who in 1902–1903 wintered in their summering area between 'Uzeyr and Rummāneh, and, in the early 1930s, by the Ṣawālḥah, who settled in the Mikmān some 6.5 km south-southwest of the Ẓahara, leaving there the Ġadāyreh with the Ṭa'awāneh and a few Ṣawālhi families.

This territorial division, however, did not develop into sociopolitical or ideological schisms because the distances involved were very small. Furthermore, the combination of the familial ideology of tribal societies in general, reinforced among the Ḥğeris by tradition and customs such as the *farīdah*[1] and the ever-present regional one-upmanship game, acted to prevent such dissolution. In fact, the dispersal not only reduced competition over resources and friction among tribesmembers, but enabled each of the segments to develop closer ties with a different neighboring village or population. In this way, when the need for a contact with that population by another segment or the Ḥğerāt as a whole arose, the segment with the appropriate connection became the relay. Differently stated, by maintaining a strong ideology of tribal unity while allowing for a maximum autonomy of tribal segments or individuals in extra-tribal relations, the political maneuverability of the whole tribe increased markedly. It should not, therefore, come as a surprise that while one segment of the tribe might be in a feud with a neighboring population, another segment might concurrently maintain amicable relations with that same population.

Regional Dynamics

As their stakes in the regional sociopolitical game increased, the Ḥğerāt continued to emphasize the traditional twin strategies—demographic weight and aggressive response—they had adopted while still in Tel al-Šummām. 'Aqīl Aga's death created a power vacuum in the region, and the eastward migration of the rest of the *'arab* al-Hanādi opened the prime area of *wādi* al-Malik for other groups. First the Ka'abīyeh (see Chapter 3), who by 1872 numbered some 200 people (Conder and Kitchner 1882:74), moved into this niche. Then, the third member of the tri-tribe alliance, the Ṭababšeh lineage, arrived in the area in the late 1880s or early 1890s.

The establishment of an alliance with the latter group provides an insight into Ḥğeri "foreign policy." Originally the Ṭababšeh numbered several families, led by Muṣtafā Ṭabāš, who fled from a blood feud in their tribe of origin, the *'arab* al-Hazaīl of the Beersheeba area. Three men of this group went to scout the area of *wādi* al-Malik and encountered Ḏiyab al-Ibrāhīm (Ġadāyreh), who was camping there during the summer. A conflict ensued and Ḏiyab shot and wounded two of the scouts (one of whom was a freed slave of Muṣtafā), while the third escaped. Ḏiyab bandaged and cared for the two wounded men and a few days later Muṣtafā Ṭabāš came to negotiate their release. A *ṣulḥa* (peace negotiation and ceremony) followed and Muṣtafā and Ḏiyab exchanged sisters. Later, the Ṭababšeh rallied around them the *'arab* al-Ḥelf, whose origin was the *'arab* al-Lağa' from Syria (Ashkenazi 1938:249, 229) and who predated the Ṭababšeh in the area (Conder and Kitchner 1882:355), and the alliance became tri-tribal.

With their increasing membership, the Ḥğerāt could put their aggressive, uncompromising reprisal policy to much more efficient use when the need arose. Thus, for example, sometime during the first decade of the twentieth century there was a conflict with the *'arab* al-Muwāsa. As a result, the latter raided the Ẓahara while the men were away with their herds. In the ensuing chase and ambushes, the Ḥğerāt succeeded in capturing three of the raiders. The Muwāsa sent a delegation offering to pay ransom in order to free their members. The Ḥğerāt refused to negotiate, but late that night the wife of the leading elder cut the ropes that bound the prisoners and set them free. When I asked if anything was done to her, the informant laughed and said, "no, she was told to do it." In other words, by refusing to negotiate, the Ḥğerāt proved that they were not afraid of the Muwāsa, which was a larger tribe (Oppenheim [1943:18, 20] lists the Ḥğerāt as 72 tents and the Muwāsa as 118 tents) and that the Muwāsa were inferior to themselves. Yet realpolitik demanded that the feud not be extended to include all of the Muwāsa and their allies, and so the prisoners were released.

Generally speaking, the Ḥğerāt did not have many overt conflicts with the neighboring villages or other bedouin tribes. In fact, they had only one major feud with the neighboring Druze, who seem to have been feuding with the bedouin on a regular basis (G.B. Naval 1920:514). This feud, which began in the early 1880s soon after their arrival at the Ẓahara, marks the beginning of the still extant rivalry between the Ḥğerāt and the Druze, and as such has some importance. According to the Ḥğerāt, the Druze were on a raid against the *'arab* al-Heīb, with whom they had a conflict. On their way they passed the Ẓahara and encountered a Ḥğeri elder sitting in front of his tent. Allegedly they asked him if he was a Heībi, and being a Ḥğeri and proud he answered, "I am a Heībi and a son of a Hebiyyah," so they killed him and went their way. Two of his cousins avenged his death by ambushing the Druze of Beyt Ğan near that village's water mill. The two are said to have killed seven or eight Druze before returning to the Ẓahara. Later a *ṣulḥa* was made and relative peace restored but the seed of a long-term conflict was sown.

On a day-to-day basis, however, the Ḥğerāt were isolationists who did not particularly look for conflicts. Their claim that they neither paid nor collected *ḫawa* may indicate that—at least at first—they could not collect it because of their small number. Their size also prevented them from raiding the larger villages and promoted amicable relations with the smaller neighboring villages, who became allies and places to secure enough water for their herds. These informal alliances, particularly with Kawkab Abū al-Hejā', Kafr Manda, 'Uzeyr, and Rummāneh, developed into a semipermanent alliance against the *fellāḥīn* of Ṣafūriyeh, which was the largest village in the area and which "terrorized the smaller villages and tribes" according to a Ḥğeri informant. The alliances, however, did not prevent individual Ḥğeris from stealing animals from their allied *fellāḥīn* or from nearby competing tribes, which was very common. In fact, informants said that when a Ḥğeri had to butcher an animal in honor of a guest, he would sneak to a nearby village and requisition one. It was also remarked that if a young man was reluctant to steal animals he was often refused a bride, with the argument that he would not be able to provide for her.

Ḥğeri Land Acquisition

The rise in their politico-military regional importance was also reflected in the Ḥğeris' ability to take over and hold on to the lands of the *fellāḥīn* of the village of Saḫnīn, one of the richer villages in the area (Conder and Kitchner 1881:286; see also Appendix B). With the decline in rural population, Saḫnīn left the Ẓahara uncultivated, using it as extra pastureland and fuel resource in times of need. When the Ḥğerāt took hold of the area, the peasants did not bother to contest the takeover. First, they possessed and cultivated fertile bottom-lands in both the Valley of Saḫnīn and the Valley of Beit Netofah. Second, while colonizing the Ẓahara, the Ḥğerāt left enough of the range for others' use so that there was no shortage in pasture or fuel when needed. Third, although some sort of land registration drive was taking place in the Valley of Jezreel, nothing of the sort was happening north of that area. Thus, the peasants of Saḫnīn did not have a legal recourse nor did they want to meddle with the Ḥğerāt militarily—the only other recourse. The Ḥğerāt were thereby able to acquire squatters' rights to these lands. They did not, however, invest much labor in changing the landscape, save for minimal forest clearing to make space for a tent or sheepfold. It was thus that when Conder and Kitchner visited the area in July of 1875, very close to the beginning of Ḥğeri occupation of the area and at a time when the Ḥğerāt would have been in the Valley of Beit Netofah, they make no mention of any signs of habitation in the area (Conder 1889b:102; Conder and Kitchner 1881:312).

During the 1890s, the Ḥğerāt, who numbered some 50 to 60 households, began to buy land in and around the Valley of Beit Netofah. For example, 'Ali al-'Aḥmed (D'eyfeh) bought some land from Kafr Manda in the Ḏmeydeh, while Nimr and Ḏiyab al-Ibrāhīm and Sleymān al-'Abed (Ġadāyreh) bought land from Saḫnīn in the Valley of Beit Netofah. According to the Ḥğerāt, these purchases were somewhat accidental. In their words, the *fellāḥīn*, who on the average cultivated between 10 and 30 *dunum* (pl.) (1 *dunam* was 900 m^2 in Palestine), or approximately 2–6 Egyptian *faddāns* per family, had more land than they needed for cultivation but not enough oxen to plow it because whenever a peasant could not meet his taxes or debt, his livestock was the first to be confiscated (cf. Conder 1878[I]:164–65). They were therefore ready to exchange 8–10 *dunum* of valley bottom-land for an ox or a cow and the richer Ḥğeris took advantage of that opportunity. The new landowners remained herders, while renting out their land either to *fellāḥīn* or to the poorer tribesmembers as sharecroppers. These acquisitions continued through the first decade of the twentieth century and intensified during the second.[2]

The following illustrates the land acquisition process described above. 'Aḥmed al-Ḥāmad of the Ġadāyreh used to summer near the village of 'Uzeyr in the southeast quadrant of the Valley of Beit Netofah, and winter in the Ẓahara. He had three sons and a daughter. One of the sons, Muḥammad, worked as a freelance tracker in addition to maintaining a herd. About 1902–1903, the family wintered in 'Uzeyr instead of returning to the Ẓahara. Thereafter they remained in that locale year around. By 1906 they had acquired squatters' rights to some 100 *dunum* of mountain land where they camped on the western slope of Mt. Ṭur'ān. During the same year, Muḥammad convinced his elder brother Ḥāmad to join him in buying some 60 *dunum* of bottom-land in the Valley of Beit Netofah; they then rented this land out to *fellāḥīn* from ʻUzeyr. They kept buying land whenever they could. In 1923 Muḥammad joined the Palestine police force as a tracker and used part of his salary to finance the acquisitions after that date. In 1938 he was the first in his family to build a house there, thereby establishing the third geographical-genealogical settlement of the Ḥğerāt south of ʻUzeyr (al-Ḏmeydeh and al-Mikmān were the first two).

To what extent these land acquisitions were motivated by a desire to forestall the effects of fluctuations in herd size and productivity—similar to those Barth (1961:103–4) reports for the Basseri—is hard to assess. The Galilean tribes had much smaller herds and their herds were not subjected to the stresses of long annual migrations as those of the Basseri. Nevertheless, violent fluctuations in herd populations were as much a danger in Palestine as among the Basseri. The British Naval Intelligence, for example, reports that in 1898 the livestock of Samaria was estimated at 210,000 heads (G.B. Naval 1920:490). By 1913, due to "a serious epidemic among sheep and cattle, the stock was very much reduced" so that by 1917 "there [was] very little stock" (G.B. Naval 1920:490). Similarly, in 1976 one of the tribe's herds suffered from *Piroplasmosis babesiaovis* (tick fever) and was reduced by half from the beginning of May to mid-June. It also seems safe to conclude that to some measure these land acquisitions were influenced by: the general milieu in the Lower Galilee; its large absentee yet very powerful landowners such as the Sursuks and the sulṭan; the land acquisition efforts of the Jewish and German settlers; and, primarily, the increase in government controls that protected such acquisitions and reduced the opportunities to acquire land by claiming squatter's rights as before. This increased control was accompanied by such visible signs as the appearance of postal services (Hizki 1957:980) and the telegraph in 1865 (Horwitz 1957:503), and railroads in the 1890s (Etingen 1957:960; Sawwaf 1938:315; Assaf 1967:34–35).

Ḥğeri House Construction

Land acquisition generated an increasing sense of stability and relative permanence as well as rental income. Around 1900 a member of the Samrāt, Ibrāhīm al-Gāsem, built the first habitable structure among the Ḥğerāt in the Ẓahara. It was a single room above a cave that he used as a goat pen. The room was used for storage and habitation. Shortly thereafter, Ḏiyab al-Ibrāhīm of the Ġadāyreh built his house (see Figure 2) and used it as his residence when wintering in the Ẓahara. House constructions, however, did not become prevalent because most Ḥğeris could not afford the expenses, which included transporting in all the materials on camels. The next house was built only in 1926; 1928 saw three more. There were five built during the 1930s, five in the 1940s, and fifteen during the 1950s.

Ḏiyab's house was built of hewn stones emulating the construction style in the villages before the advent of concrete. It had two rooms, each opening to a built platform (sort of a porch). One room served as the *dīwān* (the men's section of the tent) while the other served as *ḥarīm* (the women's section). This type of design—that is, one replicating the functional units of the tent—was maintained in all the buildings the Ḥğerāt built in the Ẓahara until 1960 when the last house was built there.

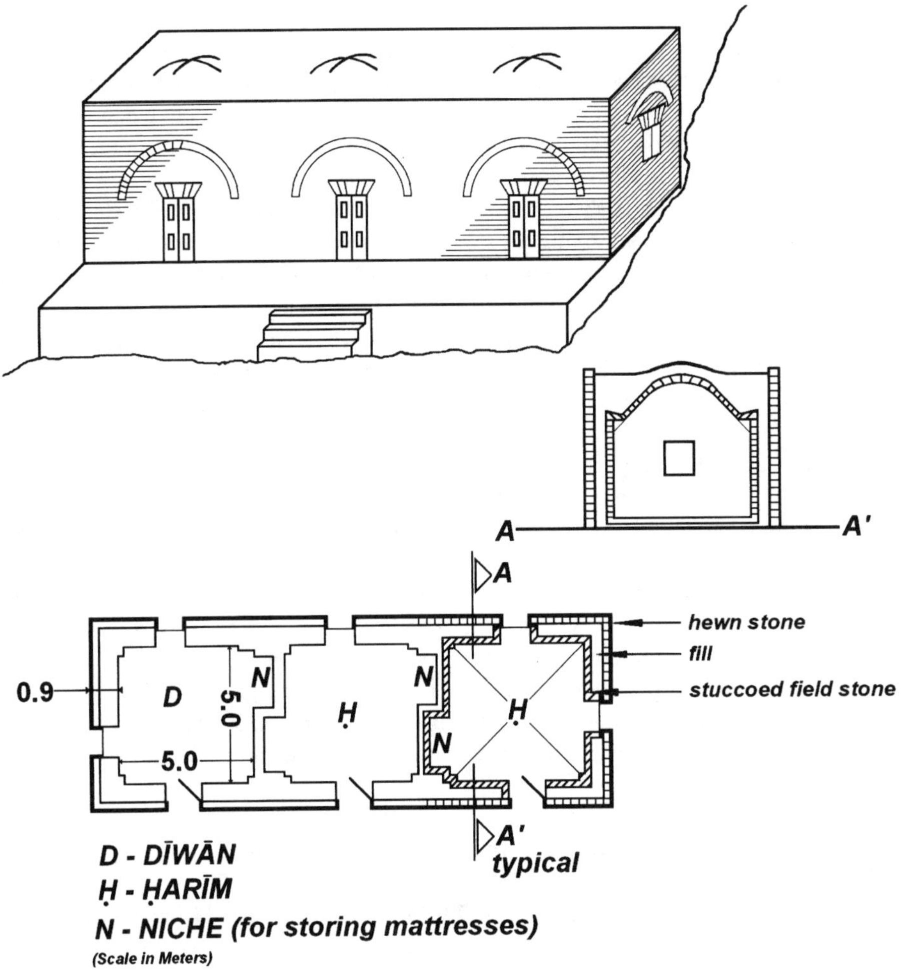

Figure 2. Traditional house construction. The first house in Bīr al-Maksūr.

Ḣğeri Economics

In spite of the economic well-being exhibited by some Ḥğeris, the tribe as a whole was neither rich nor powerful. According to their estimates, a family could live well if it owned 20 head of cattle, or 50–100 goats, or in combination 8–10 head of cattle and 30 goats, or 20–30 *dunum* of arable land, the differences between the quotes reflecting the informants' economic background. The low quotes, however, provide the lower threshold for a viable household herd. For example, an informant illustrated the sufficiency of a 50-goat herd by mentioning a generous host during the Mandate Period who used to say "I am not afraid of guests when there are 60 goats in my herd" because he could butcher in his guest's honor without cutting into his herd's minimal reproductive capacity.

This economic reality found its expression in Ḥğeri inheritance patterns. While maintaining a normative ideal of ultimogeniture and anticipatory inheritance,[3] the actual performance of these customs varied greatly. The economic inability of most Ḥğeri fathers to set up their married sons as independent households meant that at one extreme, the father would pay for his son's *mahr* and other wedding expenses but once the wedding was over, he would send off the latter empty-handed to fend for himself. At the other extreme, when he was rich (that is, had cattle, goats, and land) the father would usually provide his married sons with the traditional tents, but would keep the sons with him, until he was fairly old, to help him run the family's properties. He, thus, not only enlarged his labor pool but avoided the need to depend on hired shepherds who do not care for the animals as well as their owner (e.g., Barth 1961:103). In most cases, a marrying son received a small tent and remained a part of the father's economic enterprise. Then, when he could secure another source of income, such as being a shepherd for a rich herd owner, or had collected enough animals to start his own herd, he would establish his own independent household. A son's close cooperative ties with his father's household, however, were kept tight and rarely severed. The general inability to set up a newlywed couple as an independent productive household gave an impetus to the young males to look for wage labor (such as tracking), to steal animals or herd for a richer Ḥğeri, and if they were less enterprising, to sharecrop for a landed tribesmember. In turn, the impetus to look for other sources of income served as a selective mechanism for younger leadership.

Ḥğeri Demographic and Marriage Patterns

The marriages of Generation V (ca. 1870–1894) span the period from approximately 1890 to 1930 and correspond fairly closely to the first fifty years of Ḥğeri residence in the Ẓahara and its environs. Analyzing the pattern of these marriages provides insight into Ḥğeri demography and its influence on intra-tribal relations, and on the political aspirations of the various lineages. While maintaining tribal unity was a tradition strongly adhered to, the increase in Ḥğeri population size during this period and the growing distance from common ancestors threatened to erode the strong inter- as well as intra-lineage familial sense. It is not surprising, therefore, that the marriages of Generation V indicate an intra-tribal emphasis in reversal to the inter-tribal emphasis of its parental generation (Generation IV).

Overall, the demographic structure and marital arrangements of Generation V and Generation VI suggest that if the Ṣawālḥah had led the forming tribe by force of their larger membership, this state of affairs was beginning to change. Thus, during the period of Generation V, the ratio between the Ṣawālḥah and the Ġadāyreh was 39 and 26 males respectively and only the latter's alliance with the Ṭa'awāneh maintained a balance of 39:39 males. A policy of multiple marriages by the Ġadāyreh's Generation V resulted in 84 males in Generation VI as compared with 87 males for the Ṣawālḥah. If the Ṭa'awāneh's 28 males are added, the balance is well in favor of the Ġadāyreh, who maintain their leadership—political and demographic—to date. It should be kept in mind, however, that the competition between the two emerging lineages was probably latent rather than overt as it is, to some extent, today. Nonetheless, the changing balance of power, especially after its official recognition by the British in 1918 (see below), seems to have been a major factor in the aforementioned Ṣawālḥah's decision to move away to the Mikmān in the early 1930s.

As Table 2 shows, of the 134 marriages reported for this generation, 61.9% (83) were intra-tribal and only 38.0% (51 cases) were with non-Ḥğeris, as compared, respectively, with 44.1% (15) and 55.9% (19) of the marriages for Generation IV. However, similarly to the previous discussion of the marriages of Generation IV (see above), when considering the generational sex ratio, the apparent intra-tribal emphasis is probably a product of incomplete data (as discussed above). Thus, a total of 164 individuals (96 males and 68 females) were named for Generation V marriages. These numbers provide an adult sex ratio of .7 females/1.0 males, which is still much below the .951, .929, and .933 females/1.0 males reported before for Generations VII, VIII, and IX respectively. Since the females most likely to be forgotten are those participating in marriages with non-Ḥğeris, the total of 134 marriages is probably an underestimate and is in favor of a stronger intra-tribal emphasis on marriages than actually existed.

A further analysis of these marriages according to their lineage affiliation suggests that the reversal of the trend was not uniform across lineage lines. Rather, it depended upon the internal constitution that affected the intra-tribal balance of power, the residential conditions that affected economic and extra-tribal relations, and the aspirations of each of the three lineages. The Ġadāyreh, with the smallest number of both males and females, placed a greater emphasis on reproduction[4] and on marrying outside, either to the other two lineages or inter-tribally. At the other extreme, the Ṣawālḥah, with a larger membership as well as greater unclarity about the genealogical linkage of its sublineages, invested two-thirds of its marriages in consolidating its member sublineages. The Ḍiyabāt as a unit had a nearly equal inward and outward marital emphasis. This, however, is the

Table 2. The marriage pattern of Generation V by major categories.

Type of Marriage	**Number of Marriages**	**Percent**
endogamous*	32	23.9
intra-Ḥğerāt	51	38.1
inter-tribal	46	34.3
with villagers	5	3.7
total	*134*	*100*

*This category includes *ulād 'amm* marriages and any other marriage within a five-generation span. That is, it includes all marriage grades between FBS/D to FFFFBSSSD/S. In this specific case, there were 18 FBD/S and 14 FFBS/D marriages, or any classified as either type.

result of the Ḏiyabāt's two constituent sublineages, the D'eyfeh and the Ṭa'awāneh, and their different residential locations, the former alone in the Ḏmeydeh and the latter allied with the Ġadāyreh in the Ẓahara (see Table 3).

The inter-tribal marriages of Generation V, although more numerous in absolute number, resemble those of Generation IV in their spread. To wit: the 46 inter-tribal marriages of this generation involved 16 other small tribes; only one or two marriages were contracted with 14 of them (see Table 4).

In other words, the inter-tribal marriage policy of the three lineages was an attempt to create as many links with as many similarly small tribes—who adopted the same policy themselves—as possible. The great majority of these tribes resided in the geographic triangle formed by Acre, Haifa, and Nazareth, and were thus subjected to the same stresses—sociopolitical and demographic—as the Ḥğerāt. These inter-tribal marriages were, therefore, contracted horizontally (or in order to strengthen the present position of both contractors) rather than vertically (or to elevate the position of one of the contracting parties).

It should be kept in mind that the term "policy" is used here to refer to a general governing set of principles. Thus, in reality, so long as the chosen partner, Ḥğeri or non-Ḥğeri, was not judged by the elders to be a possible source of future problems, the decision was left in the hands of the father of the groom/bride. If, however, the choice was judged to be politically unwise or would possibly taint the lineage's honor, then the father was tactfully prevented from realizing his plans. The term "policy" thus refers to a flexible heuristic frame that tacitly directs rather than dictates the marriage of this or any other Ḥğeri generation both intra- and extra-tribally.

Nonetheless, the tacit assent of the elders to any marriage to which they did not object suggests that even if these linkages were inactive on the inter-tribal level on a day-to-day basis, they could always be activated to form an inter-tribal coordinated action if the need arose. This marriage policy should, therefore, be viewed more as a long-term insurance policy than as active recruitment of immediate political or economic support.

Finally, the fifth generation accounts for the first reported marriages between Ḥğeris and villagers. Three of these five marriages involved the Ġadāyreh taking peasant wives. Of these, two were contracted by *ulād* 'Aḥmed, who were already camping between 'Uzeyr and Rummāneh and who took one wife from the former and one from the latter. These two marriages established a pattern that was repeated and intensified in the following generations. The third wife was taken from Kafr Kaneh by a member of the Samrāt and seems to be an isolated case as no other marriages between the Ḥğerāt and this village have been contracted to 1977. The last two cases involved the giving of Ḥğeri females to *fellāḥīn*. These wives were given to each of the two leading lineages of Kafr Manda. One woman came from the D'eyfeh (Ḏiyabāt), who were settled on the western boundary of Kafr Manda's lands, and the other from *ulād* Ḥassan al-Ṣāleḥ (Ṣawālḥah) in the Ẓahara.

Table 3. The marriage pattern of the fifth generation by lineage.

Lineage	Membership			Endog-amous		Intra-Lineage		With Ġadāyreh				With Ḍiyabāt				With Ṣawālḥah				With Other Tribes				With Villages				Total*
	M	F	T	N	%	N	%	K	G	T	%	K	G	T	%	K	G	T	%	K	G	T	%	K	G	T	%	N
Ġadāyreh	26	19	45	4	8	12	24	16		16	32	4	2	6	12	5	2	7	14	12	6	18	36	3		3	6	50
Ṭa'awāneh	13	11	24	6	27.3	1	4.5		2	2	9.1	7	2	9	40.9					8	3	11	50					22
D'eyfeh	18	12	30	8	33.3	3	12.5	1	1	2	8.3	11	2	13	54.2	2	1	3	12.5	5		5	20.8		1	1	4.2	24
Ḍiyabāt	31	23	54	14	33.3	4	9.5	1	3	4	9.5	18		18	42.9	2	1	3	7.1	13	3	16	38.1		1	1	2.4	42
Ṣawālḥah	39	26	65	14	25.9	22	40.7	1	2	3	5.6		2	2	3.7	36		36	66.7	8	4	12	22.2		1	1	1.8	54

Key: M = male; F = female; T = total; N = number; K = taken from above; G = given to above

*These totals include the females who were exchanged among the lineages and who were not included in Table 2 in order to avoid duplication in counting the marriages of the tribe as a whole.

Table 4. Frequency of inter-tribal marriages of Generation V by lineage (cases).

Lineage	Number of Marriages					Total Number of Marriages	Total Number of Tribes
	1	2	3	4	5		
Ġadāyreh	5	4	0	0	1[a]	18	10
Ḍiyabāt	3	4	0	0	1[b]	16	8
Ṣawālḥah	6	3	0	0	0	12	9
total	*14*	*11*	*0*	*0*	*2*	*46*	

[a]This tribe is the *'arab* al-Ḥelf. Two of these marriages are the brother-sister (B-Z) exchanges that cemented the Ġadāyreh-Ṭababšeh alliance.

[b]This tribe is the *'arab* al-Sweytāt. As in the former case, two of the five marriages are B-Z exchanges that marked the beginning of the adoption of a Swetī splinter household by the Ḥğerāt. It would therefore be more accurate to argue that only three marriages were contracted with the Sweytāt because politically that splinter household no longer belonged to that tribe.

In Retrospect

The transfer of the base camp of the Ḥğerāt from Tel al-Šummām to the Ẓahara was a well-timed move that enabled the tribe to increase its political influence. The effects of Ottoman administrative efforts to control the bedouin, barely perceptible in the early 1870s but marked by the early 1880s, were most pronounced in the fertile areas, which provided most of the taxes. Oliphant, writing about the Valley of Jezreel in 1883, remarks that "the few Bedouins . . . have, in their turn, become the plundered and despoiled, for they are all reduced to the position of being subject to inexorable landlords" (1976:73). Conder writes "[o]n the whole . . . the settled people seem to be gaining ground, and especially in Lower Galilee; in the Sharon Plain the Bedawin are mere shadows of their forefathers" (1878[II]:271). In the relative isolation of the Ẓahara, however, the presence of the authorities was far less evident and the effects of their policies unnoticeable, leaving the Ḥğerāt to develop without any governmental intervention. At the same time, the absence of central control permitted competition with other semi-independent political entities to be commensurately fiercer, providing fertile soil for the rise of local leaders. Ḥğeri leadership of the alliance with the Ka'abīyeh and the addition of the Ḥelf to its members in the early 1890s enabled them to become such a leader in the opposition against Ṣafūriyeh and to enter the regional political scene when they were ripe for it during the 1920s. Thus, during the early years in the Ẓahara they began their political ascendancy from a small and insignificant group to the regional prominence they reached in the 1970s.

Notes

1. *Farīdah* ("decree, ordinance, *Isl. Law*, obligatory religious duty"; Madina 1973:499) was a custom according to which the *mahr* (bride-wealth) for a Ḥğeri bride was set at 40 Ottoman dinars and later at P£40.00, regardless of the individual qualities of the girl involved. As it was explained to me, this agreement among the Ḥğeris was made specifically to avoid hard feelings over unfair competition for prospective wives. It was thought that these possible conflicts could damage the unity of the tribe and, hence, should be avoided. The *farīdah* was practiced only with regard to Ḥğeris; a *mahr* of an outsider was negotiable within the accepted confines of its specific time period.
2. This land acquisition process was conducted in a piecemeal fashion. For example, the said Nimr al-Ibrāhīm bought from four different people the following: 12, 12.5, 12.5, and 12.5 *dunum* respectively. In 1918, in partnership with his brother Ḍiyab al-Ibrāhīm, he bought 13 more *dunum*, 6.5 of which were his. When he died ca. 1927, he bequeathed 56 *dunum* to his five sons, who did not divide the property until about 1940, cultivating the land and operating as a single unit until then.
3. Although the Ḥğerāt are Sunni Moslems, rather than follow the Islamic religious law (the *Šarī'a*), like the Negev bedouin (cf. Marx 1967:108), they follow the more common, anticipatory inheritance practiced among pastoralists—be they Moslems herding caprines (e.g., Barth 1961:19–20; Bates 1973:105; Irons 1975:84–85) or cattle (e.g., Stenning 1958:93–94, 98; Hopen 1958:139) or be they non-Moslems (e.g., Lattimore 1951:292). Bedouin law (*ganūn al-'aša'īr*) differs from the *Šarī'a* law in other aspects as well (e.g., cf. G.B. Naval 1920:229).
4. Although the Ġadāyreh had the smallest membership among the lineages, by using multiple marriages they contracted eight more marriages than the Ḍiyabāt and only four less than the Ṣawālḥah, who had a much larger membership. Thus the Ġadāyreh had 9 marriages involving 2 wives per husband; 1 involving 3 wives; and 2 involving 4 wives. In comparison the Ḍiyabāt had 5; 0; 1, and the Ṣawālḥah 5; 3; 0 cases respectively.

PART III

The British Mandate Period

(ca. 1917–1947)

— 5 —

The British Mandate Period

(ca. 1917–1947)

Some Historical Notes on the Rise of Palestinian Nationalism

Although the Ottoman administration collected taxes from the Ḥğerāt from at least the beginning of the twentieth century, it left them to their own devices. The Ḥğerāt thus retained their relative isolation. Even the changes that, in the wake of Sulṭan Abdulmajid's 1856 reforms, began to ferment the old Ottoman Empire in general (e.g., cf. Vinogradov 1972:125, 128–29; Assaf 1967:9–66; Berger 1962:400–401) and the *vilāyet* of Sayda (Sidon) in particular (e.g., Baer 1975; Shamir 1975; Landau 1975; Avitsur 1975; Shim'oni 1946:240–369; Elon 1971:149–85) did not affect their daily life, their sociopolitical organization, or their relations with their neighbors. The impact of the First World War, the Arab Revolt associated with it, and the temporary presence of the 5th Cavalry Division in the Lower Galilee during September 1918 (G.B. Army 1919:30–31, 50) was felt only inasmuch as more peasants in the Beit Netofah area wanted to exchange land for livestock. Such exchanges became even more crucial for the *fellāḥīn* than before, due to the devastation of the countryside by the Ottoman Army and its remnants once it was defeated (e.g., G.B. Col. 1925:4; G.B. Pls. 1937:112).

Nevertheless, to understand the fortunes of the Ḥğerāt during the British Mandate Period, one has to address the macro-forces that were shaping their environment. It is thus necessary to digress a little from their immediate history and consider the rise of Palestinian identity and the Arab-Jewish conflict—a crucial digression if one is to understand not only the internal politics of Palestine prior to 1947 but also the current differences between *fellāḥīn* and bedouin in their relations with the State of Israel.

The use of the term *vilāyet* of Sayda—rather than Palestine—above is purposeful, for it is a key to understanding the field that the various Arab leaders were facing. It had been remarked by the Shaw Commission that although "from time to time independent governments have held rule in Jerusalem . . . during by far the greater part of recorded history the country known as Palestine has formed a mere adjunct of some neighboring Empire" (G.B. Com. 1930:8). More concisely, "Palestine had not been a native sovereign state since the days of the Maccabean rulers" (Duff 1953:45), and even the name Palestine, or *falasṭīn*, is European in origin rather than an Ottoman or an Arabic native term. Prior to World War I, the present-day nation-states of the region were but provinces within the Ottoman Empire and their citizenry were divided first along religious lines and second along ethnic lines, corresponding to economic and residential lines, what Coon called "the mosaic system" (1958:5) and "an ethnic division of labor" (1958:3). Duff described that scenario as follows:

> Not that there was, in 1922, any sense of political nationality among the Palestinians. In those days the artificial States set up by their French and British masters meant less than nothing to them. Most Muslim of the illiterate masses were not conscious of being members of any nation, and if one was asked his nationality he always looked a trifle puzzled and replied, "Thanks be to God, I am Muslim." [1953:36]

and,

> [t]he main difficulty of the Arab leaders in Jerusalem during the 1920's was the lack of any cause, other than that of religion, upon which they could rouse their countrymen. . . . with no consciousness of any political nationality . . . the only unifying bond [was] that of the Faith of the Prophet. [1953:45]

Before 1920, Palestine, in fact, was considered part of Syria by the Arab National Movement. Thus, for example, Antonius (1938:83–84) mentions the major demands of the third "covering dispatch" of the "Bairut secret society" from December 31, 1880, the first of which is "the grant of independence to Syria in union with the Lebanon" (1938:84). This geopolitical framework was still evident in the "Resolutions of the General Syrian Congress" of July 2, 1919, whose first paragraph defines the boundaries of Syria in the south as "a line running from Raffah to al-Jauf and following the Syrian-Hejaz border below 'Aqaba" (Antonius 1938:440). Paragraph 8 states "we desire that there should be no dismemberment of Syria, and no separation of Palestine," and paragraph 7 refers to Palestine as "that part of southern Syria which is known as Palestine" (Antonius 1938:441).

As a result, at the beginning of the 1920s, the Arab National Movement in Palestine was confined to the local power elite and urban intelligentsia (cf. Shim'oni 1946:248; Porath 1971:14–17, 29–30, 248). This local leadership, then, tried to engender and mobilize a *popular* national sentiment and identity by using the presence of the Mandate Power and, primarily, the Jews as its rallying cause (e.g., cf. G.B. Com. 1930:172–73; Porath 1971:18–22, ch. 2). The riots of 1920–1921 and 1929 as well as the whole of the Arab Rebellion of 1936–1939 are best understood as organized attempts to create and nurture an Arab Palestinian national identity (e.g., cf. Porath 1971, 1977) parallel to the Jewish Palestinian one.

Duff, who was a police commander in the Galilee and Jerusalem during the 1920s and early 1930s, thus remarks on the major problem that faced the Palestinian leadership:

"Even the concept of their being Arabs, which all the settled peasants of the hill villages would have resented as a deadly insult in 1922, had not been enunciated" (1953:45). And even though the Supreme Arab Committee centralized the Arabs' efforts against the Jews (during the period under consideration), many did not forget that the rise of Arab political parties in the 1920s and 1930s followed the traditional rivalry of the al-Ḥusayni clan and the al-Našāšībi clan (e.g., Shim'oni 1946:278–93; Porath 1971: esp. ch. V; Porath 1977)—two notable lineages that Duff likened to "Montague and Capulets, or York and Lancaster" (Duff 1953:97)—with roots in the even earlier feuding rivalry of Qays and Yaman (e.g., Shim'oni 1947:278–93).

Of these two factions of the Palestinian Arab leadership, it was the al-Ḥusayni clan and primarily the Mufti of Jerusalem, al-Ḥāǧǧ Amīn al-Ḥusayni, who used Jewish presences as the unifying cause for Palestinian Moslems (e.g., cf. G.B. Com. 1930:158–59, esp. Mr. Snell's reservations; G.B. Com. 1930:172–73; G.B. Pls. 1937:95; Porath 1971: passim).

The Second 'Aliyah socialist Zionist pioneers (that is, those who arrived between 1904 and 1914) fitted well into the Mufti's plans by insisting on "Hebrew Labor" (as one of the slogans of those days went), which kept Arab labor away from Jewish employers, thus arousing strong resentment among the Arabs (e.g., cf. G.B. Col. 1930:51). The Zionists caused further resentment by their attitudes toward inter-gender relations, mode of dressing, and so on (Porath 1971:20). The Old Guard of the pioneers, however—those of the First 'Aliyah (1882–1903) in the Baron de Rothschild's Palestine Jewish Colonization Association (PJCA) settlements and a few members of the Second 'Aliyah such as Alexander Zaïd, who maintained friendly or amicable and cooperative relations based on mutual respect with their Arab neighbors (G.B. Col. 1930:50–51)—created a major problem for the Palestinian Arab Nationalist Movement. Consequently, from the latter point of view, selective assassinations (such as Zaïd's 1938 murder [July 10, 1938], which embroiled the Ḥğerāt) were simply seen as the removal of obstacles on the way to polarizing Arab-Jewish relations, a necessary step on the way to Palestinian Arab Nationalism.

As these processes evolved, the Ḥğerāt became increasingly enmeshed in them, like the rest of the communities in Palestine. For them, however, Palestinian identity came second to being Ḥğeris and never took precedence over Ḥğeri interests and Ḥğeri adaptation to the accumulating changes in their environment. These changes, which were barely noticeable at the onset of the Mandate Period, gained momentum as time passed, eliciting ever more changes in Ḥğeri life ways as the Ḥğerāt adapted to them.

The Establishment of the Mukhtarship

The British military administration, or the Occupied Enemy Territory Administration (the OETA), which was formed and expanded following the conquest of the area by General Allenby and his Egyptian Expeditionary Force (1917–1918), was all too preoccupied in reestablishing security and economic production (cf. G.B. Par. 1921:4). It did not, therefore, intervene in the life of small tribes such as the Ḥğerāt. The Civil Administration that replaced it in 1920 continued to emphasize public security, particularly after the riots of 1920–1921. It furthermore adopted a policy of "*[n]e pas trop gouverner* . . . particularly in an Eastern country, and above all in the early years of a new régime" (G.B. Par. 1921:10). The British, therefore, adopted the Ottoman Law and administrative organization and altered it only when deemed necessary, well after they received the Mandate to administer Palestine (Sept. 29, 1923) from the League of Nations (cf. G.B. Pls. 1937:116).

One such minor alteration, which was in line with British colonial policy everywhere, was the institution of the office of mediator between the indigenous community and the administration (e.g., Watson 1973:1–2; Howell 1951:264–65). Apart from the advantage of legitimating the colonial power by such local representatives, the main reason for the universality of this British practice seems to have been rooted in the inevitable clash between Western organizational patterns and time sense and the diametrically opposed attitudes of the indigenous populations of the colonies (for a discussion of this generic difference see Hall 1976:16–24). For example: "It has been our chief trouble during the past two years that there was no proper authority here to whom matters could be referred for immediate attention" (a British official in Iran at the turn of the twentieth century quoted in Garthwaite 1972:37). This practice, incidentally, was not limited to the British but was used by other states or colonial administrators when faced with acephalous native organizations, such as the Tsarist 1850 attempts to organize the Chukchi (Antropova and Kuznetzova 1964).

The Ottoman administrative system included such an office for the settled population—viz. the *muḫtār*, or village headman—that became an integral subunit of that administration after the institution of the 1858 Land Code (Ashkenazi 1957:59). The Ottomans, however, left the bedouin tribes (both fully and semi-nomadic) to their own leaders, *šiyuḫ* (pl.), or elders.[1] The British expanded this sedentary administrative position to include the bedouin tribes in the northern half of the country as these were not considered "strictly nomadic in habit" (Pls. Census 1933[I]:4). Thus, about 1922 the authorities nominated 'Abūd al-Ramli of the Ġadāyreh, a rich and influential member of the *ḫatyariyyeh* (the Council of Elders), to be *muḫtār* of the Ḥğerāt in the Ẓahara, as part of their drive to establish "local rather than . . . central Government" (G.B. Col. R. 1925[20]:4) in their attempt to reduce the expense of maintaining the new colonial acquisition (for example, cf. Duff 1953:166 and then G.B. Pls. 1937:117–19) (see Map 5).

In general, the creation of the office of the *muḫtār* did not alter the life of the Ḥğerāt because the British were not interested in upsetting the organization and power relations in the tribe. As the Ḥğerāt recount it, the British asked the *ḫatyariyyeh* in the Ẓahara to nominate an influential and rich member of their own number. (Being rich was necessary to ensure the efficient collection of taxes for if a tribesman failed to pay, the *muḫtār* was supposed to pay for him.) The Elders simply nominated 'Abūd al-Ramli, who had been their leader and the senior tribal Elder before the British arrived. The fact that some of the duties of the office required literacy (cf. Luke and Keith-Roach 1922:135–36; Ashkenazi 1957:61) and that none of the *maḫatīr* (pl.) of the Ḥğerāt during the Mandate Period were literate did not bother the authorities so long as the tribe maintained peace and paid its taxes.

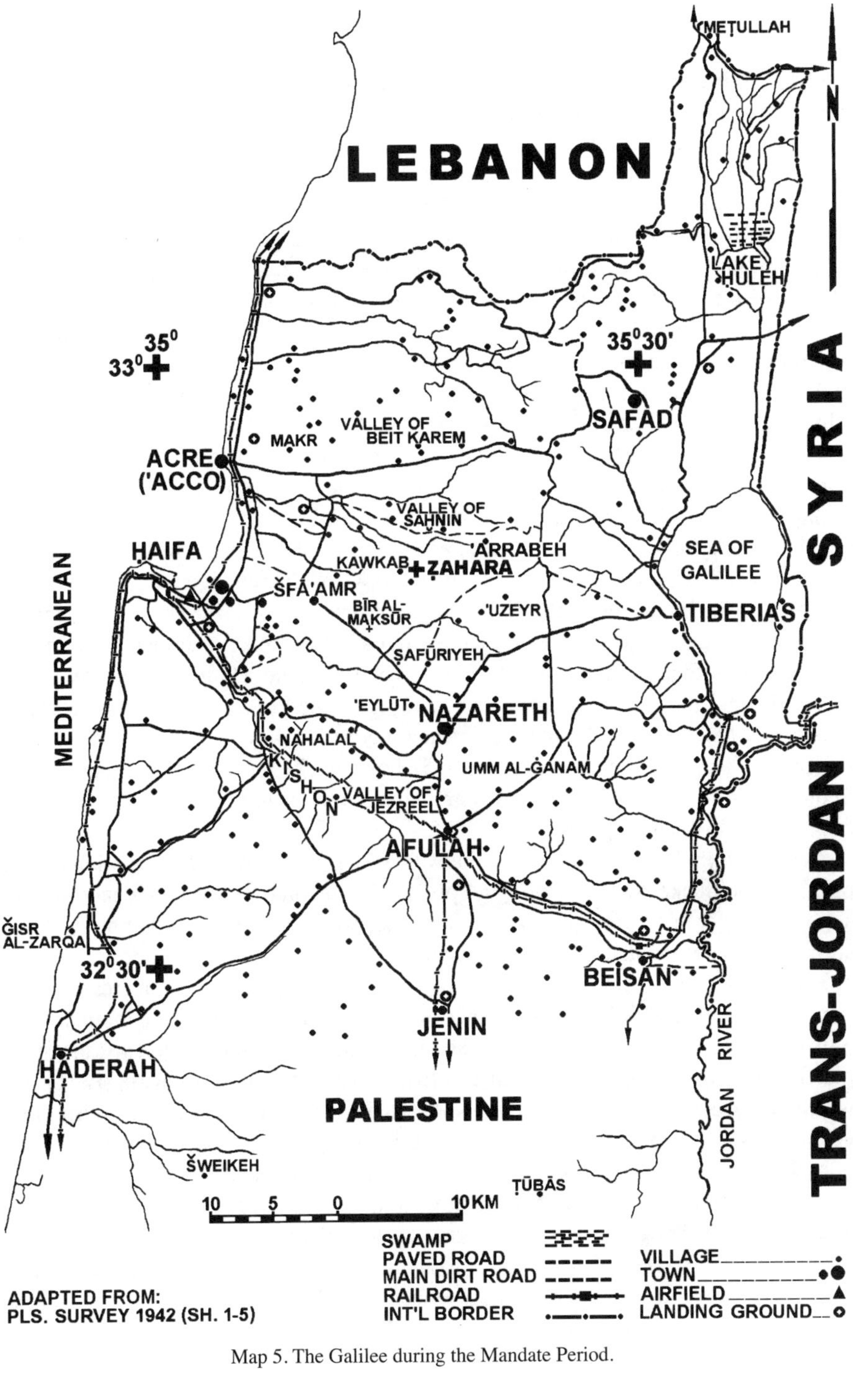

Map 5. The Galilee during the Mandate Period.

Ḥğeri Entry to Police Service

British presence in the country, however, directly affected the life of the Ḥğerāt in some other ways, most importantly through Ḥğeri employment in the Palestine police force. In 1923 a young man of the Ġadāyreh, Mūsā al-Ḍiyab, married; his father did not provide the new household with a tent and a herd. Mūsā, who was about 26 years old at the time, was already a tracker of regional fame. A few days after the wedding Mūsā was visited by a good friend, Muḥammad al-Ḥāmad, who was camping near 'Uzeyr. Muḥammad told him that Edwin G. Bryant ("Abu George"), the commander of the police in Acre and the Western Galilee, was looking for trackers. He then proceeded to convince Mūsā, who was reluctant to become an employee in general and of the British in particular, to join him in applying for the job so that he could support his wife. The two thus became the first Ḥğeris to work for the authorities on a semipermanent basis, thereby forming a link between the tribe and the British as well as with the Jews who served with them.

Neither Mūsā nor Muḥammad served continuously or for long. Both cast their lots with that of Bryant,[2] whom they loved and respected. In doing so they followed traditional bedouin behavioral patterns regarding friendship: slow to befriend, but emotional attachment and utmost loyalty when they do. Thus, Mūsā left the service when Bryant was demoted from the Acre command and although Muḥammad remained in the service to maintain the linkage with the authorities, both moved to Nazareth with Bryant when he was reinstated as the police commander in that city. Muḥammad finally left the force after Bryant's final dismissal in 1930 and when his land acquisition efforts required closer supervision. Mūsā, on the other hand, continued to join or resign according to whether he liked his supervising commander, needed money, or similar immediate considerations. During this period (1923–1945), however, he introduced seven other Ḥğeris to the Palestine police force, all of whom belonged to his lineage, including his son, his brother, one FBS and two FFBSSs.

Serving with the police had several advantages over traditional occupations. First, it provided the tracker with a steady and predictable income year round, enabling him to support a larger family on a better diet than those who lived only off their herds. It is not surprising, therefore, that six of the nine who served in the Palestine police had more than one wife; three had more than two, and two had more than three wives, greatly increasing the proportion of polygynous unions among the Ġadāyreh and even more among its policemen (see Table 5). Similarly, all had five or more children and six had ten or more (see Table 6). In other words, a steady income enabled larger families with more progeny, which in turn could influence the power relations of the following generation either through actual force (i.e., sons) or through strategic marriage alliances (i.e., daughters). Their relatively sizable income was also used to build up or expand their traditional economic resource—the herd—and, sometimes, buy land; this wealth could later be used to back up the claim for power. Furthermore, exposure to and involvement in the regional scene enabled those who served in the police to accumulate information on different trends in land availability, pasture, sociopolitical alliances, and so on—information that could be put to concrete use, economically and politically.

Table 5. The probabilities for having one wife or more among the Ḥĕrāt of Generation VI.

Number of Wives	Ḥĕrāt		Ġadāyreh		Policemen	
	Cases	Probability	Cases	Probability	Cases	Probability
1	148	0.576	53	0.505	3	0.150
2	36	0.280	16	0.305	3	0.300
3	7	0.082	4	0.114	1	0.150
4	4	0.062	2	0.076	2	0.400

Table 6. Average number of children among the Ḥĕrāt of Generation VI.

Category	Number of Households	Children/ Household
Ḥĕrāt	192	8.0
Ġadāyreh	75	8.5
Policemen	9	11.4

In addition to the direct personal advantages mentioned above, there were other benefits that emanated from the role of a policeman. In terms of "brute force," a policeman could make the lives of his opponents or enemies quite dismal while making those of his friends easier and more pleasant. Extending help, even when it was part of the official definition of duty, was an effective way to create reciprocal obligatory bonds with the recipient of such help. In other words, the juxtaposition of an impersonal, well-defined Western administrative structure on personal, defused, and traditional social relations enabled strategically placed operators to capitalize on these conflicting characteristics without stepping out of their well-defined loci or duties in the administration.

Being a native policeman in this regional context also enhanced the position of the whole tribe vis-à-vis other sociopolitical entities in the area. Whether a policeman had warned his tribesmembers of an intended police action, such as a search and/or an arrest of offenders, thereby enabling them to be involved in illegal activities that played down their opponents in the omnipresent regional one-upmanship game was relatively immaterial. More important, having to ask for an action, even if completely justified by law, rendered the one who asked it in moral debt to the one who provided the service. Since in traditional society both individuals represent their respective groups, any such action automatically received the added import of enhancing the regional status of the group of a continuous giver, that is, in this case, the native policeman.

It is very unlikely that all of these advantages were apparent to Mūsā al-Ḏiyab during the first half of the 1920s. Yet, it seems that enough of them were evident, for he introduced into the service only his close friends and lineage members rather than members of the

Ṣawālḥah or competing factions within the Ġadāyreh (for instance, members of the family of ʿAbūd al-Ramli, the *muḫtār*, who were FFBSs to Mūsā). His ability to monopolize the introduction to the police service stemmed not only from the colonial practice of minimizing communication channels between the administration and the native community, but also from the very few positions that were open for good but illiterate trackers after 1928 when "a regulation was issued, and enforced, that all our native policemen must be literates" (Duff 1953:167). His seniority, excellent work record, and character (cf. Duff 1935:186–90, 196–99) caused his immediate superiors not only to ignore his illiteracy but to depend on him for recommendations when good trackers were needed.

Regardless of their small number, the nine Ḥğeris who served in the Palestine police force, and especially Mūsā's younger brother, Ḥsēn al-Ḏiyab, laid the foundation for the relationship with the Israeli administration. This relationship not only helped *ʿulād* Ḏiyab al-Ibrāhīm monopolize political power in the tribe during the third quarter of the twentieth century, but also intensified the process of elevating the relatively small and minor tribe to regional supremacy.

Mūsā al-Ḏiyab's draft in 1923 thus heralded the beginning of the transition from the traditional means of acquiring and maintaining political power and leadership in the tribe to the "modern" (in the sense of post-colonial) means to this end. ʿAbūd al-Ramli gained the leadership, among other reasons, because of the large following of his own sublineage, the absence of suitable competition among his peers in the other sublineages of the Ġadāyreh, and his wealth, which was used for hospitality and gifts, thus tying others to him by bonds of reciprocity. Sleymān al-ʿAbed, who replaced him toward the end of 1929, although from a small sublineage, was tightly intermarried with the Ramlāt: his wife was ʿAbūd's sister and two of his own sisters were married to ʿAbūd's younger brothers. Similarly, three of his daughters were married to ʿAbūd's son and two of his paternal first cousins (FBSs). Like ʿAbūd, he was wealthy and did not have a suitable competitor of his own generation within the Ġadāyreh. The same was the case with the two *maḫatīr* of the Ṣawālḥah: ʿAbdāllah al-Ṣāleḥ, who led the Maḥāmīd—still the largest sublineage of the Ṣawālḥah—from the beginning of the 1920s (after the death of his FBS Ṭaʿamīs al-Maḥmūd), and Ḥassan al-Šhāb, the leader of *ulād* Ḥassan al-Ṣāleḥ who succeeded to the office after ʿAbdāllah's death in 1935, and who had no suitable competitors among the Maḥāmīd. As the state became more involved in the life of its citizenry, these traditional means of power (character, related membership, a following, and wealth) gave way to a new means, viz., the monopolization of the linkage between the tribe and the state's agencies controlling the sources of political power formerly embedded in the local population. During the 1920s, 1930s, and 1940s, however, involvement with the police did not change the life of the Ḥğerāt as a whole, or directly affect the mukhtarships of the tribe.

Ḥğeri Population Count in the Early 1920s

The Ḥğerāt of the 1920s and their life patterns were hardly different from those of a decade or two earlier. According to the Census of 1922, they numbered 321 persons—163 males and 158 females located in three subdistricts: Haifa (18: 8 males, 10 females), Acre (200: 107 males, 93 females), and Nazareth (103: 48 males, 55 females) (Pls. Census 1923:35, 37, 38 respectively).[3] Von Oppenheim, who visited the area in 1925, enumerates them as 72 tents—40 of which belonged to the Ġadāyreh and the remainder to the Ṣawālḥah (1943:18)—which amounts to about 350 persons in the tribe as a whole, divided as 217 and 133 between the two lineages respectively.[4] Increasing membership did not yet force them to accommodate any changes in residence or schedules. They continued to herd their sheep, goats, and cattle according to long established routines and to cultivate some land, whether their own or as sharecroppers for a richer tribesmember.

Land Registration and Economic Development in Palestine

As British presence became more established, however, several trends with profound effects on Ḥğeri life patterns began to develop. These trends were promoted by two major factors: economic policy and administrative reality. Although the Mandate Government did not become overly involved in directing Palestine's economic development, it did try to create a framework that would enable private individuals or institutions to develop the local economy (cf. Halevi and Klinov-Malul 1968:30–31; Morag 1967:2–3). At the same time, the government was unable to institute complete peace and public order in the country (cf. Duff 1934, 1935, 1953; Bowden 1975; Ashkenazi 1938:47), and, as a result, limited private wars (such as between bedouin shepherds and *fellāḥīn* cultivators) continued unabated.

From a Ḥğeri viewpoint, the most important immediate repercussion of the first of these factors was a sudden amplification in the already established trend of the expansion of cultivation and the corresponding diminution of free pasture and water. A water shortage arose as a result of the campaign undertaken by the government to combat malaria. Part of this campaign included covering infected wells and prohibiting the excavation of new ones (cf. G.B. Col. R. 1924[12]:4; Ashkenazi 1957:153). Since there were not many springs in the general area of the Ḥğerāt, competition for available water increased.

Several elements combined to intensify the reduction in free pasturage that had been occurring for half a century. In the attempt to organize the country along Western administrative principles, the government established a new land registration system that replaced the antiquated Ottoman system. To that end a law was passed in 1920 "establishing a Land Registry and providing that no disposition of immovable property should be valid unless recorded in the registry" (G.B. Col. 1937:39). By 1925 it became clear that this system was inoperative due to the lack of cadastral survey maps (G.B. Col. R. 1925[20]:5–6). Moreover, the collection of taxes and specifically the tithe proved to be a problem because "the annual estimation of crops . . . [was found by] . . . the Government . . . [to be] most cumbersome" (Pls. Gov. 1946[I]:246). Although from the cultivator's point of view the old method "had the advantage of varying according to good or bad crops" (Pls. Gov. 1946[I]:246), it was precisely these fluctuations that turned the assessment into haggling sessions and prevented the institution of predictable tax revenues deemed necessary by the administration. Consequently, in 1926 the older law regarding the tithe was amended to assess this tax on the basis of the amount of arable land owned rather than on the yield of the crop grown. This reform necessitated a detailed classification of land types and quality as well as the registration of land boundaries and ownership for the assessment to be made accurately, thus providing the necessary impetus for a cadastral survey and the establishment of land courts to settle ownership claims (G.B. Col. R. 1926[26]:5–6). An additional stimulus was generated by the drive of the Jewish national institutions to buy land and to settle it with Jewish agricultural settlements.

By forcing land registration yet eliminating conscription, and by providing incentives such as loans, subsidies, seed gifts, advice, and other services, the government was quite successful in its attempts to encourage the intensification and expansion of agriculture, the mainstay of at least 54 percent of the population in 1931 (Pls. Census 1933[I]:282).

While not wholly successful in instituting peace and security within the boundary of Palestine, the Mandate Government ended organized bedouin raids both inside the country and from Trans-Jordan, and by 1924 it could claim that "there have been . . . no raids from Transjordan [sic]" (G.B. Col. R. 1924[12]:4). This accomplishment was achieved through the use of the Royal Air Force (RAF) in cooperation with the Palestine Gendarmerie from 1924 on (G.B. Col. R. 1925[20]:33–34, [31]:47, [82]:66, etc.), as well as through the financing of the Trans-Jordan Frontier Force, which was charged with control of the desert bedouin tribes (G.B. Col. R. 1926[26]:8). Thus, for the first time in many centuries the peasants of Palestine could be sure of harvesting their crops.

An added pressure on the availability of open pasture was the massive purchasing of land by Jews, notably by the Jewish National Fund (JNF), whose primary purpose was to acquire land for the Zionist project (Orni 1974:17). This drive influenced diminishing pastures both directly and indirectly. Directly, it established Jewish agricultural settlements that turned uncultivated and lightly cultivated land to intensive cultivation (e.g., G.B. Col. R. 1924[12]:4) and did not recognize the post-harvest rights of the herdsman (Porath 1971:18). Indirectly, it set an example of the economic rewards of Western agricultural techniques, which combined with the government's efforts to influence the Arab peasant to increase his own production.

Another factor influencing pasture availability was the rapid increase in the Moslem rural population, the dominant fraction of the non-urban sector in the country. Thus, the total rural population, which in 1931 numbered 648,530 persons, reached an estimated 872,090 people in 1944 (Warriner 1948:57). Although rural-urban migration siphoned off some of the increase (Pls. Gov. 1946[I]:157), this did not alleviate the pressure to any measurable degree.

Ḥğeri Relations with Ṣafūriyeh

The expansion in cultivated area, however, was concurrent with the increase in Ḥğeri population size, which enabled the tribe to increase its protective force. During the 1920s and 1930s, the competition between land cultivation and herding in the Beit Netofah and Saḫnīn areas was still relatively relaxed, although pressures were mounting steadily. In general during that period, the Ḥğerāt continued to maintain their amiable relations with those small villages in the area too weak to fight back and with which the tribe had been slowly intermarrying. Already strained relations with neighboring Ṣafūriyeh, however, deteriorated markedly.

Ṣafūriyeh, the largest village[5] north of the Valley of Jezreel, controlled much of the land in the western half of the Valley of Beit Netofah to the north of the village as well as a large tract of land to its south into *wādi* al-Malik. On the west these lands were flanked by *wādi* al-Malik's tributary, *wādi* al-Ḫaldiyeh. Simply put, much of the Ḥğeri traditional summer pasture was on fallow Ṣafūrian land and on its open range. Conflict was therefore inevitable, especially because the Ṣafūrians could amass more men than the Ḥğerāt, and hence did not shy away from violent confrontation. The Ḥğerāt, however, maintain today that winning these conflicts did not depend on absolute numbers but on unity, courage, and ferocity when fighting, superior tactics, and cunning, in all of which attributes they surpassed the Ṣafūrian peasants. Conflicts between the two adversaries usually took the form of skirmishes between Ḥğeri shepherds and either Ṣafūrian cultivators or shepherds. Every so often such skirmishes resulted in the loss of human life. One such major incident started when the Ṣafūrians chased the herds of the Ṣawālḥah back to the Mikmān where four Ḥğeris fired on them, chasing them away, killing one Ṣafūrian and wounding several others. The ensuing feud continued for several years, during which, according to the Ḥğerāt, most of the Ṣafūrians could not cultivate their fields or collect the crops in the Valley of Beit Netofah in safety.

The Purchase of the Lands of Bīr al-Maksūr

The government's cadastral survey and land registration drive affected the Ḥğerāt in an even more profound manner—the resulting purchase of the lands of Bīr al-Maksūr in 1942. Originally these lands belonged to the Druze of Šfā'amr. When the government enacted the land laws, effectively making land registration mandatory, the Moslems of Šfā'amr tried to deprive the Druze of their ownership by making claims to that land. The case went to court but the Druze, who traditionally were a weak minority (Falah 1975:42),[6] could not finance the lawsuit. They therefore approached a rich Moslem landowner, one Ṣāleḥ al-Šibl of Kafr Makr near Acre, and offered him half the land on the condition that he would go to court and win the case against the Moslems of Šfā'amr. Ṣāleḥ Effendi took the challenge and won the case. One Friday in 1934, however, while coming out of the mosque in Šfā'amr, he was axed down by some angry peasants. In 1935 his three sons and two daughters, who had inherited the land, tried to sell it cheaply to peasants of other local villages in order to avenge their father's death on the Shfar'ameans. The villages did not accept the offer either because they did not want to enter into conflict with the Shfar'ameans or because they already had enough land or perhaps because they lacked the necessary funds. By 1940 the opportunity was offered to the Ḥğerāt, who jointly bought the land in 1942. The total deal amounted to 1875 *dunum* (417.6 acres) at P£3.5/*dunam* or a little over P£6500.00 for the whole parcel to be paid in three installments over the following five years. The area was registered as *muša'* (communal land) and there were 85.25 original shares for the 85 families who paid the full price and one who participated in only one-quarter of a share. Following the registration of the land, the Ḥğerāt immediately began to cultivate the new property, and in 1945 the first house was built on the hill that was to become the center of the tribe from 1960 to the present.

The lands of Bīr al-Maksūr were not conceived as privately owned property of the 86 families who participated in their purchase. Rather, these were communal lands belonging to *all* the Ḥğerāt, even though they were not *muša'* in the formal sense of the term (cf. Baer 1971:67–68 for the legal definition of *muša'*). Any tribesman who wanted to cultivate the land was therefore free to do so as long as there was no counterclaim on that plot of land. Nor did he have to compensate any other tribesmember for using the land; hence, no sharecropping arrangements developed around these lands during the 1940s and early 1950s.

The purchase of the lands of Bīr al-Maksūr did not greatly change the migratory cycle of the Ḥğerāt. Before the purchase, each herding camp would return to its wintering area according to its own schedule. Now, when the end of summer drew near, all the tribe would congregate at Bīr al-Maksūr. Following the first autumn rain they would plow and sow the land. Using the traditional "heavy plow" (cf. Avitsur 1976:20–22), they would start (usually in mid-November) and continue until the work was completed. If they were interrupted by early heavy rains, they would temporarily stop but would complete the plowing and sowing no later than the end of January. Once done, they would return to their respective wintering grounds. The Ṣawālḥah, who moved their base camp to the Mikmān in 1930 (see below), did not have to change their migratory pattern at all, as the Mikmān is a little over one kilometer north of Maksūr. In the spring they would return to Maksūr, camping on the hills to its east and maintaining their traditional spring activities. By the end of May they would harvest the barley and toward the end of June, the wheat, thresh it in the fields, and store the grain in their wintering areas before breaking up camp and resuming their summer movement. The smaller herds would graze on the stubble before leaving for the valley, trampling some manure into these fields.

In addition to involving the whole tribe more closely with agriculture, purchasing Maksūr enabled those tribesmen who did not have adequate herds for independent economic survival to shift completely to independent cultivation, rather than be dependent on sharecropping. Thus, for the first time some members of the tribe became conceptually fully sedentary, investing the crux of their efforts in land cultivation rather than in herding, and no longer redirecting agricultural income into building up a herd. Purchasing Maksūr also marked the establishment of a common minimum property base so that no Ḥğeri household was truly property-less as long as the *muša'* was in force.

The year 1942 similarly marked the time when agriculture became a more important economic resource in the Ẓahara as well. The Ẓahara was, as mentioned above, a maquis of *Q. calliprinos-P. palaestina* association. This vegetation survived the deforestation that intensified toward the end of the nineteenth century as a result of the increased demand for charcoal (e.g., Oliphant 1976:72, 154–55; G.B. Naval 1920:506), and which culminated in the massive consumption of wood during the First World War by the Ottoman railway system (G.B. Naval 1920:542; Pls. Forests 1946:8). The Ḥğerāt did little to alter the tree cover, although over time the little patches that were cleared in order to pitch a tent or construct a pen were expanded to include small areas for kitchen gardens. Thus, although some cultivation was practiced, it never reached any significant measure, and the natural cover was preserved.

The massive concentration of British troops during World War II, however, created an increased demand for firewood and charcoal for heating and cooking (Pls. Forests 1946), which aggravated the cumulative destruction of the preceding centuries. So it was that in 1942, the charcoal-makers from Kafr Ṭubās[7] reached the Yotvat mountain range and cut down the trees throughout, thus clearing the Ẓahara for possible agriculture.

Before 1950, however, while most Ḥğeris practiced some cultivation and some of them depended on it for their livelihood, none produced on a large enough scale for marketing. The main crop was wheat, used for home consumption in bread, with barley and tobacco as secondary crops. In their land in the Valley of Beit Netofah they grew some durra (*Sorghum bicolor*). They also grew vegetables, sesame, and watermelons in small kitchen gardens.

The importance of their gradual introduction to cultivation in slow piecemeal fashion was to legitimatize agriculture as an acceptable endeavor for a bedouin, thus preparing them for its adoption as a major economic pursuit later on.

The Beginnings of Ḥğeri Market Orientation

Eventually, a few enterprising individuals took advantage of the opportunities created by the economic development of the country as a whole. This development was spurred primarily by the Jewish immigrants who, with engineering and managerial experience and imported capital, gave the impetus to intensified market-oriented agricultural production (Veicmanas 1938:346) and to the development of local industry (e.g., G.B. Col. R. 1924[12]:3, 1926[26]:3, 1927[31]:4; G.B. Com. 1930:174; G.B. Pls. 1937:90–94; Himadeh 1938:228–29; Halevi and Klinov-Malul 1968:18–22). The taxes and customs paid by these new and intensified production schemes were the government's two main revenue sources (e.g., cf. G.B. Com. 1930:19, 134; G.B. Col. R. 1928[40]:18 for 1920–1928; Col. R. 1932[82]:145 for 1929–1930; Col. R. 1935[112]:202 for 1931–1932/33; Col. R. 1938[166]:210 for 1933/34–1937/38) and as such financed many of the governmental programs in the rural areas (e.g., cf. Duff 1953:166).

Some enterprising Ḥğeris responded to the expanding market by providing transport services with their camels; others collected goat and cattle manure from their herds and sold it to merchants who distributed the fertilizer. A few became traders and "fences" for smugglers who imported contraband from Lebanon, and several supplemented their income by participating in and often winning the horse races that began in Acre in 1930 and continued all over the country until the Arab Rebellion broke out in 1936.

These activities, however, were intermittent in character and were used primarily as a means to build up or expand a herd, buy land, and supplement the family income, much like the economic aspect of service in the police. As such, these activities did not constitute a radical break from the traditional pattern of economic activities nor did they induce the Ḥğerāt to become more deeply involved in the fast developing market-oriented regional economy.

The Ḥğerāt and the 1936–1939 Arab Rebellion

While some Ḥğeris became more involved in the regional economic network or gained public exposure through their service with the police, the majority of the tribe kept to its traditional isolation during the first half of the Mandate Period. Though its numbers were increasing, the Ḥğerāt was still a relatively small tribe in terms of size, and not yet very influential in the regional political arena. To its advantage, however, the larger, stronger, and more important tribes such as the *'arab* al-Ṣbeyḥ or the *'arab* al-Muwāsa were living in the eastern half of the Lower Galilee and the Valley of Beisan. So while the Ḥğerāt tell of one conflict with the Muwāsa, and of once being raided by a bedouin tribe from the Lağa' (Syria), both occurred during the first decade of the Mandate Period and were the exception rather than the rule. Usually the Ḥğerāt had to contend only with relatively small tribes similar to themselves, and while these relations were competitive, they were nonbelligerent (although they included a large measure of animal theft at which, the Ḥğeris claim, they were the best). In these relations the Ḥğerāt, moreover, had the advantage of leading the alliance with the Ka'abīyeh and the Ḥelf, which could have enabled them to amass a larger number of fighters than other small local tribes had the need arisen. As time passed, however, and as relations with Ṣafūriyeh became increasingly strained, they slowly became more involved in the regional sociopolitical and economic networks, both as individuals and as larger groups, because even individual bedouin who seemingly act as unattached self-interested entities are nonetheless formal representatives of their respective lineages and tribes. In this respect bedouin always become involved as larger sociopolitical units even if only one person makes an appearance.

The decline in inter-tribal belligerence was the outcome of the general waning of the autonomous politico-military power of the bedouin tribes, which was already noticeable in the 1880s (e.g., Oliphant 1976:73–75; Conder 1878[II]:271–72) and which became all the more pronounced with the Mandate Government's success in curbing the traditional inter-tribal and village raids (the *ġāzu*). Similarly, the collection of "protection fees" (the *ḫawa*) was disappearing, although the Ḥğerāt said that the *'arab* al-Ṣbeyḥ were still exacting it from both small tribes and villages well into the 1930s and several other tribes were reported to have collected it from some Jewish settlements (Duff 1953:167). As the practice of *ḫawa* collection diminished, there was a parallel decrease in the intense competition over its exaction and its symbolic attributes of nobler versus commoner tribes with corresponding degrees of political autonomy and power. Now the government exacted "*ḫawa*" in the form of the Animal Tax and the Tithe. It also forbade carrying firearms in public, so although practically every bedouin had a gun, these were kept in hiding. Animal stealing and smuggling became more remunerative and respectable in inverse relation to the amount of control the government could exercise over the prevention of highway robbery, the *ġāzu*, and the other traditionally more respectable bedouin occupations.

The tribe's growing involvement in the regional scene became very discernible during the 1936–1939 Arab Rebellion. While the majority of the tribe maintained their daily routines, the young men joined the rebels and seven of them became commanders in the rebel bands (Porath 1977:388–403). Maintaining daily routines did not mean that the tribe as a unit did not condone the fighting. The type of warfare favored continued economic production in order to supply the bands. It therefore seems that although there was no formal decision to participate in the rebellion, there was a tacit approval of and agreement with the youth. For example, the son of the *muḫtār* of the Ẓahara, who with his brother lived with their father to help run the family properties, was one of the sub-band commanders mentioned by Porath (Porath 1977:402).

It is hard to establish details of Ḥğeri rebel organization due to their understandable reluctance to address the subject. However, it is important to explain their participation in the rebellion because while the tribe had adopted an isolationist policy until then, seven Ḥğeris (six sub-band commanders and one band commander) are listed in Porath's Appendix B ("Officers of the Revolt," 1977:388–403). This list includes 281 names, 22 (or 7.8%) of which belonged to bedouin (Porath 1977:261). In other words, the Ḥğerāt provided a lion's share, or 31.8%, of the listed bedouin commanders. Only two villages provided a comparable number (that is, seven) of commanders for the rebellion: Silat al-Ẓahr in the Nablus area and Ṣafūriyeh (Porath 1977:262).

The heavy Ḥğeri participation becomes clearer when viewed against the regional setting. The rebel bands, which originally belonged to the organization of the Mufti al-Ḥāğğ Amīn of the al-Ḥusayni family, adopted a policy of terror that included settling personal accounts with competing Arab families while polarizing Jewish-Arab relations and ensuring the provision of supplies and money by the civil, often village, population. To defend themselves and to fight back against that campaign, many villages (especially those aligned with the rivals of the al-Ḥusayni clan, the al-Našāšībi family) formed "peace bands." Most of these bands fought the rebel bands outright. Some, however, like the one of the Zu'bīyeh lineage of the lower Galilee, outwardly participated in the rebellion but, in fact, were formed to protect their villages from the rebel bands (cf. Porath 1977:251–57).

Undoubtedly, many youths joined the fighting having been influenced by their neighbors from Kawkab Abū al-Hejā', Kafr Manda, 'Uzeyr, Rummāneh, and so on, as well as for the fame, glory, and riches that wars are thought to bestow on heroes. Nevertheless, it seems that a prominent reason among the several that prompted the tribes to participate was concern over the Ṣafūrian bands and, similar to the Zu'bīyeh, the need for self-defense. Regardless of the reasons for their participation, the important fact was that they became involved in the feuds spurred by the rebellion (cf. Porath 1977:257–58), and it is this fact that bears upon the ensuing events and on Ḥğeri adaptation during the third quarter of the twentieth century.

It was in their role as rebels that the Ḥğerāt were again pitted against the Druze. During the rebellion, the Druze either remained neutral or, like the Mt. Carmel villages, had "cordial relationships" with the Jews (Porath 1977:271). In either case they were identified, according to the Ḥğerāt, with the British and the Jews during the rebellion (also, cf. Porath 1977:271–73). To coerce Druze villages to supply provisions to rebel bands, to take a pro-rebel stand, and, as part of a more general policy of terrorizing opponents to force compliance with their demands, the rebels raided Druze villages in the fall of 1936 and winter of 1937 (Porath 1977:271). It was against this background that in 1937 five Druze were murdered in Šfā'amr and their bodies thrown into a well. The son of the most prominent among them, Ṣāleḥ Ḥassan al-Ḫnefes, accused the Ḥğerāt of the murder, and based on his testimony, two Ḥğeris were sent to the gallows at Acre prison in 1939. Today the Ḥğerāt say they had nothing to do with the murder of Ḥassan al-Ḫnefes and his co-religionists and that it was the work of Moslem peasants from Šfā'amr who took their revenge on the Druze on account of the Ṣāleḥ al-Šibl and the lands of Bīr al-Maksūr case and because the Druze were "friends of the English."

To complicate matters even further, in 1938 a rebel who was a member of the Ṭababšeh (the leading lineage of the Ḥelf) was instructed by the officers of the rebellion (from its headquarters in Jerusalem) to murder Alexander Zaïd, the forest guard of the hill area south of Šfā'amr and a famous figure in the Jewish sector. Zaïd, who in 1907 was one of the seven founders of "Bar Giora," the first in a series of Jewish guard and defense organizations, lived in a farmhouse on a hill not far from the village of Sheikh Abreik and was no longer active in the Jewish defense effort. He was, nonetheless, a legendary figure among the Jews and was highly respected and influential among his Arab neighbors, particularly among the bedouin. The order for his murder was thus an attempt to polarize Arab-Jewish relations in the area. As the leaders of the tripartite alliance, this murder automatically implicated the Ḥğerāt in the ensuing blood feud with the Jews.

Of the two developments—Ḫnefes' murder and the Zaïd assassination—the latter was more assumed than real and was grounded on the terms of the alliance rather than on actual, day-to-day, realpolitik. Zaïd's death was avenged later that year when three people approached a camp of the Ḥelf at night and called the killer, Gāsem al-Muḥammad, who was sitting near the fire. He went to see who they were and was shot and killed. Since he was the killer, his death, according to tradition, would have signaled the end of the feud had such an end been desired. The Ḥğerāt, however, were prompted by the Ḥelf not to let the case die. Moreover, the Ḥğerāt suspected the three killers to be Zaïd's firstborn and two members of the *'arab* al-Ṣbeyḥ so the case took on inter-tribal overtones with its regional one-upmanship game implications. Regardless of the specific reasons, the Ḥğerāt swore to avenge Gāsem's death and kill Zaïd's firstborn. The latter, incidentally, said that the three killers were members of the *PalMaH* (the elite units of the *Haganah*), that it was this organization that took it upon itself to avenge his father's murder, and that once done, the Jews viewed the case closed.

The Ḫnefes case, however, was of very immediate and grave consequence for the Ḥğerāt. Their relations with the Druze had been strained ever since the Druze had raided the Ẓahara and mistakenly killed a Ḥğeri in the last quarter of the nineteenth century (see above). The death was avenged, only to be followed by other deaths several years later. Finally, a *ṣulḥa* was negotiated under the auspices of a *šeyḫ* from Jebel al-Druze in Syria and a strained peace prevailed. After the British conquered the country and instituted some measure of law and order, the old rivalries assumed a more peaceful expression during the *fantaziyeh* (festivities) and horse races in neighboring village weddings and later in the official race courses. Ṣāleḥ Ḥassan al-Ḫnefes' testimony, whether true or not, brought blood to the foreground and the Ḥğerāt, led by the Ġadāyreh, swore blood revenge. Notwithstanding, a member of the Ṣawālḥah, a friend of the Druze leader prior to the case, maintained his friendship with Ṣāleḥ al-Ḥassan after it as well.

Not only did macro-relations such as Jewish-Arab, Arab-Druze, and so on become more strained as time passed, but micro-relations such as Ḥğerāt-Ṣafūriyeh also became more belligerent. For example, in 1941 the Ṣafūrians attacked the Ḥelf to avenge the elopement of one of their young women with her husband's young Ḥelfi laborer. The Ḥelf were away at a wedding and the Ṣafūrians killed the one who was left to guard the encampment. At that point a young Ḥğeri who was camping with the Ḥelf intervened, killing four Ṣafūrians and five horses before they were able to get away. The *ṣulḥa* that followed restored peace to the area only nominally because continuous shepherds' conflicts threatened the continuity of any peace arrangement.

These events of the second half of the 1930s gained more importance with the purchase of the lands of Bīr al-Maksūr. The processes that gave rise to the events, however, continued to evolve and to intensify, culminating during the 1948 Israel's War of Independence.

The Yearly Round in the Ẓahara and Bīr al-Maksūr

These excitements, however, while pointing to areas of tension and danger in Ḥğeri life and extra-tribal relations, were not the common fare. In fact, Ḥğeri life throughout the period was usually monotonous, occasionally punctuated by a trip to Nazareth and several nights of stories about that adventure. Life followed the seasonal cycle of their herds and land; their days started early and often ended late. A spring or summer day began typically with the women starting the fire at about 03:30–04:00. By the time tea was ready, the rest of the family would be up, and after some tea the herd would be inspected, milked if in season, and set to pasture. Since in general security was good and tribal raids a thing of the past, there was no need for young adults or older teenagers to herd. Instead, the shepherds were the younger teenage males if the range was further away (for instance, in the Valley of Saḫnīn) or of either sex if the herd was pastured closer to the tent or in the Ẓahara. This arrangement meant that males were more likely to herd the more mobile flocks of sheep and goats while females and younger males were more likely to care for the lambs and kids kept closer to home and the cattle herded on the Ẓahara itself.

Once the herd was on its way the young men (to middle age if a person were poor), with the help of the older female members of the household, would leave for the fields—their own, in partnership, or in sharecropping. Those females who stayed at home would collect firewood and edible wild plants in season; bring the water, often from afar (for example, from Kafr Manda, the Ḏmeydeh, and even Bīr al-Badawiyyeh to the Ẓahara); cook; and look after the babies. The women were also charged with milking the herd and processing the milk into *laban* (yogurt), *labne* (drained *laban* cream cheese), *ǧibneh* (cheese), and *samneh* (clarified butter). The last three products were the only way to preserve the milk for use during the summer, fall, and most of the winter when the herds went dry.

In late afternoon and early evening the people from the fields and the herds would return to camp. The herds would be milked if in season. After supper, the men would congregate in one tent or another and spend the evening together talking. Like other northern tribes (cf. Ashkenazi 1938:117), the Ḥǧerāt did not maintain a *šig* (a central guest tent) as did the tribes in the center of the country (e.g., Diqs 1969:15, et passim; Kressel 1976:27, et passim), or the Negev bedouin (e.g., Marx 1967:82, et passim; Randolph 1963:84–86). Each Ḥǧeri tent could become the social center for an evening, and each tent could receive its own guests, tribesmembers or outsiders. Consequently, practically every Ḥǧeri tent would make the ceremonial bedouin bitter coffee, the *sa'adah* or *gahwa murra*; if the males were too busy, it was prepared by those females who stayed at home. Nor was an evening's get-together (the *sahara*) barred to the tribe's women unconditionally. If no strangers were present and if the women felt like joining the gathering, they would congregate in a corner of the *dīwān* (the males' section) rather than in the *ḥarīm* (the females' section). Alternatively, those who had finished their chores or had some free time between one task and another would get together at a friend's *ḥarīm*. The day would often end at about 22:00 when most people would go to sleep. This informality was, to a large extent, the result of the small size of their *ḥama'il* (lineages) for most of their history and of the sense of being one family, as one of them remarked years later: "*mā bu ḥama'il 'andina, bu ḥamūleh wāḥdah, ḥamūlat al-ḥǧerāt*" ("We do not have lineages. We have one lineage, the lineage of the Ḥǧerāt.").

This daily schedule would shift with the seasons. During the winter there was only work with the herds. With some annual fluctuations as a result of the rains and pasture availability (cf. also Hirsch 1933:24, 57), from mid-November the sheep would start to drop the lambs and from mid-December the goats would join them. Lambing added much work in caring for and feeding the lambs and kids before the herd left in the morning and following its return in the evening. Apart from that, however, most of the day would be spent socializing.

If free time was abundant, food was scarce and not very interesting. Meat was hardly seen during the winter months because rarely would a guest worthy of a feast arrive when the weather was cold and gray and the paths all but washed out. Without guests one was very reluctant to cut into his producing capital—the herd. Nor was it great fun to go out on a rainy night to steal an animal from the villagers or a competing tribe, especially since during such winter nights the animals were likely to be kept in a cave or in the cellar under a peasant's house. Winter was a time to eat preserved foods such as dried okra, *mluḫiyeh* (mallow leaves or Lebanese spinach), and figs as well as olives, *labne* preserved in olive oil, cheese, butter, *burġul* (cracked wheat), and so on. Before the rainy season each family would try to stock up both food and firewood for the whole period (about three months) so that they would not have to go out to resupply when it was rainy, cold, and muddy.

While some of the produce was grown by the Ḥğerāt, some of it had to be procured from the nearby villages. Thus, for example, yogurt (*laban*) would be exchanged by volume at a ratio of 1:1 with *burġul* while *labne* would be exchanged at 1:1 with olive oil. Whereas *burġul* was exchanged often and in large quantities, olive oil was bartered less frequently because the main source of fat in the diet was homemade clarified butter (*samneh*) while olive oil was used primarily to preserve the *labne*. Okra, lentils, figs, *mluḫiyeh* (*Corchorus olitorius*) and other vegetable material not grown by the Ḥğerāt in their kitchen gardens were also bartered with the neighboring villages. Coffee, tea, sugar, and other such necessities were bought in Nazareth or Šfā'amr. In the 1920s, the tribesmembers began purchasing kerosene and oil lamps, thereby replacing the hearth as the main source of light after darkness and increasing their dependence on the market.

Spring (March) was always a welcome change after the dreariness and boredom of winter. The lambs and kids would have grown and could be sent out to pasture, and milk was plentiful. The world was green and fresh plant food could be procured. People were no longer confined to their tents by the discomfort outside and would visit friends in the villages, collect wild edible plants, steal animals, and engage in other outdoor activities. In April, the herds would move down from the Ẓahara to Maksūr and the wedding season would start, reuniting the Ḥğeris from the Ẓahara with the Ḍmeydeh, the Mikmān, and even the more solitary households from 'Uzeyr's environs, who would come to participate in the festivities.

Weddings during the Mandate Period and especially after ca. 1930 would usually be celebrated over a 24- to 30-hour period starting about noon one day and ending between noon and evening of the following day. During the Ottoman and early Mandate Period, in comparison, the celebrations would start some 10 to 14 days before the nuptial night. During this period, every evening after supper people would come to the celebrating family to sing and dance the *dabchah* (or *dabkah*) until about midnight when even the young would depart to sleep. During the Mandate Period, pre-wedding celebrations became increasingly shorter both in duration and in scope as free time grew shorter due to the increase in daily activities that faced the tribesmembers.

Like most other aspects of Ḥğeri life, weddings followed a fairly set routine. The guests would start arriving at noon and be received by the groom's father while the groom, who acted as the "active" host, was in charge of making sure they were made comfortable and cared for. The father would thus calmly, slowly oversee the event while the groom would be constantly on the move, unshaven and tired.

The gifts brought by the guests would be duly recorded,[8] some being returns on gifts the groom's father might have given out years before the groom was born, others being returns on gifts the groom might have given, and yet others being new gifts, which the groom, or his son, would have to reciprocate in the future. Gifts thus played both intrafamilial and interfamilial roles. Intrafamilial, they served to tie the younger generations to their elders and vice versa, creating continuity in time and enmeshing the son in his father's and grandfather's network of friends, allies, and acquaintances (often expressed in the size and value of the gift). They thus ensured continuity to economic and political relations aside from and beyond the immediate social ones. Interfamilial, wedding gifts tied different families in reciprocal exchange obligations, which were revalidated by the son's assuming the obligations of his father.

The guests would be entertained with horse races and a bard (*ša'er*), who sang about great events of the past and about the noble qualities of the tribe he was staying with at the time, accompanying himself on a *rabābah* (the single-string forerunner of the fiddle). After a big feast the *ḫadaya*, or the rhymesters, would take over the entertainment. There have always been at least two *ḫadaya*, each trying to compose a better, funnier, or more profound rhyme with which to challenge the other, who has to answer by a comparable verse while the audience serves as jury, clapping their hands in approval and shouting encouragements. The rhyming couplets generally praised the courage and generosity of the tribe, the groom's father, and the groom, as well as other qualities of the hosts.[9] The practice of employing *ḫadaya*, who were usually *fellāḥīn*, was adopted from the villagers by the Ḥğerāt and other local tribes only during the beginning of the second quarter of the twentieth century, and since these rhymesters were hired, they represent another service linkage between the tribe and the villages.

With the male guests thus entertained, the bride would sit in her father's tent, accompanied by the household's women, her friends, and other female members of her sublineage, who would be singing; she would be visited by other women of the tribe and those who came with male guests. Like the groom, she would not be especially dressed or ornamented.

The first evening, after most of the guests left, the *ḥenna* would start. The *ḥenna* was a private, intra-lineage affair to celebrate the event with song and dance. Its name derives from the custom of applying *ḥenna* to the hands of the couple and any other person present, a practice that is considered to bestow good luck. The *ḥenna* would be celebrated separately first in honor of the bride, and later for the groom. When the celebration ended the groom would be taken to a friend's tent, washed, and given a place to sleep accompanied by his best friend(s). Similarly, the bride would spend the night accompanied by her best friend and some of her female relatives.

In the morning the bride would be brought from her father's tent (although this was not an exclusive location) in a procession, called the *fārdah*, to the tent where the new couple would spend their first nuptial night. This tent was not necessarily the groom's new tent. More often it was makeshift, as the groom's father could not provide his son with a new tent. Shortly after the bride's arrival at about noon, the *zaffah*, or groom's procession, would start. This procession would be much more sonorous, joyous, and active as the men would form parallel rows ten to fifteen persons wide, clapping their hands and singing praises to the groom and more general wedding songs. When the groom entered the tent the young people would dance before the new couple. This phase, the *daḫlah*, would continue for about an hour or two and then the couple would be left to themselves while the relatives who had worked through the wedding had their feast and celebration.

Spring was also the time when people, like lambs, gained weight after the lean winter and before the hard summer. Then came the *ḥamsīn*, or the fifty days of hot dry desert wind, which desiccates everything and ripens the wheat. Harvest time after the acquisition of Maksūr was harder but more joyous than in earlier days. People would rise before dawn, work until noon, rest for two to three hours, then continue harvesting. This period was especially difficult for the women who, in addition to their usual chores, also helped in the harvest.

After the harvest in July, summer was at its height and families would break off in groups of two to three (and sometimes more) households for mutual help and company as they searched for dried pasture and stubble, or invaded the fields of Ṣafūriyeh. The herds were watered every day and were brought back to camp every evening to prevent animal thefts. The heat and the dry pasturage had their effect on the sheep and the milk supply began to dwindle from the beginning of July. Cheese, *labne*, vegetables, and fruits became the seasonal staple, and people began to lose the weight they put on during the spring.

Ḥğeri Demographic Patterns during the Mandate Period

The harsh climate and the physical exercise associated with herding and outdoor life, combined with the fluctuations in the quantity and richness of their diet, kept most of the men lean and fit. They would gorge themselves at each wedding feast or hospitality banquet (*nzaleh*) but, like their sheep, all the fat they had put on would disappear by the end of summer. The women were taxed more heavily because in addition to the climate and their workload, they continuously bore and nursed children.

The elder Ḥğeris reported that during the Mandate Period, women spaced their children between three and five years, depending on the sex of the last infant. The reason given for this practice was that women did not lactate as much during that period as they do today (in the 1970s), for they worked much harder and ate less well and less regularly. They consequently weaned their female infants at the age of 1.5–2 years while a male child was weaned at 2.5–3 years "*miš'an yekun gawī*" ("so that he'd be strong"). Females, therefore, usually did not conceive for two to four years after childbearing although there was no religious or customary prohibition against sexual intercourse beyond the customary observance after the first postpartum menstrual cycle.[10]

Although the average Ḥğeri female today has more children than ever before, the demographic pattern of the Ḥğerāt during the Mandate Period was very similar to the general pattern of the Moslem population, which Mills characterized as "progressive" (Pls. Census 1933[I]:129), whose "birth rates of today are abnormally high" (Pls. Census 1933[I]:128). Thus, even though the diet of the *fellāḥ* was described as "poor and monotonous"—predominantly consisting of (whole wheat) "cake of unleavened bread," some vegetables, olive oil, and, occasionally, a little meat (G.B. Col. 1930:65)—his average household size was 4.5 persons (Pls. Census 1933[I]:32). The diet of the Ḥğerāt, although as monotonous, was far richer in animal protein, for milk products were present in practically every meal and the average household size of Generation V parents (ca. 1870–1895) was 7.0 persons, of which 4.9 were children.[11] Hence, although in comparison with the mid-1970s the fertility of Ḥğeri women during the Mandate Period was lower and Ḥğeri population growth was further depressed by the more than 17% infant mortality rate (Pls. Census 1933[I]:146), Ḥğeri population was by no means stationary, almost tripling from the estimated 350 persons for 1919 to some 950 persons by 1949.

Ḥğeri Marriage Patterns during the Mandate Period

The rapid increase of the Ḥğeri population is also reflected in the number of marriages contracted by Generation VI. Two hundred and ninety-two marriages, spanning from about 1910 to the mid-1970s, were recorded for this generation. The majority of these marriages were made between 1930 and 1959—for example, scattering the 145 marriages of this generation for which the year of marriage is known, the distribution indicated in Table 7 emerges.

In spite of the rise in the absolute frequency of these marriages, the increasingly greater public security combined with the need to unify their growing membership tended to maintain the overall marriage pattern of this generation similar to that of their fathers: 64.7% intra-Ḥğerāt and 35.2% extra-Ḥğerāt marriages for Generation VI's marriages, as compared with 62.0% and 38.0% of Generation V's marriages, a slightly greater emphasis on intra-tribal marriages. Since the processes of population increase and increased public security were evolving from the second half of the nineteenth century, it seems that the two marriage categories may have reached a state of equilibrium.

However, the internal constitution of these categories has changed greatly, as Table 8 indicates. Two trends are evident in this table. First is the reversal in the relations between the "endogamous" and the "intra-Ḥğerāt" subcategories. The second is a rise in the relative number of marriages with the settled population at the expense of those with other bedouin tribes.

The reversal between "endogamous" and "intra-Ḥğerāt" marriages is primarily an artifact of the increasing generational depth of the tribe and the genealogical knowledge of its members reinforced by Ḥğeri population increase. To wit, since genealogical relationships before Generation III (in the case of the Ṣawālḥah, before Generation IV) are no longer remembered, the maximum possible accurate depth of genealogical connections between Generation V marital partners was two generations as compared with a depth of three generations for Generation VI. This issue becomes more pronounced when one compares the endogamous marriages of Generations IV–VII (see Table 9). Moreover, Generation II, the grandparental generation of Generation V, includes most of the founders of the current major sublineages resulting in—due to lack of concrete information—the marriages of Generation V being counted as between sublineages rather than endogamous. Thus, to a large measure this reversal seems to be imputed rather than actual in character, as each sublineage continued to unite its membership vis-à-vis the other sublineages in what might be viewed as a typical segmentary lineage organizational strategy.

Similarly, the significance of the general rise in marriages with the settled population, while indicating increased regional involvement, is somewhat misleading for three reasons. First, this involvement is not uniform across sublineage lines. Nine, or 31%, of the total of 29 marriages made with villages were contracted by *ulād* 'Aḥmed, who comprised only 3.3% (14 out of 426) of the membership of Generation VI. *Ulād* 'Aḥmed, residing between the villages of 'Uzeyr and Rummāneh, invested in fact more than half (9 out of 17) of its Generation VI marriages in unions with villagers, thereby repeating a similar pattern (2 out of 5 marriages with villagers) a generation earlier. The second

Table 7. The temporal distribution of Generation VI marriages.

Period	Marriages (N)
1919	1
1920–1929	7
1930–1939	39
1940–1949	41
1950–1959	37
1960–1969	13
1970–1977	7

Table 8. The marriage pattern of Generation VI by major categories and in comparison with that of Generation V.

Type of Marriage	Number of Marriages of Generation VI	Generation VI (%)	Generation V (%)	Delta (%)
endogamous	104	35.6	23.9	+11.7
intra-Ḥğerāt	85	29.1	38.1	-9
subtotal	*189*	*64.7*	*62.0*	*+2.8*
inter-tribal	71	24.3	34.3	-10
with villages	29	9.9	3.7	+6.2
with towns	3	1	—	+1
subtotal	*103*	*35.2*	*38.0*	*-2.9*
total	*292*	*100*	*100*	—

Table 9. A comparison by categories of generational distance of the endogamous marriages of Generation IV through Generation VII (cases).

Generation	FBD etc.	FFBD etc.	FFFBD etc.	FFFFBD etc.	Total
IV	1	—	—	—	1
V	18	14	—	—	32
VI	59	34	11	—	104
VII	63	70	35	24	192

reason is that 5 of the 20 (or 25.0%) remaining marriages, if those of *ulād* 'Aḥmed are subtracted, and 6 of 29 (or 20.9%) if they are not, were second marriages mostly by widowers. These marriages are not considered to have the importance of first marriages and are left to the discretion of the marrying individual and his/her siblings. Finally, there is the problem of the distribution of Generation VI marriages over time. As was mentioned before, these marriages span all of both the Mandate and the Israeli Periods and the transition between the two, which included the major population shifts caused by the 1948 War, when whole tribes and villages left the country. These shifts changed not only former patterns of political alliances but also the demographic availability of suitable marriage partners within politically permissible confines. About a third of the marriages with the villagers and all three marriages with townspeople are thus post-1948 events not governed by the same logic of the pre-1948 ones (for instance, one such marriage is with an ex-resident of Ṣafūriyeh, with which village the Ḥğerāt were at odds throughout the Mandate Period).

The above problems notwithstanding, 20 of the 29 marriages with sedentary communities were made with four neighboring villages: 'Uzeyr (9), Kafr Manda (6), Kawkab Abū al-Hejā' (3), and I'billin (2), and very possibly had an effect on the services that the Ḥğerāt needed from their inhabitants (see below). The last 9 were made with other villages across the Lower Galilee.

The internal differences between the marriage patterns of the three lineages seen in Table 10 noted earlier for Generation IV and Generation V were maintained during this generation as well (see Table 11). The Ġadāyreh, although less than before, still directed over half (56.1%) of its marriages toward the outside, either to the other two lineages (13.8%) or extra-Ḥğerāt altogether (42.3%). The Ṣawālḥah, again the reverse, invested 63.7% of its Generation VI marriages in uniting its membership and only 36.3% in marrying out. The Ḏiyabāt's marriage pattern is much more similar to that of the Ġadāyreh than it was a generation ago, and although it has already been noted that its two sublineages behave independently of each other, it is interesting to note that their respective patterns are now practically in opposition. The Ṭa'awāneh, allied much closer with the Ġadāyreh, for the second consecutive generation in a row did not give to or take females from the Ṣawālḥah, while placing far less emphasis than before on extra-Ḥğerāt marriages. The D'eyfeh, by contrast, reduced its emphasis on intra-lineage marriages and placed its primary emphasis on extra-Ḥğerāt marriages (see Table 10), while maintaining balanced relations with the other two lineages, as it had a generation earlier. The increased emphasis of the D'eyfeh on extra-Ḥğerāt marriages is most pronounced when the Generation VI marriage patterns of the three lineages are compared with those of Generation V (see Table 12). In this case the D'eyfeh's pattern is almost in complete reversal of that of the Ṭa'awāneh and the other two lineages (that is, the whole tribe), with a general decrease in the relative number of endogamous and intra-Ḥğerāt marriages, and with the only relative increase among the other units' inter-tribal marriages.

The difference in patterns between the lineages seems to be largely the consequence of their residence. Those in the relative security and isolation of the Ẓahara, faced with the problems of growing membership and latent competition for the leadership of the tribe between the Ṣawālḥah and the Ġadāyreh, directed their marriages toward internal unifica-

Table 11. A comparison of the direction of marriages among the three lineages of the Ḥğerāt.

Direction	**Ġadāyreh** (%)		**Ḏiyabāt** (%)		**Ṣawālḥah** (%)
		Ṭa'awāneh	D'eyfeh	Total	
intra-lineage	43.9	45.9	43.6	44.7	63.7
inter-lineage	13.8	18.9	10.3	14.5	18.6
intra-Ḥğerāt	57.7	64.8	53.8	59.2	82.3
extra-Ḥğerāt	42.3	35.1	46.2	40.8	17.7
extra-lineage	56.1	54.1	56.4	55.3	36.3

tion. *Ulād* 'Aḥmed, on the other hand, small in number and camping away from the Ẓahara on the outskirts of 'Uzeyr, needed much more help, goodwill, and cooperation from the villagers around them. They therefore invested more than half of their available marriages in creating marital links with the villages to their east and primarily with 'Uzeyr (4 out of 9). The D'eyfeh in the Ḏmeydeh, in a similar predicament to that of *ulād* 'Aḥmed, found itself partly isolated from the tribe topographically and out of the leadership competition politically. Although by the early 1930s, with the Ṣawālḥah's move to the Mikmān, the D'eyfeh was no longer isolated, the pursuit of its marriage policy, as argued by Aswad (1971: esp. ch. 14, et passim), is best understood as an answer to the relative isolation experienced by the parental generation, and which finds its expression in the marital arrangements of the filial generation. Thus, the D'eyfeh's daily concerns were a paramount factor in its marriage strategy, which was centered upon its neighbors: Kafr Manda to the east, I'billin to the west, Kawkab Abū al-Hejā' to its north on the mountain and in possession of the only three springs in the area (cf. Pls. Survey, 1941: sheet 17–24), and several small tribes to the west and south. They consequently followed a marrying-out policy to form a network of goodwill and mutual help with the neighboring populations. The extensive strategy is evident in the extra-Ḥğerāt marriage distribution of this sub-lineage. Three of the 4 marriages with *fellāḥīn* (2 wives taken; 2 daughters given) were made with their closest neighbors in Kafr Manda (1; 2 respectively) and the fourth with Kawkab Abū al-Hejā'. Their 11 (4; 7 respectively) marriages with other bedouin tribes prior to 1948 are less distinctly local. Nonetheless, 4 (2; 2 respectively) of these were with the *'arab* al-Mreysāt who camped to their northwest and east of Acre (Ashkenazi 1938: appendix D, p. 251, #55). Two more wives were taken from the Ḥelf who camped around Šfā'amr (Ashkenazi 1938: appendix D, p. 249, #49) to their west-southwest and one daughter was given to the *'arab* al-Heb Battūf, who camped west of Rummāneh.

In Retrospect

The Mandate Period was thus a period of increasing Ḥğeri involvement in the local scene of the Lower Galilee. They tripled their membership, which in traditional terms meant an increase in their regional political weight, for they could amass more men should

Table 10. The marriages of Generation VI by lineage.

Lineage	Membership			Endog-amous		Intra-Lineage		With Ġadāyreh				With Ḍiyabāt				With Ṣawālḥah				With Other Tribes				With Villages				With Towns				Total*
	M	F	T	N	%	N	%	K	G	T	%	K	G	T	%	K	G	T	%	K	G	T	%	K	G	T	%	K	G	T	%	N
Ġadāyreh	84	60	144	36	29.3	18	14.6	54		54	43.9	8		8	6.5	6	3	9	7.3	26	8	34	27.6	11	6	17	13.8		1	1	0.8	123
Ṭa'awāneh	28	23	51	13	35.1	4	10.8	2	5	7	18.9	17		17	45.9					7	3	10	27	2	1	3	8.1					37
D'eyfeh	26	29	55	12	30.8	5	12.8	1	1	2	5.1	17		17	43.6	2		2	5.1	6	7	13	33.3	2	2	4	10.3		1	1	2.6	39
Ḍiyabāt	54	52	106	25	32.9	9	11.8	3	6	9	11.8	34		34	44.7	2		2	2.6	13	10	23	30.3	4	3	7	9.2		1	1	1.3	76
Ṣawālḥah	87	89	176	43	38.1	29	25.7	4	9	13	11.5	6	2	8	7.1	72		72	63.7	9	5	14	12.4	3	2	5	4.4	1		1	0.9	113

Key: M = male; F = female; T = total; N = number; K = taken; G = given

*These totals include the females who were exchanged among the lineages and who were not included in Table 8 in order to avoid duplication in counting the marriages of the tribe as a whole.

Table 12. A comparison between the marriage patterns of Generation V and Generation VI by lineage.

Lineage	Endogamous (%)			Intra-Lineage (%)			With Ġadāyreh (%)			With Ḍiyabāt (%)			With Ṣawālḥah (%)			With Other Tribes (%)			With Villages (%)		
	G. V	G. VI	Delta	G. V	G. VI	Delta	G. V	G. VI	Delta	G. V	G. VI	Delta	G. V	G. VI	Delta	G. V	G. VI	Delta	G. V	G. VI	Delta
Ġadāyreh	8	29.3	+21.3	24	14.6	-9.4	32	43.9	+11.9	12	6.5	-5.5	14	7.3	-6.7	36	27.6	-8.4	6	13.8	+7.8
Ṭa'awāneh	27.3	35.1	+7.8	4.5	10.8	+6.3	9.1	18.9	+9.8	40.9	45.9	+5.0				50	27	-23.0		8.1	+8.1
D'eyfeh	33.3	30.8	-2.5	12.5	12.8	+0.3	8.3	5.6	-2.7	54.2	43.6	-10.6	12.5	5.1	-7.4	20.8	33.3	+12.5	4.2	10.3	+6.1
Ḍiyabāt	33.3	32.9	-0.4	9.5	11.8	+2.3	9.5	11.8	+2.3	42.9	44.7	+1.8	7.1	2.6	-4.5	38.1	30.3	-7.8	2.4	9.2	+6.8
Ṣawālḥah	25.9	38.1	+12.2	40.7	25.7	-15.0	5.6	11.5	+5.9	3.7	7.1	+3.4	66.7	63.7	-3.0	22.2	12.4	-9.8	1.8	4.4	+2.6

the occasion arise. The increase in their male population also decided the internal balance of power in the tribe, thus eliminating the ambiguity and waste inherent in undecided power struggles and facilitating the claim for the leadership of the tribe by any suitable member of the Ġadāyreh. Within the Ġadāyreh itself during that period, power rested with the Ramlāt, the senior and largest of its sublineages. Nonetheless, the service of Mūsā al-Ḏiyab of *ulād* Ġadīr and his close relatives and friends in the police and the ties they formed via the police with their Jewish colleagues prepared the way for the rise of this sublineage to the leadership of the tribe.

The service with the police, as well as involvement in economic enterprises in the region, not only provided for the tribe's needs and raised their standard of living but provided them with capital for land purchases, the largest of which was the acquisition of the lands of Bīr al-Maksūr. It was also their service with the police that, among other reasons, probably convinced the heirs of Ṣāleḥ al-Šibl to sell them the land and arrange for the payment in three installments, which made that purchase possible. The ownership of a large tract of land, for which they had almost finished payment, was a strong incentive to try to find a modus vivendi with the Jews once the decision between leaving Palestine or staying in Israel became inevitable. Their contacts with Jews made, in their minds, reaching such an understanding with the new government a real possibility so that they actually initiated the discussion rather than simply giving in and leaving the country as others had done.

Finally, during this period they became more involved with both settled life and the settled population, which helped them cope with the continuous decrease in free pasturage and the gradual increase in governmental control.

Notes

1. Ashkenazi (1957:59) reports that the small bedouin tribes of the north had *maḫatīr* (pl.) during the Ottoman Period. The Ḥǧerāt, however, emphasized that formal mukhtarship came only with the British. Similarly, members of other small tribes whom I questioned on this point confirmed the Ḥǧeri version.
2. Douglas V. Duff's book *Galilee Galloper* (1935) is about Bryant's tenure in Palestine. He describes some of the Bryant-Mūsā relations as well as some of Mūsā's tracking feats. He, nevertheless, mistook Mūsā to be a member of the *'arab* al-'Arāmšeh and not a Ḥǧeri.
3. Unfortunately, it is impossible to evaluate the relative membership of the three lineages by using the census figures, due to two factors. First, the census was taken on October 23, 1922. This date falls during the period when the Ḥǧerāt were returning to winter in the Ẓahara. Since this migration was not organized and was not conducted according to lineage affiliation, some families of either lineage had already returned while others were slowly winding their way to the Ẓahara. Second, the Ẓahara was divided administratively between the subdistricts of Acre and Nazareth, while Ḏmeydeh was divided between the subdistricts of Acre, Nazareth, and Haifa (cf. Pls. Survey 1941: sheet 17–24). Therefore, when the census was taken the respective lineages of the Ḥǧerāt were intermixed both in time and in space and any attempt to untangle these figures is futile from the onset. (Incidentally, the other two members of the alliance, the Ka'abīyeh and the Ḥelf, numbered 320 [161 males and 159 females] and 67 [38 males, 29 females] persons respectively [Pls. Census 1923:35].)
4. This figure was arrived at as follows: assuming an annual population rate of increase of 2.6 percent (Hopkins 1938:16), and computing it cumulatively for 1923, 1924, and 1925 using

the 1922 Census figures, one arrives at 215 and 132 persons in the two lineages, or 347 for the tribe as a whole. This figure is somewhat larger than the one that would result if we were to use the average number of residents per house for the subdistrict of Nazareth computed from the 1931 Census returns, that is, 4.67 persons per house (Pls. Census 1933[I]:43) and 336 persons for the whole tribe. If, however, one is to use Schumacher's (1887:170) estimate of 5 persons per one adult male (16–60 years old) and assuming only one such male per tent (i.e., an underestimate), one arrives at a figure of 360 for the whole tribe. Notwithstanding, counting the members of the 5th, 6th, and the beginning of the 7th generations (i.e., those assumed to have been born between 1870 and 1924) that are remembered in the tribe's genealogy, one arrives at 478 souls. It would thus seem that the 1922 Census is an underrepresentation and a likely figure would be about 450 souls. This figure was arrived at by assuming a ratio of 1.25 adult males ages 16–60 per tent. The possibility should be kept in mind, however, that von Oppenheim—who omitted the Ḏiyabāt altogether and who interchanged the names of the "sheykhs" of the two lineages—simply did not count all the tents. (The Ḏiyabāt, incidentally, he lumped with the Ġadāyreh [the Ṭa'awāneh] and the Ṣawālḥah [the D'eyfeh].)

5. Ṣafūriyeh's 1922 population was 2574 (1250 males, 1324 females; Pls. Census 1923:38); its 1931 population increased to 3147 (1468 males, 1679 females; Pls. Census 1932:76).
6. For example, in 1922 the population of Šfā'amr numbered 2288 persons, of whom 623 were Moslems, 1263 Christians, and 402 Druze (Pls. Census 1923:33). By 1931 the population was 2824, with Moslems comprising 1006, Christians 1321, and Druze 496 (Pls. Census 1932:95). In other words, the Druze were not only a minority, but the rapid growth rate of the Moslem population made them ever more so as time passed.
7. Ṭubās, some 17 km SSE of Jenin in today's West Bank, was one of several "specialized" villages in the region. It was famous for its charcoal industry, which dominated other economic activities in the village except agriculture. In the mid-1970s there were still some "specialized" villages, e.g., *ṭur'ān* (manure) and *umm al-ġanam* (straw). Such specialization clearly becomes an important supplement to agriculture, and when the pressure on available land reaches a critical threshold, it serves to absorb excess labor.
8. While it is very hard to ascertain to what extent the presents were recorded in writing during the Mandate Period, they were definitely recorded in the memory of those concerned. In 1977 an illiterate Ḥğeri father quoted from memory the list of the presents given them on the occasion of his second son's wedding (1966) while the son and I checked his list against the copybook in which the presents were registered. He had a complete recall of all the items. He could also state which of the gifts was a return, a partial return, or a new one. It is highly likely, therefore, that while the groom was making sure that the guests were well cared for, his father was registering the gifts in his head and, hence, appeared slow-moving and calm.
9. This form of entertainment is quite ancient, very popular, and is not limited to weddings and professional rhymesters. One can hear these rhyming matches between friends in an informal social gathering in a house or tent, or in a car on the way to a quail hunt. Similarly, they are a popular pastime in coffeehouses, where the young men often give them a bawdy slant. Rhyming couplets can be turned into a political device when the *ḫadaya* decides to sing about the foreign government, police, nationalism, or any other such topic. His audience, who are attuned to the form and quality of the verses, soon begin to respond to the political content of the messages he may send.
10. Although the Ḥğeri explanation implicates nutrition as the cause for this practice, it is only during famine or near-famine shortages that nutrition seems to affect lactation. Under normal circumstances the body of the mother serves as a homeostatic mechanism that buffers her baby's diet from fluctuation (Gunther 1968:77–82). Lactation (Donovan 1979:584) and high frequency of nursing (Konner and Worthman 1980:790–91) rather than endemic low level nutrition were identified as temporary depressants of ovulation (cf. Bongaarts 1980:566–67; Harrell 1981:797–802). Moreover, delayed weaning was not a characteristic peculiar to the Ḥğerāt, or even to bedouin. Mills, for example, reports that "it is usual to moslem mothers to

keep their babies at the breast for two or more years" (Pls. Census 1933[I]:101). In other words, it was a common practice, whether among city mothers, peasants, or bedouin ones, regardless of their workload or dietary patterns. In fact, prolonged suckling seems to be common to most, if not all, traditional societies (Donovan 1979:583).

11. The Ḥğeri data and that of the 1931 Census are not strictly comparable because the latter refers to the average household size at the specific time of the census and hence includes only "live" people present at that time, whereas the former was computed from their genealogy and is not, therefore, time dependent and includes "surviving"— i.e., members of Generation V and their children born before 1949 and who were remembered in the tribal genealogy—rather than "live" people. I nevertheless make this comparison because although the Ḥğeri figure is probably higher than the 1931 Census statistic (for it was picked at the maximum expansion of Ḥğeri families, whereas that of the census was not), it does illuminate the demographic pattern of the Ḥğerāt in the general absence of such information on bedouin and other pastoral tribes.

PART IV

The Israeli Period
(1947–1977)

– 6 –

The Military Government Era
(1947–1966)

The 1948 War and Its Aftermath

On November 29, 1947, when the General Assembly of the United Nations voted for the partition of Palestine, the Ḥĝerāt were hardly aware of that event's significance for their future. They did know about the rapidly mounting tensions between the Jews and the Arabs in Palestine, especially since 1936. In fact, they were involved in the schism through their participation in the rebel bands and their direct involvement in the Alexander Zaïd assassination and its repercussions. Nonetheless, for most of them, the increasing tension after the rebellion's apparent failure was the concern of the *fellāḥīn* (that is, Arabs) and not of the *'arab* (that is, bedouin). They were thus once again more involved with preserving their traditional semiautonomy, which they maintained by not meddling in "global" affairs not directly related to their well-being and by keeping a low profile vis-à-vis the government, which had some eight years earlier executed two of their members.

For the Ḥĝerāt as a tribe to again become enmeshed in the Jewish-Arab conflict was antithetical to their traditional policies and practice. As individuals some youth joined the troops of Fawzi al-Qāwuqĝi, the Syrian officer who led the Palestinian Rescue Army (*ĝayš al-inqaḏ al-'arabi*, or PRA), while others smuggled cattle through its outposts to sell to the Jews. In general, however, the Ḥĝerāt adopted a policy of "sit and watch"—not committing themselves to anyone or acting as a corporate entity—in order to preserve their political maneuverability.

In reality, the Ḥĝerāt adopted the non-intervention policy because no safer or better alternative was available to them. Between the arrival of al-Qāwuqĝi and the PRA at the beginning of April 1948 and the departure of the British on May 14—and in spite of claims to the contrary—Haifa, Tiberias, and Safad were in Jewish hands, and by May

17 Acre was also captured. The invasion of Israel by the armies of the neighboring Arab states on May 15–16 went practically unnoticed where the Ḥğerāt lived. Indeed, their greatest concern was that their traditional enemies, the Ṣafūrians, were left to man the PRA posts when al-Qāwuqği took the majority of his troops to help conquer Jerusalem at the end of April. On June 6, the main PRA units returned north and became a threat to the local Jewish settlements and transportation lines. Consequently, as soon as the First Cease Fire (June 11–July 8, 1948) ended, the newly formed Israel Defense Army (*tzva hagana le-israel/TZaHaL*, or IDA) launched Operation *deqel* (July 9–18) to clear the area. During those ten days Shfar'am, Ṣafūriyeh, and Nazareth were conquered and the war arrived at the Ḥğeri heartland, leaving Bīr al-Maksūr, the Mikmān, and the Ḏmeydeh and their water sources under Jewish control while the Ẓahara remained in PRA territory.

This turn of events ended the period of corporate noncommitment for it became clear that something had to be done, and that any course of action would commit the whole tribe one way or the other. The general feeling was to follow al-Qāwuqği, who kept saying the PRA was going to win in the end. It was not al-Qāwuqği's opinion, however, that swayed the Ḥğerāt; rather, it was the general state of affairs, both intra- and extra-tribal, that made this option seem the logical one.

Throughout the 1930s and 1940s, a new contender for the leadership of the Ġadāyreh had risen. Ibrāhīm al-Nimr, a member of the VI generation, was the eldest of five brothers and a successful entrepreneur who became rich through horse racing, trade, and fencing for smugglers. He was also a successful leader, a sub-band commander during the 1936–1939 Rebellion (Porath 1977:399); by deploying his brothers, he became increasingly influential in intra-tribal affairs. He was aspiring for the role of *muḫtār* when the aging Sleymān al-'Abed vacated that office.

When al-Qāwuqği invaded in early 1948, Muḥammad al-Nimr, the third brother and Ibrāhīm's right-hand man, joined the PRA, leading the Ḥğeri youth who wanted to join those units. After the British left Tiberias, Muḥammad was joined by his FBSS, Mūsā al-Ḏiyab's son Muḥammad, who was left without a job when the police force in that city was disbanded. By joining with Muḥammad al-Nimr, Muḥammad al-Mūsā supported the claim to leadership of Ibrāhīm al-Nimr, who was leading the faction that sided with al-Qāwuqği. At the same time, however, Muḥammad al-Mūsā was monitoring his cousins' quest for leadership, for *ulād* Ḏiyab themselves were vying for the leadership (as a result of their central role as the link to the police and their genealogical precedence over *ulād* Nimr).

Ultimately, their extra-tribal relations influenced the Ḥğerāt to throw their support behind the council of the *ulād* Nimr's faction. The Jews, with whom there was a general sense of uneasiness due to the 1936–1939 Rebellion and the blood feud resulting from the Zaïd affair, were winning. The Druze, with whom there was another feud on account of the Ḫnefes affair, and who at first were uncommitted to either side, finally made up their minds when it became certain the Jews were winning (cf. Allon 1965:254) and began sending their youth to help the IDA and join in its battles. And the Ḥğerāt's traditional bedouin rivals, the *'arab* al-Heīb, were fighting openly on the side of the Jews since before the departure of the British (Allon 1965:220, 237).

Of these potential dangers, the Druze posed the most prominent threat to the Ḥğerāt. First, the animosity with them included blood and extended over some fifty years or more. Second, Ṣāleḥ Ḥassan al-Ḫnefes, who became one of their leaders, harbored animosity toward the Ġadāyreh, whom he accused of his father's murder. Ṣāleḥ, according to the Ġadāyreh, made it public knowledge that when victory came he would ensure that the Ġadāyreh paid for his father's death in full and with interest. It was this threat that lay heaviest on the minds of the Ḥğerāt and provided the pro-al-Qāwuqği faction with its best argument.

Openly there was no opposition to the pro-al-Qāwuqği faction because to be publicly pro-Jewish at that time amounted to suicide. Nonetheless, a small group led by Mūsā al-Ḏiyab's younger brother Ḥsēn argued against committing the tribe to following the PRA and argued for maintaining their semi-neutrality. While this group's council was pro-Ḥğeri rather than pro-Jewish, it was considered subversive in the polarized political atmosphere of the region. For example, according to the Ḥğerāt, during Operation *deqel*, a PRA officer, Kamāl Bek, established a small camp near the house of Sleymān al-ʿAbed, on the border between the Ẓahara and *ğabel Daydabe*. He invited the Ḥğeri elders, including Ḥsēn al-Ḏiyab. After a while the PRA men began to rebuke Ḥsēn al-Ḏiyab, charging that his group's council "comes to destroy and not to help," and they wanted to arrest and punish him. The Ḥğeri elders, however, led by the *muḫtār* made it clear that if any harm were caused to Ḥsēn al-Ḏiyab (or any other Ḥğeri), there would be a feud between the Ḥğerāt and the PRA men. After a short while the PRA folded its camp and moved away.

Ḥsēn al-Ḏiyab met Jews through his police service at the station in the Jewish settlement of Nahalal. There he developed close friendships with two Jewish policemen, and was a casual acquaintance of several others. If before Operation *deqel* he advocated isolation and noncommittal, after its completion it became clear to him that the Jews would win the war and that when that happened there would be only two options open to the Ḥğerāt: leave the country or stay. Siding with al-Qāwuqği would necessitate the first option; if the Ḥğerāt wanted to stay they would have to make peace with the Jews. From his pre-war contact with them he knew that as far as the Jews were concerned, the Zaïd affair was closed, they did not hold the tribe's participation in the rebellion against them, and they wanted the Ḥğerāt to remain in the country. The Druze, however, were a different matter.

Consequently, one night toward mid-August 1948, accompanied by the son of the *muḫtār*, Muḥammad al-Sleymān, Ḥsēn al-Ḏiyab rode to the Mikmān to pay a visit to Ḥsēn al-Gāsem, a member of the Ṣawālḥah and a friend of Ṣāleḥ Ḥassan al-Ḫnefes. The two asked Ḥsēn al-Gāsem to intervene with Ṣāleḥ on behalf of the Ḥğerāt in general and the Ġadāyreh in particular. Ḥsēn al-Gāsem rode to Shfarʿam to talk with the Druze leader while the two waited in his tent. Later that night he returned with Ṣāleḥ's negative answer—if he were able to avenge his father he would, so the Ġadāyreh had better flee while they could. Ḥsēn al-Ḏiyab sent Muḥammad al-Sleymān back to the Ẓahara and continued to the Nahalal station, which had become the local IDA headquarters, where he met with his friends. He told them of Ṣāleḥ's answer and was told to stay and not to fear the Druze because they would have to abide by the law like any other citizen in the new state.

By the time Ḥsēn al-Ḏiyab returned to the Ẓahara, another problem took precedence over the tribe's long-term political commitments—the war had interfered with their migratory pattern and there was no more water in the Ẓahara's cisterns.[1] This problem did not affect the Ḥğeri tribal segments equally. The Ṣawālḥah in the Mikmān and Maksūr were under Israeli control and could maintain their traditional herding patterns unchanged, especially since the mass exodus of the villagers of Ṣafūriyeh left ample pasturage on unharvested fields and full cisterns. The D'eyfeh in the Ḏmeydeh, located in the border zone between the two adversaries, moved to the Jewish-held territory in search of water and pasture. The Ẓahara in the PRA territory, however, experienced a water shortage that grew increasingly severe as the summer wore on, and by mid-August the herd owners of the Ġadāyreh and the Ṭa'awāneh moved camp to *wādi* Salāmeh northeast of 'Arrabeh, leaving behind herdless members to guard Ḥğeri property. By November (cf. Ashbel 1950:7–8), after the rains arrived and new grass sprouted, the herds were back in the Ẓahara and the discussion of politics resumed dominance in each gathering, social or formal.

During this period Ḥsēn al-Ḏiyab maintained his council of nonintervention while sporadically keeping in touch with Nahalal. After their return to the Ẓahara, he intensified his contact with Nahalal and he communicated more regularly with the IDA, using his first wife as the messenger. These later contacts were known to only a select few, including the *muḫtār*. According to his sons, Ḥsēn was notified before the final assault on the PRA (Operation *Ḥirām* from the night of October 28–29 to October 31, 1948), enabling him to warn the tribe not to flee.

The Early Years

After the war ended in the North, the Ḥğerāt resumed their daily routines, trying to stay as quiet as possible because of their number who fought with the PRA, as well as being chary of governments in general and of the new regime in particular. Later, the new authorities arrived to demand the surrender of their weapons, to issue identification (ID) cards, and to reinstitute the office of the *muḫtār* in the Ẓahara and the Mikmān. The Ḥğerāt surrendered some thirty antiquated rifles while hiding the rest of the tribe's arsenal; grafted to their genealogy individuals, families, and a sublineage left behind by the fleeing *'arab* tribes; and helped the authorities select a *muḫtār*.

In the Ẓahara the job offer focused on *ulād* Ḏiyab, due to their role during the war, which the authorities considered a sign of loyalty, while the aging *muḫtār*, Sleymān al-'Abed, was uncommitted in this respect and Ibrāhīm al-Nimr an outright suspect. Thus, the job was first offered to Mūsā al-Ḏiyab, who was renown and highly respected among the Jews (two of whom were from the Nahalal station and were friends of Ḥsēn, Mūsā al-Ḏiyab's younger brother) who came that day to the Ẓahara. Although it was Ḥsēn who maintained the contact with the Jews, it was considered a breach of etiquette to jump over Mūsā and offer the office to his younger brother, especially when it was assumed that Ḥsēn would not have contacted them without Mūsā's consent and encouragement.

Mūsā, however, refused the offer. It was then offered to Ḥsēn al-Ḏiyab, who also refused the job. When asked "*min?*" ("who?," meaning "who do you suggest?"), Ḥsēn reportedly answered "*ḥuḏ al-walad*" ("take the child"), pointing to his seventeen- or eighteen-year-old firstborn Muḥammad. Ḥsēn himself consented to reenlist with the Israeli police.

Ḥsēn's reenlistment with the police and the allocation of his son as *muḫtār* are best understood as responses to the prevalent conditions of maintaining and controlling access to the authorities during the Mandate Period. Being a policeman in those days was more advantageous than being a *muḫtār* because the policeman belonged to the authorities. It soon became apparent, however, that the relative position of the two roles had reversed as a result of differences between British and Israeli approaches to administering the country. A brief review will clarify this shift.

British interests, as previously mentioned, were centered on Palestine as a communication link in a mercantile empire. Palestine was important in ensuring the physical continuity from India via Iran, Iraq, and Jordan in the northeast to Egypt and East Africa in the south. This linkage, important for the traditional nineteenth-century trade items, had become increasingly more crucial after 1914 with the Admiralty's transition to oil as fuel for its ships (Garthwaite 1972:36) and the development of motor vehicle and airplane transportation. In addition, Palestine was also very important as a buffer zone for the Suez Canal, "the jugular vein of the British Empire" (Arthur 1920[III]:95), as the British had learned from experience during World War I when Major von Kressenstein raided the canal and its zone from the north in 1915/16 and brought Field Marshall Lord Kitchner to ask "who defends whom here, you the Canal or the Canal you?" (quoted in Gichon 1969:102).

Since this scale of interests was supra-regional it was essential, from the Colonial Office point of view, that the Civil Administration in Palestine not meddle in local affairs or antagonize the population more than was absolutely necessary. It was also the politically advantageous course of least resistance, which became necessary to comply with the ambiguities and contradictory terms that abounded in the Mandate Charter.[2] Finally, intensified Jewish-Arab animosity—especially the inexperience and inefficiency of the administration itself (G.B. Pls. 1937:117–18 et passim; Duff 1953:205–8; Bowden 1975)—left the latter isolated from the population at large (cf. Duff 1953:187–89; Bowden 1975:119–20).

The result of this state of affairs was that in spite of the Mandate Charter and its stipulation of promoting self-rule, the government of Palestine was, straight and simple, a colonial administration that did not integrate the local community to its structure because the latter was viewed as an antithesis to the former. Consequently, "the present link between the Government official and the peasantry is the *muḫtār* or village headman, elected as under the Turkish rule and giving his loyalty to the village rather than to the Government" (G.B. Pls. 1937:119). In other words, the Mandate Period *muḫtār* answered to his sources of power located solely in the local community that he represented, even though the government routed both economic assistance and official decrees through him. He was, therefore, kept in check by his relatives and bound by inter-lineage considerations and intrigues.

The policeman, on the other hand, was part of the administration. His political power was derived from an external source, making him relatively independent of the members of the community if he so wished. Moreover, his word carried more weight with the authorities than that of a *muḫtār*.

Under the newly formed Israeli state administration, the general situation was radically changed and the relative power of the two roles reversed. The Rhodes Armistice Agreements, which ended the 1948–1949 War, did not normalize relations in the Middle East. As a result, the Israeli authorities were locked between two contradictory goals. On the one hand, most of those Arabs who stayed in Israel were a priori suspects as likely allies of the state's antagonistic neighbors. On the other hand, the new government was dominated by late nineteenth-/early twentieth-century socialist ideology combined with a Judaic sense of mission as dispensers of humanitarian justice. This humanitarian ideology was intensified by a claim to the leadership of the global Jewish community and a sense of having to be exemplary, an image fueled by continuously being in the limelight of the Western World whose support, both political and economic, was crucial to the state's survival. These two contradictory forces in the Israeli government permeated the scene to the mid-1970s: they provided welfare state services to all its citizens, while at the same time monitoring "the Arab sector" very closely. In the early 1950s these forces were skewed toward the latter and the result was a very powerful and watchful Military Government (MG) that "was in fact the only form of government in the Arab districts" (Ben Porath 1966:51).

The MG maintained complete control over the Arab sector in two ways: by an elaborate complex of permits, first and foremost among which was the Travel Permit; and through the deployment of an extensive network of informants. And since any elaborate bureaucracy calls for special favors, either to shortcut red tape or to provide more lenient interpretations to strict laws, the MG became self-supportive by rewarding its informants with such favors.

Through the manipulation of favors and informants the MG attempted to achieve three major goals. Militarily it kept a well-informed intelligence and counter-intelligence service. Economically it kept the cheaper Arab labor force in their villages and reserved the scarce jobs of the early 1950s for demobilized army veterans and Jewish immigrants (cf. Ben Porath 1966:51–52; Marx 1967:46–51; Tadmor 1952:41–42; Levy 1955:63–65, 125–27; Halevi and Klinov-Malul 1968:64–71). Finally, politically it tried to enlist the support of the Arab vote to Israel's Workers Party (*Mifleget Po'alei Yisrael* or *MaPal*), the ruling political party, during the parliamentary elections of the 1950s and early 1960s.

Since the majority of the Arab sector in those days was rural and to a large measure economically self-sufficient, it was those who worked in the services who were most dependent on the MG for travel permits, jobs, and so on. Teachers, *maḫatīr*, and the like thus had the closest contacts with the MG and if "they played their cards right" they were likely to procure the necessary permits, help their fellow Arabs in getting jobs, and so on, all of which were to a greater or lesser degree controlled by the MG.

While teachers maintained their contacts with the MG in relative secrecy, the *maḫatīr* maintained theirs quite openly. They were, in fact, expected by their community members to intervene successfully on their behalf and to maintain good relations with the officials of the MG for that purpose. The MG, for its part, used the *maḫatīr*—who were part of the administrative structure of the Ministry of the Interior—as the official channel of communication between the local community and the MG. The *maḫatīr*, therefore, were supposed to corroborate and authenticate any request made by a community member and, often, actually present the case for the applicant. This policy was required to reduce the amount of information generated by each applicant (which determined the amount of time it took to process an application) to amounts manageable by the relatively small staff of the MG.[3] By becoming the mediators between the community and the MG, the *maḫatīr* succeeded in accumulating extensive political and economic power. This power was de facto, legitimated by their community members who used the services of the *maḫatīr* because they needed an access to the MG, and who very often preferred to have the *muḫtār* approach the alien administration rather than do so themselves.

In opposition to the omnipotent MG, which could handle semi-legitimate items under a claim of necessary evil for the sake of national security, the police of Israel was neither omnipotent nor free in its conduct. Being itself a ministry and in the limelight, it was bound by laws and regulations ensuring its rights, obligations, and proper and accountable behavior in the Civil Administration. If the MG was operating in the Arab sector and, therefore, in relative secrecy from the Jewish sector whose media reporters for various reasons usually let the MG be, the police, operating primarily in the Jewish sector, was constantly in the public eye. Consequently, an Israeli policeman had neither the status nor the relative power enjoyed by his Mandate predecessor; the relations between an Arab policeman and his *muḫtār* in this period became a replica of those between the police and the MG in the Arab sector.

The Rise to Power of *ulād* Ḏiyab al-Ibrāhīm

This role reversal between Ḥsēn al-Ḏiyab and his son Muḥammad took about five years to reach completion and was symbolically concluded when on November 30, 1954, the former did not renew his service contract with the police and introduced his fourth son, Ibrāhīm, in his stead. During the first three or four years the role reversal was secondary in importance to the final phase in the covert power struggle over the tribe's leadership between *ulād* Ḏiyab al-Ibrāhīm, nominally led by Ḥsēn, and their cousins *ulād* Nimr al-Ibrāhīm, led by Ibrāhīm al-Nimr.

By the end of 1949 Ibrāhīm al-Nimr's ambitions were blunted by the death of his brother Muḥammad in the last days of the war and the nomination of Muḥammad al-Ḥsēn as *muḫtār* of the Ẓahara by the new authorities. These two events not only severely hurt Ibrāhīm personally but were also a strategic setback. Of the two, Muḥammad's death, in addition to its emotional impact (for he was Ibrāhīm's most beloved and trusted sibling), was the major blow because he was also his most reliable deputy. Muḥammad al-Ḥsēn's mukhtarship, from Ibrāhīm's perspective, was more of a serious disappointment than a debilitating strategic setback. The mukhtarship was a temporary appointment pending reconfirmation every year; Muḥammad was young and a strong opponent in the community could replace an incumbent *muḫtār* by arousing enough antagonism against him.

Thus, in 1949–1950, while still mourning Muḥammad, Ibrāhīm reestablished his old smuggling operations, sending two of the three remaining brothers to smuggle coffee, sugar, and cloth, and to drive herds of sheep, goats, and cattle from Lebanon into economically rationed Israel. These two were joined by several other young Ḥǧeris including Muḥammad al-Mūsā, who had been with Muḥammad al-Nimr when he was killed.

Smuggling was easy: they would cross the border at night; spend the day rounding up goods and animals; rest the following night in Lebanon, completing whatever other business or errands they had to accomplish; drive the herd to the border during the second day and evening; and at night cross the border back into Israel. Once the herd and other commodities were in the Ẓahara, Ibrāhīm al-Nimr, as the "fence," would sell them and after a few days of rest they would make another run. The problems they encountered were not generated by the authorities but by rival smuggling gangs who would try to hijack the herds and goods once they were inside Israel.

Smuggling in those days was a very lucrative profession due to the shortages generated by the war and by the massive increase in consumption in the Jewish sector caused by the rapid increase of population, which had doubled by December 1951.[4] It was also an act of defiance against the new authorities and in line with the traditional bedouin ideal of independent occupation and economic success. In this respect Ibrāhīm al-Nimr still led the now defunct pro-al-Qāwuqǧi faction and as such was a major threat to the newly installed young *muḫtār*. Thus, for example, in 1951 the Ṣawālḥah had a wedding in the Mikmān to which the Druze were invited. The Druze, who were serving in the IDA, came with their Bren guns, thus boasting their supremacy over the Ḥǧerāt, who could not come with their own rifles in the open. Ibrāhīm al-Nimr allegedly slapped the groom's father on his cheek for inviting the Druze to a Ḥǧeri wedding and "gave his opinion" about the Druze, their ancestry, and so on to Ṣāleḥ Ḥassan al-Ḫnefes (their leader and the Ġadāyreh's nemesis) because he allowed his men to come armed to a wedding that was not theirs. In this manner he stood up to the Druze challenge and saved the honor of the Ġadāyreh and the Ḥǧerāt. That done, he and the Ġadāyreh left the wedding and returned to the Ẓahara. (That this incident was recounted by a leading member of *ulād* Ḏiyab without any mention of the *muḫtār* is rather enlightening.)

Consequently, by mid-1952 Ḥsēn al-Ḏiyab convinced his nephew, Muḥammad al-Mūsā, to end his smuggling operations. He told him the police knew about the activities but did not act because they needed trackers and hoped that he would return to police service. Muḥammad consented and on August 15, 1952, he reenlisted. Then, Ibrāhīm al-Nimr's two brothers were called in to the MG and asked to hand over their rifles. The two denied the charge and were detained for questioning for a month before they were released. The police next began to express interest in Ibrāhīm's smuggling enterprises and in 1955 he decided to leave the Ẓahara to Muḥammad al-Ḥsēn and to move to Bīr al-Maksūr.

While *ulād* Ḏiyab were consolidating their position of leadership in the Ġadāyreh, their nemesis Ṣāleḥ Ḥassan al-Ḫnefes, who became a Member of Knesset (MK) in 1951, was trying to erode their power by cultivating a schism between them and the Ṣawālḥah.

He thus became the influential power behind the 1951 transfer of the mukhtarship of the Mikmān from Ḥassan al-Šhāb (who became *muḫtār* in 1933 and was reconfirmed by the authorities in 1949) to his old-time friend Ḥsēn al-Gāsem. The friendship with Ḥsēn al-Gāsem, a member of a small sublineage of the Ṣawālḥah, began before Ṣāleḥ's father's murder, and was the reason Ḥsēn al-Ḏiyab asked Ḥsēn al-Gāsem to intervene with Ṣāleḥ in August of 1948 on the Ġadāyreh's behalf. Ṣāleḥ Ḥassan al-Ḫnefes' reasons in installing Ḥsēn al-Gāsem as *muḫtār* of the Mikmān and kindling his aspirations for independence from the primacy of the *muḫtār* of the Ẓahara (who was also the tribal *muḫtār* by force of leading the Ġadāyreh and the Ḏiyabāt) were oriented at eroding the power of the latter and of the tribe as a whole.

The Rise of Muḥammad al-Ḥsēn to Power

Political struggles and intrigues aside, during those early years the Ḥğerāt tried to maintain their old lifestyle and seasonal migration pattern. They soon encountered a major obstacle in that their traditional territory was located in three administrative subdistricts. The Ẓahara, the Ḏmeydeh, and 'Uzeyr fell mostly within the Nazareth subdistrict, with some parts in the Acre subdistrict. The Mikmān and Bīr al-Maksūr fell mostly within the boundaries of the Haifa subdistrict, with some edges in the east belonging to the Nazareth subdistrict. Practically, this meant that the ability to move within their territory unencumbered by travel permits necessitated a collective permanent or semipermanent permit that could be arranged only through their *muḫtār*. With the help of some of Mūsā and Ḥsēn al-Ḏiyab's friends in the MG, such an understanding was achieved and the Ḥğerāt were allowed to move freely within their territory as well as, in special cases, to other parts of the Galilee. If, however, a tribesmember did not comply with the *muḫtār* he could easily lose this freedom of movement, or face even more severe restrictions and sanctions.

At first, save for travel permits, people did not often approach the *muḫtār*. Although he was always courteous and accommodating and paid people their due respect, the life the Ḥğerāt led did not demand much contact with the authorities, nor were the people anxious to develop such contacts with the new and yet unknown regime. As the tribe got used to the new situation, however, and as individuals became involved in cash cropping, shopping trips to Nazareth, and other necessary economic transactions, the dependence on the *muḫtār* increased. Such dependence was inevitable as MG permits were necessary for practically every economic transaction, including the sale or purchase of agricultural and pastoral products.[5] Moreover, the multitude of new rules and regulations meant that people were bound to transgress the law, whether wittingly or unwillingly, and hence needed the *muḫtār* to be their advocate in the MG. Similarly, after 1954–1955, when the younger generation began to seek work outside the traditional occupations of animal husbandry and agriculture, the *muḫtār* was needed both to recommend a person to the employing agency and to secure a "permanent" travel permit for that person.

Muḥammad al-Ḥsēn, for his part, was careful not to embarrass those who sought his help. He was always civil and understanding and when a person requested help he would usually answer "leave it [the matter] with me," and once he had taken upon himself to resolve an issue he would follow the matter until it was concluded to his satisfaction, much as he would follow a private matter of his own. He did not, however, take it upon himself to clear up anything he was not sure the authorities would accept. Similarly, unlike many other *maḫatīr*, he did not ask for gifts or services in return for his "help," although such returns were socially acceptable and often demanded. Thus, since gifts are given "to put people under obligations and to win followers" (Mauss 1969:73), by providing his tribesmembers with services, a *muḫtār* gained followers, and by not enabling people to reciprocate, he left them in his debt, thereby ever increasing his following.[6] Nevertheless, when the national parliamentary election came around, the *muḫtār* would cash in on his help. He would not, however, ask people to return a favor and vote for *MaPal* or one of its associated minorities' lists. Rather, he would advocate that such a vote "is good for us." Most Ḥğeris did not have a sense of the relations between the one-in-four-years election and the daily realities embodied in the MG. Consequently, voting one way or another meant little to them. For those who understood the relationship, it was important to keep the *muḫtār* in good relations with the MG; if that meant voting for *MaPal*, they did it. In either case, Muḥammad al-Ḥsēn elicited a majority of the Ġadāyri vote for *MaPal* each election during the 1950s and 1960s (see Table 30).

Muḥammad al-Ḥsēn emphasized the tradition of Ḥğeri unity and left the management of traditional intra-tribal affairs (that is, conflict resolution) to the Council of Elders, the *ḫatyariyyeh*. He thus avoided antagonizing the elders and their following while using this traditional institution to help him maintain peace and relative quiet in the tribe as was expected of a good *muḫtār*, thereby increasing his esteem in the MG.

In spite of, or maybe because of, his age Muḥammad al-Ḥsēn proved to be a great asset to the MG. He maintained the tribe in peace and cooperation with the authorities. He served as a filter, shielding MG officers from the onslaught of individual tribesmembers who would have consumed an amount of time disproportionate to whatever they wanted accomplished.[7] He did part of the MG officers' work by grouping requests according to subjects and addressing each group to the officer in charge of the respective subject. And, he brought in his share of votes for *MaPal* every parliamentary election. It was thus in the interest of the MG to promote Muḥammad al-Ḥsēn and a reinforcing loop developed: the more the MG granted his requests, the more the tribesmembers channeled their requests through him, the greater control he gained over the tribe, the more of service he was to the MG, and so on.

For most Ḥğeris the political or administrative considerations of the MG were no more a part of their daily worries than the national parliamentary election. They led their lives the way they had before the war. They paid the last installment for the lands of Bīr al-Maksūr; they cultivated that and their other lands and herded their animals. While not a major problem yet, pastures began to be somewhat more scarce. The lands of Ṣafūriyeh, the traditional summer pasture of the Ḥğerāt, now belonged to the state and were cultivated by two new Jewish agricultural settlements—Tzipori and Hasolelim—which were founded in 1949. The invasion of the settlements' green fields by bedouin herds ended before they even had a chance to start. The agriculturalists simply complained to the police, the police routed the problem to the MG, and the latter called in the *maḫatīr*. For the time being, however, there was still enough pasture in the environs of Bīr al-Maksūr and after the harvest they could graze on the stubble of Kafr Manda and other villages in the Valley of Beit Netofah.

The situation in the Ẓahara was somewhat better after some small encounters with the peasants of Saḫnīn. That village's new *muḫtār*, *šeyḫ* ʻAwad, had decided to take advantage of Muḥammad al-Ḥsēn's youth and "put the Ḥğerāt in their place." Consequently, he publicly declared he would bar the Ḥğerāt from using the pastures in the Valley of Saḫnīn (which they had traditionally used as winter and early spring pasture) and restore them to Saḫnini ownership. He was soon put in an awkward position. First, Muḥammad al-Ḥsēn did not come to see him to talk things over but sent him a written note stating the traditional claim of the Ḥğerāt to the valley's natural pastures; if *šeyḫ* ʻAwad did not like it, it was just too bad. Second, shortly after, he was quietly told by the MG not to look for conflicts and to leave the Ḥğerāt alone. This incident raised the prestige of Muḥammad al-Ḥsēn not only within the Ḥğerāt but among other tribes and villages in the area as well.

Changes in the Ẓahara

The suppression of inter-community conflicts by the MG, the good relations with that administration, and the rapid return to daily routines soon found a visible expression in the resumption of house construction by the richer Ḥğeris (see Map 6). The rate was very slow because apart from the reluctance to convert a productive resource (i.e., animals) to not very productive real estate, the expenses incurred in transporting materials by pack animals over a long mountain track to the Ẓahara were quite prohibitive. These houses were constructed of hewn stone walls backed by concrete and topped with a concrete roof about five to six centimeters thick supported by a steel I-beam in the center of each room. They, thus, had to bring in the stone, cement, mixing sand, gravel, lime, steel beams, wooden doors, window frames, and shutters. To reduce transportation expenses, in 1951 most of the Ġadāyreh, led by Ḥsēn al-Ḏiyab, leveled a dirt road for trucks and four-wheel drive vehicles. In 1952 *ulād* Ḏiyab al-Ibrāhīm (that is, Mūsā and Ḥsēn al-Ḏiyab and their descendants) joined together to buy (in equal shares) a truck to transport the necessary goods and construction materials. The tangible profits to be derived from such an enterprise were already known to them, for not only they but other Ḥğeris used camels to transport in whatever they needed. However, the majority of the few transport camels in the area belonged to their cousin and political competitor, Ibrāhīm al-Nimr. The purchase of the truck, for which one needed a complex of MG permits, was thus not only an economic investment toward the development of a practical monopoly on transportation but also a setback for Ibrāhīm al-Nimr, who could not use his camels for generating reciprocal debts. It is not surprising therefore that three out of the five houses that were constructed during the next two years (1953–1954) belonged to members of *ulād* Ḏiyab.

In 1954, with encouragement and a loan from the MG, the community in the Ẓahara got together to build a two-room school. Before that date school had convened in differ-

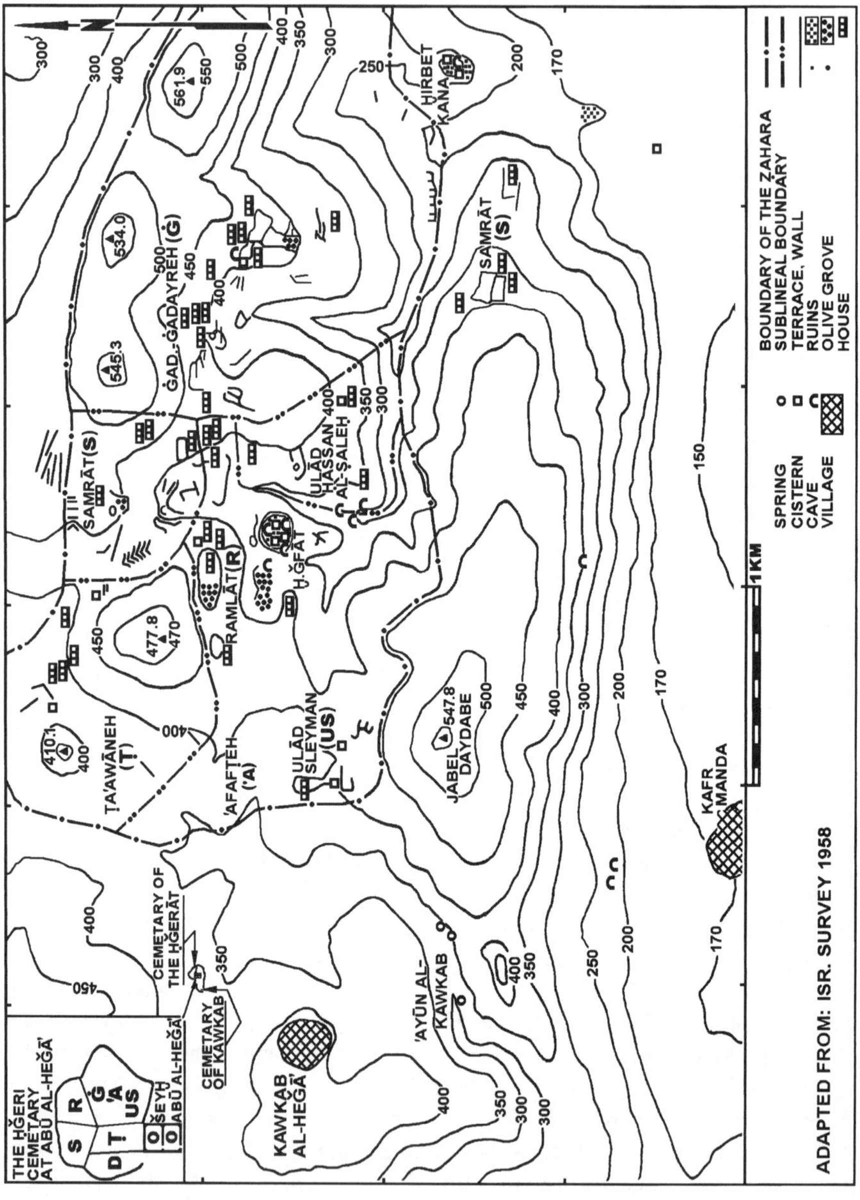

Map 6. The Ẕahara in 1968.

ent houses or tents and was organized after the older semi-formal village Koran school, which emphasized memorizing the Koran and some writing. The Ḥğerāt began voluntarily to employ a *ḫaṭīb* ("orator; preacher; speaker; lecturer"; Madina 1973:195) during the mid-1930s when their economic involvement in the regional network increased markedly once the fourth generation—that of Mūsā al-Ḏiyab and Ibrāhīm al-Nimr—began to expand the tribe's contacts.[8] After the State of Israel took over, it was about two years before compulsory elementary education could be even nominally enforced. The lack of trained teachers (most of whom fled the country), the paucity of adequate structures and furniture (much of which was destroyed during the war), the financial straits in which the new government found itself, and the tense Jewish-Arab relations in the country during the 1950s made the task of adequately enforcing education laws in the Arab sector practically impossible.

Schooling in the Ẓahara in 1954 was still for males only, irregular (because fathers would pull their sons from school and send them to herd or help in seasonal agricultural work), and inadequate (due to untrained or undertrained teachers). Teachers came from the nearby villages and often did not have even a high school diploma because their own schooling was disrupted by the war. Several factors contributed to the irregularity of schooling, and seem to have continued to affect this phenomenon after this date: (1) reluctance to invest time and effort in an intangible long-term project like formal education (cf. Ben Porath 1966:15), all the more so when at that time the country as a whole "had a 'surplus' of education in relation to tangible capital" (Klinov-Malul 1966:15); (2) the strong control the father exerted on household management and its labor force deployment, which was further sanctified by the Moslem tradition that leaves the child's education in his father's hands (Levy 1957:218); (3) the lack of a strong tradition that sanctified formal education so that when the fourth factor was in operation, there was little to keep it viable; and (4) the age structure of the Moslem population of Israel in general and the Ḥğerāt in particular (see Table 13). Ben Porath remarked that "the Arab population in Israel today is one of the youngest in the world" (1966:13); such an age distribution places a heavy burden on the population's productive sector. Under these

Table 13. Ḥğeri age structure, 1959 and 1964.

	Age Cohort			
	0–14 years (%)	15–29 years (%)	30–44 years (%)	45–64 years (%)
Ḥğerāt				
1959	47.4	27.4	11.8	13.64
1964	51.1	24.6	10.7	13.6
Arab Sector*				
1961	48.6	26.1	12.3	9

*Arab sector data: Isr. CBS Abs. 1962[13]:45.

circumstances it is no surprise that fathers pulled their sons out of school to increase the family's labor pool and reduce the consumer/producer ratio. The long-term effects of this action, however, were to markedly limit the next generation's ability to acquire better paying professional jobs in the industrial sector, as well as white-collar or academic careers.

Similarly, two categories of factors combined to affect teacher inadequacy, a problem endemic to the whole Arab sector's rural education in the 1950s and early 1960s. The first category was the educational tradition of Moslem education in the Arab sector, which primarily affected teacher quality, while the second was a combination of external factors, which primarily affected teacher availability. Similar to other traditional educational systems that had their roots in religious instruction, the teacher-student relationship in the traditional Moslem educational system is more accurately described as following the "master-disciple" model. One of the characteristics of this form of relationship is that the "master" authorizes his graduating disciples "to teach others what they had learned from him" (Gibb 1971:98). In the rural Arab sector of the 1950s, this tradition was expressed in high school graduates teaching elementary school classes what they had learned from their teachers without any specialized teacher's training. To a large extent the untrained teachers were responsible for the emphasis on recitation and memorization, which de facto perpetuated the *ḫaṭīb* system long after it was called "primary education." For its part, the community accepted this teaching style as the proper way because it conformed with tradition, and as late as the mid-1970s, middle-aged parents did not understand the drive of the government in demanding teacher's training as a condition for employment.

The second category of factors had its roots in the Mandate administration's refusal to view education as one of its duties, for the most part leaving it to the country's different religious communities. This policy resulted in a shortage of trained teachers in, primarily, the Moslem rural areas, a problem aggravated by the 1948 mass exodus. From the Israeli government's point of view, the shortage in trained teachers during the 1950s was not confined to the Arab sector. The mass immigration of the early 1950s and the lower educational level of that population (cf. Ben Porath 1966:10, tb. 1–3; Klinov-Malul 1966:12–13), many of whom were educated by the similar Jewish religious education, generated a similar—although smaller—shortage in the Jewish sector. Moreover, since all through the Mandate Period the Jews and the Arabs comprised separate sectors, and with the MG functioning to maintain that separation, there was little reason to assume that even had there been a surplus of trained Jewish teachers, the Ministry of Education would have assigned them to the Arab sector. Much like the British, the Israeli authorities tried to meddle as little as possible in what might be interpreted as the religious instruction of a state's minority. And last but not least, the MG used teaching positions as part of its reward and surveillance strategies. Such a practice practically eliminated professional aptitude as the primary consideration in assigning teachers to schools. The effects of the type of instruction the children received were to manifest themselves, however, only when this generation joined the labor force.

Consequently, much as during the earlier period, the emphasis in school was primarily on memorization of material as the basic learning technique and the four Rs—the traditional three plus religion—as the subject matter, with only scant attention to other subjects such as geography or history. These problems also faced the school in the Mikmān, which met on the ground floor of the local *muḫtār*'s house. Nevertheless, setting aside a place for formal instruction added to the prestige of education and to the realization of its necessity—as well as to the awkwardness of pulling a child out of a class in session to send him off with the herd.

The Moving of the Tribal Center to Bīr al-Maksūr

At about the same time, the process of shifting the tribal center from the Ẓahara to Bīr al-Maksūr began to gain momentum. As part of the state's attempts to establish new settlements, both as a continuation of the pre-state ideology (cf. Halevi and Klinov-Malul 1968:34–35) and as defensive strategy, in 1953 a new Jewish settlement, Segev, was established some 3.5 km northwest of the Ẓahara (see Map 7). For the first three years of its existence Segev was populated by a unit of the agricultural corps of the IDA, the *NaḤaL*, and was a link in the civil defense settlement network that had proven so successful in holding back the invading armies during the War of 1948. Located on the western hills overlooking the Valley of Saḫnīn, it was the only Jewish settlement in that area during the 1950s. To alleviate the isolation of Segev, which had both social and politico-military repercussions, it was necessary to establish at least one other Jewish settlement in that area. The Ẓahara—close by, mountainous, and predominantly state lands—was the logical choice. Consequently, early in 1955 the director of the Jewish National Fund (JNF) in northern Israel, Yosef Naḥmani, arrived for an overnight visit in the Ẓahara as a guest of the *muḫtār*.

In their private discussion Naḥmani pointed out to Muḥammad al-Ḥsēn that the Ẓahara, legally speaking, belonged to the government because most of the Ḥğerāt had not bothered to register their plots when the Mandate administration pursued its land ownership settlement program. The state, however, recognized Ḥğeri squatters' rights whenever a person could prove them. But this problem, according to Naḥmani, was only secondary in relation to a major problem. The real issue was twofold. First, agriculture had been expanding and natural free pasture diminishing proportionally for the previous thirty years, and this process would continue and intensify as time passed. Second, the Ḥğerāt had been investing much money, time, and effort in building houses that thus far formed a dispersed settlement, which the government would not be able to provide with civil services. Naḥmani pointed to the rugged mountainous character of the landscape and to the practice of individual houseowners of building away from each other so that the twenty-five houses that made up the Ḥğeri settlement there dotted a triangular area of close to seven square kilometers. The government, with its small budget, could not provide roads, running water, and electricity to each house.[9] He then suggested that the young *muḫtār* move the Ḥğerāt to the hill of Ḫirbet al-Maksūr, which is located virtually on the Shfar'am-Nazareth road. The hill would be planned as a modern village with roads, running water, electricity, mosque, clinic, and the like, and it would cost much less than in the Ẓahara because the houses would be closer together. Furthermore, he

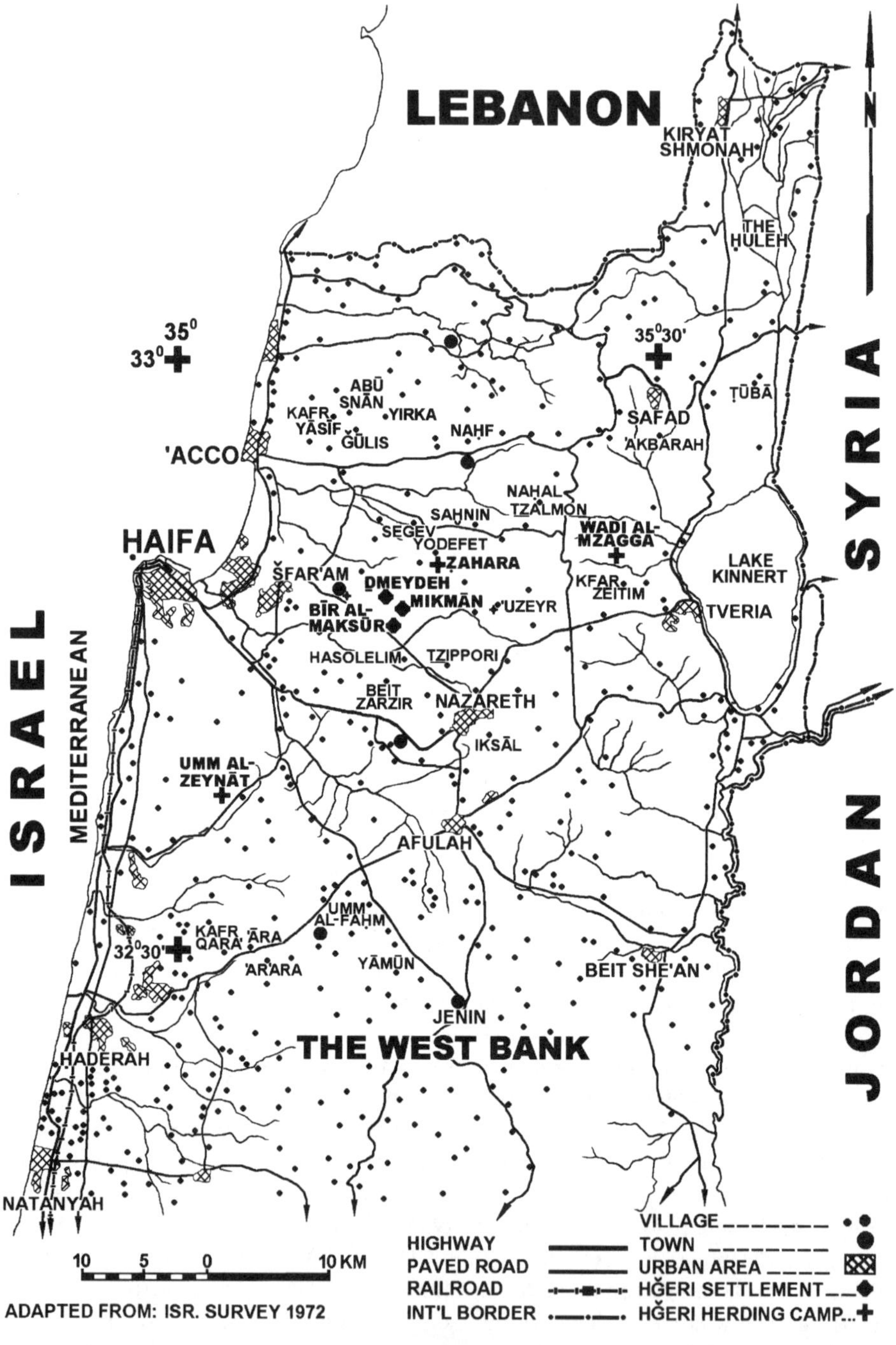

Map 7. The Galilee in the 1970s.

pointed out, in Maksūr the Ḥğerāt would be mostly on their own land and next to their arable fields so they would not have to travel from the Ẓahara to cultivate them. The *muḫtār* told Naḥmani he would think the matter over and the next day Naḥmani returned to Tiberias where he lived.

By 1953–1954, life in the Ẓahara began to show discernible differences from what the older generation remembered. The MG was practically everywhere, and although some animal theft still occurred it was no longer on any major scale. In general, public security was high. The population of the Ḥğerāt, in both the Ẓahara and the Mikmān, was increasing rapidly as a result of the wave of marriages that had been delayed by the war and the parental generation's investment in the purchase of the lands of Bīr al-Maksūr. Now, as new households were set up, the physical space of those already established diminished proportionally as the tribe could not expand beyond the original enclave into which its forefathers had moved some eighty years earlier. And as space diminished, there was increased competition over the meager economic resources, especially within the Ẓahara. Finally, a host of personal reasons—ranging from unhappiness with the rise of *ulād* Ḏiyab, through economic necessity, to polygamous marital arrangements—served as catalysts to bring some of the middle-aged people to move to Ḫirbet al-Maksūr and join the two sublineages of the Ṣawālḥah, the Masa'īd and Sama'neh, already settled there.

This migration began in 1953 when three families moved from the Ẓahara and settled in Maksūr. These were joined by two families from the Mikmān and during 1954 five more families from the Ẓahara. None of these families had land in the Ẓahara or in the Mikmān; their mainstay was the cultivation of the lands of Bīr al-Maksūr augmented by a few animals to provide the home with milk products. They settled on the rocky hill of Ḫirbet al-Maksūr, which overlooked the *wādi* where the *bir* (well) and their arable lands were located and where a few houses of the Sama'neh were already built. On the next hill to their east they could see the households of the Masa'īd. There were thus some twenty-five settled households, plus two more permanently camped to the south, when Ibrāhīm al-Nimr joined them after leaving the Ẓahara to the control of Muḥammad al-Ḥsēn.

By the end of 1955 those in Maksūr began to talk about the need to have a local *muḫtār* to mediate between themselves and the MG because Muḥammad al-Ḥsēn was living in the Ẓahara and could not take good care of their daily dealing with the authorities. This initial discussion soon gained momentum under the remote influence of Ṣāleḥ Ḥassan al-Ḫnefes, who had not lost his interest in weakening the Ḥğerāt in general and the Ġadāyreh in particular. The discussions about a *muḫtār* for Maksūr were of great interest not only to Ṣāleḥ al-Ḫnefes and Ḥsēn al-Gāsem, but to Ibrāhīm al-Nimr as well. Not surprisingly, he saw an opportunity to get back at *ulād* Ḏiyab and acquire a mukhtarship for himself all in one swoop.

The settlers, using the connections of one of their members (who hoped to gain the mukhtarship for himself), approached the elders of the Christian community of Shfar'am to gain access to one of its members, an aide to the military governor in Shfar'am. With the help of this person and a word from Ṣāleḥ al-Ḫnefes, MK, an envoy was received by the governor. The envoy requested that the governor nominate a *muḫtār* for Maksūr, and stated their reasons. The governor was sympathetic and told them that he would look into the matter and make his recommendations to the authorities concerned, the Ministry of the Interior. He then sent a message to Muḥammad al-Ḥsēn, notifying him of the request and saying that if he stayed in the Ẓahara the MG would have to recommend a *muḫtār* for Maksūr because the hamlet was growing rapidly.

A few nights later, Mūsā al-Ḏiyab, accompanied by his brother, Ḥsēn, and nephew, the *muḫtār*, paid a visit to Ibrāhīm al-Nimr. Mūsā, who kept out of the power struggle in the Ẓahara and maintained his friendship with Ibrāhīm, did the talking. He pointed to the tradition of unity in the Ḥğerāt, that Ġadāyreh were all one family, and that if they let a rift develop between them the whole lineage would suffer, and not merely this or that individual. He pointed to the continuous vigilance that the Ġadāyreh had to exercise to maintain the leadership in its hands, and that the Ramlāt, not to mention the Ṣawālḥah, would be happy if the Ġadāyreh were divided. Moreover, the only ones standing to gain from a quarrel in the Ġadāyreh were the Druze, who wanted to weaken the Ḥğerāt in order to keep them in check. He ended by advocating "forgive and forget," and Ibrāhīm al-Nimr, Ḥsēn, and Muḥammad shook hands and the past was put to rest.[10]

When Muḥammad al-Ḥsēn returned to the Ẓahara he halted the preparations to build his second house, which was to be a large hewn stone house befitting a *muḫtār*. He bought a traditional goat-hair tent and started to migrate. He would spend part of the year in Maksūr and the rest elsewhere, including Rosh Pinah, Hittin near Tiberias, and the Valley of Beisan where, in 1958, he met the commander of the local police station with whom he struck up a friendship, which was to help him in later years. Finally, in the fall of 1958 he bought three *dunum* (3000 m^2) from another tribesmember on the south end of the hill of Maksūr overlooking the Shfar'am-Nazareth road and built a small house there. He himself, however, continued living in his tent except for rare occasions. Earlier that same year he also used his influence with the MG to secure a recommendation for a permit to build a school in Maksūr. The school was requested by the settlers there in order to save their children the two-kilometer walk to the school in the Mikmān—an onerous task during the winter, and a point lost in the ever-present one-upmanship game with the Ṣawālḥah.[11] The school, which was built in 1958 next to the *muḫtār*'s house, included a four-room poured concrete structure accompanied by a two-room frame house containing the school's office and a teachers' room.

Although the *muḫtār* himself continued to migrate with his herd, he left two of his brothers to reside in Maksūr, one making his living from agriculture and the other a tracker in the police. He then began a campaign to convince the tribesmembers to move their residence from the Ẓahara to Maksūr. At first, only those of his friends and younger relations who owned no stone houses in the Ẓahara followed him, pitching their tents on the hill of Ḫirbet al-Maksūr. These were reinforced by members of the poorer families and minor sublineages who did not have a solid economic base in the Ẓahara and who moved to be closer to their fields and to the Shfar'am-Nazareth road. It was this transportation artery connecting Nazareth and the industrial areas of the Bay of Haifa that was gaining importance as the younger generation sought work outside the limited opportunities within the tribal territory and the Arab sector, and as the Jewish sector was opening up to Arab labor (cf. Ben Porath 1966:52–57).

Notes

1. In general, 1947/48 had smaller amounts of rainfall and fewer rainy days than the annual averages (Ashbel 1949:3, tb. A), which meant that although the cisterns were full, the water table was lower than usual because much of the rain ran off and the springs were less plentiful. This was amplified by a drier year than usual in 1945/46 (Ashbel 1947:1) and a relative drought in 1946/47 when not only was there less rainfall than the average but most of it fell during a single month—January (Ashbel 1948:1–2, tb. A). Nazareth, for example, received only 45% of its annual average, of which 49% fell in January and 27% in December (Ashbel 1948:5).
2. These contradictions had been noted before; various British commissioners pointed to them in practically every report on Palestine (e.g., G.B. Pls. 1937:161 et passim). More precisely, Articles 2 and 6 are contradictory in providing for "the establishment of the Jewish national home" while "safe-guarding the civil and religious right of all the inhabitants of Palestine" (Article 2) and "Jewish immigration," "while ensuring that the rights and position of other sections of the population are not prejudiced" (Article 6). Article 11, for example, is ambiguous in demanding that "[t]he Administration of Palestine shall take all necessary measures to safeguard the interests of the *community* in connection with the development of the country" (G.B. Par. 1922:3–4, emphasis mine).
3. This problem is not unique to military and/or colonial administrations. It arises whenever relatively small administrations attempt to "attenuate" (cf. Beer 1974:23–29) the amount of information that is generated by the population at large. This situation becomes more pronounced when Western administrations, which work on "monochronic" principles, confront kin-based societies, which are governed by "polychronic" principles (see Hall 1976:17–24 for an elaboration of this topic). Consequently, the more evolved the state organization, the greater the gulf between the two entities, and the more acute the problem.
4. While the total population size declined from an estimated 1,899,000 (not including the Negev bedouin) in 1947 to an estimated 914,700 in 1948, rising to a total of 1,577,800 in 1951 (Halevi and Klinov-Malul 1968:15, 52 respectively), due to the mass departure of the Arab population, production and consumption patterns changed, leading to shortages in foodstuffs and other commodities. Prior to 1947 the predominant Arab population was rural (70% in 1944; Pls. Gov. 1946[I]:157), producing most of the food consumed. The mass immigration that characterized the first three and a half years, May 1948–1951 (101,800; 239,600; 170,200; and 175,100 respectively; Isr. CBS Abs. 1966[17]:91) doubled the Jewish population, which was estimated at 650,000 in May 1948 (Isr. CBS Abs. 1966[17]:22). The absorption of this wave was further aggravated by the fact that an "estimated 30 per cent of the established Jewish population of Israel in 1947 . . . [was] not as yet productively rooted in the economy" (Levy 1955:12), and by the demobilization of the army after the war ended. To cope with these tasks, which included providing food, clothing, and shelter to some 686,700 immigrants, an austerity program was instituted whereby food and other necessities were rationed (Halevi and Klinov-Malul 1968:5–7). At the same time, to finance the country during that period, the government printed money quite liberally (Halevi and Klinov-Malul 1968:253). Much of this money ended in public hands, which could not spend it legally due to the general scarcity generated by the doubling of the number of consumers, coupled with the rationing program. The result was the florescence of black marketeering (Halevi and Klinov-Malul 1968:258) on a fairly massive scale, in which enterprising individuals such as *ulād* Nimr could find a lucrative subsistence.
5. Until the last quarter of 1952, many of the economic regulations and restrictions were part of the general rationing program that governed the whole economy. Some of the essential foodstuffs were rationed even later (cf. Tadmor 1953:16). Yet many of the regulations resulted from the evolution of the MG itself and the control it exerted over the Arab sector. In the words of one of the people who were intimately involved with the MG and the Arab sector in those days, "[whether] to sell a sheep in Nazareth or to urinate in Shfar'am, you needed a permit from the *mīmšal* [MG]."

6. The Ḥğerāt were well aware of this tactic. Thus, in July 1976, when the *muḫtār* wanted to make public that he did not want any gifts on the occasion of his firstborn's wedding, one of his brothers raised the point that people wanted to give him gifts because for so long he helped without receiving any gifts in return and this occasion was the first time that etiquette sanctioned such reciprocation. He also mentioned that "it is not good not to let people bring [wedding] presents," meaning that it is a bad policy not to let people discharge some of their debts of honor. The family council (the *muḫtār*'s father and some of his brothers) accepted that brother's opinion and it was recommended to the *muḫtār* not to declare anything in public in regard to gifts.
7. For example, as late as 1976 a Ministry of Agriculture official told the members of a Ḥğeri herding camp to approach him through one of their members who had similar qualities to the *muḫtār*. He told me he did so because whenever that individual came with a batch of requests and problems, he could go through the pile relatively quickly, but whenever the camp members came in person it took him "forever" because each had to tell his own story and he did not have the time or the patience to deal with each of them separately or in a group.
8. Formal education was nonexistent for the Ḥğerāt during the Ottoman Period. The attempts of the Occupied Enemy Territory Administration (OETA) to reconstruct Palestine's educational system were too low-keyed—with only P£53,000 for the country's educational budget for 1919/20 (G.B. Col. 1937:117)—to affect the backwoods. The Mandate administration tried to institute a semi-self-help system according to which the settlement would provide the building and its upkeep while the administration paid the salaries and other costs (G.B. Par. 1921:16). The administration however soon developed a very restricted view of its legitimate functions (Morag 1967:5) and the actual educational budget was very small (e.g., cf. G.B. Col. 1930:79, 149; G.B. Pls. 1937:251–52; Halevi and Klinov-Malul 1968:37). As part of this policy it enacted the Education Ordinance in 1933 under which municipalities and "local councils" became the educational authorities in the areas of their jurisdiction (Pls. Gov. 1946[I]:640). In general, however, the local Arab councils were reluctant to impose a tax for financing education, and the program's implementation was very slow (cf. Pls. Gov. 1947:6–7). In particular, the Ḥğerāt were within the jurisdiction of the "council" of Ṣafūriyeh, with whose peasants they were in conflict. The *ḫaṭīb* was, thus, a self-help enterprise promoted by the more religious elders and financed by the increasing relative affluence of the tribe.
9. For a more comprehensive discussion of the problem of spontaneous settlement of bedouin in Israel and the West Bank, see Amiran and Ben Arieh (1963:173–74 et passim) and Shmueli (1970:71–108, 1973:82–112).
10. According to Ibrāhīm al-Nimr he butchered a lamb in their honor. I asked him repeatedly if it was a *ṣulḥa* (formal reconciliation) and he answered, "No, there was no fight between us, it was just so that we understand each other." By rules of proper conduct, however, the fact of *ulād* Ḍiyab coming to his tent meant that they acknowledged him as the wronged party, thereby restoring his honor (although not his former power).
11. Superfluous as it may look, in 1975 a school was opened in Beit Zarzir, a planned bedouin settlement for four tribes. The school was built closer to two of the four tribes than to the other two. Consequently, the latter two tribes refused to send their children to the school and tried to have the authorities establish another school nearer to their neighborhood.

— 7 —

Ḥğeri Economics

Overview

The development of Bīr al-Maksūr as the tribal center marked the Ḥğerāt's growing involvement in the Israeli economic and political environments. From Ḥğeri perspective, the salient characteristic of this environment was its industrialization and the opportunities it afforded wage labor seekers. At the same time it impacted their agricultural practices, reorienting them toward mechanized cultivation and market production, and effected a gradual decrease in pasture availability, with major consequences for their traditional occupation—herding. The integrated character of the Israeli State environment meant that increasingly the Ḥğerāt needed to respond to changes that originated in other sectors of the Israeli system of which they were not aware but to which they nevertheless needed to adapt. Ḥğeri economy was thus the bull's-eye within three concentric rings: the Arab sector economy, the Israeli economy, and other national economies with which Israel traded. Consequently, the following discussion will incorporate these three levels in the analysis of the Ḥğeri economy in its adaptations. Following a general discussion of the Arab sector and Ḥğeri economies during the MG Period, a gestation period with only little apparent change, a more detailed discussion of Ḥğeri involvement in wage labor, agriculture, and herding from the early 1960s to 1977 will be concluded with a discussion of the Ḥğeri labor force and economy as a whole.

Broadly speaking, the MG Period afforded the Ḥğerāt a gradual transition from their traditional involvement in herding mixed with some agriculture to, by 1977, a primary involvement in wage labor and secondary involvement in agriculture. The process can be said to have begun with the few Ḥğeris who became involved in wage labor as police trackers during the Mandate Period. From the early 1950s, an increasing number became involved in intermittent wage labor in reforestation, as guards, and as trackers with the police and the Border Guard after its formation in 1955. In those days, however, except for jobs in the security branches, this activity was a supplement to the income they derived from their herds and land rather than a major resource in and of itself. Similarly, it was easily incorporated into their traditional work patterns and schedules and did not require any major adjustment in their practices.

The gradual development of Ḥğeri wage labor followed the pattern of the general Arab sector movement into the Jewish sector's labor market during the 1950s. In general, Arab involvement was restricted and controlled by the country's bisectoral sociopolitical and economic organization, which survived the Mandate Period in which it developed (cf. Ben Porath 1966:47–57; Halevi and Klinov-Malul 1968:60; Horowitz and Lissak 1978:19–21). Consequently, while the Arab labor force, the Ḥğerāt included, was looking in varying degrees of intensity for ways first to augment their income from agriculture and, later, to derive most of their income from wage labor in the Jewish sector, the MG was tightly controlling the ability of this labor force to move, an activity in which the MG "was guided by and co-operated with the Ministry of Labor" (Ben Porath 1966:51–52). The pursuance of this policy was largely a continuation of the pre-state general doctrine of "Hebrew Labor" and it helped emphasize and maintain the distinction between the Jewish sector and its Arab counterpart. During the early 1950s the transition from this sectoral pre-state ideology to a state administrative ideology was aggravated by the mass influx of immigrants whose caring and absorption emphasized sectarian loyalties. Parallel to the influx of immigrants, the increasingly tense security conditions that reached their climax in the 1956 Sinai Campaign helped polarize Jewish-Arab relations, thereby perpetuating the pre-state conditions (cf. Ben Porath 1966:56–57).

Other, less historical and parochial reasons also existed. The MG and the Ministry of Labor were responsive to the demands of the *Histadrut*, which took care of the Jewish worker and provided him with employment services. The *Histadrut*, however, also represented the political and/or ideological calculations of the socialist political parties that created it in 1920 and that dominated and governed its conference, departments, and other constituting bodies thereafter (cf. Medding 1972:9–10, 237–42). The relations of the *Histadrut* and the work-seeker, thus, were not completely free and devoid of courting prospective members or sympathetic voters. It suggests itself that since the Arab voters were largely controlled by the MG through their *maḫatīr*, there was less political need to provide work to job-seeking Arabs. It is not surprising, therefore, that it was the small parliamentary parties and parties in the opposition who proposed abolishing the MG in 1962.

During the early 1950s the general attitude of the authorities was to reserve the available work for the Jewish unemployed, whose number peaked in 1953 to 11.5% of the Jewish labor force (Halevi and Klinov-Malul 1968:66, tb.). There was thus reluctance on the part of the authorities and open hostility on the part of organized labor (Ben Porath 1966:55) to allow Arab labor access to the Jewish sector, including the allocation of relief work days to Arabs. It was not surprising, therefore, that when unemployed Arabs did receive relief work it was much less than their Jewish counterparts, a difference which in 1961 was "about 35 work days . . . per unemployed person" to "a little over 100" days respectively (Ben Porath 1966:53, n. 10). The competition within the Arab sector on the available relief work days was relatively intense and could serve as a general measure of the local leader's quality of relations with the MG and other related government offices. At the same time, the distribution of the allocated relief work days among community members could be used to increase the following of such local leaders.

Among the Ḥğerāt, the process of centralization of local power during the early 1950s was still in flux. Not only such competitors as *ulād* Nimr but also other individuals who did not want to appeal to the young *muḫtār* were developing their own linkages to the authorities, which were not always coordinating their activities with the MG. One such example was the partial reforestation of the Yotvat mountain range and its environs by the JNF, and forest guarding once an area was planted. On the Ḥğeri side the *muḫtār* was competing with other tribesmembers who had contacts with the JNF or the authorities in order to monopolize this access. On the authorities' side, the JNF was not as strict as the MG in dealing with the community via its *muḫtār*. If one had his own contacts with the JNF Forestation Department one could independently secure a job, usually as a forest guard, with that organization. Characteristically, these jobs were confined to a small area and did not require a movement permit. From the JNF point of view this arrangement was attractive on two counts. First, it was an effective preventive measure to protect the young groves because the Ḥğerāt would interpret any attempt to destroy the trees as an attempt to undermine the position of a Ḥğeri guard vis-à-vis his employer, hence an insult against the tribe as a whole. Potential transgressors, therefore, were far less likely to damage the saplings or other property under his responsibility for fear that a theft might escalate into a sociopolitical conflict with the tribe. The remedy of the law, by way of contrast, could be taken only once the forest had been damaged. Second, by letting the herdsman guard the forest, the JNF was trying to control the saplings' worst enemy—the goat—using the tactic of having the cat guard the milk. From a Ḥğeri point of view a guard job was a source of income without any work. All one had to do was pitch one's tent there and sometimes it was enough just to make it public knowledge that the area was under his guardianship. Secondly, being a guard was a source of authority, which one could use either to help friends a little or harass non-friends, especially if they were *fellāḥīn*.[1]

By and large Ḥğeri wage jobs were the traditional wage labor opportunities, that is, the work came to the Ḥğerāt in their own camps and territory rather than vice versa. Thus, if a source of income appeared near the village or a herding camp, older Ḥğeris would become temporarily employed for as long as the work lasted, they were present in the area, they felt they made enough money, they felt they had enough strenuous work, or some other such immediate reason. For example, when *Mekorot* (the National Water Company) excavated the Kinneret-Negev Conduit through the Valley of Beit Netofah in the late 1950s and early 1960s, some Ḥğeris dug trenches while others guarded its equipment for as long as the project lasted in the area. The same held true when working for the JNF reforestation efforts or as agricultural migrant labor for the Jewish settlements in the neighborhood of their camps. In other words, for the Ḥğerāt, wage labor in the 1950s was an opportunity rather than a necessity. This was not true for the Arab villagers who were subjected to rapidly increasing pressure for wage labor as their productive resources dwindled and their population increased.

Until the late 1950s most of the Ḥğerāt lived comparatively well off their herds and land. The lands of Bīr al-Maksūr, although in cultivation since 1942/43, were still under-utilized and served as a reservoir of arable land, which was gradually put to use as more men decided to allocate land to their maturing sons. While these lands had been under cereal cultivation from their time of purchase, they were used only where no preparation other than plowing was necessary, and were not cultivated year round. As more people began to cultivate smaller plots, hill areas were cleared of stones and put to the plow, crop rotation was introduced, and from 1959 when the first tractor was purchased, more intensive methods and seeds were incorporated into the local agricultural technology.

Although free pasture was slowly diminishing, it was still abundant during this decade due to the deserted villages and tribal lands resulting from the 1948 War. The facility with which Muḥammad al-Ḥsēn could arrange for travel permits enabled the majority of the tribe to use these abandoned lands and to maintain herding as their major economic endeavor. This, however, was not true for the Ṣawālḥah. Although Muḥammad al-Ḥsēn occupied the senior position of the tribe's two *maḫatīr*, there was much tension between him and Ḥsēn al-Gāsem, the *muḫtār* of the Mikmān where the Ṣawālḥah resided. First, there was the traditional rivalry inherent in segmentary lineage organization. More importantly, Ḥsēn al-Gāsem was supported by Ṣāleḥ al-Ḫnefes, the Ġadāyreh's sworn enemy. Muḥammad al-Ḥsēn would, therefore, use his influence with the MG mostly on behalf of his own lineage members, leaving the Ṣawālḥah to their own *muḫtār*, who was not nearly as influential. Occasionally Muḥammad al-Ḥsēn would help a member of the Ṣawālḥah, provided he was a friend or in order to make a follower while playing down Ḥsēn al-Gāsem.

Those helped by Muḥammad al-Ḥsēn were much freer in their ability to move than the majority of the Arab sector. For example, in 1956 a member of the Ṭa'awāneh began to rent some pastureland in *wādi* al-Mzagga (north of Tiberias in the former tribal territory of the *'arab* al-Muwāsa) and secured the necessary permits with Muḥammad al-Ḥsēn's help. A year later the Ṭa'awāni was joined by his nephew and between 1961 and 1963 by eleven additional Ġadāyri households, forming a permanent herding camp there. One of these households left the Ẓahara in 1957; spent 1957/58 near Safad; camped during 1958/59 in Naḥal Tabor near Mt. Tabor; and relocated to south of Shfar'am in 1959/60 before moving to *wādi* al-Mzagga in 1961.

The increasing participation of the Ḥğerāt in a market-oriented regional economy had a more solid foundation in their growing involvement in market-oriented agricultural production. Their agricultural efforts during the Mandate Period, as previously mentioned, were primarily oriented toward self-sufficiency with an emphasis on grain production (wheat for bread, some barley—at a ratio of 2:1 respectively—and, in the Valley of Beit Netofah, durra) and tobacco accompanied by kitchen gardens in which they grew some vegetables, sesame, and watermelons. Sometimes, if a crop was plentiful and in excess of household needs, as was often the case with watermelons, they would sell off the excess to other Ḥğeri families or to nearby village middlemen who would ship it to Nazareth or Shfar'am with their own crop.

The decline in Arab agricultural landed population as a result of the 1948 War and the increase in the semi-urban Jewish population created an increased demand for marketed agricultural foodstuffs, making market-oriented production attractive. This became all the more true when the movement inherent in herding was curtailed. It was thus that in 1950 the Ṣawālḥah in the Mikmān and in Maksūr who owned some fertile bottom-lands in *wādi* I'billin in addition to the lands of Bīr al-Maksūr, who were close to neighboring villages with their agricultural orientation and skills, and who had a less influential *muḫtār* who could not arrange for the free movement required for herding, started instead to grow grain, vegetables, and watermelons for sale. By 1954 they were joined by those settlers who came to Maksūr from the Ẓahara, and as time passed, increasing numbers of Ḥğeris who could not establish or maintain a herd and who thus shifted the emphasis of their economic efforts to market-oriented agriculture.[2]

During the 1950s, market orientation was still secondary to household consumption and in a large measure was an expansion of the production of traditional items grown for household use combined with the sale of the excess. As time passed, however, calculations of market profitability entered the agricultural decision-making processes. If there was demand and the price was good they would increase the production of a previously secondary crop over a primary one. For example, it was marketing considerations that brought about the reversal from the predominance of wheat cultivation to one of barley, leaving wheat production oriented toward household consumption. The reason for this reversal was the problems encountered in disposing of excess wheat crop due to *Tnuva*'s (the major Jewish agricultural marketing cooperative) adherence to the general reluctance of its parent organization (the *Histadrut*) to incorporate the Arab sector in its activities prior to 1959 (cf. Ben Porath 1966:54–56). (*Tnuva*, as of 1977, was still constrained in its dealings in the Arab sector by the problems of Jewish dietary laws [*kashrut*], which were closely watched over by the regional Rabbinical Councils.) Barley, on the other hand, was disposed of much more easily as animal feed within both the tribe and the region. At the level of the Arab sector, barley was not only disposed of as animal feed but was absorbed by the beer industry, which bought the grain directly from private middlemen rather than routing its purchases via *Tnuva*. From 1960/61 this industry began producing beer on a much larger scale (Isr. CBS 1961:348, n. 6), thus encouraging barley production. It is not surprising, therefore, that in 1959/60 the Arab sector sowed some 268,500 *dunam* of barley and in 1960/61 that figure rose to 391,200 *dunam* (Isr. CBS 1970:22). Interestingly, there was a decline in barley production in the Jewish sector during this period with the respective figures being 327,000 and 306,100 *dunam* respectively (Isr. CBS 1970:22).

Finally, Ḥğeri demography was still in balance with its traditional economic pursuits. The economic burden of unproductive children was generally not too onerous to force middle-aged Ḥğeris to actively look for wage labor to support their families or to help maintain their old levels of consumption when an increasing number of consumers threatened to reduce it.[3] Consequently, the Ḥğerāt lagged by two to three years behind the rest of the Arab sector that, from about 1957 to 1959 when the MG relaxed its control on travel and Jewish unemployment was declining rapidly (Ben Porath 1966:52), was entering the wage labor market of the Jewish sector in increasing numbers (Ben Porath 1966:59, tb.).

With no immediate pressure to seek salaried jobs, the first few Ḥğeris to enter the Jewish sector's labor market during the 1950s were characteristically young (15–20 years old), unmarried or newly-married males. They were just entering the adult working period and did not have a herd or land to support them nor were they as constrained as their elders by past habits and memories. Often they started to work before marriage to supplement their paternal household's income or to help collect the *mahr* (bride's wealth) and other expenses for their own weddings, while younger siblings took over caring for the family herd and land cultivation. They all lived close to a bus route, which was essential to commute daily to the Bay of Haifa area where most of the jobs were.[4] While they would take whatever job was available, the majority of the jobs they secured were in the construction industry—where unskilled labor could be absorbed with ease, where periodic absenteeism could be tolerated, and where work was easily found due to the demand for apartments generated by both immigration and natural population growth. The process began in 1954 when a few individuals from the Ḏmeydeh and the Mikmān started working in trench digging, cinder block manufacture, and other unskilled and low-paying construction jobs in the Bay area. By 1959 a few youth became employed as apprentices in somewhat more professional jobs such as mechanic apprentices and factory work both in Nazareth and the Bay area, and with this development the character of Ḥğeri involvement in wage labor changed. Whereas in the old pattern paid work came to the Ḥğerāt in their own camps and territory, in the new pattern young Ḥğeris sought out work and became increasingly more exposed to and influenced by the values of the Jewish sector.

Wage Labor

Overview

As the 1960s wore on, the involvement with the Jewish sector increased rapidly as both the younger age cohorts and early middle-aged individuals looked for wage labor in growing numbers. Thus, by 1977, 59.3% of the Ḥğeri labor force was involved in wage labor, overturning the traditional balance among the various income sources of the tribe's economy. In the following I will first discuss the pressures to seek wage labor and the pattern of involvement in the wage labor market. I will then focus on Ḥğeri employment in the security forces, female employment, and the evolving pattern of civilian wage labor in the third quarter of the 1970s. The discussion of these three areas will focus on their economic aspect although it is important to remember that all three had wider ramifications beyond the economic sphere—in inter- and intra-tribal politics, gender relations, and intergenerational relations—to be discussed in later sections.

Pressure to Seek Wage Labor

The pressures to look for wage labor resulted from intensifying endogenous Ḥğeri demands to find new sources of income combined with a growing hunger for unskilled labor in the Jewish sector. The intra-Ḥğeri pressures included population growth, reduced demand for labor in agriculture and herding, and changing lifestyle. The Jewish sector reversed its demand for Arab labor when the immigration waves of the early 1950s were finally absorbed and unemployment hovered at about 3.6% (Halevi and Klinov-Malul 1968:66, tb.). Thus, this new state of "full employment" (Ben Porath 1966:47) encouraged the search for wage labor and facilitated the incorporation of the Arab worker into the Jewish workplace.

Most important among the endogenous pressures was the expansion of the Ḥğeri population and its working segment, which was rapidly exhausting the traditional jobs available within the tribe's economic enterprises. This population increase impacted the need for wage labor in two ways, an increase demand fueled by the growing number of non-productive consumers and by an increased supply of participants in the available labor force. By 1961 the Ḥğerāt numbered 1618 individuals in their core settlements (see Table 14). Of that population 53% were consumers (ages 1–14 and 65+) and 47% were in the labor force (24% males and 22.9% females).

The natural growth of the Ḥğeri labor force and its demand for jobs was further aggravated by a declining demand for labor in both agriculture and herding. In agriculture the labor demand declined as a result of mechanization. Not only did more people acquire tractors to cultivate their fields but in 1964 the first harvester combine was added to the tribe's agricultural technology. Concurrently, with the gradual withdrawal of the MG from everyday life, the civilian governmental ministries commensurately increased their presence and exerted more influence in the Arab sector. In particular, the Ministry of Agriculture in the Galilee conducted an educational campaign to make agriculture and animal husbandry more productive, thereby increasing both the level of Ḥğeri agricultural technology (machines, seeds, breeds, and techniques) and their market orientation. An-

Table 14. The 1961 distribution of Ḥğeri population in its core settlements (by age and sex).*

	Total	**Age** (years)											
		0–4	5–9	10–14	15–19	20–24	25–29	30–34	35–44	45–54	55–64	65–74	75+
males	864	218	149	79	90	76	58	37	58	40	30	15	14
females	754	179	104	79	89	64	48	44	60	47	19	12	9
total	*1618*	*397*	*253*	*158*	*179*	*140*	*106*	*81*	*118*	*87*	*49*	*27*	*23*

(Source: Isr. CBS 1963b:164–65, tb.)

*The census was conducted by settlement; hence, Ḥğeris who resided elsewhere ('Uzeyr, Shfar'am, herding camps, etc.) are not included in these figures. This fact accounts for the occasional discrepancies between my figures, which included all of the Ḥğerāt, and the official figures, which enumerated only those in the Ẓahara, the Ḍmeydeh, the Mikmān, and Maksūr.

other source of influence were the Jewish agricultural settlements with which the Ḥǧerāt were coming in ever-closer contact via their guard and other jobs. Thus, as agriculture became more labor efficient, it required less labor.

The steady decline in pasture availability, which impacted herding, was made worse by the general increase in the number of animals of both Jewish and Arab herds. The problem of diminishing pastures was caused by two related factors. First, there was the continuous increase in cultivated land, which went from an area of 1,650,000 *dunam* in 1948/49 to some 4,138,000 *dunam* in 1966/67 (Isr. CBS 1970:9), an increase of some 250%. Similarly, "built-on area" and "forested area" each increased by 55% during the same period (Isr. CBS 1970:9). As a result, the category of "natural pasture and unused land" decreased by 17.6% (Isr. CBS 1970:9). While the magnitude of this decline was calculated using the total amount of unused land in Israel (that is, subtracting the used land from the total land area of the country) (Isr. CBS 1970:9, n.) most of the unused land lay in the semi-arid and arid south. Consequently, the reduction in pasturage was felt disproportionately in the center and the north of the country, where most of the expansion in all three categories (cultivated, forested, and built-on land) took place. Moreover, the drive to bring all suitable available land under the plow or irrigation pipe was not confined to the Jewish sector, which established some 446 new agricultural settlements between 1949 and 1965 (Horwitz 1967:465–66, tb.), but was pursued with equal zeal in the agricultural Arab sector (cf. Isr. CBS 1970:10–11).

While open pasture was declining, in both sectors there was a continuous increase in livestock populations during the 1950s. Arab cattle (breed: *baladi*) increased from some 20,000 head in 1951 to 41,500 in 1961 (Isr. CBS 1970:74), an increase of over 200%, while Jewish cattle increased by over 300% (from 61,000 to 191,000; Isr. CBS 1970:74). Traditionally, however, the majority of the Jewish cattle herd was dairy cattle, primarily fed on improved pasture lots and cultivated fodder and, hence, not competing with the Arab cattle, which predominately used natural pasture. Nevertheless, from a mere 1.3% of the Jewish cattle herd in 1951, the beef industry's cattle herd grew rapidly throughout the 1950s and increasingly competed with the Arab cattle herd for the available natural pasture. This competition was most intense in the north (the districts of Haifa and the North) where 70.6% of the Jewish beef cattle and 87.6% of the Arab *baladi* cattle were concentrated in 1971 (Isr. CBS 1974a:6–7). By 1961 the competition was won by the beef industry and the Arab cattle herd declined from 41,500 head that year to 27,300 head in 1969 (Isr. CBS Abs. 24:408) to 16,735 in 1971 (Isr. CBS 1974a:6–7), remaining under 20,000 head as of 1976/77 (cf. Isr. CBS Abs. 24:408; 25:400; 26:389; 27:384; 28:388; 29:429 for the years 1972–1977 respectively).

The pressures on the available pasturage were further aggravated by an increased sheep and goat population in the country as a whole (sheep by more than 330% and goats by about 235% in 1961; Isr. CBS 1970:76). While most of the Jewish sheep herds were lot-fed, hence not heavily competing with the Arab herds, the latter were competing among themselves, further reducing pasture availability. With the decrease in open pasturage and the continuous increase in rental fees of natural pasture and stubble due to both the rising cost of living and the competition over access to the available pasturage, aggravated by the growing shortage of trained shepherds, small herd owners were slowly forced out of this traditional economic pursuit.

Finally, changes in lifestyles and increased consumerism created a need for liquid cash. The tightening contact with the markets of Nazareth, Shfar'am, and Haifa and the intensification of the sedentary mode of life, which more Ḥğeris were adopting and which did not sanction against accumulating consumer durables, resulted in increased acquisition of these goods (cf. Kressel 1976:46 for a similar process among the Central Region bedouin). Moreover, as more Ḥğeris decided to build houses, the need for liquid cash increased. The rising cost of living (cf. Halevi 1968:110, tb.) affected the cost of building materials as well as other facets of life such as marriage, where the increased cost was expressed both in the continuous rise of the *mahr* (bride's-wealth, progeny price, or *feḏ*)[5] and in other wedding expenses be they the *ğhāz* (the dowry) or the expenses of hospitality. Thus, a reinforcing loop developed where intermittent wage labor created an appetite for consumerism that combined with the other pressures on the traditional economic pursuits to seek wage labor ever more intensely.

Patterns of Involvement in the Wage Labor Market

The pattern of Ḥğeri involvement in the wage labor market, although slower, generally followed that of the Arab sector at large with the exception of bedouin involvement with Israel's security forces. Lacking in Western education and industrial skills, they found work in professions where these were not required, especially in construction where they could receive pay equal to or even higher than that of their Jewish counterparts (cf. Ben Porath 1966:64), and where skill could be acquired on the job. By the end of the 1960s and the beginning of the 1970s, some of those in construction had become skilled workers and foremen, and with the increase in house construction in Bīr al-Maksūr and the Mikmān, the more enterprising became small-scale building contractors.

The majority of the wage laborers during the 1960s, however, maintained a high rate of job mobility. For example:

(1) A member of the 'Afafṭeh (born 1945): 1958 (6 months) worked in a bakery in a Jewish settlement; 1958–1962 apprenticed in a tannery; 1962–1970 self-employed in agriculture (rented land 1962–1967 around Maksūr and 1967–1970 in the area of Haderah); 1971–1973 was a tracker in the IDA (disabled veteran); 1973–1977 worked as a foreman in a construction equipment company.

(2) A member of the Ramlāt (born 1942): 1964–1966 Border Guard; 1966–1970 civilian guard for a guard company in Haifa (guarded a variety of establishments); 1970–1974 contractor for cutting trees for the JNF and a charcoal maker; 1974–1976 herded sheep (self-employed); 1976–1977 herded cattle (partnership with an elder of the Ġadāyreh).

(3) A member of the Ġadāyreh (born 1936): until 1963 herded his sheep and goats; 1963–1967 worked in construction; 1967–1968 was in the Border Guard; 1968–1969 worked as unskilled labor for the JNF; 1969–1977 was in construction again.

Ben Porath (1966:67–68) has argued that the high rate of job mobility was the result of the employment of Arabs in industries with a characteristically high rate of turnover (construction and seasonal agriculture) superimposed on the intersectoral mobility between their Arab homes and Jewish workplaces. Nevertheless, it was precisely their ability to shift between the two sectors and among jobs that allowed the Ḥğerāt (and other Arabs) to be enmeshed in industrial wage labor in the Jewish sector while maintaining their economic activities in the village (cf. Boneh 1983:211–58; Jakubowska 1985:159–220). Such dual sector economic involvement widened their economic base and increased their economic stability (that is, their ability to withstand short perturbations in the Jewish labor market and the state's economic cycles such as the 1966/67 recession).

Like the general pattern in the Arab sector during the 1950s (Ben Porath 1966:53) and in the late 1960s and early 1970s (Isr. CBS 1972a:98, tb.), Ḥğeris looking for and finding work usually did so on an individual basis rather than through the Ministry of Labor's Employment Service Labor Exchanges. While the 1959 Employment Service Law required both potential employers and job seekers to make use of the exchanges (Isr. Laws 13:32–33, Sec. 32), a worker would often locate a job by himself and only then visit the exchange with a note from his new employer to validate the position. Instead of the exchange, individuals would use whatever source of job information was available, be it hearsay in the villages or intra-tribally, a shot-gun approach to visiting and asking at probable worksites, or tips from friends or relatives. This last method was preferred among the youth because the job seeker could enter an alien environment able to use the social network developed by his friends.[6] As self-assurance and experience increased, the youth might look for work regardless whether he had friends at a given workplace.

Employment in the Security Forces

The 1967 Six-Day War opened a new set of job opportunities in the security complex for the Ḥğerāt and other bedouin tribes in Israel. Some of them became trackers for the IDA, under whose Military Government's responsibility were the "Administered Territories" occupied during that war. The involvement of the Ḥğerāt with the state's security forces, as mentioned before, had been primarily with the police and, from 1955, its Border Guard. The former, however, could employ only a handful of trackers and even though usually it was a Ḥğeri who got the job when a new position became available, not many found employment in the police. The formation of the Border Guard to help (among other purposes and responsibilities) seal the borders against the 1954–1956 Fedayeen created a few more tracking positions that were rapidly manned by Ḥğeris and other bedouin tribesmen. The 1956 Sinai Campaign, however, all but ended Fedayeen activity, and the Border Guard, especially after the Kafr Qāsim Massacre, were confined to relatively quiet borders that did not require a large pool of trackers. Nor could they fuel demands for an increased budget to expand the force. Consequently, from 1956 to 1967 the Border Guard mostly replaced older trackers (who graduated into the police proper or resigned altogether) rather than create new jobs.

Although the IDA had its own trackers, until 1967 these positions were generally manned by the Ḥğerāt's traditional rivals, the *'arab* al-Heīb.[7] The Six-Day War left shorter borders than the pre-1967 ones but a larger occupied territory to watch and administer, requiring more trackers than the Heīb could supply. Moreover, the renewed terrorist activities of the Palestine Liberation Organization (PLO) and similar organizations placed tracking in growing demand because once a terrorist unit crossed the border the fastest way of finding it was by tracking. Trackers were also important for the discovery of plastic mines and other such nonmetallic devices. Consequently, not only did the Border Guard hire more trackers but the IDA, in whose jurisdiction laid the Administered Territories and the terrorists, began to use them in numbers not seen before.

From the bedouin point of view, employment in the IDF was economically attractive on several accounts. First, since most of the Ḥğerāt (as well as other tribesmen) were employed as civilian personnel rather than as draftees, their salaries and added benefits were more than competitive with those in the civilian labor market. Thus, Ḥğeri civilian military salaries in 1976 ranged around the I£4000+ mark. By comparison, the average civilian salary in 1976 Israel was I£2851 while the average salary in agriculture was I£2012; construction I£2703; educational services I£2312; public and community services I£2568; and industry I£3039 (Isr. CBS Abs. 28:338–39). This comparison, moreover, does not take into account the other benefits such as clothing, full room and board while on the job, transportation services, PX stores, insurance and medical care, low-interest loans, and the like, which were part of the IDA package. Moreover, trackers' salaries were relatively unaffected by lack of seniority when compared with the civilian workplace, and the specific experience needed to perform the job well could be rapidly acquired while working.[8] Nor did their lack of secondary education hamper their advancement up the noncommissioned officers' (NCO) ranks with respective economic benefits, and although the lack of such education would prevent their promotion into officers' ranks, the army provided time and facilities for those who wanted to study and complete their matriculation examinations, which one Ḥğeri made use of and was accepted to officers' course just before I left the tribe. (Other Ḥğeri IDF trackers, however, did not avail themselves of these opportunities because they did not have the patience, the desire, or a sufficient educational base to pursue their formal education.) In addition, although military discipline was strict, the employment contracts were commonly annual in duration so that a person could join for a year, make some money, and return to the laxer atmosphere of the civilian labor force when he wished. The army, in short, provided a lucrative salary that enabled a youth to become economically independent from his family if he so wished.

Notwithstanding, in contrast with the civilian labor market, where finding work was an independent initiative of the individual concerned, joining the police and its Border Guard or the IDF was, due to reasons of security, dependent upon a recommendation by Muḥammad al-Ḥsēn, the *muḫtār*. Consequently, the relations between a job-seeker and his potential employer were much more complex than the simple labor-market models of supply and demand can account for. These relations involved, on one level, the internal balance of power within the Ḥğerāt and the maintenance of the leadership in the hands of *ulād* Ḏiyab al-Ibrāhīm of the Ġadāyreh. On another level they involved the needs of the Ḥğerāt (as a tribe vis-à-vis its Arab and bedouin neighbors and vis-à-vis the State of Israel) on the one hand, and the state itself (its security, its relations with its Arab minorities, and its resultant world image) on the other. I will return to these topics when discussing their relation to the tribe's political dynamics. For the present, these considerations served to control free access to the attractive military labor market.

These economic incentives and the bedouin cultural image of the male as a fighter combined to make service in the security forces a preferred occupation, with a consequent surplus of applicants in relation to the available positions. There was thus a "waiting list" of applicants to tracking jobs in the IDA. The reasons given by Ḥğeris for wanting to join were quite varied and ranged from "need money to finish the house"; through "am sick and tired of construction work," and other such job related reasons; to at least one applicant where a young wife (age 17) convinced her husband (age 22) to join the IDF to get him away from working with his father in a low-esteem profession; and others who answered "the army is the work for a bedouin."

With such popularity it is of little surprise that, in 1977, of the 459 Ḥğeri males aged 18–47 for whom occupational data were recorded, 116 (25.3%) had served in the security forces since 1967 and of those, 62 (or 13.5% of the recorded labor force) were in service in 1977. This high rate of job mobility (54 individuals, or 46.6% of those who had served since 1967) was characteristic of the service in the IDF, which was especially preferred by the youth. By way of contrast, only one person (0.9%) of those serving in the police after 1967 was no longer in service in 1977. The difference between the police and the IDF was all the more pronounced when considering the age distribution of those who were in service in 1977 (see Table 15). These differences are the result of the availability of tracking positions before and after 1967 and the lifelong career orientation of police service versus the generally temporary character of the employment in the IDF in combination with their respective work conditions.

The Civilian Wage Labor in the 1970s

Concurrent with the spreading employment in the security complex during the 1970s, the Ḥğeri labor force intensified and diversified its general involvement in the wage labor market. The growing number of Ḥğeris who sought salaried jobs was caused by the continuous accretion in the size of the tribe's labor force as successively younger age cohorts joined it and as members of the elder age groups abandoned herding and looked for other sources of income. This last group consisted of people who found it increasingly difficult to secure pasture and shepherds, and who decided to sell their herds in order to

Table 15. Age distribution of Ḥğeris in the security forces in 1977 by branch.

Branch	Total (N = 100%)	Range (by age)	Age 18–27 years		Age 28–47 years		Statistical Mode	
			N	%	N	%	Age Bracket	N
IDA	44	18–37	34	77.3	10	22.7	23–27	21
Police	18	23–47	4	22.2	14	77.8	38–42	7

build houses in Bīr al-Maksūr, which had grown from a hamlet to a comfortable village equipped with running water, roads, electricity, and school.

Formal education, in fact, became both a drawing force for those young parents in the herding camps who wanted their youngsters to be educated among relatives and a causal factor in the intensifying scarcity of shepherds, the increasing need for salaried jobs, and a greater diversity of professions. Like the rest of the Arab sector where the continuous decline of the 14–17 years age cohort in the labor force (1975: 29.1%; 1976: 27.9%; 1977: 26.9%; Isr. CBS Abs. 29:350) mapped the rising commitment to formal education, a burgeoning fraction of Ḥğeris under age 18 continued their education through high school, placing their parental households under increased economic burden. First, they withdrew their otherwise salaried labor from the family pool. Second, their families had to cover their schooling expenses (such as transportation, school uniforms, and books) that were not covered by the academic grants of the state. Upon completing their studies (and regardless of the level completed) they became increasingly reluctant to go into herding because shepherding was considered to be "work for idiots"—or, as a bedouin proverb goes, "*sārāḫt yūm—btayst sanah*" ("herd for a day—be a billy goat [= stupid, fool] for a year"). Similarly they did not find their place in agriculture, both for reasons of self-esteem and because of the growing efficiency of agricultural production, which called for a smaller work force. Hence, they looked for work in the service industry rather than in manufacturing or construction, which were associated with lower educational levels. While this trend was only in its initial phase in 1975–1977, the employment of some young Ḥğeris in banks, insurance, secretarial positions, the merchant marine, and trained hotel work, to mention but a few, suggests a growing sense of the range of available jobs for high school educated personnel beyond the traditional occupation of such individuals (namely, teaching).

Female Participation in Wage Labor

Another trend that was beginning to gain momentum in the mid-1970s was the increasing participation of females in the salaried labor market. Unlike *fellāḥīn* women who had already been involved in wage labor seasonal agriculture during the Mandate Period (Ben Porath 1966:54, n. 13), bedouin women were kept closer to home. Even *fellāḥīn* female participation in the salaried labor force of the Arab sector had traditionally been low, fluctuating between a low of 8.6% in 1970 and a high of 11.9% in 1973 (Isr. CBS Abs. 23:313 and 28:313 respectively). Two major factors seem to account for the low rate of female participation. The first was demographic and involved early marriage and large family size, which tied females to their homes. The second was "that traditional societies frown on women . . . working outside the home" (Ben Porath 1966:17) due to their gender (e.g., Abou-Zeid 1965) and their place in Moslem cosmology (cf. Mernissi 1975, esp. Part I). When bedouin women did work for cash return, it was either at home in crafts for sale, such as the Ġawārneh of the Ḥulah Basin who made and sold reed mats (Ashkenazi 1938:46), or with their male family members and close relatives who rented land for cultivation or crops for harvesting, such as the Negev bedouin in the Central

Region during the early 1960s (Kressel 1976:44). To send bedouin females to work away from home was considered to be too risky for the survival of the family's honor, as well as an unpleasant reminder of their household's low degree of economic independence.

What made possible greater female participation in the wage labor market was the *ra'īs* (lit. manager, leader, etc.)—the labor contractor. During the 1950s the role of the *ra'īs*—who during the Mandate Period was just an entrepreneur linking the available rural worker with potential workplaces—was elevated as a result of the institution of the MG and the need for travel permits. In this milieu only members of influential families with ties to the authorities could secure the necessary permits and vehicles for transporting the teams of workers, so the *'arus* (pl.) were few and more respected. Relaxed restrictions on travel and the country's economic development—which created a growing demand for cheap labor in agriculture in the early 1960s[9]—enabled the return of entrepreneurs from poorer and less influential families, provided they were trustworthy individuals in matters of family honor. For the bedouin, such a person was invariably a member of the tribe. He often started his career as a *ra'īs* by contracting first his own family labor, enlarged by some female members of his siblings' households. It was precisely the respect and trust commanded by the *ra'īs* that enabled the poorer families to send away their daughters, often in the company of young males, to earn the much needed cash, while being assured that the honor of the family would not be compromised.[10]

The settlement of the poorer families in Bīr al-Maksūr during the 1960s left female labor, formerly used in tending the herd, under-utilized. Similarly, those among them who had access to some land did not have enough to use the available family labor completely, a situation that was only aggravated by the mechanization of agriculture.[11] With the growing dependence on cash income, reinforced by escalating inflation, which jumped from 192 points in 1968 to 1087 points in 1977 (Isr. CBS Abs. 29:267; see also appendix C), the issue of the degree of economic independence through self-sufficiency lost its importance, and when assured their honor would not be compromised, these families sent their daughters to work under a *ra'īs*' supervision.

At first only young unmarried daughters went to work for the JNF Forestation Department, with which the Ḥğerāt had long-standing relations. They weeded the nurseries and trimmed the young trees. At that time the *ra'īs* would stay with his team of workers throughout the workday, supervising both the deployment of their labor and the social interaction between the males and the females in the group. With the passage of time, as happened with the younger cohorts of the male labor force, the deployment of female salaried labor diversified into semiskilled mechanized factory work. By 1977, although only thirty to forty females were involved in wage labor, only one team out of three still worked for the JNF Forestation Department. The other two worked in industry: one in a canned food factory in the industrial area of Haifa Bay (nine females) and the other in a large textile factory in Nazareth (eight females). Moreover, a few young married women prior to childbearing joined the team that worked for the JNF, thus introducing a new trend in this growing involvement. In the factory, the *ra'īs* could no longer stay with his team during the workday to personally supervise their behavior. Instead, he would recruit an older woman to keep a watchful eye, or rely on his own and his siblings' daughters and on intra-team gossip to keep informed of unbecoming behavior of his wards while he himself pursued other economic activities. Thus, for example, the team working in the canned food factory in March 1977 was made of two daughters of the *ra'īs*, ages 15 and 17; two daughters, one of each of two of his brothers, ages 15 and 19; and one woman from another sublineage 59 years old. Nonetheless, the exposure to the laxer atmosphere of the factory milieu relaxed the inter-gender discipline of the younger females and although as of 1977 Ḥğeri honor had not been compromised, other bedouin tribes in the region encountered problems in this regard.

For most Ḥğeris, however, the *ra'īs* had not been an acceptable solution to the problem of women working because, as one informant worded the concern, "in the factory everything can happen." This attitude resulted in a large portion of the available female labor force's being left untapped. Notwithstanding, in 1977 a successful entrepreneur and a member of the leading family of the Ġadāyreh began plans to tap this under-utilized resource by opening a sewing workshop in Bīr al-Maksūr, inspired by similar enterprises in several Druze and Arab villages by local businessmen. These entrepreneurs were encouraged by officials from the Ministries of Industry and Development, who not only pointed to this reservoir of under-utilized labor but also provided the local businesses with tax concessions and easy-term industrial development loans to launch these projects. Thus, in June 1979 the workshop opened, employing thirty local female workers.

Ḥğeri Employment Characteristics

The general process of occupational transition that the Ḥğeri male labor force was involved in since the beginning of the Israeli Period becomes clearer when this force is distributed by age in the different professional categories (see Table 16).

The predominance of land cultivation among the 1900–1919 age group was primarily the result of their owning most of the tribal lands, because it was their generation who purchased the lands of Bīr al-Maksūr. While in 1977 this group was generally no longer involved in actual cultivation and the related decision-making processes, they usually retained a general supervisory function (if not actual management) of the cultivation, which was done by an older son or a partner. By way of contrast, the herdsmen in this age group tended to concentrate on the younger end of this cohort. Herding was also dominant in the next age cohort (1920–1924), which was just setting itself up when Maksūr was bought. It is within this age group that the pressures to sell the herd due to diminishing pasture, scarcity of shepherds, and age were mounting. The following two cohorts (1925–1929 and 1930–1934) were the groups that, from the mid-1960s, had been slowly shifting to wage labor, particularly into construction for lack of productive skills beyond herding and land cultivation. The members of the 1935–1939 age group were those individuals who first entered the labor market in the Jewish sector, hence the ratio of almost 2:1 between the employees and self-employed categories. The succeeding age groups continued this trend until the 1950–1954 cohort, whose members were born after the establishment of the State of Israel and had increasingly greater exposure to formal education. This group was also the one whose members were closest to age 18 in 1968 when job opportunities in the IDA became available. It is of little surprise, therefore, that this age group had the largest segment of its membership in services when compared with the other cohorts. The increase in the agricultural and industrial categories in the next cell (1955–1959) was partly related to this cohort's inability to enter the security branches as freely as their predecessors did and partly due to their still being tied to their parental households. The former factor tended to orient them toward work in construction and manufacturing while the latter led to an involvement in agriculture, primarily seasonal agricultural wage labor.

The immersion of the Ḥğeri labor force in the state's economic and bureaucratic structures[12] and the different degrees of access to the administration enjoyed by each of the lineages had immediate effects on the relative involvement of their respective labor forces in the various professional categories (see Table 17). From the Ḥğerāt's tribal point of view, ties with the administration were important in two areas: land rental and employment in the security forces, because access to industry and non-security related services was much freer. The economic advantages of employment in the security forces have already been discussed. The rental of state lands and lands of Arab refugees held in custody by the Office of the Custodian was managed by the Israel Land Administration (ILA), which was also involved in the bedouin sedentarization program. While both arable land and natural open pastures were leased, the latter was by far the more important category due to the increased productivity of agriculture in Israel, which reduced the importance of the size of the lot-viable (the amount of arable land needed to sustain an independent farm). Open range herding, contrarily, was directly dependent on the size of the available natural pasture. The number of herd owners in each lineage was, therefore, related to their relative ability to secure extra pasture on state lands.

The Ṣawālḥah, whose *muḫtār* did not have close ties with the administration, were much more involved in the industrial sector than in either agriculture or services, and in services they were more involved in non-security related work than with the security forces. Similarly, in agriculture they were more committed to land cultivation than to herding, reflecting their inability to compete effectively for the rental of open pastures due to their weaker contacts with the state agencies controlling these rentals. Although their ability to rent arable state lands was more limited than the other two lineages, they did own some land and both lease and buy more land from the villagers of I'billin, their neighbors to the northwest.

The Ḏiyabāt, being allied with the Ġadāyreh and their *muḫtār*, succeeded in maintaining herding as the largest single occupational category of its members. The predominance of herding in this lineage resulted from the more rural character of the Ḏmeydeh and the presence of its members in both herding camps: *wādi* al-Mzagga and Umm al-Zīnāt. There were fewer land cultivators among them because there were fewer landowners, although each landowner had relatively large holdings. The difference in residence of its two sublineages, the D'eyfeh in the Ḏmeydeh and the Ṭa'awāneh in Bīr al-Maksūr, was also reflected in the occupational distribution of their labor force. The D'eyfeh, owning larger land holdings and living in a more rural setting, deployed 12.9% of its labor force in land cultivation as compared with only 6.4% among the Ṭa'awāneh. The reverse is the case in industry, with the Ṭa'awāneh deploying 46.8% of its labor force in that category to 31.4% of the D'eyfeh. In general, 68.1% (32 of 47 individuals) of the Ṭa'awāneh were salaried labor as compared with 60.0% (42 out of 70 individuals) of the D'eyfeh.

The Ġadāyreh, with the closest ties to the administration, had 42 herd owners to the Ḏiyabāt's 31 and the Ṣawālḥah's 16. Similarly, they had 40 individuals in the security forces to respectively 3 and 19 of the other two lineages.[13] Similar differences existed among the sublineages of the Ġadāyreh with the *ulād* Ġadīr occupying the most favored position and the 'Afafṭeh the least.

The last column in Table 17 compares the general occupational distribution of the male labor force of the Arab sector at large with that of the Ḥĝerāt. While there was a rough similarity in their respective self-employed/employees ratios, there was a marked difference in their degree of involvement both in "Agriculture" and in "Services." Whereas the Ḥĝeri self-employed concentrated in the agriculture/herding category (154 individuals, or 27.3% of the total labor force) with only 11 (or 1.9%) self-employed individuals in "Services," most of the 30.7% self-employed in the Arab sector were in the "Services" category, working as neighborhood storekeepers, professionals, and the like (cf. Isr. CBS Abs. 29:351, tb. XII/10 [males, 1977]). While the involvement of the Ḥĝerāt in the "Services" was divided almost half and half between "Security" and "Other" service occupations (11.0% and 13.6% respectively), the involvement of the Arab sector was almost totally in the "Other" category. Were we to compare only their relative involvement in the "Other" category, then the Arab sector was almost three times as involved in "Services" as the Ḥĝerāt. The difference in their respective occupational involvement is partly a methodological result of comparing the small contingent of the Ḥĝeri labor force with that of the Arab sector at large and partly the result of objective differences between the Ḥĝerāt and like-size groups. The rapid growth of villages in the Arab sector into "urban settlements" generated an intensifying demand for services. Such demand was far weaker in the category of the smaller villages, which included the Ḥĝeri settlements. At the same time, within this category: (1) the Ḥĝerāt had better contacts with the administration, hence greater ability to rent arable land and to receive greater amounts of practical assistance of different kinds; and (2) the tribe's land management (particularly its inheritance practices) enabled its members to preserve their lots at a viable size in contrast with the villagers whose lots became increasingly fragmented as a result of *Šarī'a* inheritance laws, forcing them to abandon agriculture and move into industry and services.

The Agricultural Sector

Overview

The Ḥĝerāt's ability to adjust gradually to wage labor was a result of their success in maintaining their traditional economic base in herding and agriculture. This success was predicated on interplay between their *muḫtār*'s political and administrative efficacy in dealing

Table 16. The distribution of the Ḥğeri active labor force (males) in the different occupational categories and the degree of involvement in wage labor by age group (percent) in 1977.

	Year of Birth										Total
	1900-1919	1920-1924	1925-1929	1930-1934	1935-1939	1940-1944	1945-1949	1950-1954	1955-1959	1960-1964	
Number[a]	29	21	27	39	60	82	54	116	108	29[b]	565
%	100.0	100.0	100.0	100.0	100.0	100.0	100.0	100.0	100.0	100.0	100.0
Agriculture											
self-employed											
land cultivation	0.5	14.3	22.2	15.4	15.0	9.8	13.0	4.3	3.7	(6.9)[c]	11.2
herding	34.5	57.1	22.2	25.6	20.0	7.3	7.4	9.5	10.9	(24.1)[c]	14.5
subtotal self-employed	*86.2*	*71.4*	*44.4*	*41.0*	*35.0*	*17.1*	*20.4*	*13.8*	*13.9*	*(31.0)*[c]	*25.7*
wage labor	3.4	14.3	7.4	15.4	8.3	14.6	5.6	8.6	14.8	24.1	11.5
subtotal agriculture	*89.7*	*85.7*	*51.9*	*81.5*	*43.3*	*31.7*	*25.9*	*22.4*	*28.7*	*55.2*	*38.8*
Industry											
construction and unskilled	3.4	14.3	67.0	23.1	31.7	37.8	35.2	22.4	23.1	6.9	25.7
mfg and mech equip	–	–	–	–	5.0	9.8	7.4	16.4	19.4	24.1	11.0
subtotal industry	*3.4*	*14.3*	*37.0*	*23.1*	*36.7*	*47.6*	*42.6*	*38.8*	*42.6*	*31.0*	*36.6*
Services											
security											
Police and B.G.	–	–	–	7.7	11.7	3.7	1.9	3.4	–	–	3.2
IDA	–	–	–	–	–	6.1	9.3	18.1	12.0	–	7.8
subtotal security	–	–	–	*7.7*	*11.7*	*9.6*	*11.1*	*21.5*	*12.0*	–	*11.0*
other	6.9	–	11.1	12.8	8.3	11.0	20.4	17.2	16.7	13.8	13.6
subtotal services	*6.9*	–	*11.1*	*20.5*	*20.0*	*20.7*	*31.5*	*38.8*	*28.7*	*13.8*	*24.6*
Involvement in Wage Labor											
self-employed	86.2	71.4	44.4	41.0	35.0	17.1	20.4	13.8	13.9	(31.0)[c]	27.6 (1.6)[d]
employed	13.8	28.6	55.6	59.0	65.0	82.9	79.6	86.2	86.1	69.0	70.8

[a]The size of the sample that was used to construct this table and Table 17 is 77.0% of the total Ḥğeri male population age 13 and over (690 of 896 individuals). Of these, 111 were still in school and 14 were disabled individuals who did not work, leaving an active male labor force of 565 individuals or 63.1% of the above total population. Since the 1977 figure for Moslem male labor force participation in Israel was 68.2% of the Moslem male population age 14 and over (Isr. CBS Abs. 29:350), the Ḥğeri sample can be assumed to portray accurately the process under discussion.

[b]This age group includes 201 males ages 13 to 17. Of these, 107 were still in school while most of the rest were only partially, if at all, involved with the labor force on any continuous basis.

[c]These 31.0% (9 individuals) are unpaid family members. Consequently, they are neither self-employed nor employees. Nevertheless, in order not to lose them altogether, they are presented in parentheses.

[d]Same as footnote c, but here they are calculated as a percentage of the total labor force.

Table 17. The distribution of the Ḥğeri active labor force (males) in the different occupational categories and the degree of involvement in wage labor by lineage in 1977.

	Lineage								
	Ġadāyreh		Ḍiyabāt		Ṣawālḥah		Total		Arab Sector[a]
	N	%	N	%	N	%	N	%	%
Number	224	100	117	100	224	100	565	100	
Agriculture									
self-employed									
land cultivation	30	13.4	12	10.3	23	10.3	65	(11.5)[b]	–
herding	42	18.8	31	26.5	16	7.1	89	(15.8)[b]	–
subtotal self-employed	*72*	*32.1*	*43*	*36.8*	*39*	*17.4*	*154*	*(27.3)*[b]	–
wage labor	33	14.7	11	9.4	21	9.4	65	11.5	–
subtotal agriculture	*105*	*46.9*	*54*	*46.2*	*60*	*26.8*	*219*	*38.8*	*15.6*
Industry									
construction and unskilled	27	21.1	28	23.9	90	40.2	145	25.7	26.4
mfg and mech equip	21	9.4	16	13.7	25	11.2	62	11.0	16.9
subtotal industry	*48*	*21.4*	*44*	*37.6*	*115*	*51.3*	*207*	*36.6*	*43.3*
Services									
security									
Police and B.G.	13	5.8	1	0.9	4	1.8	18	3.2	–
IDA	27	12.0	2	1.7	15	6.7	44	7.8	–
subtotal security	*40*	*17.9*	*3*	*2.6*	*19*	*8.5*	*62*	*11.0*	–
other	31	13.8	16	13.7	30	13.4	77	13.6	40.9
subtotal services	*71*	*31.7*	*19*	*16.2*	*49*	*21.9*	*139*	*24.6*	*40.9*
Involvement in Wage Labor									
self-employed	79	35.3	46	39.3	40	17.9	165	27.6 +(1.6)[c]	26.5 +(4.2)[c]
employed	145	64.7	71	60.7	184	82.1	400	70.8	69.3

[a]Source: Isr. CBS Abs. 29:351, tb. XII/10 (males, 1977).
[b]Including unpaid family members.
[c]Unpaid family members.

with the MG and their success in keeping their land holdings large enough to keep agricultural lots viable. Consequently, the ensuing discussion will focus first on access to agricultural land, both in terms of the pressures on land ownership in the Arab sector and among the Ḥğerāt and in terms of land rental agreements. I will then focus on the changing agricultural technology of the Ḥğerāt, first on mechanization and then on the crops they raised and sold.

By far the major problem facing the Arab agriculturalist in Israel was access to arable land. Here, the Ḥğerāt had two major advantages—a cultural one and a historical one, derived from their bedouin tradition—in addition to their highly instrumental link to the authorities through their *muḫtār*. Culturally, although Sunni Moslems, they did not follow the land inheritance rules of the *Šarīʻa*, and historically they did not own their agricultural land for long. To appreciate the import of these two advantages it is necessary to understand the land access problems of the Arab sector in general.

Access to Land in the Arab Sector

A steadily intensifying problem faced by the Arab agricultural sector was the fragmentation and dispersal of its arable land due to the application of the inheritance rules of the *Šarīʻa*, which provide for the inheritance by all the children of the deceased plus some other relatives (cf. Ben Shemesh 1979, *Koran* 4:11–12, 177; Fyzee 1964: ch. XIII). The ensuing land tenure problems included the decline in actual size of the holding, the fragmentation of each holding, and the dispersal of the fragments over a relatively large area, resulting in a gradual reduction of the farm's viability. Warriner, for example, reports that the average size of a farm in Palestine declined 16% from 1930 to 1942 (1948:57). By 1971, although the mean size of a farm of "non-Jews" was 65.4 *dunam*, the median size and the statistical mode of such farms fell within the 11–20 *dunam* category (Isr. CBS 1973:255).

The reduction in actual size of individual patrimonies was further aggravated by the *Šarīʻa* demand that the inherited segments be of same type and quality (for example: alluvial, hillside; fields, orchards, pasture) to prevent discrimination between the heirs. Consequently, an individual might end up with a 60-*dunam* farm divided into thirteen or so fragments distributed over an area of several scores of square kilometers or even in different villages (cf. Pls. Census 1933[I]:26). The Mandate authorities, who collected land plot fragmentation statistics, found an average of nine fragments per holding and a positive correlation between the size of the holding and the number of fragments that composed it (cf. Pls. Gov. 1946[I]:275–78).

The resulting small, striplike fields so characteristic of Middle Eastern rural areas made mechanization wasteful and pipe-irrigation problematic. With so many adjacent small plots without intervening spaces, access routes for agricultural machinery took increasingly larger relative shares of the total cultivable land. Similarly, the large number of fields and owners made securing right-of-way for irrigation waterlines a major task—so much so that the Mandate authorities bemoaned that "in the exploitation of his scattered holding [the *fellāḥ*] is excluded from the advantages of mechanization and irrigation" (Pls. Gov. 1946[I]:278). Field fragmentation and dispersal was then aggravated by the traditional emphasis on field crops most amenable to mechanization, which brought the Mandate Authorities to talk of the "extravagant use of land" (Pls. Gov. 1946[I]:278).

As the economic viability of Arab farm units declined, the competitive advantage of the wage-labor market increased, and although it is hard to estimate the income level of an independent farmer, in 1977 the average salary was I£2833 in agriculture, I£3635 in construction, and I£4327 in industry (Isr. CBS Abs. 29:378–79). More importantly, regardless of the income level in question, as a farm's viability declines, its owner will reach a stage where it will be more profitable to rent out his land and seek a salaried job elsewhere. Thus, a new pattern evolved whereby landowners rented out their fields while they themselves found salaried jobs in the Jewish sector. This practice became so widespread that the directors of the Census of Agriculture in 1971 noted the difficulties they encountered in obtaining their data in the Arab sector because "a sizable segment of the landowners work away from their farms and rent out their land to various people" (Isr. CBS Census 1972b: XXXI).

Access to Land among the Ḥğerāt

As of 1977, these problems had not yet beset the Ḥğerāt for several reasons. First, most of the landed property of the Ḥğerāt in 1977 had been purchased during the previous fifty years and in most cases had not yet been subjected to fragmentation through inheritance. Moreover, the lands of Bīr al-Maksūr, the tribe's largest single landholding, were registered under a communal title (*muša'*). Therefore, although each family knew its land plots, theirs was a de facto ownership through cultivation rather than a de jure one; that is, it was the right of usufruct rather than actual ownership (which was subject to the inheritance laws). Third, traditionally among Palestinian bedouin, females did not inherit (Levy 1957:146), nor did bedouin women inherit in Israel as of 1977 (e.g., Marx 1967:185 for the Negev), thus reducing the circle of inheritors. For example, a woman in her 50s commented that she would be ashamed to demand a share from her brothers and that she would not like to antagonize them by making such a demand because it might make them angry at her. Moreover, she said, if she took a share of her father's estate, for which he labored all his life, it would go to her husband, who is not her father's son, and it would be as if her father worked to make others rich. It is, therefore, better that her brothers divide her father's estate among themselves so that it stays in the family. Indeed, if she demanded her share and thereby antagonized her brothers, she would jeopardize her legal and political rights as a member of her patrilineage and would be left at the mercy of her husband for whom her *legal* rights end with being the mother of his sons.

Another factor retarding the fragmentation of Ḥğeri land holdings was the early orientation of the sons to the various economic pursuits available to the family during the father's lifetime. This set patterns that survived his death for two reasons. First, the orientation, and the allotment of family owned resources that it may entail, was done with the son's tacit, if not verbal, consent. Second, with the passage of time each son was established with a source of income that reduced, if not eliminated, the need to self-manage his share in the land in order to provide his household with sustenance. There was, therefore, less need to separate the parts and a greater tendency to leave decisions concerned with cultivation with the brother who actually cultivated the land.

For example, one landowning father "F" (born ca. 1910) had his firstborn "A" (born 1934) work the land while his other children took care of his cattle herd between their classes in school. In 1961, shortly after his marriage, "A" decided to become a livestock merchant and left his duties to "F"'s second son, "B" (born 1945), who had just completed his tenth grade. In 1964, at nineteen, "B" joined the police and "F" made a "type-2 partnership" (see below) with another tribesman ("P1"). "F," then, had his third son "C" (born 1952) take care of field preparation (leaving the rest of the cultivation process to "P1") while the younger children took care of the herd. When "C" was about 20 years old he became involved in plumbing in the construction industry, work that fitted with his agricultural schedule. In 1974, at age 22, he married and, through a friend, found a job as a heavy equipment operator in road construction, leaving agriculture altogether. At that time "F"'s fourth son, "D" (born 1958), took over preparing the fields while the herd was given in partnership to another tribesman ("P2"). In 1977 the disposition of "F"'s sons was as follows: "A" was a livestock merchant and, with the connection of Maksūr to the country's electrical network, the village butcher. He was making a good living and had no plans to return to agriculture. "B" was very successful in his job, was planning to go to police officer's school, and considered his police work as a lifelong career. "C," on the other hand, after three years in a well-paying job, decided that it did not allow him enough time with his family and was talking about returning and taking over the family agricultural operation as "D" was beginning to look for a job in the wage-labor market. About that time "F" began talking about dividing his land among his sons and "A" and "B" informed me that they would be satisfied if "C" would take over the management and would give them their share (according to type-1 partnership) in the crop.

If none of the brothers were interested in agriculture they usually made sharecropping partnerships with other tribesmembers or *fellāḥīn*. Family HY is a case in point. The family was composed of seven adult brothers (ages ranging from 22 to 55 in 1977) who inherited their father's land when he died in the early 1960s. Of the seven, four had herds and three of these were also employed as field guards by Jewish agricultural settlements in the vicinity of their herding camps. Of the remaining three brothers, one was a first-sergeant in the police; one was a sergeant major in the IDA; and the youngest worked with one of his herd owning brothers and was considering a herding vocation. Consequently, the brothers contracted peasants to cultivate (mostly tobacco) their land as partners.

Another factor that retarded fragmentation was a practice among the elders of the sixth generation who owned land (other than their share in the lands of Bīr al-Maksūr) to divide it among their sons during their own lifetimes rather than leave it until after their death. In this manner they kept the *Šarī'a* Court away; reduced future conflicts, hard feelings, and a sense of deprivation among the sons over the inheritance; and set the pattern of cooperative management of the land while they still had influence over their sons. Finally, the memory of the deceased father, his honor, and his role as the focus around which the sons rally vis-à-vis the other families of the tribe were often strong enough inducements to prevent the separation of the landed patrimony due to small disagreements. Major personality conflict among the heirs was very rare because these were foreseen and resolved during the father's lifetime by giving a quarrelsome son his share while leaving the rest for his other sons to work together. In most cases,[14] therefore, the sons avoided the fragmentation of their inherited land for as long as possible.

If division of the patrimony among the heirs was seriously discussed, it was usually the result of disagreements about major decisions concerning investments in the land and policies of cultivation. For example, in the early 1970s a group of six brothers had a debate concerning an investment in aluminum irrigation pipes in order to convert some of their land into irrigated fields. Three of the brothers dissented and there was talk about dividing the land, which was inherited around 1960. Later the three reversed their position and the land remained in one block, about a third of which was irrigated. In 1977 they renewed the talk about investing in more pipes in order to irrigate the whole block. Two of the brothers dissented. Then another brother began pushing for dividing the land because he wanted to build a small storeroom near the field and the others objected. At the time of my departure the controversy was still in negotiation.

In general, thus, the sons tried to keep their inherited land as a single unit and although the income from the land was properly divided, from the point of view of cultivation the land remained as one plot, which was amenable to mechanized cultivation.

Finally, the Ḥğerāt continued to buy land whenever and wherever possible. They did so for two reasons: (1) unlike salaried labor, agriculture allowed for independent subsistence, which more closely approximated the bedouin ideal of independence; and (2) with the continuously mounting pressures on herding, there was a tendency to convert the herd to land if the right deal came along, especially since such a transaction did not entail much loss, or interest on bank loans. It is thus that the Ṣawālḥah in the Mikmān bought from I'billin, the D'eyfeh from Kafr Manda, and the Ġadāyreh from all over but predominantly in the Valley of Beit Netofah and south of Bīr al-Maksūr from the people of Shfar'am.

In 1977, most of these acquisitions were made with agriculture in mind and not for land speculation or as an investment to hedge against inflation. Nevertheless, a few individuals began buying land specifically for these purposes. It can be safely assumed, therefore, that given enough time the Ḥğerāt will experience a growing discrepancy between rich landed families and poorer landless ones, which tribal solidarity would find harder to bridge. This discrepancy will receive a boost when the communal title to the lands of Bīr al-Maksūr becomes divided among its shareholders, and a discussion about this course of action began to surface during the last month of my stay in the village.

Land Rental Contracts

Land acquisition, however, was not a daily occurrence. More regularly the extra land that was needed to support the tribe's agriculturalists was rented from whatever source was available—the state or other farmers, Jews or Arabs. Leasing state lands was cheaper but was increasingly more difficult because with each new Jewish agricultural settlement, arable land became scarcer. Then, due to its economic attractiveness and scarcity, leasing state lands was usually dependent on contacts with the authorities, which often required the *muḫtār*'s intervention on the applicant's behalf. Consequently, not only was the access to such rentals more restricted because members of the leading families had a greater probability of securing a rental contract, but it often left the applicant in a reciprocal debt to the *muḫtār*.

It was therefore preferable from the tribesmember's point of view to rent land from Jewish farmers who had better paying salaried jobs and who had abandoned agriculture. Not only were the fields of these farmers larger and better shaped than those of Arab *fellāḥīn*, but most rental arrangements violated the conditions of the landholding charter of the Jewish farmer,[15] thus often giving the transaction a somewhat clandestine character. This affected the specific terms of the rental agreement aside from personalizing it, an important end in itself in the context of Middle Eastern traditional society (e.g., cf. Hall 1959:106–7, 127–29; 1966:162–63; 1976:17–18, 22–23).

Land rental agreements in agriculture were of two general types: cash contracts and sharecropping, or *šarikah* (partnership), contracts. Cash contracts were commonly used when dealing with Jewish farmers, had no standard rules, and were contracted "as agreed" between the individuals concerned. Categorically, cash contracts were struck whenever the owner could not or did not want to deal with the land itself. Jews who held a better paying job usually did not want to spend the time necessary for tilling the field or disposing of the crop, so they used this type of contract. It was, however, by no means confined to contracts with Jews.

Partnership contracts, on the other hand, were of three standard kinds:

(1) The landowner tilled the land, but rented out the tending of the crop and its harvest. The crop was divided 2/3:1/3 between the owner and the partner respectively.

(2) The owner plowed and removed the stones, and divided in half the price of the fertilizer and seeds with the partner who invested all the necessary labor. The crop was divided 1/2:1/2 respectively.

(3) The owner gave the land unprepared and the partner took care of all the work and expenses. The crop was divided 1/3:2/3 respectively.

All these kinds of land rental contracts were used both intra- and extra-tribally. The most common arrangement intra-tribally was the second partnership type in which a landed family that could not cultivate all its land gave part of it to a landless tribesmember. The same type of contract was also used to enlist peasants to work the land of a family whose adult sons had independent sources of income (for instance, the HY family, above). This type was favored even when none of the family cultivated the land. Profit-wise it was advantageous for them to hire someone to plow the land and contract a peasant to grow a labor-intensive high-return cash crop such as tobacco, dividing with him cash outlays but having him invest the labor, which was the major expense.

Partnership contracts emphasized the personal aspect of the rental transaction and thus emphasized the status relations between the contracting individuals, and were pregnant with political power play and its symbolism. Nowhere was this clearer than in the Ḥğeri practice of giving a *nzaleh* (hospitality banquet) in honor of the peasant partners who came to work for them. Such a ceremonial dinner established the peasant as a protégé of his Ḥğeri landed partner and through him, of the whole tribe.

If the Ḥğerāt let their land in partnership contracts, they rented it from the outside solely under cash contracts, whether rented from the ILA and Jewish farmers as far south as Haderah or from Arab peasants. While rental from the Jewish sector was under cash contracts by default, rental from the Arab sector was contracted in cash to expressively eliminate the personal and political connotations of partnership contracts. Cash contracts were market transactions devoid of personal or political connotations and were negotiated and concluded within a much shorter span of time. They, thus, did not present the Ḥğeri renter as a protégé of the peasant landed partner. In this context, therefore, cash contracts were more compatible with the Ḥğerāt's claim for independence and leadership. By employing partnership or cash rental contract judiciously, the Ḥğerāt succeeded in reinforcing their regional status, helping to convert their land ownership to political preeminence.

The Mechanization of Agriculture

Since the early 1960s, as mentioned above, the Ḥğerāt, like the rest of the Arab sector, became increasingly committed to mechanized land cultivation. By 1977 this trend was so well established that practically every landowning family had a tractor, and those of the non-landed individuals who were committed to agriculture usually owned one as well. Heavier equipment like bulldozers, used to level land or clear large stones from the fields, was rented as needed from the appropriate operating companies in the region while grain, pulses, and sunflowers were harvested by Ḥğeri-owned grain combine harvesters and balers.

The mechanization of Ḥğeri agriculture affords an insight into the transition from traditional to market-oriented cash economy. The tractors used by the Ḥğerāt were multipurpose agricultural tools employed in a variety of circumstances, from plowing, harrowing, and sowing to transportation, and were especially adapted to the area's stony hills. They were, thus, an efficiently employed investment. This was not true of the Ḥğeri-owned self-propelled grain combine harvesters.

The number of combines in Israel as a whole declined after an all-time high of 1025 units in 1962 (470 of which were the drawn type and 555 the self-propelled type; Isr. CBS 1970:78) to a low of 500 self-propelled units in 1972 (Isr. CBS Abs. 25:400), rising to 540 self-propelled, high capacity machines in 1977 (Isr. CBS Abs. 29:429). By comparison, in 1977 the Ḥğerāt owned 14 self-propelled units, 10 of which were operative to various degrees. Although they were old, second- and third-hand machines and of relatively low capacity, they nonetheless had much greater capacity than was needed to harvest the tribe's fields. Furthermore, this excess capacity could not be used to harvest other Arabs' fields in Israel because other bedouin and *fellāḥīn* had their own combines and faced the same tough competition in unloading the excess capacity of their machines. While West Bank fields offered some alleviation of the problem, the short harvest periods and the sheer size of the fleet made combines a wasteful and inefficient economic investment. This waste was all the more pronounced when viewed against the practices in the Jewish sector where agricultural establishments increasingly preferred to hire an operator and his new high capacity combine rather than own one (due to its high price and excess capacity for any single establishment).

According to the Ḥğeri who drew my attention to this phenomenon, the reason for this apparently paradoxical situation was that "they [local Arabs] don't like to be dependent on the one they hired to do the job." That is, even though the combine owner may not play one person against another by having one wait with his ripened crop while he harvested a latecomer's field first, the mere possibility of such behavior placed one's honor in jeopardy and emphasized the traditional bedouin ideal of independence: economic and political.

The working of ideals such as honor and independence on Ḥğeri economic activities however, was not, as this informant thought, an independent end in itself. Rather, it was a symptom of a much more profound conflict that results from the juxtaposition of a traditional nonmarket-oriented economy, with its ideological precepts, on an industrial cash market, with its economic reality. Traditional economy, as pointed out by Sahlins (1972: ch. 2–3), is characterized by a "domestic mode of production" (DMP), where each household owns and controls the means of production necessary for its viability. No less important, its members conceive these means to be a part of the household's *necessary* toolkit. Since the technology associated with DMP is relatively simple and cheap, when a new tool is introduced to the productive process it can spread in the population rapidly, with no major investment, while maintaining technological equality among the households. Once large, efficient, and expensive machines such as combine harvesters enter the productive process, the above no longer holds true because these machines have to work continuously in order to pay back the original investment, their maintenance, and depreciation before they begin to make profit.

In 1964 a Ḥğeri bought his first second-hand combine from the Jew he hired to harvest his fields and as it was the only Arab-owned such machine in the area, he made a good profit. When other Ḥğeris bought similar machines—thinking they could realize similar profits, not wanting to be dependent, and relying on their own lineal relatives to provide them with work—no combine could realize the profit it could before, if it realized a profit at all. Incidentally, this same scenario repeated itself with Ḥğeri grocery shops in Bīr al-Maksūr. Once the first opened and succeeded, six other enterprising individuals opened such shops, thereby reducing the volume and profit of every store in the village.

This kind of economic behavior is but a variant of what Hardin (1968) called "the tragedy of the Commons" and seems to be among the major reasons underlying the failures in attempts to industrialize and establish market-oriented economies in traditional societies.

The Crops

Much like the rest of the Arab sector,[16] in 1975 the Ḥğerāt cultivated predominately field crops. Foremost among these were wheat and barley because, as one informant remarked, they required the least amount of work, were most amenable to mechanized cultivation, and brought good profit. Secondary crops were sunflowers and tobacco, followed by watermelon, vegetables, legumes, and occasionally sesame. Nevertheless, by 1977 orchards were planted and new cultivation methods introduced, signaling a change in the traditional balance in favor of higher return crops such as vegetable and fruits.

Three categories of factors—general, functional tactics, and individual experience—determined the specific crop combination in a given year and the absorption of innovations in crops and tillage into Ḥğeri agriculture. A basic set of variables delineated the options open to the Ḥğeri farmer (as with any other cultivator), and included: the type of land, the type of crop grown last on the field in question (that is, summer or winter crop), and the predicted climatic conditions of the seasons to come. These variables, however, left much room for tactical variation and it was at this intermediary level that marketing opportunities and the Ministry of Agriculture's guidance and incentives, as well as the influence of observing agriculturalists in the Jewish sector, had their greatest effect. Nevertheless, the final decision lay with the individual farmer and was heavily influenced by his character and experience.

Thus, the two major sources for innovations in Ḥğeri agriculture were enterprising individuals and the Ministry of Agriculture. It is of note that all the innovations in Ḥğeri agriculture—machines, crops, and techniques—were introduced by a few individuals, who mostly observed them among Jewish cultivators or learned about them from the guides of the Ministry of Agriculture. Once they tried the innovation and succeeded, other tribesmen followed and adopted the item in question. For example, the individual who bought the first tractor also bought the first combine, introduced several new breeds (including new varieties of wheat and tobacco), was the first to use chemical fertilizers and herbicides, was the first to cultivate potatoes (which had not caught on yet in 1977), and was the leader of a group in a venture to grow tomatoes for industrial production in 1975.

With the steady increase in economic exchange with the European Common Market in general and agricultural produce in particular, the Ministry of Agriculture moved toward a greater degree of direction and coordination of the country's agricultural production. For example, in 1973/74 it was realized that tobacco production was declining due to the exploitative practices of the tobacco companies who graded the quality of the crop, set the prices of the various grades, weighed the tobacco bales, and bought the crop. To undermine this cartel the ministry established the Tobacco Commission—empowered to weigh the tobacco by the 1924 Tobacco Ordinance of the Mandate Department of Customs and Excise—to encourage the growers to cultivate the crop and supervise its marketing. Subsequently, a general grading framework was established for the various subregions and the prices set annually by the commission in negotiations with the companies. Then, in each specific sale a representative of the companies graded the crop in the presence of the grower and a commission man who then weighed again the bales that the company man later transported to their destination. In this way, for example, grade II tobacco increased in price per kilo from I£5.4 in 1974 to I£18.5 in 1976, a rise of 342.6% (by comparison, the CPI rose by only 182.9% during that period). Not surprisingly, the tobacco companies did not like the new arrangement and in 1976 they did not buy the crop, hoping to break the resistance of the commission and the growers. This tactic backfired when the commission was authorized to buy the crop from the growers with the explicit intention of later selling it (with storage fees and so on) to the companies when they ran out of their stock, while alleviating the pressures on the growers. Another way in which the commission encouraged tobacco cultivation was by giving incentives—such as prepayment on the crop according to the area cultivated. In this way the growers received immediately usable cash with no interest, and which, due to inflation, would be cheaper to repay when that year's crop was sold. These measures helped increase tobacco production at the expense of less exportable crops such as sunflowers and watermelons, which were grown on the same types of soils in the same area of Bīr al-Maksūr. One farmer, for example, cultivated 10 *dunam* of his land in tobacco in 1975, 30 *dunam* in 1976, and 60 *dunam* in 1977.

Although cereal grains, occupying more than half the cultivated land, were the major crop of the tribe, the Ḥğerāt avoided monocropping and used summer crops such as tobacco, sunflowers, and watermelons to balance the risks entailed in winter grain crops, which were more susceptible to the region's characteristic erratic rain patterns and semi-droughts (Ashbel 1957:166–67). Thus, for example, in 1976 one of the more enterprising farmers cultivated 60 *dunam* of wheat, 50 of barley, 30 of tobacco, 10 of sunflowers, and 60 of watermelons. All the land but that for watermelons was rented from the ILA while the watermelons were grown on his father's land under type-3 partnership contract. He also privately owned 7 *dunam* around his house on which he cultivated maize (for his few head of cattle) and a kitchen garden. It should be noted that although this crop combination included both winter and summer crops, they did not, properly speaking, form a crop rotation cycle because no legumes or other nitrogen-fixing plants were included. Indeed, this person added about one metric ton of urea chemical fertilizer each to his wheat and his barley fields to compensate for the missing nutrients. Thus, the traditional rule of thumb for deciding on the type of crop was: if the last crop was a winter crop the land has to rest through the next winter before cultivation can resume with a summer crop, while if the last crop was a summer crop it can be followed by late winter grains. These calculations, however, started losing importance as increasing numbers adopted chemical fertilizers and herbicides.

Of these two crop types, most of the grain crop was disposed of within the tribe while most of the summer crops were marketed. For example, one market-oriented farmer had in 1976 a crop of 10 metric tons each of wheat and barley. He disposed of the wheat as follows: 2 tons were kept for home use; 1.5 tons each were given to his father and one of his brothers as a payment on type-3 partnership; 1 ton each was sold to two tribesmembers; and the remaining 3 tons were sold to a grain merchant in Jenin in the West Bank. Seventy percent of his wheat crop remained in the tribe. (Ḥğeris who were less market oriented disposed of their grain crops entirely within the tribe.) The same farmer disposed of his entire barley crop within his family, giving 3 and 1.5 metric tons each to two of his brothers who raised sheep and goats, and keeping the remainder for his own animals.

The grain crop that remained in the tribe was consumed as bread and *burġul* (cracked wheat) if it was wheat and as animal feed if it was barley. The rest was sold to grain merchants in the area and as far southeast as Jenin, depending on the competitive prices offered. Sunflowers were marketed to the oil industry through middlemen in Nazareth and the Bay of Haifa area while tobacco bales were disposed of through the Tobacco Commission. Watermelons, on the other hand, were sold in the field under the *ḍamān*[17] type of contract because marketing this crop was based on mutual trust between the city merchant and his supplier, and the Ḥğerāt did not have such a network for disposing of the fruit.

In 1974 a new trend was established with the planting of an almond orchard in the south of the Ḏmeydeh. This was followed by the planting of a small olive grove southwest of Bīr al-Maksūr in 1976 and discussions about almond and a variety of nut tree orchards on the hillside property of the ʻUzeyr branch of the Ġadāyreh. This development was largely a response to the continuous efforts of the Ministry of Agriculture to develop and promote export-oriented high-return agricultural, horticultural, and arboricultural production. These efforts included loans on easy terms to finance the planting of these orchards.

At the beginning of 1977 the *muḫtār* began requesting financial assistance from the Ministry of Agriculture in order to connect the lands of Bīr al-Maksūr to the irrigation network in the region. His intent was to develop pipe-irrigated vegetable cultivation in the bottom-lands around the village to provide for both higher income from the tribal lands and a more intensive utilization of the youth and female components of the tribal labor force in Maksūr and the Mikmān. Whether the *muḫtār*'s plan materialized or not, Ḥğeri agriculture had reached maturity: it responded to modern cultivation technologies and to market forces as far as the Common Market, it did not shy from long-term investments (such as olive and almond groves), and it occupied an independent niche in the tribe's economic domain.

The Herding Sector

Overview

While the transformation of Ḥğeri agriculture from subsistence occupation to market-oriented production was accelerating—increasing in diversity, complexity, and volume—Ḥğeri herding was changing at a much slower rate and in an altogether different direction. Whereas agriculture was becoming a more popular occupation, herding was steadily declining from its traditional role as the backbone of Ḥğeri economy, gradually becoming the enterprise of a select few but relatively major herd owners/merchants.

Four clusters of structural factors underlay the herdsman inability to convert to market-oriented herding and to successfully compete with his Jewish counterpart: pasture availability versus converting to feed lots, herd health and preventive veterinary, the limited productive unit, and labor availability. The first two clusters were the outcome of increasing governmental control over agricultural production and herding, the third was a result of kin-based cultural attitudes, and the fourth was a result of the tribe's intensified participation in wage labor. In the following paragraphs I will discuss each of these clusters before discussing the state of Ḥğeri herding in the 1970s.

Pasture Availability and Lot Feed

Several sets of factors underlay these diametrical trends. Foremost among these was the respective difference between the intensive and extensive patterns of land usage between agricultural production and herding. This difference was all the more pronounced in the north where elevations were not high enough to promote vertical transhumance or the soils were too marginal to make their cultivation profitable when population size increased and modern agricultural technology was introduced. Moreover, many of the crops grown on these lands (for example, tobacco) could be exported, earning the state much needed foreign currency whereas all the meat produced by local herds was consumed within the country. Consequently, governmental incentives in the north favored agriculture over herding and fenced-in over free-ranging herds. In addition to the economic importance of agricultural settlements in general, the Jewish ones represented two additional properties. The first was demographic, dispersing the population more evenly over the land. The second property touched directly on state security in case of war; these settlements formed a spatial defense lattice as well as balanced Arab village populations that might join an invading neighboring army.

A second set of factors was the intensifying competition with Jewish herdsmen for diminishing pastureland. Several elements tipped the balance in favor of the latter even aside from their closer affiliation and connection with the authorities. Traditionally the local Arab herdsman relied almost exclusively on natural pasture for his animals and as late as 1977 he used open range or stubble whenever possible. His Jewish counterpart, conversely, cultivated rough fodder, as only a very few Arab farmers did (in 1971, Jewish settlements cultivated 535,511 *dunam*, or 23.4%, while Arabs cultivated 5165 *dunam*, or 0.8%, of their total agricultural production; Isr. CBS 1973:4). Additionally, the Jewish herdsman relied on supplementary feed, which not only kept his animals in better health and higher productivity, but enabled him to use a smaller range for a comparable number of animals. Moreover, most of the supplemental feed was the organic refuse of the food industry such as sugar beet and tomato pulp or chicken droppings, which became the most popular cattle feed due to its availability and very high nutritional value. A metric ton of this feed in 1976 cost I£150. By way of comparison, a fattened *baladi* calf, which consumed 0.5 ton of the feed, sold for an average of I£2000 during the summer of that year. The feed was known to Arab herd owners and was used by a few large cattle herders so the reluctance of the average owner to invest in such supplementary feed cannot be attributed to ignorance or inaccessibility. Rather, it was attitudinal and, as one informant pointed out, was derived from an unwillingness to invest in higher future returns when present profits were deemed sufficient. Thus, when the cooperation of the Jewish herdsman with the Veterinary Service (below) was added to land use pattern, it is hardly surprising that the Ministry of Agriculture and the ILA were more lenient in pasture rentals to Jewish than to Arab herd owners, even before sectoral affiliation is introduced into this equation.

Herd Health and the Relationship with the Veterinary Service

Supplementary feed lots also helped protect the herd's health. The Jewish herdsman was much more aware of the impact of diseases on herd productivity than his bedouin counterpart, and worked in close cooperation with the Veterinary Service of the Ministry of Agriculture. The local Arab, in most cases, still mistrusted modern veterinarian practices and usually did not cooperate willingly with the service. In fact, he often viewed the veterinarian as a spy for the Income Tax Service—otherwise why would the veterinarian want to know where all his animals were?

Three distinct attitudes underlay this mistrust. First, many did not believe in vaccine efficacy because the concept of preventive medicine did not exist in their frame of reference. Consequently, the average herd owner did not understand the need for an injection when no signs of disease were evident or when he knew his herd to be healthy at the time. This immediate approach to the herd's well-being was promoted by a second, fatalistic, attitude illustrated by the following proverb quoted by a Ḥğeri: "*min 'endo—yamūt, wa-min laysa 'endo—la' yamūt*" ("he who has—will lose [lit. it will die], and he who does not have—will not lose [lit. it will not die]"). In other words, dead animals were a testimony to their owner's wealth, an attitude that facilitated coping with rapid fluctuations in herd populations under traditional herding practices.

The second attitude regarded the perception of causality as immediate. Thus, once the veterinarian had taken care of a herd, should death occur it was considered to be his fault even when traditionally its cause had been accepted as "the hand of the Almighty." Similarly, if he injected a sick animal and it died, often the death was not considered to be the outcome of the disease but of the injection.

The third attitude that promoted mistrust between the Arab herdsman and the Veterinarian Service had to do with the role of the service as a public guardian of the health of *all* the animals in its domain. More specifically, being tuned to conceiving natural events in terms of their immediate perceivable cause-and-effect, the Galilean Arab herdsman did not see his sick herd as a threat to other herds in the area and was angered when the veterinarian had it destroyed due to—for him—an insufficient cause, such as a lethal contagious disease. A case in point was the notorious foot-and-mouth disease (aphthous fever). The *baladi* is a hardy breed, wholly or partly immune to many diseases including this viral fever. Thus, if an animal contracted it during the winter when there was ample young and tender grass, it could survive by staying off its hoofs, lying down, and grazing the young grass around it until its legs and mouth recovered. Since the herdsman knew his cattle would survive, he did not generally bother to notify the service about the epizootic because he also knew that the sick animals would be destroyed in order to contain the disease, which was lethal to the thoroughbred breeds such as Hollander milch herds in the area. When, incidentally, the disease struck in the summer when the grass was dry, tough, and in short supply and the sick animal would not survive, the same herdsman would notify the service in order to save whatever could be saved of his herd and to receive some cash compensation for his condemned cattle.

This mistrust deepened the concern of Ḥğeri herd owners when in 1976 the Veterinary Service began a campaign to register and issue identification tags and certificates to all cattle in Israel. The reasons for the campaign were threefold. Specifically it was directed at eradicating *Brucellosis abortus*. This disease is transferable to humans, and induces spontaneous abortions in cattle, causing large financial losses when the Jewish sector's high yielding but low resistance breeds contracted it. On a more general level the campaign was an attempt to have the Arab herdsmen butcher their animals in officially approved slaughterhouses where some health and sanitation standards were mandatory, thus preventing human consumption of sick animals and curtailing the spread of diseases, food poisoning, and other health hazards due to butchering in unsanitary places (such as fields) and improper transportation in ill-equipped vehicles. Finally, the registration was instituted to establish a regular procedure for checking the country's herds to combat epizootics and diseases at an early stage and to facilitate the establishment of standardized registration and practical applications of veterinarian procedures. In short, the project was to leave the Ministry of Agriculture with a very large measure of control over the transfer and disposition of the animals. Not surprisingly, in December of 1976 one informant told me that his family intended to sell their cattle after they fatted on the coming spring pasture because "with the new ID system [for cattle], it is no deal raising them." The issue was not profits, because often a herdsman was better compensated for an emaciated cow on its way to destruction than for the same animal sold on the open market. The problem, rather, seems to have been the perceived excess control the veterinarian *could* exercise by telling the owner what to do with his cattle.

The Productive Unit

The results of the competition over dominance in meat production favored the Jewish herdsmen for yet other reasons. Jewish growers were usually corporate bodies, whether kibbutzim, communal moshavim, or commercial companies, whereas the Arab herdsmen were private owners. Consequently, their relative political leverage was weaker because they competed as individuals against corporate bodies. Further, because the Jewish herds were larger, they were more efficient per owner[18] in converting investment into marketable produce, and so Jewish herdsmen had a stronger economic argument to support their demand for more pastures.

The Arab herdsmen did not incorporate in order to compete more effectively with the Jewish herding corporations because they were generally apprehensive about partnerships. A good illustration of this attitude was provided in proverb by the *muḫtār* in response to my question "why don't the Ḥğerāt form a cattle company which will enable them to compete with the Jews on pasture?" He said that the bedouin do not like companies and added "*lawā šarāki mliḥah lakan kul thnen šarāku bi-ḥormah*" (lit. "if partnerships were good every two would share in a wife"). Another illustration was provided by the ministry's veterinarian for the Galilean Arabs in general. He suggested to a few local prominent Arabs that they form a company for processing and marketing milk, with the ministry's blessing. His idea was to prevent the loss of the milk produced in the Arab sector, which could not find its way to the processing plants of *Tnuva* due to the Rabbinical Council's *kashrut* laws. A second reason was to organize milk processing within the Arab sector so as to ensure pasteurization and sanitary handling of production, thereby preventing *B. abortus* and *B. militensis* transmission to humans. The Arab businessmen declined the offer due to unworkability rather than unprofitability. They said that after a period of initial excitement the *fellāḥīn* would sell their milk in the villages more often than bring it to the plant. They also did not think that the veterinarian's suggestion that the milk supply could be made predictable by using legally binding contracts between the company and the suppliers was workable.

The difference in approach between the Jewish and Arab sectors lies in the contradiction between a non-kin, relatively anonymous industrial corporate model and the kin-oriented universe of the rural Galilean Arab. In other words, partnerships could easily pit an individual's economic aspirations against familial obligations and unity, disrupting the latter when lines of allegiance had to be drawn. Hence the negative social attitude toward partnership, as expressed in the *muḫtār*'s proverb. Similarly, businessmen were uncomfortable with using legal contracts to bind the villagers because they would in any case have to sell/give their milk to relatives before supplying it to the company should such conflicting demands be made. That is, if a binding legal contract was invoked to force a *fellāḥ* to bring his milk to the processing plant, he would view it as an act of coercion, threatening his independence and compromising his honor. It would irreparably damage the relations between him and the individuals who owned or ran the company. Since these individuals lived in the region and derived their prominence from converting their wealth to sociopolitical ends, while such an economic venture would add to their wealth, it would be disastrous to their sociopolitical status and aspirations.

Labor Availability

The differences between Jewish and bedouin herd size also highlight the problem of hiring trained personnel to care for the herds. First, within the aforementioned size ranges, larger herds more efficiently used the shepherd or cowhand. Second, Jewish growers usually fenced in their cattle, so very little continuous attention was required from the herdsman. Third, having pasture, Jewish companies often attracted an Arab herd owner with a small herd to care for their herd and paid part of his salary in kind—feed and water—while he managed both herds together.

By contrast, the traditional Arab herd owner who pastured his herd on an open, unfenced range increasingly faced a shortage in shepherds as his traditional hands—his sons—looked for economic independence in salaried jobs, and who as trained hired adults demanded increasingly higher wages for their labor.

The pressures that were generated by the shortage of pasture; the need to rent most of the available pasturage; the consequent growing investment in supplemental feed; the rising cost of personnel; and myriad expenses not known before (such as transportation to truck the herds as the distance between pastures increased, chemicals for pest control, veterinarian services when not part of the Ministry of Agriculture services and for medicines injected when part of these services, and so on) gradually eliminated the small herd owners, leaving fewer but larger herds that were handled increasingly often as marketable commodity rather than as a "family herd." It is interesting to note that a similar process was observed in rural France (Elgazi, pers. comm.) and the Negev (Marx 1981:38), and might prove to be a general pattern in the transition from traditional extensive herding to modern intensive animal husbandry.

Ḥǧeri Herding in the 1970s

During the second half of the 1970s, the visible results of this process among the Ḥǧerāt formed a continuum along which three categories of herd owners could be discerned. The first category included those herdsmen who were involved in the traditional style of herding, which heavily relied on open natural pasture (although occasionally supplemented with purchased feed when no other alternative presented itself) and family labor. Members of this category were found primarily in the permanent herding camps in *wādi* al-Mzagga, where sheep were the principal species, and in Umm al-Zīnāt,[19] which was a predominately *baladi* cattle herding camp. There was also a remnant still found in the Ẓahara, where they herded goats and some cattle. Finally, a few individuals had private arrangements with independent Jewish farmers or agricultural settlements from Kiryat Shmonah in the north to Haderah in the south. These individuals rented at a low cost or, sometimes, freely used local pasturage (in return for guarding and/or herding the local properties) while paying for water and for damage caused by their herds. As a category these herdsmen were the least receptive to veterinarian practices and Western concepts of animal husbandry. They were also the most exposed to the shortage in shepherds and the competition over pasture with their Jewish counterparts or with state agencies.

In *wādi* al-Mzagga, for example, as part of its campaign to increase the Jewish population in the Galilee, the Jewish Agency decided to establish a new agricultural settlement in the area, and the Ḥǧeri herd owners were asked to leave. The camp members sought help from the *muḫtār* to prevent the exodus. He argued their case in the ILA and as a result it was decided to divide the land of al-Mzagga in half between the new kibbutz and the Ḥǧeri camp in recognition of their rights of usufruct in these pastures. The *muḫtār* then told them to reduce their herd sizes and reorganize the grazing pattern so as to more fully use their half of the area and to reduce the chances of conflicts with the new kibbutz. Although for a time his actions averted the camp's demise, conflicts over pasture with the new kibbutz, combined with the established rivalry and conflicts with the older nearby settlement of Kfar Zeytim, and combined with the Green Patrol after 1977 accumulated by 1982 to deliver the coup de grâce to this camp.

In Umm al-Zīnāt the herds had already been shifted from their old pastures to a new place, in the same general area, as a result of the JNF's afforestation campaign. At the same time growing tensions due to competition over the rental of agricultural land with some members of the nearby moshav of Elyaqim necessitated the involvement of the local police and the Ministry of Agriculture, which had a stake in this area. Although for small encounters these agencies preferred dealing with a single representative of the camp members, thereby introducing political clientism into the camp, for any major intervention on their behalf camp members had to approach the *muḫtār* for help. Consequently, members of this category were among those most dependent on his services, almost as much as during the period of the MG and its travel permits.

Members of the second category resided in the three tribal settlements and kept their predominately sheep herds there. Due to the limited pasturage in the surrounding area, these herds were kept relatively small and were given supplementary feed. The expenses incurred by the feed were augmented by the cost of water near the villages that, being for residential use, was much more expensive than that for agricultural use available in the herding camps. By and large, members of this category were more receptive to modern ideas of animal husbandry and veterinary practices emanating from nearby Nazareth where the regional offices of the Ministry of Agriculture were located. For example, a member of this group (who unfortunately died before realizing this plan) was planning to completely trough-feed his herd of sheep and to gradually replace the Awassi breed he had with more productive ones, which regularly drop twins. Although such a change would have ended his revenues from milk, he reasoned that the boost to his income from the sale of lambs would more than compensate him. This man also used veterinarian services quite regularly, and other pest control measures. In general, the idea of reducing herd size in order to completely trough-feed was heard increasingly more often toward the end of 1977.

The third category consisted of the emerging group of large herd owner/animal merchants who could secure the increasingly scarcer labor; who had the necessary connections to secure enough pasture; and who could meet the growing number of additional expenses involved in this occupation. Most importantly, members in this group were entrepreneurs who treated their herds as a commodity and might buy or sell a whole herd at once if a profit could be realized. For example, a member of this category exchanged a herd of pregnant goats for a herd of heifers of the same value. He then sent a herd of calves, which he had bought from another Ḥğeri in *wādi* al-Mzagga, to Umm al-Zīnāt under the care of an employed Ḥğeri herder who did not know of the first transaction. When the latter arrived at Umm al-Zīnāt and learned he was supposed to receive the herd of heifers, which doubled the number of animals under his responsibility, he packed and left the entrepreneur without a cowhand on very short notice. Without much ado the entrepreneur turned around and sold, without a loss, both herds to another tribesman who was present in the camp at the time. The same individual also bought a herd of sheep in order to engage its competent teenage shepherd, who was bound to it by an annual contract with its former owner and transferable with the herd until the contract's termination.

Herding Contracts

Securing labor was by far the most demanding of the requirements that faced a herd owner/merchant, for if he had initial cash he could finance both pasture on private land and the necessary extra expenses. Skilled personnel, however, was increasingly in shorter supply, not only because of the lowered social image of the shepherd and its abandonment by tribal youth but also because the herd owner had to compete with the salaries of the organized labor market, which were beyond his means. Thus, the average 1976 annual salary in the employed labor market in Israel was I£34,212 and in agriculture it was I£24,144 (Isr. CBS Abs. 28:338–39). By comparison, a shepherd received an annual salary of I£10,000. It is not surprising, therefore, that most shepherds were brought from the West Bank, where labor was unorganized, salaries were much lower, and there was a labor surplus that had only limited access to the Jewish sector's labor demands. The rest of the shepherds employed by Ḥğeri herd owners were their young sons and close relatives who had not yet left that occupation.

Herding partnerships were contracted between a herd owner and, usually, another tribesmember of his choice who may or may not have animals of his own. According to agreements of this type, the herd owner may provide the entire herd or, if the partner owned a small herd, the two herds were merged into the single unit of the partnership, its total value then serving as the basis for the agreement's financial calculations. The partner provided the labor (valued as the salary of a skilled shepherd), which included contracting for pasture, while cash expenses and produce were shared equally. For example, if only the owner provided the herd of 100 animals valued at X, then each owned 0.5X, which was the sum the partner owed the owner. If they combined their herds and the owner gave 150 animals and the partner 50 and the combined herd was valued at X, then each owned 0.5X of the herd but the partner, having brought one quarter of the animals, owed the owner only 0.25X for his share. During the period of the agreement the herd's size was kept constant. Once the partner paid for his half of the herd's value, the herd was divided and then he could leave and become an independent small herd owner or he could negotiate a new contract.

Partnership arrangements of this sort were advantageous to both parties. From the herding partner's point of view, the partnership enabled him to build up a herd, in exchange for labor and responsibility, without any capital investment on his part. The herd owner, although he lost half the produce of the herd, preferred this type of contract for three major reasons. First he engaged a shepherd who was highly motivated to increase the production of the herd without damaging it—because the animals belonged to both. Moreover, a partner was not likely to cheat him because the relationship was as much a sociopolitical one as it was economic. Second, having several partners camping at different places made it easier to locate pasture because one needed several smaller plots rather than a single large range—which also reduced the risk of epizootics decimating all of his herds (as happened to one herd owner who lost over 150 sheep due to an attack of tic fever, *Piroplasmosis babesiaovis*, during a single spring month). Third, since for the contract's duration the herding partner represented the herd (for instance, in signing pasture contracts), it was considered to be under his titular ownership and was not counted as part of the herd owner's property. Any produce of the herd could not be considered as taxable income of the herd owner and could not be added to the revenues he may derive from other sources, an all-important calculation in Israel where income tax is of the rapidly escalating graduated type.

Although partnerships were an attractive arrangement that helped recycle older herdsmen and introduced younger ones back into this occupation, the general decline in herding also affected this form of contract so that Ḥğeri herd owners/merchants increasingly looked for partners among members of other tribes. In this respect herding partnerships were similar to agricultural partnerships with the *fellāḥīn*; here, the Ḥğerāt used their connections with the authorities to secure access to pasture that members of other smaller tribes often could not achieve. As in the case of agriculture, these contracts formed a linkage of clientism that was simultaneously economic and political and that helped substantiate the Ḥğeri claim to regional leadership.

Disposition of Herd Produce

The differences in herding practices and the resulting difference in locations were also reflected in the disposition of herd produce by the three categories of herd owners. While all three sold the progeny of their herds to animal merchants, butchers, and private individuals as far south as Jerusalem, and similarly disposed of the wool of their sheep and hair of the goats, and while none sold the *labne* (drained yogurt cream cheese), which was made for home use only, members of the first category did not usually sell milk or milk products from their herds. Two reasons accounted for this practice. First was the reluctance of *Tnuva* to market fresh milk from the Arab sector, which meant that it could not be processed in time to prevent spoilage. The second was the distance from Nazareth—the major urban center that could absorb the home-processed *ǧibneh* (cheese)—because the added transportation costs rendered it noncompetitive with cheese from the nearby villages including the three tribal settlements. Instead, members of this category fed more milk to the lambs, kids, and calves and processed the rest into *labne* and *ǧibneh* for home use and as presents to close relatives who no longer had producing animals of their own.

Of the third herd owner category, only a few sold milk or its derivatives from their sheep and goat herds, for much the same reasons as above. Those who did sell had developed the necessary transportation links and sold it either as fresh milk[20] or as fresh unsalted *ǧibneh*. Herd owners of the second category, unlike the others, did not have a problem of distance due to their proximity to Nazareth. They sold their herd's milk as fresh *laban* (yogurt) in the old market of Nazareth if they lacked the necessary outlets (or if it was the "pocket money" of the wife), or they might dispose of it as *ǧibneh* preserved in brine if they had developed a network of customers, both private households and small grocery stores. Lastly, none of the herd owners sold manure from their herds. It was not competitive with available chemical fertilizers because it contained seeds and pollen of wild plants and grasses, which invade the fields, effectively eliminating the demand for it.

Characteristics of Ḥǧeri Economic Adaptation

Overview

Viewed as a whole, two complementary features characterized the Ḥǧeri economy in the second half of the 1970s. The first was the maintenance of the traditional approach of multiple resource extraction expressed by most members of the tribe's labor force holding a salaried job concurrently with being self-employed in agriculture, herding, or trade. The second was their intensifying integration into the regional economic network and growing involvement with the related state agencies, the effects of which have far transcended the purely economic.

Multi-Resource Economic Involvement

Multiple source income strategy was as characteristic of Ḥğeris in the herding camps as of those in the permanent tribal settlements. In *wādi* al-Mzagga, for example, all the tribesmembers herded and some cultivated cereal grains, while practically each tent sent one or two members to work in the nearby Kibbutzim. In Umm al-Zīnāt they herded and cultivated wheat and barley, and a few worked in nearby Yoqne'am, Haifa, and the Bay area. In the four tribal settlements the variety was even greater as a single individual might have several sources of income. For example, in 1976 one person cultivated his land (cereal grains), worked as skilled labor in the construction industry, and owned a grocery store managed by his wife; another person worked in construction and agriculture, and owned a tractor that he rented out; yet a third worked in a textile factory in the Bay area and owned a herd cared for by his teenage son.

Multiple resource extraction was an important component in an individual's adaptation to the volatile Israeli economy, and it gained an even greater socioeconomic importance at the household level through the cooperation and sharing of its members. Although from the state's perspective such individualized occupational diversity was counterproductive because it maintained an underspecialized, less efficient, and more expensive labor force (cf. Arad 1975:86), from the individual's point of view this approach was preferable. First, it may be the individual's only economic alternative to make ends meet. Second, as pointed out by Rappaport (1970:53–54), the "hyper-integration" that results from specialization and simplification of the systemic structure causes instability, which might be "lethal" to the organization's lower orders. In an economic sense, instability takes the form of recessions, which might be weathered by complex organizations while having dire effects on the welfare of their individual human constituents. Third, being continuously productive, even at lower levels, the individual is less likely to suffer from the varied side effects of unemployment, which usually plague the more specialized unemployed worker who does not have an alternative occupation.

A Ḥğeri household's ability to maintain this traditional approach in the face of a changing environment was linked to the development of a general practice of keeping the sons at home after they had children, and often after they had built their own house, as the four examples below show. As a result, a household with several mature sons could rely on income from several sources to accomplish its tasks, be they daily subsistence, marrying off a member, house construction, or capital investment. For example, two months before his wedding, a firstborn son who was planning to build his house was approached by his father, who convinced him to delay his house construction for a year or so in order to pool the family money and buy a combine "because money in a house does not bring more money while the combine will work." The son consented and postponed his plans for more than two years.

Furthermore, a household could expand its own active labor pool and increase its ability to diversify economic resources by deploying its teenagers in sporadic activities (such as agriculture) that fit in with their academic schedule. And, by maintaining part of its resources in primary food production, the household could retain a basic level of stability that served to buffer it from, and allowed it to weather out, periods of perturbation in the state economic system.

Below are four households at different stages of their domestic cycle in 1977, exemplifying these adaptive elements:

(1) *Beginning*. Members: father (b. 1950); mother (b. 1955); three children (b. 1974, 1975, 1976 respectively). Married: 1975. First (ground) level of house: 1975. Second (elaborate) level added 1977/78 (younger brother of father with his wife moved into the first level). Resources of household: 1 salaried job (father). Remarks: father's father was relatively wealthy and put up much of the money that went into construction.

(2) *End of first quarter*. Members: father (b. 1937); mother (b. 1940); first son (b. 1965) in 5th grade of school; plus 6 others (4 females, 2 males) born 1967–1976. Resources: a small herd plus 2 salaried jobs in the same workplace (a worker and a resident guard) held by the father. Remarks: family resided away from tribal settlements but was constructing its house in Bīr al-Maksūr (1977/78) next to father's elder brother's house on father's father's land.

(3) *End of second quarter (height of its productive cycle)*. Members: father (b. 1933); mother (b. 1935); 1st son (b. 1955) married 1976 and his wife (b. 1961); 2nd son (b. 1956); 3rd son (b. 1959); plus 8 more children born 1961–1977. Resources: agriculture and renting out agricultural machinery with its operators (the three sons with occasional help from the father as well as other household members); transportation (father and one son); salaried jobs (the three sons).

(4) *End of third and into the fourth quarter*. Members: father (b. 1893); mother (b. 1896); the last three sons (b. 1949, 1952, and 1955 respectively), two with their families. The last son married in 1973 and had two children; the first married in 1976 and had one child. Resources: agriculture (land cultivated by eldest son who lived next door); salaried jobs (2 sons); self-employed contractor (1 son).

The preservation of the Ḥğeri extended household coordinated even after the sons married was the exact opposite of the process documented by Rosenfeld (1958; 1969) for the *fellāḥīn* he studied in the same general area (Lower Galilee). Whereas Rosenfeld's data suggest that the changing economic patterns under Israeli rule and the lack of landed property or its equal division among inheritors of unequal expectations and demands cause the fission of extended family households, among the Ḥğerāt—conversely—the less a household had, the longer sons were likely to remain with their father.

To explain the Ḥğeri adaptive success we need to look at the interaction of three factors: sedentarization, the traditional ideal of private residence for the newly wed, and the ideal and politics of tribal and familial solidarity, which were embedded in segmentary lineage structures. Since sedentarization and the intensified use of their landed resources were almost concurrent with their increasing ability to seek salaried jobs, the tradition of intergenerational rivalry over the available family resources, such as documented by Rosenfeld (e.g., 1958:1133–34), had not yet developed. Concurrently, "segmentary sociability" (Sahlins 1961:331–32), validated and reinforced by traditional sharing and cooperation patterns, helped perpetuate the intergenerational relationship developed since childhood and which united the family in "complementary opposition" (Sahlins

1961:332–33) to other like units. Second, prior to sedentarization a son could readily erect a small tent or a reed hut next to his father's, thereby establishing an independent residence even though it may have been a temporary one, and patterns of food sharing maintained him closely tied to his paternal household. House construction, on the other hand, was an expensive undertaking even in the Arab sector where prices were lower than in its Jewish counterpart. It may thus take several years before a son could amass, with the help of his father, siblings, and other close relatives, the necessary funds. It may also be cheaper and easier to add another story to the father's house than to buy or rent a new land plot. The son therefore stayed in his father's house and shared in its resources, services, and upkeep. These patterns of cooperation and sharing continued after the son established a separate household (usually in close proximity to his father's), linking the extended family after its spatial separation.

Finally, multi-resource extraction was not a new strategy for the Ḥǧerāt; they traditionally used it to adapt to their marginal environments. Nor is it surprising, for it is a basic adaptive strategy to "scarcity," real or imagined (e.g., Sahlins 1972:4–5). First they had to adapt to the instabilities inherent in the marginal existence of pastoralism. Then, within the context of the Israeli economy, the approach proved useful in making use of whatever limited resources were available to them, both as participants in an unstable industrial economic system and as members of the Arab sector, albeit with special ties to the authorities.

Circles of Cooperation

While households were expected to and did tend to operate independently of one another, patterns of sharing and cooperation tied the individual households and wove them into concentric rings. These rings, as Sahlins (1968:81) observed, followed fairly closely the layout of the tribe's segmentary pattern, occasionally short-circuited by links of friendship. Acts of sharing ranged from sharing food and lending cars or money to acts of cooperation such as helping in concrete roof-casting. For example, any person present when food was served at the home was invited to partake in the meal. These meals were the family's daily food and the invitation was not considered formal hospitality but was normal everyday behavior expected of the host by force of the ideal of generosity. (The best indicator of its character is that the host ate with those present, a behavior not seen in formal hospitality).

Lending cars, helping in roof-castings, and the like were more closely bound to kin-distance and friendship. Several of the services in the tribal settlements—such as driving a sick tribesmember in one of the three local taxis to a hospital in Haifa, delivering a water tank to another tribesmember when the water reservoir was shut because of unpaid bills, or plowing a sick person's field—were sometimes extended as neighborly assistance and sometimes as paid services. In the latter case, it was often dependent on the service provider but may also have been the choice of the recipient to pay and so be free of moral debts. In the camps these acts were never paid for.

In this manner society's kinship base enhanced the ability of individual households to withstand the economic reality of rampant inflation, recessions, and similar hardships, while economic cooperation reaffirmed the tribe's kin-ideology. Thus, while alternating multiple sources of income and taking advantage of opportunities to develop such resources portray the Ḥğerāt as economic entrepreneurs, their patterns of sharing, cooperation, and consumption set them apart from the Western entrepreneurial model and its Jewish variety in Israel.

The most visible to a Western observer among such acts of sharing were financial loans sans interest, mortgage, pawn, countersignatures, and other banking practices. All a person had to do was to ask, and whenever possible fairly large sums were given to siblings, friends, and other relatives. For example, one person in March 1977 talked about building his house sometime during the following year. Arriving at the financial aspects of the enterprise, he commented that he had to start collecting some I£35,000 he had loaned to several tribesmembers; to ask two of his brothers for I£10,000 each; and to apply for a I£20,000 low-interest, easy-term loan from his workplace in order to build stage I of the house.

It must be noted that these money transfers were made with full knowledge of their Western banking characteristics. In other words, a Ḥğeri would seek a loan from the Ministry of Agriculture, the police, the IDA, or any other such state agency but not from a commercial bank because the former loans were low interest and were given out on easy terms, that is, untied to the CPI and other such benchmarks, and hence, lagged behind the rate of inflation. (For example, I£1000 in January of 1977 depreciated to some I£650 by the end of that year, whereas salaries, being tied to the CPI, increased proportionally.)

Such charge-free transfers enabled a Ḥğeri household to maintain a much broader financial base than that of a household in the more Western Jewish sector. Moreover, this financial fluidity was important to the perpetuation of the Ḥğeri lifestyle, not only because it fostered kin sentiments and in some respects served to equalize the ownership of material possessions, but also because the spending patterns of the Ḥğerāt were sporadic in character. A household could retain a fairly low expenditure level until a worthy cause such as a wedding, house construction, or land purchase presented itself. At that time it would unload its savings, may very well borrow, and then worked to recuperate its economic independence. In large measure, this type of spending pattern was in accord with Sahlins' Production for Livelihood, "the traditional economy of finite objectives insists on asserting itself even as it is broken and harnessed to the market" (1972:85). Thus, even as households and individuals tried to amass wealth, they continuously used it to finance hospitality and to show generosity in order to convert their economic possessions to sociopolitical preeminence and the personal satisfaction of approaching the ideal of being a "true bedouin."

The wealth deployment differences between the two sectors had immediate effects on the shape, orientation, and intensity of their respective consumption patterns. Among the Ḥğerāt and the rural Arab sector, the orientation was toward sociopolitical ends, while within the Jewish sector, it was directed toward individualized material comfort, which then served to indicate social status and superiority. There is probably no better example of these opposing perspectives than the commonly used measure of the standard of living used by the Central Bureau of Statistics (CBS). Ben Porath, for instance, citing the bureau's data, reports as one measure of the standard that the average housing density among Arabs and Jews in 1961 was 3.6 and 1.9 persons/room respectively (1966:76–77). Both he and the CBS seem to have overlooked that the standard was a set of Western criteria imposed on the local Arabs, who built larger rooms and had different values regarding privacy, space, its uses, and so on (for instance, see Hall 1966:154–64 for the question of Middle Eastern space use and Said 1978 for the general issue of imposing Western "reality" on non-Western phenomena). Notwithstanding, one should be aware of a possible alternative explanation, namely, that state agencies such as the CBS treated their diverse data in accordance with a single set of criteria to express the population's conformity with the ideals of the state itself.

The State Economic Impact

The Ḥğerāt's economic involvement at regional and national levels had, as has been mentioned, two complementary aspects or directions. The first was the multiple resource extraction—increased emphasis on salaried employment, reorientation of economic production toward the market, and so on—that emanated from the tribe, linking it to the regional economic network and beyond. The other aspect was oriented in the opposite direction—from state agencies to the tribe.

The state's intervention and involvement in the life of the Ḥğerāt proceeded both on the level of individuals in their households and on the level of the community as a whole. The former ranged from providing advice and support in production and produce disposal to health related allowances, national insurance programs, educational stipends, and the like. The latter case included various subsidies and grants directed at helping the tribe to sedentarize.

Starting from the perspective of the household's economic health, the most important and regular among these monies were the programs of the Institute for National Insurance. These included various allowances and pensions that in 1976–1977 channeled some I£3,000,000–4,000,000 to the tribe each month. While these sums, the result of the welfare character of the state, were directed at ensuring a basic standard of living, they promoted other changes in their wake.

Family Allowance

Of the Institute's monies that reached the Ḥğerāt, "Family Allowance"[21] was by far the major source. For example, in April, May, and June of 1977 the allowance cash receipts paid in Bīr al-Maksūr and the Mikmān were I£246,869; I£240,395; and I£238,520 respectively. By comparison, the combined receipt of "Senior Citizens' and Widows' Pensions" and "Invalids' and Work-disabled Pensions" for the same three months was I£137,348; I£136,189; and I£132,917 respectively. On the average, each Ḥğeri family with children received I£1073 (N = 231; range I£157 to I£2902) during these three months. The monthly receipt of family allowance slowly began redefining interactional patterns because its recipient was the mother, who previously had no independent economic identity.

This process was very slow and operated in combination with other factors such as age, the family's income level, emotional ties and trust between the couple, and education. In general most informants concurred that this was "the wife's money" and in the few cases where a man used it for other purposes he usually answered with the justification that "anyway we are one family." In practice, among older people the husbands usually collected the sum at the post office where it was paid out through the Postal Bank. If they were relatively well off they handed it over to their wives. The more traditional or less well off kept it and gave money to the wife whenever she asked for it. Most younger husbands either had their wives pick up the allowance or if they themselves had picked it up, they handed it over to their wives on their return to the house. As mentioned, only a handful used it for purposes other than food and clothing for the children.

In terms of changes in Ḥğeri culture, the allowance was more important when considering the conceptual framework and ideology of the Ḥğerāt than at the purely economic level. Although either way the money was spent on the children, it was the first time that the tribe's women had a source of income that was formally independent of their husbands. Moreover, due to a series of post office branch robberies in several Arab villages in the Galilee where the robbers walked off with several millions of Israeli *lirôt* in allowance money in mid-1976, the Institute began a campaign to convince recipients to open bank accounts for direct deposit of the allowance.

Senior Citizens' and Widows' Pensions

The monthly senior citizens' and widows' pensions (Isr. Laws 19:126–149, Amendment No. 11), which averaged I£1189 (N = 98) per person in June 1977, provided the elderly with a source of income independent of their descendants. Since no elderly person in the tribe lived alone and their basic daily expenses were met within the household as a whole, the pensions were used for personal expenses and gifts that enabled the elderly to interact with their descendants on a reciprocal basis instead of having to depend on the younger generation's reverence at a time when the dynamics of intergenerational relations were under pressure to reformulate.

Major among these pressures was the growing disparity between the types of problems that faced the younger generations in their everyday life and the traditional answers that the elder generation had to offer. Consequently, if in the past reverence was based on the elderly's experience and economic wealth, reverence became more dependent on tradition, socialization, and the realization of the political necessity of unity, which still placed a high premium on the life experience of the elders.

While on an intergenerational plane the pension reduced tension by alleviating economic pressures on the household and thus retarded change, on the inter-sexual plane it promoted change. In providing a widow with an independent income, the pension (as well as other types of insurance money and allowances paid to widows of government employees) made it possible for a few females to be economically independent of their own or husband's relatives for the first time in Ḥğeri history. In the mid-1970s, the tensions thus generated were latent—more a sense of uneasiness than actual worry.

Notwithstanding, the impact of these pensions, combined with increased education and a general movement away from orthodox Moslem religious precepts, added to the pressures to equalize male-female status among the Ḥğerāt.

Use of Banks

Finally, employment by state agencies such as the police, IDA, and the Ministry of Education promoted establishing bank accounts to facilitate the receipt of monthly salaries. With the passage of time the use of banking services became more popular, fostered also, as mentioned before, by the Institute for National Insurance, which in 1976 began to promote use of banks for the receipt of its allowances and pensions.

By and large, most tribesmembers were conservative in their use of banking services and tended to establish checking and/or saving accounts that, due to the rate of inflation, only superficially increased their capital. A few individuals, however, began to invest in (usually) conservative commercial and/or industrial stocks, an activity that better protected the value of their money. As a general rule, however, the Ḥğerāt did not like to gamble with their money, and the extent to which an individual would invest in stock, albeit conservative and very solid, was primarily dependent on his interpersonal relations with the bank branch manager, and his trust in him.

Notes

1. Ironically, while in the early 1950s this work provided the tribesmembers with extra income, in the long run its outcome reduced the available pasture on this mountain range, especially because goats, which predominated in their herds, were banned from reforested areas. Reduction in pasture availability increased the pressure to reduce herd size and ultimately to abandon herding altogether and enter the wage labor market.
2. While the Ḥğerāt viewed and usually became involved in their respective economic pursuits as individuals, it is misleading to consider this scenario in such discrete terms. Their strong kin ideology and family cohesiveness promoted cooperation, which served as the setting for individual activities. Although a young man might feel that his chances for economic independence lay in agriculture and hence move into this occupation, he usually represented the broadening economic base of his paternal household, particularly if his father was still alive. It was not uncommon, therefore, to see one son cultivating all of the family's lands while another kept a herd and yet others moved into industrial wage labor. While each of these would usually make his own productive and consumptive decisions independently, there were regular distributions of part of the crop, gifts from the herd, or a loan without interest between the father and his sons and among the sibling group.
3. In 1955 the Ḥğerāt numbered 1220 persons (Ashkenazi 1957:215–16). Of these, 244 (20.0%) were infants 1–5 years of age; 141 (11.6%) were aged 6–10 years (the age bracket when children began to help in household chores and herding); and 186 (15.2%) were 11–15 years old (the age cohort that entered the tribe's labor force). In other words, less than 30% of the tribe's membership were completely nonproductive consumers.
4. The need to be close to a bus route was a major incentive to settle in Maksūr, both for people from the Ẓahara and those from the Ḏmeydeh and the Mikmān. In the words of a person from the Mikmān who first moved to the outskirts of Shfar'am and then to Maksūr, "It took an hour

to get from the Mikmān to the road, an hour of dust in summer and mud in winter, so I moved to Shfar'am." The small settlement (some twelve Ḥğeri families in 1977 plus families from other tribes) on the eastern edge of Shfar'am grew, in fact, in response to the need to be near a bus.

5. Ben Porath, using unpublished CBS data, quotes a compounded annual average increase of 8.8% for the whole country and 8.1%, 7.7%, and 11.9% for the Northern, Haifa, and Central Districts respectively for the period 1950–1961 (1966:80, tb.). The compounded annual average increase derived from the Ḥğeri data is 13.3% for all marriages (i.e., intra- and inter-tribal and with *fellāḥīn*) on which *mahr* data was available (N = 72) and 13.2% for intra-Ḥğeri marriages (N = 53). In constant prices (1955 = 100) the increase was from an average of I£549 in 1950 to an average of I£2165 in 1961.
6. For example, the two mechanized earth removal companies in the Galilee that employed Ḥğeris were entered in this manner. In 1971 one member of the Ġadāyreh joined one of these companies through a non-Ḥğeri friend. Later he introduced four more individuals who introduced other Ḥğeris who eventually joined the other company, making it easier for other Ḥğeris to join it. By 1977 eleven Ḥğeris, two of whom were working for a similar company in Jerusalem, were involved in this well-paid profession (about I£5000.00 a month in 1977; cf. Isr. CBS Abs. 29:378–79).
7. Since Druze and Circassians also served in the IDA, a distinction must be made between tracking positions, which were usually attached to Jewish units, and the Minorities Brigade, which were predominantly manned by Druze and Circassians. The bedouin, who were involved with the former, generally served as hired civilian personnel. The Druze and Circassians, on the other hand, were conscripted to their military service the same way their Jewish counterparts were, served as a regular military unit, and were paid according to the same pay scales, which were much lower than those of career and civilian personnel.
8. Tracking is a profession composed of two closely interrelated skills: an inductive-deductive analytical approach, which emphasizes pattern recognition and acute visual sensitivity. Both skills were acquired among bedouin living in open country from infancy during their socialization process as part of the behaviors that were meaningful for a bedouin herdsman. Once these skills were mastered, adding new patterns, such as the tactics of terrorism, was relatively easy because the analytical framework for handling the pattern was already there.
9. As noted by Kressel, the adoption of the Arabic term *ra'īs* by Hebrew speakers in reference to the labor contractor during the 1960s bears witness to the rapid transition of "most of the agricultural cultivation activities . . . from Jewish to Arab hands" (1976:45).
10. Much like the erroneous Jewish sector's interpretation of Ḥğeri involvement with the IDF attributing it to Israel proving its "invincibility" in 1967, so is its understanding of the role of the *ra'īs*. As Ben Porath observes, the "Employment Service is trying . . . to deal with seasonal Arab labor and Arab women's labor and at the same time to abolish the institution of the *ra'īs*" (Ben Porath 1966:54).
11. The mechanization of agriculture was not a strictly economic issue. Rather, issues of honor played an important role in the process (see below). A man might have been poor enough to send his unmarried daughters to work—and yet own a tractor and other such labor-saving devices in order not to be dependent on his neighbor's goodwill, instead of soundly deploying his economic resources for future gain. This behavioral pattern suggests that the concept of honor is not monolithic or absolute but a gradation of relative states and nuances.
12. For a general discussion of the degree of control of economic activities and other aspects of life in the country exercised by Israel's Labor Party and the governmental bureaucracies, see Medding (1972:239–41 et passim), Aronoff (1977:132, 138–39 et passim), Evron et al. (1975), and Zohar (1974), to mention but a few.
13. While the Ḏiyabāt has a better showing percentage-wise, a case-by-case comparison seems more appropriate in this instance because, in reality, both pasture rental and security jobs are dealt with by case and not by lineage.
14. I have recorded only two cases of relatively early divisions of landed patrimony. In both cases there were only two brothers and both pairs were members of the 6th generation, which preceded the generation beginning to seek wage labor in the Jewish sector.

15. Most Jewish agricultural settlements in Israel were located on state lands (the JNF's, the ILA's, or the Custodian of Absentees' Property's). When an agricultural settlement was established, its members declared or actually signed a contract (depending on the type of the settlement) containing an article that stipulated that they manage and work the land in person and not rent it to others. Letting the land to others was, thus, a violation of their charter or, if signed, a breach of their contract with JNF or the state (cf. Kressel 1976:44).
16. In 1971 (a census year) the "non-Jew" agriculturalists cultivated 676,693 *dunam* of which 87.5% were field crops. Of these, 529,989 *dunam* (89.6% of the field crops or 78.3% of the grand total) were sown with "grains and pulses" (Isr. CBS 1973:4), 61.2% of which were wheat and 36.7% barley (Isr. CBS 1973:5).
17. *Ḍamān* (lit. "be responsible," "guaranty," etc.) among the Ḥğerāt referred to cash contract according to which the contractor bought the crop while still in the field ("on the plant"), harvested and marketed it, and pocketed all the proceeds. In this usage they differed somewhat from the Central Region where the term also referred to contracting a person to perform routine maintenance cultivation such as watering and weeding (cf. Kressel 1976:44), activities that among the Ḥğerāt fell under *šarikah* contracts. *Ḍamān* contracts were used both within the tribe (3 of the 30-*dunam* tobacco crop mentioned above were *ḍamān* from another tribesmember) as well as for marketing tribal-grown watermelons, and as completely entrepreneurial endeavors of harvesting and marketing crops grown by other Arab *fellāḥīn* or Jewish farmers. Generally speaking, however, the use of this type of contract was, as of 1977, rather limited.
18. In 1971 the average herd size of *baladi* cattle among "non-Jews" was 9.0 head and the median was in the 36–50 head herd size category (approximately 48 head). By comparison, among Jewish producers the average herd size was 50.5 head overall and 55.0 head for the "others" (growers not organized in settlements, i.e., companies) subcategory and the median was in the 201–300 head herd size cell at approximately 205 head per herd (Isr. CBS 1974a:65). Moreover, only 21 Jewish producers owned this breed whereas the majority of the beef herd (32.8 of 49.5 thousand head) was in other, higher yielding breeds (Isr. CBS 1974a:5).
19. Umm al-Zīnāt is located at the foothills of Mt. Carmel, about 22.5 km southeast of Haifa (see Map 1). The camp was established in 1961 when a Christian herd owner from Shfar'am rented some JNF pastureland and hired a Ḥğeri from the Masa'īd to herd his cattle there. Later the Ḥğeri was joined by a relative, followed by two small herd owners from the 'Afafṭeh in 1964 and 1966 respectively, and a large herd owner from the D'eyfeh in 1969. During the first half of the 1970s, several other tribesmen joined them and in January of 1977 the camp consisted of ten Ḥğeri tents (two D'eyfeh, two Ramlāt, three 'Afafṭeh, and two Masa'īd) and four tents from other tribes.
20. Fresh milk was sold either to small private cheese factories in the Galilee, which were not under as strict supervision by the local Rabbinical Councils as *Tnuva*, or through a Jewish herd owner who acted as a middleman for several large herd owners from the Ḥğerāt. This man collected the milk daily from their herds, as well as from others, and marketed it to *Tnuva* together with his own milk as if it were all derived from Jewish owned herds.
21. The Institute paid family allowance to each family with children according to a sliding scale determined by the number of children. The function of the allowance was to ensure the children's basic level of consumption. The allowance began in 1959 as "large Family Insurance" and was paid for each child past the third one (Isr. Laws 13:168–73, Amendment No. 4). In 1965, under the name of "Children's Pension," it was expanded to include all children of employees (Isr. Laws 19:215–23, Amendment No. 12) and later for those of the self-employed as well. In 1975 its title was changed to "Family Allowance" and its scope expanded to include all the children in Israel, regardless of their parents' employment or income level (Isr. Laws 29:189–98, Amendment No. 17).

– 8 –

Bīr al-Maksūr

Overview

The changes in the economy of the Ḥğerāt, described in Chapter 7, were intertwined with their increased commitment to sedentarization and the gradually accelerating development of Bīr al-Maksūr from the early 1960s to the present. In large measure, until 1966 the associated growth of the village corresponded to the loosening controls exercised by the MG and their assumption by the civilian governmental ministries. Thereafter, its development resulted from the combination of the government's bedouin sedentarization policy (see Appendix G) and the tribesmembers' response to the civil services and comfort offered by the village.

It has already been mentioned that the replacement of the MG by the civilian authorities was gradual and approximated the lifting of the restrictions of the Travel Permits starting in 1957. Nevertheless, throughout the period when it held control (that is, 1949–1966), the MG was entrusted with administrating the status quo and not with promoting change. Consequently, while some civilian involvement in local Arab affairs was always exercised, it was under the MG's constraining supervision and was kept minimal. With relaxing MG controls, especially after the beginning of the 1960s when the country's economic state ameliorated, the transition of authority gained momentum and with it the generation of change in local lifestyles and affairs, as each of the government's ministries was assuming and exercising its full powers under the law. Among these changes was the sedentarization of the northern bedouin as part of the regional development master plan, which directly affected the growth and development of tribal settlements.

As of 1977, Bīr al-Maksūr's development was far more advanced than that of either the Mikmān or the Ḏmeydeh. Several factors account for these differences. Succinctly, Bīr al-Maksūr was *the* planned tribal settlement, the largest village in terms of population, and the seat of its political power. The Mikmān, conversely, had a smaller population and was a quite dispersed spontaneous settlement, lacking a recognizable settlement core. It, therefore, was originally planned as a subdivision of Bīr al-Maksūr. Although by 1977 both places were connected to the regional water, electrical, and telephone networks and the Mikmān boasted a mosque, Bīr al-Maksūr had paved roads, a post office, a modern school, and a Mother and Child Clinic, which the former lacked. By contrast, the growth of the Ḏmeydeh had been arrested and its population was under covert pressures to move their residence to the Mikmān or to Maksūr. This pressure was expressed by the refusal to formally recognize the Ḏmeydeh as a settlement, a recognition that would entail its provision with civil services. Similarly, no construction permits were granted to settlement members, thereby forcing the younger people to build elsewhere. As a result, the Ḏmeydeans schooled in the Mikmān, and collected their mail and national insurance benefits in nearby Kafr Manda or I'billin, where they also received their mother-child care and public transportation linkage. Due to the lack of services and the declared position of the authorities regarding its future, its landless and younger members slowly deserted the Ḏmeydeh and moved to Maksūr, I'billin, and other places (except for the Mikmān, which was not much more developed). In appearance the Ḏmeydeh looked like other spontaneous bedouin settlements, namely, scattered houses with no recognizable center, and without electricity, running water, fenced yards, paved roads or paths, and the like, and was, thus, a relic of the pre-sedentarization policy era. Therefore, since Bīr al-Maksūr was the tribe's sedentarization vanguard and the most developed of the three, the following discussion centers on this settlement.

Until 1960 the lack of incentives to move to the hill of Ḥirbet al-Maksūr—whether because of the meager services offered by the settlement; the region's general slow economic development and the availability of salaried jobs; population pressure in the Ẓahara; or the lack of imposed, overt or covert, pressures to sedentarize—made the alternative of Maksūr incompatible with the traditional ties to the Ẓahara for most people. As a result, in 1961 the hamlet numbered 54 families (Golani 1961:9), using 3 tents and 88 structures (65 made of hewn stone, concrete, or cinder blocks; 22 of corrugated iron; and one of frame [Golani 1961:4] as part of the school). The houses among these structures were mostly low-ceilinged two-room structures very similar to those built in the Ẓahara (that is, the rooms arranged in a row and open to a common open, cast platform) that were strewn over the almost 1000-*dunam* hill.

However, the combination of the example set by Muḥammad al-Ḥsēn, the establishment of the Jewish settlement of Yodfāt[1] on the Ẓahara's western edge, population increase in that place, the gradual opening of the Jewish industrial sector to Arab labor, and the presence of some relatives or friends in the hamlet increased the trickle of settlers after 1960. By the abrogation of the MG in 1966, over a hundred houses and some tents stood on the hill.

Since Bīr al-Maksūr was a well-defined site, half private tribal property and only half state lands, and was already in the process of development, the authorities began planning for their part of the hill (this was among the first bedouin sites to be planned). To lend teeth to the project, the Ministry of the Interior froze the granting of construction permits until the planning stage of both zones (state and private) were completed, and threatened to follow the letter of the law in cases of illegal house construction (consequently, two houses were torn down).[2] Concurrently, in 1966, the authorities convinced Muḥammad al-Ḥsēn of the need to parcel the private land section so that no houses would be built on future road sites and so that some areas would be designated for public use. The *muḫtār* consequently convened the tribesmen and convinced them to hire an architect from Nazareth—a former government employee of the regional planning operation—to provide a master plan for the private lands. By the beginning of 1967 the plans for both zones were approved and the Ministry of the Interior resumed the issue of construction permits (see Figure 3).

To make the settlement process more attractive, the ILA extended the duration of the residential land rental contracts in the village to 99 years with a right of renewal. Save for their duration clause, these contracts were identical to those signed by Jews and other non-bedouin for 49 years. The 50-year difference was a concession by the state (which does not sell any of its lands) to the different orientation and self-assurance of Jews and Arabs in the country and was one of the inducements offered to sedentarize the bedouin in general. In short, whereas a Jew was assured of his right of renewal so long as the state remains Israel and was not inclined to think that any of his descendants would live in the same house, the local Arab was less assured of the continual commitment of any government and was more inclined to build and think of his house as the homestead of his descendants. A 99-year contract thus meant that after his death and while the contract was still in force one of his sons would reside in the house without possible eviction and when the contract expired the heir would have an easier time renewing it.

Another ILA incentive to render settling in the village more attractive to landowners in the Ẓahara was the land exchange value. This incentive made land exchanges more advantageous for the bedouin than for the rest of the population. While the general exchange rate was established according to current values of the respective land plots, exchanges with bedouin were usually done on a *dunam* per *dunam* basis irrespective of the specific values of the two plots.

Even though the government played a prominent role in making Bīr al-Maksūr attractive for settlement, the project would not have succeeded nor the policy have had much effect without its legitimization by—that is, the consent of—the tribesmembers themselves. For if a bedouin tribe decided to outwait the government, expecting a better deal for its land or usufruct rights, its members easily located the fissures between different agencies that constituted the Northern Supreme Bedouin Committee (NSBC), and by playing one against its bureaucratic or political rivals, bided their time leisurely. For example, as of July 1977, most of the *'arab* al-Sawā'ed had refused to move to the newly prepared planned settlement of Naḥal Tzalmon with its roads, running water, and school building, arguing that the price of house plots was too high. In response the authorities reduced plot price but the tribesmembers still refused to move in and kept building illegally anywhere but in the parceled area. Then, before the 1977 elections, a subgroup of that tribe, which resided some 400 m from the planned settlement, received an unofficial recognition as a "settlement" (that is, promised infrastructure, and so on) from the district commissioner of the Ministry of the Interior and a member of the NSBC in return for their voting for his political party during the elections.

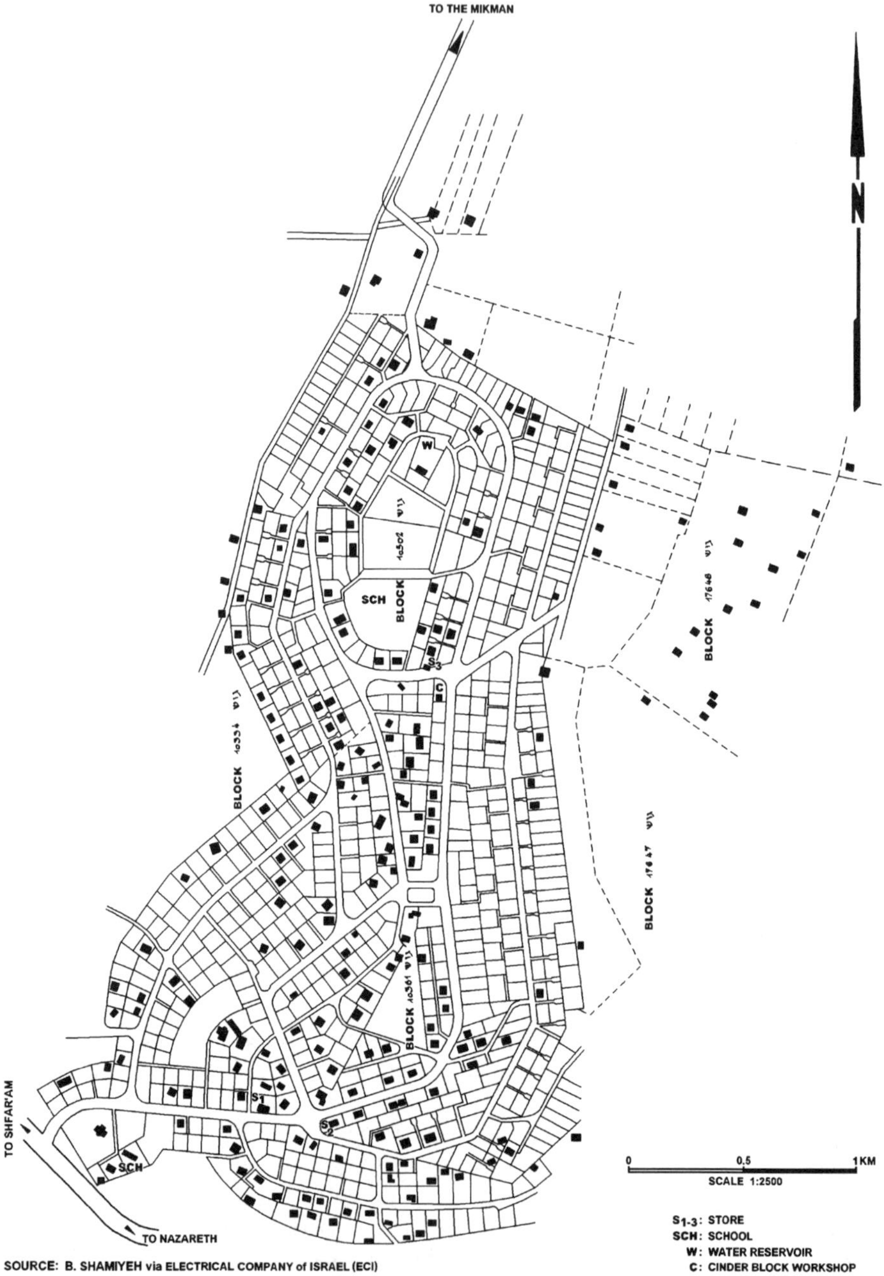

Figure 3a. The master plan of Bīr al-Maksūr.

Figure 3b. Aerial view of Bīr al-Maksūr in 1975.

Figure 3c. Bīr al-Maksūr in 1976.

The migration of the Ḥğerāt to Bīr al-Maksūr was thus a measure of the *muḫtār*'s influence and his acumen in guiding their settlement there. More specifically: first, by not forcing the tribesmembers, he avoided provoking antagonism to the project. Second, by convincing his own sublineage to relocate first, he transferred much of the wealth and the political center of the tribe to Maksūr. Third, by furnishing the village with services he provided the necessary attractions to bring those who did not need to settle there. Once this trend was set in motion it was just a question of time before the more stubborn individuals would begin to feel somewhat left out of the tribe's sociopolitical life, and as herding became increasingly restrictive, would make plans to join the village.

The Development of Bīr al-Maksūr

Following the approval of the master plan, a Water Co-Operative Society was formed to contract *Mekorot* (the National Water Company) to connect the new village to its regional water network, and in March 1971 the village was connected. Establishing the Water Co-Operative Society was in line with the practice of the authorities to promote cooperative societies for practically any activity requiring concerted public action by a settlement's constituting lineages, both *fellāḥīn* and bedouin. Such societies were advantageous from the state's point of view. First, they were functionally attractive because they transcended the inherent interfamilial factionalism and saved the administration both time and expenses, ensuring the collection of fees, shares, and so on, while getting the job done. Second, they were ideologically attractive because they were part of local self-government, which was not only a part of the model of a socialistic state, but since kin-organized villages were predominately Arab, such self-government was good for the administration's image vis-à-vis world opinion. From the tribe's point of view, co-op societies were attractive because they were commensurable with the mode and means of the traditional decision making processes, while getting the service the settlement wanted more cheaply than it could get on the open market (due to governmental grants and subsidies).

Notwithstanding these advantages, such societies had legal identities. That is, they were founded under and bound by the rules and laws pertaining to non-profit organizations and could be investigated by the Bureau of the State Comptroller. They thus provided the younger generations with some legal recourse to limit the freedom of the leaders who traditionally tended to concentrate the political power inherent in decision making in their hands. In fact, due to these bureaucratic aspects, the elders often tended to have younger (that is, middle-aged) trusted lineage members represent them on co-operative governing bodies. (For example, the 9-member executive committee of the Water Co-Op Society of the Ḥğerāt had a mean age of 41.2 years [range 31–47; median and mode 43 years; membership: 4 Ġad., 3 Ṣawl., 1 Ḏiyabāt, 1 Samrāt] and only one of its members had real power.) Moreover, the younger the generation, the better educated it was and the more disgruntled its members became because they felt disenfranchised of the status to which they felt entitled by their education. Consequently, although these societies cleaved vertically along lineage lines, the growing discontent of the youth bridged these lineage boundaries and created horizontal age-based alliances of the younger age brackets against the older ones. For example, on December 18, 1976, the village's water supply was cut off due to unpaid bills totaling some I£47,000. On the 22nd, a group of 11 young men (5 of whom I recognized: mean age 27.8; range 22–32; median 28.0; membership: 2 Ġad., 2 Ṭa'awāneh, 1 D'eyfeh) discussed a way to mobilize the youth against the Water Co-Op executive committee. On January 5, 1977, they mailed a formal complaint to the Registrar of Co-Operative Societies at the Ministry of Agriculture in Jerusalem and to the Supervisory Board of Co-Operative Societies of the *Histadrut* in Tel Aviv (see Appendix H). Of the 8 signatories to the complaint, I identified 7, of whom 3 were present at the original meeting (the mean age of these 7 was 28.3 years; range 24–32; median 28.0; membership: 4 Ġad., 2 D'eyfeh, 1 Ṣawl.).

In other words, although functionally cooperative societies were an attractive solution for both the administration and the community, when viewed against a continuous timescale they promoted instability in the community by furthering the realignment of interests according to criteria other than kinship. In this respect cooperation added to the advantages derived by the state because it promoted dissolution of the tribe's politically competitive organization.

Next in the development of the village the main road site was prepared and the village began to take on the image of a spacious Western-style rural settlement. These improvements added weight to the *muḫtār*'s words and by 1968 his own sublineage, who resided in hewn stone houses and owned land in the Ẓahara, began to negotiate with the ILA to exchange their properties for land in and near Maksūr. Their transfer to the village over the next two years—and especially that of Ḥsēn al-Ḏiyab, their patriarch (and following Mūsā al-Ḏiyab's death on 12/8/1960, the tribe's most prominent elder)—shifted the Ġadāyreh's geographical locus of power to Bīr al-Maksūr, boosting the village's attractiveness and its residents' claim for recognition. More significantly, with Ḥsēn al-Ḏiyab's arrival, the village residents included the elders of the Ġadāyreh, Samrāt, Ṭa'awāneh, Masa'īd, and Sama'neh. Thereafter, individual decisions about moving to the settlement no longer revolved about "whether to move" but about "when to move," and increasing numbers of Ḥğeris settled in the village each year. Thus, by 1972 there were 137 households in Bīr al-Maksūr (Isr. CBS 1974b:12–13) and by 1977 there were 213 households.

The Ḥğerāt's growing commitment to settling in Maksūr (whose population in 1977 numbered almost half of the tribe's total population and represented all of its sublineages) and the prominence of their *muḫtār* endowed the village with a favored status after the consolidation of the government's sedentarization policy, when more resources became available for the development of planned bedouin settlements. Thus, the development of Maksūr provides yet another insight into the interaction between Western state administration and traditional society and politics. As was remarked by a number of the NSBC (the committee in charge of the bedouin sedentarization in the north), it would have been more rewarding from the state's point of view to funnel the necessary funds and complete the development of Maksūr—namely, roads, core civic buildings, phase II of the school, and so on—as fast as possible by diverting one year's budget for the project. In this way the administration could use the village both as a showcase for foreign visitors, donors, critics, and so on, and to entice more recalcitrant bedouin tribes to settle in planned settlements.

The *muḫtār* repeatedly argued successfully against such a move on the grounds that it would not be fair to the other tribes, who would be envious. It seems, however, that fairness was only half of the argument. That is, it would be politically unwise to promote envy if the *muḫtār* strived to represent all the Galilean bedouin. In other words, while the *muḫtār* had to—and did—attract financial support to satisfy his own tribesmembers, he was very careful to slow the rate to below that desired by the administration. Such an approach served him in two ways: it maintained the dependence of village members on his connections with the administration, and it avoided antagonizing other local tribes while increasing their dependence on him and promoting his status as a regional patron.

Even with the *muḫtār* slowing down the process, the modifications in the village's appearance accumulated rapidly after 1972. Thus, in April 1973, the village post office branch opened with a 21-year-old member of the Ramlāt as postmaster. In 1974 a Mother and Child Clinic opened, replacing the mobile clinic that visited the village monthly to vaccinate (against polio, diphtheria, tetanus, variola, tuberculosis, and the like) babies and children to age six. The clinic was open five days a week and employed a full-time nurse and a physician who visited it three days a week. Its primary function was to provide maternal care through post-delivery for mothers and their babies; its secondary task was to vaccinate village children through primary school age. Unobtrusively it also provided birth control information and referral to the regional birth control clinic in Acre as part of the family planning campaign undertaken by the Ministry of Health.

The year 1975 saw the beginning of a new structure for a 12- (phase I) to 20- (phase II) classroom modern school building to replace the old structures and the assortment of rooms rented around the village once the original five rooms were insufficient to handle the growing student body. Also in 1975 the Electricity Co-Operative Society was established to contract the Israel Electric Corporation (IEC) to connect Maksūr to its national grid. By mid-1977 both these projects were completed and Maksūr had all the basic civic services—that is, running water, electricity, telephone, school, clinic, and paved main and secondary (in the state's lands) roads including a paved connecting road to the Mikmān. In October of 1976, after the death of a prominent tribesmember, the village residents began talking about needing a mosque and collected money for the project, for which the ILA provided a land plot in 1977. During that year a soccer/football field was also added to the village scene, providing the youth with an athletic outlet.

Although any of these public projects might have been initiated practically by anyone—for example, a governmental ministry (the clinic), the *muḫtār* (irrigation water for the village's agriculturalists), the elders (the mosque), or the youth (the soccer field)—as of 1977 its successful realization depended on the *muḫtār*'s willingness to see it through. First, most state agencies preferred to channel the projects through him because they trusted his ability to neutralize any opposition, should it arise, and to mobilize village support for the project. Second, he himself tried to monopolize the channels between the authorities and the tribe, making himself indispensable for any interaction between the two. Third, no one in the tribe knew as well as he the administration's labyrinthine structure and where financial support in grants, matching funds, subsidies, and so on could be tapped. Consequently, the elders preferred to approach the authorities through him both because he buffered them from the unknown world of the government and because without his support little, if anything, would be accomplished. Similarly, while each project added to his prestige, it also added to the prestige of tribe as a whole because the two were closely tied. The youth, on the other hand, had to go through him because they lacked knowledge of how the government worked and lacked connections with the right loci of power, and because the administration refused to deal with them as representatives of the village.

Private Enterprise in the Village

The rapid development of the infrastructure of Bīr al-Maksūr and its provision with social services were closely followed by local enterprise. Until 1973 the village was served by a single grocery store, which carried an assortment of products from sweets and dry foods to various household goods and clothing (see Appendix D for its 1975 inventory). The store, however, remained small and did not expand to cater to the village's growing population because village members usually did their shopping in nearby Shfarʿam or Nazareth where there was more variety, bulk purchases were cheaper, and other services such as health care were available. The store owner himself considered the store a secondary economic resource and left its management to his wife and elder daughters while he rented and cultivated land from another tribesmember.

In 1973 a similar store opened some 200 meters up the road from the first (see Figure 3a), similarly managed by the wife while the husband dealt with agriculture. By the end of 1975 four such stores were open, three of which were within a 100-meter radius on the south side of the hill. In 1975, the chronologically second store was best stocked among the four, followed by its chronological senior. The third store opened in 1974 on the hill's saddle, catering for those living on the saddle and the northern side of the hill. It was a solitary structure rather than the ground floor of a house, and the smallest in terms of space, but it was third in the amount and variety of its stock. The fourth was opened for an elderly woman by her son, in whose house she lived. This store was the least stocked (see Appendix E for a comparison between the inventories of the second and fourth stores). All four stores were managed by women and/or children of their male owners and were supplementary income sources. Similarly all had a slow turnover of stock as most families did their major food and clothing shopping away from the village.

Concurrently, from the beginning of the 1970s itinerant fresh produce merchants and dry goods peddlers from the West Bank slowly began to incorporate the Arab villages in Israel within their circles of wandering, selling their wares cheaper than Israeli produced goods and services. This form of trade had disappeared from the Arab sector after 1949 due to the restrictions on movement and because an efficient public transportation network connected the villages with urban commercial centers. After the tensions of the 1967 War had subsided, West Bank small tradesmen who still practiced peddlery were looking for other markets to replace the Jordanian one, which had been closed by the war. With no native competition they found their welcome in Israeli Arab villages, both for their cheaper wares and for the stories and information they carried with their stock. Similarly, small agriculturalists who could not dispose of their surplus crops in the West Bank or through the 'Abdāllah Bridge to Jordan found open markets for their cheaper vegetables for two related reasons. First, the scarcity of arable land caused a greater proportion of the expanding village population to shift to non-agricultural employment, thus becoming a market for West Bank agricultural produce. Second, most of those who remained in agriculture became specialized in cash crops and developed market orientation, which made it more attractive to sell their crops in the Jewish market and buy cheaper West Bank produce for themselves than to use their available land for crops for home consumption.

The two types of peddlers could be distinguished on three major axes: their wares (fresh produce vs. dry goods), their mode of transportation (pickup van or truck vs. pedestrian), and number (2–3 men vs. a single individual). These combined characteristics determined their mode of interaction on the Israeli side of the border. Due to their great mobility, fresh produce merchants returned to the West Bank every night, and due to their number, did not need to be sociable outside their group. Hence, they rarely developed a social network in the villages. The pedestrian peddlers, by contrast, might spend twenty days or more on the road before returning home to rest and restock. They, thus, slept at hospitable households where they spent social evenings, thereby developing a network of acquaintances over time.

During my stay in Bīr al-Maksūr I could not find any regularity in individual visits of either type, or coordination of schedules between tradesmen of similar wares. Most conspicuous in this regard were the fresh produce merchants, two to three groups of whom might come in one day, and then none appearing for a week or two. Dry goods peddlers did not compete as intensely because they moved about more slowly and were usually quite specialized in their wares (for example, cloth, clothes, brass, notions). A few of them seemed to be more regular in the frequency of their visits.

Finally, in 1974 a one-man cinder block manufacturing operation began catering to some of the villagers' building needs. A few other services such as construction and some metal work were provided by individual village members as supplementary income to their main jobs outside the village.

The opening of the new school building in the fall of 1976 inspired two of its neighbors to open stands on both sides of the schoolyard and sell *falāfel* (chickpea patties) to the youngsters. With the availability of electricity, a month later, another neighbor of the school bought two large refrigerators, which he stocked with soft drinks for sale. Next, a new grocery store opened in the northwest quadrant of the village, equipped with a large commercial refrigerator and dealing with foodstuffs only. In March of 1977, the brother of that store owner opened a stationary/textbook store next door, which he, being an insurance sub-agent, also used as his base for insurance operations. This person (born 1953) was involved at the time in building his own house, the second floor of which he said he rented out to *Kupāt Ḥolim* (the *Histadrut*'s HMO) as clinic space for which he would serve as branch secretary. He planned to live in the third level and open a larger stationary/bookstore on the ground level.[3]

Similarly, in November 1976, the postmaster completed the first level of his house, which he divided into three stores: (1) the post office; (2) his own insurance sub-agency, working for a certified agent from Nazareth; and (3) reserved for his elder brother who was a labor contractor contemplating a diversification of his activities.

When the southern half of the village was provided with electricity, three individuals installed commercial (380 volts) rather than residential (220 volts) current in their houses. One planned to open a mechanic/metal shop; the second was inconclusive as to what type of a operation he wanted to establish; while the third, an animal merchant, opened a butcher shop. Shortly thereafter, a young son of the owner of the second grocery store invested in a large commercial refrigerator, stocked it with beer and soft drinks among other perishable items, added two folding card tables for comfortable drinking, and opened the first beer-room in the village. Within a month he expanded to an adjacent room, which became the popular meeting place for adolescents and young adults. His idea that the clientèle would not be satisfied with a single can of beer was proven right when occasionally they drank the place dry. More importantly, the place provided the village youth with a social center in a period of growing estrangement between the lifestyles of the elder and younger generations.

Although electricity and the entrepreneurial younger generations did much to increase and diversify the volume of commerce and services provided in the village, the Ḥğerāt still often shopped for goods and services far away from the village. This is hardly surprising since travel by privately owned vehicles, buses, or taxis was easy and popular, thus leaving availability, variety, and price as the determining factors in the decision where to shop. Most often they went to Nazareth (13 km southeast) with its large marketplace, hospitals, regional administrative offices, and other services. Shfar'am, 6 km to the northwest, was a secondary center, providing the medical services of *Kupāt Ḥolim*, various stores, and one bank. For larger single investments or specialized medical services, they would travel to Jenin in the West Bank, Jerusalem, Haifa, or wherever else they could find what they were looking for.

Maksurean Population Dynamics

Throughout this period the physical growth of Bīr al-Maksūr was intimately interwoven with the increase in its population size—both natural and through settlement. The behavior of these two modes of population accretion shifted over time and the difference between and within them influenced the structure of the village's population and some of its social dynamics between 1961 (when the survey of the village for planning purposes was conducted),[4] 1972 (the last year before the consolidation of the bedouin sedentarization program, the beginning of the rapid development of the village's infrastructure, and its provision with social services), and 1977 (when immigration and settlement were in full swing) (see Table 18).

The most prominent characteristic of Bīr al-Maksūr's population was its youthfulness (see Figure 4), even when compared with the rest of the bedouin or the Moslem populations in Israel. Nonetheless, as Table 18 suggests, this trait fluctuated between 1961 and 1977, first declining between 1961[5] and 1972 and then moderately rising during the remainder of the period.[6] The high rate of natural increase in this instance was caused by two factors. First was the increasing rate of infant survivorship, which resulted from the expanding practice of prenatal care, hospital births, better medical attention during infancy and childhood, and the reduced risk-laden lifestyle in the village. There was also a reduction in birth-spacing (to 18–24 months) due to better diet, lighter female workloads, earlier weaning of babies, and so on. Of these factors the use of hospitals for deliveries was the only complete innovation, and not a direct consequence of sedentarization and the growing involvement in wage labor. In fact, the practice began as medical care for difficult births, which required professional medical expertise. The first hospital birth involving a Ḥğeri family took place on February 23, 1955, in a Nazarene hospital, and was the result of a needed cesarean section. Within the next two years the same woman delivered two more sons by this method. Her hospital experience involved a few days of rest and the privileged status of being sick. The advantages of the new experience were quickly perceived by the hamlet's women but their realization was delayed by the lack of easy transportation to the hospitals and their husbands' reluctance to increase expense and energy where these were not necessary before. By the beginning of the 1960s, however, the practice began to spread in Bīr al-Maksūr, and as more families moved to the village it accelerated. By the close of that decade hospital deliveries became the norm even in the herding camps.

The second reason for the village population's youthfulness in the 1960s was the settlement of predominately young families who came to be close to the Nazareth-Shfar'am road and the wage labor market in the Bay of Haifa or who simply followed their *muḫtār*'s advice. With the arrival of increasingly older families (as they decided to abandon herding and settle in the village), the average age of the population reversed and began to rise after 1972. Furthermore, the expanding adoption of birth control measures as young and lower middle-age couples tried to limit their family size[7] emphasized the population's rising average age as the lower age bracket failed to replenish at the necessary rate to maintain the 1972 status quo, as is suggested by the increase of the median age at a faster rate than the average age.

Table 18. The population of Bīr al-Maksūr by age and sex in 1961, 1972, and 1977.

		Bīr al-Maksūr															Comparative Median Ages				
		Total		0–14 yrs		15–29 yrs		30–44 yrs		45–65 yrs		65+ yrs		Ave. Age	Med. Age	Ḥğerāt	Bedouin			Moslems
		N	%	N	%	N	%	N	%	N	%	N	%				North	South	Both	
April 1961[a]	male	186	54.2	98	52.7	46	24.7	20	10.8	18	9.7	4	2.2	19	13.9	14.1				
	female[b]	157	45.8	72	45.9	39	24.8	26	16.6	16	10.2	4	2.5	21.8	16.8	15.8				
	total	*343*	*100*	*170*	*49.6*	*85*	*24.8*	*46*	*13.4*	*34*	*9.9*	*8*	*2.3*	*20.3*	*15.2*	*15.0*[c]			*15.9*[d]	*15.6*[e]
May 1972[f]	male	437	50.3	238	54.5	109	24.9	55	12.6	26	5.9	9	2.1	17.6	13.2		12.6	12.2	12.3	13.7
	female	432	49.7	254	58.8	101	23.9	47	10.9	24	5.6	6	1.4	16.2	9.9		13.6	13.2	13.4	14.2
	total	*869*	*100*	*492*	*56.6*	*210*	*24.2*	*102*	*11.7*	*50*	*5.8*	*15*	*1.7*	*16.9*	*11.4*		*13.1*[g]	*12.7*[g]	*12.8*[g]	*13.9*[h]
April 1977[i]	male	763	50.2	389	51.0	208	27.3	111	14.7	38	5.0	17	2.2	18.4	14.6	16.4				
	female	758	49.8	432	57.0	170	22.4	95	12.5	42	5.5	19	2.5	17.9	12.9	15.6				
	total	*1521*[j]	*100*	*821*	*54.0*	*378*	*24.9*	*206*	*13.5*	*80*	*5.3*	*36*	*2.4*	*18.1*	*13.7*	*16*				

[a] Golani 1961:5.
[b] The low count of females seems to be a result of the procedure of data collection rather than of Ḥğeri sex ratio.
[c] Calculated from Isr. CBS 1963b:164–65.
[d] Isr. CBS 1964:22.
[e] Isr. CBS 1964:6.
[f] Isr. CBS 1976:16–17.
[g] Isr. CBS 1975:112–15.
[h] Isr. CBS 1975:236–37.
[i] Personal data.
[j] The total number should include an additional 17 males and 18 females for whom no birth data were available.

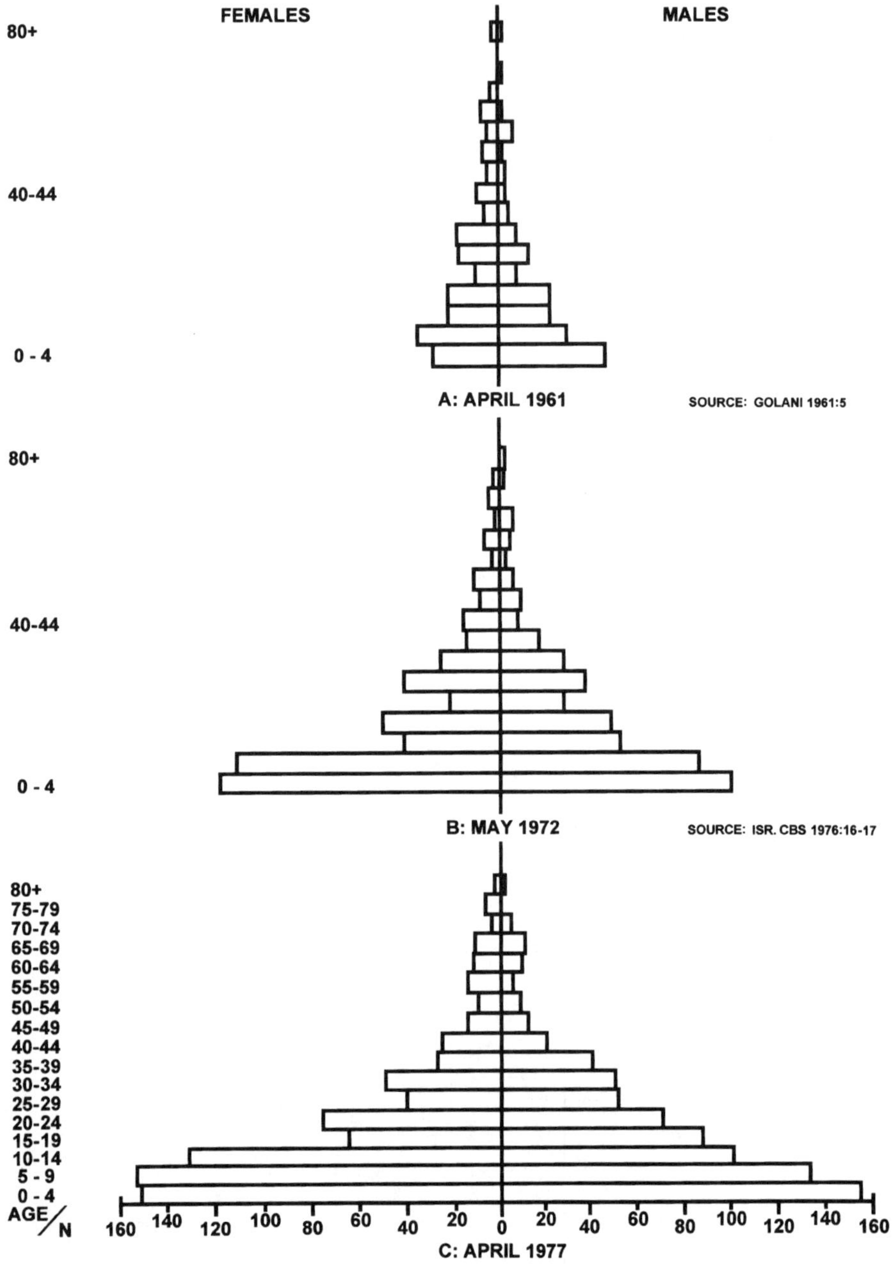

Figure 4. The population structure of Bīr al-Maksūr.

Family planning information was available to Ḥğeri husbands predominately through peer network or their wives, who usually got it in the village's Mother and Child Clinic. The clinic employed "positive suggestion" (such as more time with individual children, easier economic burden as the demands of raising children increased, more time for oneself and one's spouse) to convince women of the need for birth control. Other sources of information and influence were provided by the regional radio and television networks as far south as Egypt. These provided both direct information and propaganda on the need for, and advantages of, smaller families, and indirect suggestion through models of small families in other features such as movies.

As of 1977 the predominant birth control method was to tie the wife's oviducts; this operation was provided by a free clinic of the Ministry of Health in Acre, by private physicians, and by the hospitals in Nazareth. Interestingly, very few Ḥğeris used the ministry's free services because the clinic was visible whereas private physicians or hospitals were not. Not surprisingly, none of these agencies would provide its services without the husband's permission.

Several Ḥğeri husbands remarked that in general the men were more open to family planning than their wives because they were more aware of the economic burdens imposed on a large family when the future of the children was considered, whereas their wives worried that later in life their husbands might want more children and would take second wives. The younger women with whom I discussed the matter, however, were aware of the economic aspect of having children and were more confident about their marriages, and thus usually remarked that they would be satisfied with two to three children in whom they would invest more time individually, keep well dressed, and provide with a good education.

Although the data in the 0–14 years age bracket column (Table 18) suggest that the Ḥğeris of Bīr al-Maksūr gave birth to more females than males at a rate of 4.3% in 1972 and 6% in 1977, the conclusiveness of such an observation of sexual disparity is unclear. Not only is the 1977 overall sex-ratio of the Ḥğerāt as a whole in practical parity (763 males to 758 females), but when the Maksurean 0–14 years age group is broken down to its three constituting age brackets (0–4, 5–9, and 10–14), the male to female ratios are 155:152, 133:153, and 101:127 respectively (see Appendix F). Of these the most accurate ratio figures are those of the first age bracket because all of its members were born in hospitals and were registered immediately by both the hospital bureaucracy and their parents (in order to increase the household's National Insurance family allowance).

The reversal of the sex ratio in the following age brackets in Table 18 points to the scarcity of marriageable females in especially the 15–29 years age group, thus shifting from a demographic observation to a social problem. This sex-ratio turnabout seems to be the result of the earlier marriage age of females in comparison to males, combined with the greater attractiveness of Ḥğeri females raised in Maksūr (thus having some education) to Ḥğeri males from outlying settlements and camps as well as for members of other tribes. The young men of the village met this shortage either by invoking the FBS-right and claiming their female relatives[8] or by looking for a wife outside the Ḥğerāt, altering the more traditional, political, and kin orientation of marriage in favor of more personalized and private motives. If, incidentally, they chose to marry a relative, they often had to wait for her to mature and/or complete her schooling, thus increasing the disparity between the marriage age of their respective sexes even further, an increase that would help perpetuate the shortage of marriageable females for the next generation as well. Looking for a wife in the surrounding villages or towns, on the other hand, had been greatly facilitated by sedentarization because the special skills formerly needed by a Ḥğeri herdswoman were no longer required for most village wives, whose tasks centered about the home. Similarly, education that made Maksurean females more attractive to the less educated Ḥğeri males made townswomen, who were more accomplished than rural females in this regard, more attractive to Maksurean males. Thus, the emphasis shifted from economic specialization of female roles to those female characteristics of Arab women in Israel in general. Politically such marriages were facilitated by the need for more extensive extra-tribal economic-political networks as workplaces and political involvement of the tribe extended beyond its boundaries.

Nonetheless, these two strategies, especially the second one, were altering the more traditional, political, and kin orientation of marriage in favor of more personalized and private motives. The young village men were aware of the shortage and in more than one case argued away their parents saying that they could not get married because there were no suitable Ḥğeri women available. In this way they gained relative freedom and some time to play around instead of establishing a household. Later they would tell the parents that they were tired of waiting and that they loved "X" in Shfar'am or Nazareth. By then the parents were usually anxious to have their son married because his bachelorhood was a bad social stigma ("What? Can't they marry their son? Why?!!?") and often gave their consent. In this manner the son exercised more freedom in the choice of his spouse than ever before.

Finally, a new trend that developed after 1972 was the reversal in the population's sex ratio in favor of females 45 years and older, as the 1977 entries in Table 18 show. This trend indicates an increase in the death rate of males of comparative age. It can only be suggested that this may be due to an increase in the incidence of death caused by heart disease and hypertension as a result of sedentarization combined with the amplification of their traditional diet. The impact of sedentarization on Ḥğeri health suggested by the data is but an educated guess because very few statistics about causes of death among the Ḥğerāt are reliable. Although a cause of death was always cited, the physician issuing the legally required death certificate often did not see the corpse before signing and relied on information provided for him by the person applying for the document. The Ḥğerāt, for their part, had only one term for adult invisible (that is, unexplainable by traditional methods) cause of death—*sakto galbiyeh* (~heart attack). Consequently, if a sudden death was not violent it was invariably classified as a heart attack whether it was or not.

The Ḥğerāt, in fact, seemed to be prone to congenital heart diseases and at least one family whose parents were patrilineal cross-cousins lost six out of twelve children before age 14 due to heart attacks. Other less dramatic cases were also brought to my attention. Increased male death in the older age brackets, however, was a new phenomenon and seemed to result from a combination of their more intense and intensive social interaction that characterized the more confined area of the village, their traditional diet that included much oil and animal fats, and their increasingly sedentary way of life that did not provide enough exercise. The mismatch was all the more severe as the more expensive olive oil was replaced by cheaper processed hydrogenated oil and they consumed more animal fats as their standard of living rose and meat became more available. Similarly, the wedding season that had been confined to late spring/early summer, enabling the people to lose the excess fat they gained in the feasts as summer wore on, had been extended from early spring to fairly late autumn because the tribesmembers no longer relied on nature's bounty to finance the feasts. In addition, as their diet became richer and food more plentiful than ever before, motor vehicles became the popular means of transportation even when the distance in question was 300–500 m and the occasion was the common social evening. Although as of 1977 the impacts of these lifestyle changes and demographic trend on the Ḥğeri social organization were not obvious, their continuation and intensification could be expected to add to the mounting pressures on the traditional Ḥğeri organization and increase its instability.

At least two major types of such pressures could be expected. First was the possible development of a power vacuum because during middle age, individuals began to accumulate the traditional type of political power and became involved in the tribe's politics. If the number of middle-aged males decreased, the resulting vacuum could transform the advance of individuals in the tribal political hierarchy from a gradual one to an uneven one. This might cause a polarization of the hierarchy as younger and more action-oriented men faced older and more strategy-oriented elders without sufficient mediation by the middle-aged. This pressure had already been aggravated by the development of new sources of political power that lay outside the community and that took little or no account of the age component in the traditional power structure.

The second type of pressure on the traditional Ḥğeri cultural system was the continual increase in the number of widows in a social setting that was no longer geared to deal with such a pressure. The old customs of levirate and widow inheritance were no longer practiced because levirate by a younger single brother of the deceased (if one was available) was shunned by the youth who had his own aspirations, and because widow inheritance by married brothers, like all polygamous unions, was prohibited by state laws. Other possible remarriages were similarly unrealistic because by tradition the widow would lose her children to her husband's kinsmen, thus giving up the major emotional and social support in old age that these children would provide. The problem, incidentally, would not be an economic one because widows remained the managers of their late husbands' estates in the name of their children and received governmental widow allowance, life insurance benefits, and help from relatives. If, however, there were a significant increase in their number, and especially if a major proportion of this population was in the middle of their reproductive life (as they tended to be), such a situation could be expected—when combined with education, birth control, and exposure to models of other lifestyles—to increase the pressure on the alteration of the sexual mores (and thus inter-sexual dynamics) of the tribe. This pressure was already mounting in the 15–20 years age bracket.

Table 19. Comparative distribution of Maksurean family size, 1961 and 1977.*

		Total	Persons per Family: 1	2	3	4	5	6	7	8	9	10	11	12	13+	Ave.	Med.
1961	N	54		2	7	4	6	9	12	4	2	7		1			
	%	100.0		3.7	13.0	7.4	11.1	16.7	22.2	7.4	3.7	13.0		1.9		6.4	6.9
1977	N	239		27	20	26	29	25	21	26	23	22	8	6	6		
	%	100.0		11.3	8.4	10.9	12.1	10.5	8.8	10.9	9.6	9.2	3.3	2.5	2.5	6.5	6.7

(Sources: 1961: Golani 1961:10; 1977: personal notes)

*Unfortunately, the CBS 1972 census data do not include information on family sizes because they were collected on the basis of households. Consequently, it is impossible here to break down the processes involved into the two periods that were argued to illuminate the development of the village.

The antagonistic effects of the sources of Maksurean population growth—natural increase versus settlement—are apparent not only in its aggregate characteristics of average age and sex ratio but also in the demographic characteristics of the village's families. To wit, the influx of larger families who came to settle reinforced the older hence larger families of the village and together they balanced the growing number of the younger and smaller families to maintain the 1961 average family size of 6.4 persons per family (P/F) with little change in 1977 (6.5 P/F), although a reduction in this ratio would be expected (see Table 19). Nevertheless, the increase in the number of younger families, reflected in the shift of the mode of the frequency distribution of Maksurean family sizes from 7.0 P/F in 1961 to 5.0 P/F in 1977, is also evident in their balancing influence on the general shape of that distribution as well (see Figure 5). In other words, while the difference between the 1961 mean and median (6.4 and 6.9 P/F respectively) was on the order of 0.5 P/F, thus indicating a greater frequency of large families than might be expected (i.e., negative skew), the 1977 value of the difference was only 0.2 P/F (6.5 and 6.7 P/F respectively), indicating a reduction in the degree of skew and a pull toward symmetry or normal distribution of family sizes as a result of the more rapid increase in the number of smaller families.

The increase in the number of younger families, however, intensified a social strain that was expressed in the growing discrepancy between the traditional ideal of establishing a newly formed nuclear family in a private residence and the reality of house construction costs. While a shortage in houses was usually met by a son's family co-residing with his parents, the resulting fluctuations in household size (that is, all

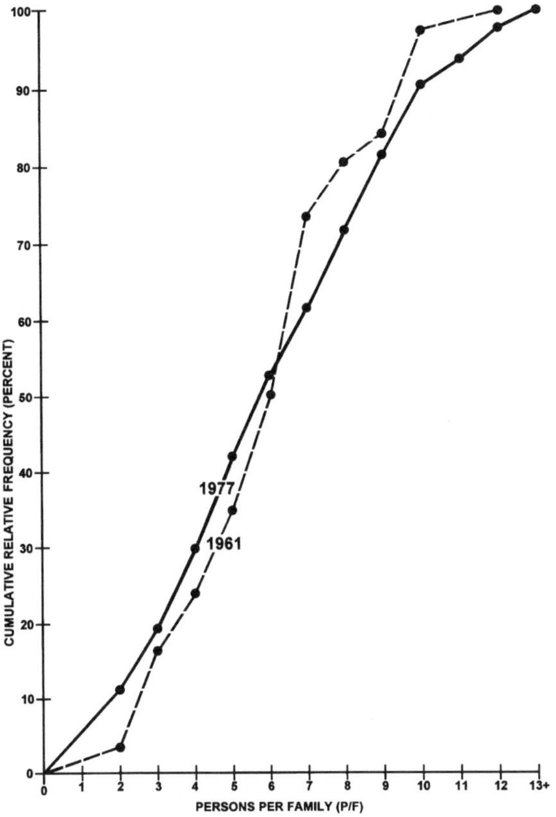

Figure 5. Frequency distribution of family sizes (1961 and 1977).

the individuals who reside in one house and use a single kitchen) describe the physical growth of the village itself. This view is predicated on the assumption that houses serve as living spaces for humans and are, therefore, meaningful here only in relation to human needs. Thus, it is not the growth of the village per se but its growth as a result of individual families setting up their independent households and the interplay between this process and governmental intervention that is of interest here. In this sense, as long as families can establish their independent quarters, they do not face the stress that is inherent in the discrepancy between ideal and reality, and the growth of the village is gradual. If, however, a household has two or more concurrent construction projects that it cannot meet, a problem arises and finds expression in the rising value of the person per household (P/HH) ratio. Since the families that settled in the village during the 1961–1972 period were predominantly young (a trait that is also indicated by this population's average and median ages), they did not have married sons and could move in slowly, that is, first build a two-room structure (that would later serve for lower level storage) and settle in it, and later build the house on the second level. Consequently, while the rate of growth increased, the discrepancy between residential independence and economic constraints was primarily the problem of the village's established older families. Local families, however, had more time to space the demands of their maturing sons and to meet them successfully, and as a result there should be a reduced discrepancy between ideal and reality and the stresses that such discrepancy generates.

In 1961, nineteen years after the first house was built on the hill, the village consisted of 88 structures (Golani 1961:4) including 48 houses that, together with 3 tents, accommodated 54 families.[9] Consequently, 6 families shared their quarters (Golani 1961:10–11) and the resulting 51 households averaged 6.7 persons per household (P/HH) (see Table 20). Assuming that had the co-resident families been able to afford to construct their own houses they would have done so, the discrepancy between the number of households and that of the families represents a measure of the inability of 3 (or 5.6%) of the village families to meet the ideal of private residence due to economic constraints.[10]

While the 1972 Census figures do not separate families from households, thus permitting a derivation of the 1972 measure of the discrepancy between ideal and reality, the 137 households they list average 6.3 P/HH (Isr. CBS 1974b:12–13), or very close to the 6.2 P/HH national average for "non-Jews" (Isr. CBS 1974b: XII). By way of comparison, the Maksurean population in its 1961 definition (that is, Maksūr, the Mikmān, and the Ḏmeydeh) averaged 5.7 P/HH (calculated from Isr. CBS 1963b:32) whereas the general Moslem population had a mean of 5.4 P/HH (Isr. CBS 1964:23). In other words, there seems to have been a growing similarity between the sedentarized Ḥğeris and the general "non-Jew" settled population in the country during the 1961–1972 period.

Since the families that are expected to have difficulties in building their houses are young couples, the relatively high 8.8% of P/HH = 2 households in the 1972 returns, as compared with 1961 (3.7%) and 1977 (5.6%), suggest that they were able to meet house construction expenses between 1972 and 1977. In view of the fact that this period coincided with their movement into the military labor market with its high salaries and other benefits, their ability to finance such endeavors is not too surprising. It should be noted that the possibility of a solitary elderly couple whose children reside in their own private residences is highly unlikely due to inheritance patterns and because it did not exist at all during 1975–1977. The three P/HH = 1 households in 1972 can only be young men who resided in their fathers' houses while the latter with the rest of the family camped elsewhere.

The population influx in the following period, however, placed the economic resources of individual families under strain as both settling families and their married sons attempted to build their houses as fast as possible. The strain was further aggravated by the rising cost of materials and labor as a result of the country's escalating inflation, the increase in price of the ILA land plots to meet the expenses incurred by providing the village with its infrastructure, and the decreasing availability of the well-paid tracking jobs with the IDA once the original openings had been filled. The combination of these factors brought about an increase in the average size of a Maksurean household to P/HH = 7.3, as 26 (10.9%) of the village's 239 resident families failed to meet the ideal of residential independence.

Table 20. Comparative household size distribution in 1961, 1972, and 1977: comparison of Bīr al-Maksūr (BM) with household sizes in the herding camps (HCs).[a]

	Popu-lation Size	**Number of House-holds**	**Household Size** (persons/household)																										Ave.	Med.
			1		2		3		4		5		6		7		8		9		10		11		12		13+			
			N	%	N	%	N	%	N	%	N	%	N	%	N	%	N	%	N	%	N	%	N	%	N	%	N	%		
BM																														
1961	343	51			2	3.9	4	7.8	4	7.8	5	9.8	9	17.6	12	23.5	4	7.8	2	3.9	6	11.8	1	2	1	2	1	2	6.7	7.1
1972	869	137	3	2	12	8.8	12	8.8	11	8	17	12	14	10.2	68[b]	49.6													6.3	7
1977	1556	213			12	5.6	13	6.1	22	10.3	24	11	19	8.9	22	10.3	26	12	21	9.9	20	9.4	14	6.6	9	4	11	5	7.3	7.8
HCs																														
1977	275	32					2	6.3	3	9.4			5	15.6			3	9.4	5	16	6	18.6	4	13	1	3	3	9	8.6	9.6

(Sources: 1961: Golani 1961:10–11; 1972: Isr. CBS 1974b:12–13; 1977: personal data)

[a]Data include the herding camps in the Ẓahara, *wādi* al-Mzagga, and Umm al-Zīnāt.

[b]Collapsed categories: 7+

The Social Dimensions of the Village

By 1977 the intensifying rate of house construction, both to establish young families on their own and to provide habitations to settling households, started to obliterate the grouping of houses according to their owner's lineage affiliation. In fact, the location of a house according to strict lineage membership was never overly emphasized in Bīr al-Maksūr. Although the hill, like the agricultural part of the property, was conscientiously divided among the sublineages, it was treated at first somewhat contemptuously as an open domain (namely, whoever wanted to settle and become an agriculturalist there could choose his house site as he pleased). Thus, when the sublineages later began to be stricter about their shares, some members of other subgroups were already present in their assigned areas. This was further confounded by private deals between members of different sublineages who transferred their rights to land either in exchange for land elsewhere or for money. As a result, by the late 1960s a member of the *ulād* Ġadīr could be found next door to a member of the Sama'neh who owned the first house there, and the *muḫtār,* who bought some land from a member of the Samrāt, was located with his two brothers and away from the rest of his relatives between the Samrāt, the Ṭa'awāneh, and the Shfar'am-Nazareth road.

The ILA's planning of the village and the attempts to induce the Ḥğerāt to move from the Ẓahara to Bīr al-Maksūr further added to the obliteration of clear-cut lineal spatial division. Not only did the ILA's policy dictate a free-for-all approach in its part of the village, thus enabling an individual to choose whichever available house plot he pleased to rent, but land exchange deals with landowners from the Ẓahara enabled the formation of some small "islands" of one sublineage in an area predominantly inhabited by members of another. Although as of 1977 these "islands" were visible only when land exchange contracts were plotted on the village map and were not yet an observable fact, such "islands" will become observable as the descendants of such a landowner are allotted their shares to build houses. By and large, however, whether in the tribal property or whether in the ILA section, one strived to build his house next to a favorite close relative or a friend whenever possible. Nonetheless, as increasingly more houses were built on the hill, the ability to choose one's neighbor became commensurably more difficult and the degree of mixing of different lineages increased proportionately.

In summary, by April of 1977 Bīr al-Maksūr was a comfortable and thriving village boasting a population of over 1556 residents plus about 225 others whose houses were in the village but who camped elsewhere. These individuals were members of, respectively, 239 and 25 families that represented all the tribe's sublineages belonging to the Ġadāyreh (126 and 18 respectively), Ḏiyabāt (37:2), Ṣawālḥah (73:3), and 5 non-Ḥğeri immigrants (2 *'arab* al-Ğanādi, 1 Ḥelf, 1 Ka'abīyeh, and a villager from Ša'ab). These 264 families owned 246 residential buildings, of which 213 were in use (113, 32, 65, 3 respectively) and 33 were empty (8 of these belonged to unmarried sons who still resided in their parental household). Finally, some 15 new houses were in different stages of construction while over a score of individuals had signed rental contracts with the ILA, according to which they had to begin construction within a year.

House Construction and Use

The development of Bīr al-Maksūr as a village was accompanied by a gradual change in the floor plan of its houses, which in turn caused some shifts in the patterned use of the space comprising the habitation. As previously mentioned, the houses in the Ẓahara and those built during the 1950s and early 1960s in the Mikmān and Maksūr followed the general layout of the traditional bipart division of the space in the tent: the public/guest/male half (the *dīwān*) and the private/domestic/female half (the *ḥarīm*).[11] These two rooms (or more in a polygamous household when more private rooms, *aḥrām* [pl.], were added) opened to a flat platform/porch that, hill slope permitting, topped a space used to house the animals and/or their feed. The greater number of rooms, however, did not increase the variety in or complexity of use of the habitational space but simply multiplied the number of independent modules that made up the house space. In the Mikmān, the Ḏmeydeh, and Maksūr, these houses were constructed of hewn stone, poured concrete, cinder blocks daubed with cement mortar, or corrugated metal, with a window in each outer wall to provide an open view of the surroundings and for ventilation. As a household needed more space, or when it could afford an addition, either the platform was wholly or partially enclosed and converted into a new *dīwān* or a new larger room was added. Later, more rooms or a whole second level might be added in this piecemeal fashion (cf. Shmueli 1970:71, 1973:113–114 for a similar phenomenon among the Judean Desert tribes).[12]

Similar to the tent, the use of these living spaces emphasized communality and served more than a single functional end. The *dīwān* was, thus, where the ceremonial *sa'adah* coffee was prepared and where the household guests were received. It was also used as the family's living area when no formal guests were present. It was here that the *lux* (the kerosene mantle lamp) was lit and, therefore, the children prepared their homework while half listening to the adults spending the evening discussing politics or economics, gossiping, or playing cards. Finally, it served as sleeping quarters for the adult males and, occasionally, a young son if his father allowed him to bed with himself. The *ḥarīm*, on the other hand, served as the sleeping area of the wife, adult unmarried daughters, and young children. Here, in a corner, the food was prepared on a kerosene burner and the women got together to chat and gossip during the day, often helping each other with cooking chores while talking. When wood burning was used for cooking, such as when baking bread, it was done outside in the open air during the summer and in a small lean-to in the winter.

From about 1967, the planning of Bīr al-Maksūr and the need to secure construction permits from the Ministry of the Interior, as well as experience gleaned from work in the construction industry, promoted several changes both in the floor plan of the house and in the conception of its role (and that of comfort in general). To wit, the requirement to provide the ministry with a plan of the future building forced the Ḥğeris, first, to retain the services of a certified architect,[13] who exerted some influence on the planning of the habitation and, second, to perceive the house as an integrated unit subdivided along functional lines rather than a conglomerate of semi-independent all-purpose modules. The change in conceiving the house as an integrated unit did not, at first, affect the piecemeal fashion in which it was constructed. Thus, while the plans and permits were ready, rooms were added when the household could afford them. Among the 20- to 30-year-old age group, however, there was an increasing practice of building in a single drive, if not a whole house, at least each of its levels as an autonomous and complete habitational space.

The most visible influence of the architect, undoubtedly, lay in convincing his clientèle of the need to willingly obey the government's construction code. As a result, each house was built no less than 3 m from its plot border and 4–5 m from the street. This construction style, as previously mentioned, conveyed a sense of spaciousness and openness with its infrastructural corollaries without having the authorities intervene overtly in the village's residential construction. Moreover, in as much as this scenery set up the early visual and spatial landscape to which the present and future younger generations would be exposed, thus influencing the development of their visual and spatial perception (e.g., cf. Hall 1966, esp. ch. 9–10; Brazelton 1969, 1974), it could be expected to change these in comparison to those of their elders, thereby adding to the accumulating differences and estrangements between their respective life experiences.

The architect also introduced less visible yet as profound changes, as he explained in an interview:

> before, they used to build such large rooms, 5 × 5 meters, [and a house was] 2–3 rooms and a veranda [porch, platform] along all its length. That was long ago. Now I explained to them that . . . if you build a room 5 × 5 [meter] it is 25 square meters and if you build a room 4 × 4 [meter] it is 16 square meters, that is about half. . . . [and] if it is large, 5 meters, you need to give good iron [i.e., steel reinforcement in concrete column, beam, and roof casts] and I worry if I do not supervise they will not give enough iron and that would not be good [i.e., it will be dangerous]. They do not pay much for supervision of the construction. There is a contractor and he does [whatever the owner wants].

As a result, for a lower price (both in materials and in permit fees) one could build more, although smaller, rooms in a same size house. More rooms allowed for specialized quarters such as a kitchen, which was the only location of plumbing in the house (hence hosted the enclosures for a shower and a toilet, and laundry once the house connected to electricity). Smaller rooms, however, meant that they were often not large enough to accommodate the sleeping arrangements of a relatively small family of five in one room when Western-style beds were introduced. Consequently, if the parental generation of such a family was about 35 years or younger (that is, the age brackets most likely to adopt beds), the primacy of the traditional sexual division of the sleeping quarters often gave way to a generational division with its subsequent impact on socialization. Thus, smaller room size not only underwrote and promoted greater specialization in the utilization of the habitational space but also influenced more strictly defined social dynamics.

The predominant floor plan in Bīr al-Maksūr in 1977 (see Figure 6) still emphasized an all-purpose public space—*dīwān*—that often occupied one-third of the total floor area. Usually this room was about 4 m wide, oblong, and occupied the whole length of the house. This room's width was such that it could accommodate two lines of mattresses, head to tail, each along one of the long walls (a mattress measures approximately 1.80

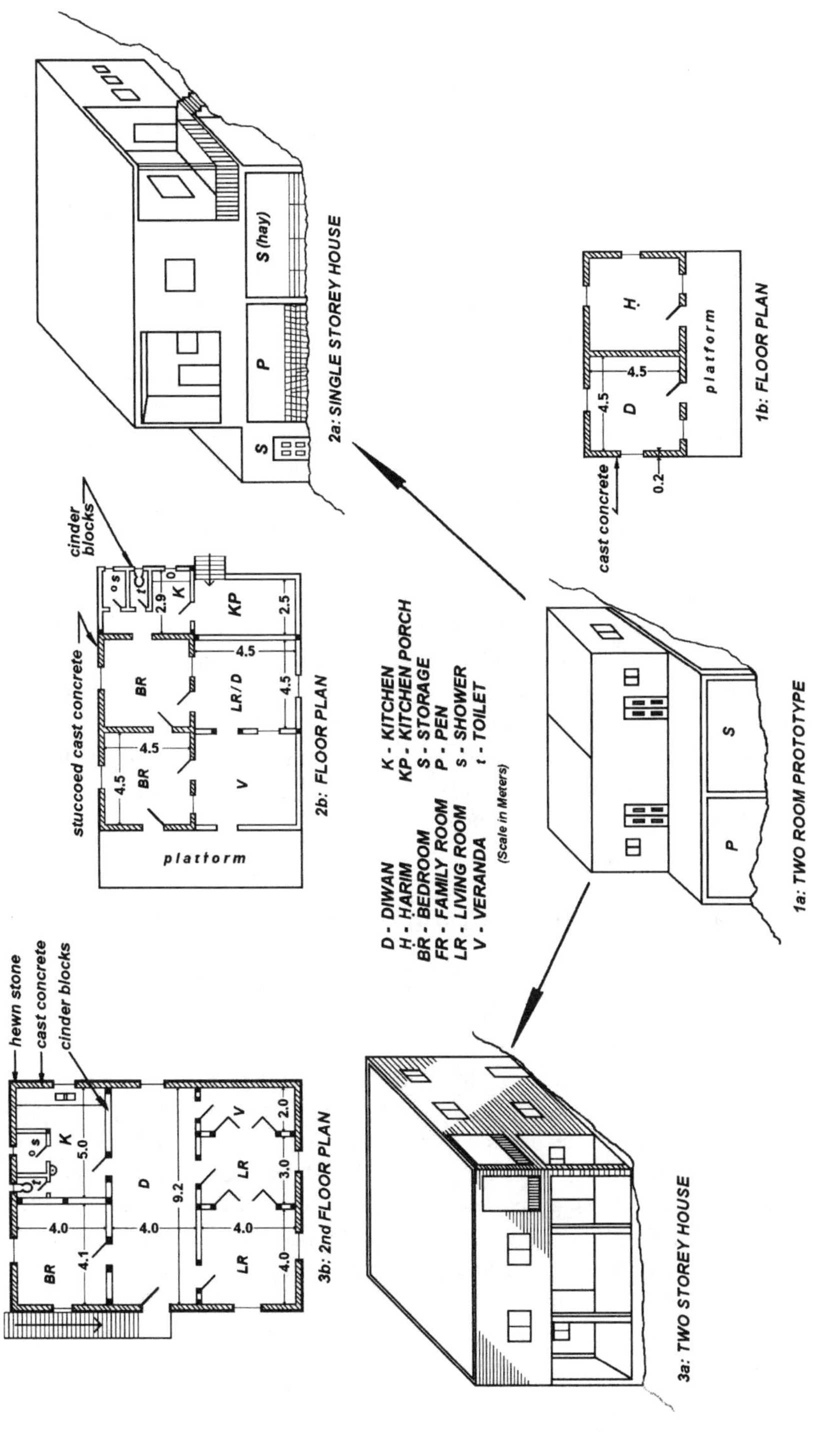

Figure 6. A schematic development of a house.

× 1.10 × 0.10 m) and an open space of about 2 m between them. Thus, it was both comfortable to talk across the dividing space and convenient to serve food from the center to the sides when eating. If, as usual, the *dīwān* was located in the building's center, each of its long sides had two doors that led into two smaller spaces that may or may not be interconnected: a room, a veranda, or a kitchen/shower/toilet/ unit.[14] A habitational unit, thus, encompassed a large public space of about 32–40 m^2; 2–3 rooms of approximately 16 m^2 each; a kitchen/shower/toilet unit of about 20 m^2; and a veranda of roughly 8 m^2. Later, the veranda was often enclosed with aluminum and plastic sliding shutters to provide a flexible extra closed space (for instance, in the rainy season). This method of adding to an apartment's space was very popular throughout Israel both along the rural/urban and the Jew/Arab axes. In general the floor area fluctuated between 100 and 110 m^2, which was 20% or less of the building plot area. A few houses reached 115 m^2 per floor area and only three houses exceeded this measure, ranging between 175 and 200 m^2. Often this unit was built as a second level while the ground level was enclosed to serve as storage area, animal enclosure, business units, and so on, as mentioned before (for example, the Mother and Child Clinic and the sewing workshop).

Living on the second level permitted an open view of the horizon and let the breeze ventilate the house; thus, each house had many large windows in practically every outer wall. Besides allowing for sunlight and breeze to pass through, these windows enabled the occupants to monitor almost everything outside. When sitting with Ḥğeris in a house, one is continuously aware of their casual but frequent scanning of the visual field outside their windows. This became, therefore, the preferred construction style after the beginning of the 1970s when more money became available for construction. When I asked the architect about the windows in connection with the thermal properties of the buildings, he answered that "if you plan fewer windows they say 'why? I will not take the building,' if you close a window they say 'no, we want a window.'"

Habitational Space Use

At first, the greater availability of habitable space had little effect on patterns of its use due to both long-established habits and the limitation imposed by the lack of electricity, which caused people to gather after dark in the single room where the mantle lamp was placed. Thus, among the elder and more tradition-bound individuals, the *dīwān* was set with mattresses and cushions whenever guests appeared during the day or the evening and was easily converted into sleeping quarters for the adult males at night. Sometimes this room also included a few pieces of Western-style furniture—a sofa, two or four armchairs, and a coffee table—at one end to accommodate Western-oriented visitors (Jews and Arabs). Among the younger and less tradition-bound individuals, the *dīwān* served as hallway most of the time, assuming its traditional role only occasionally, while the whole family slept together in one of the smaller rooms. In these houses one room was furnished as a Western-style living room with a sofa, armchairs, a coffee table, and a china cabinet to store and display the family glassware and other valuables, and was used for receiving the household's visitors. The area assigned for receiving guests was thus doubly reduced: first the actual size of the room was about half of the *dīwān*, and, second, the furniture reduced the available space even further. It is hardly surprising, therefore, that throughout my stay in the village I did not observe the younger generation entertaining in their living rooms more than ten individuals at any one time, and they usually entertained fewer. By contrast, those village members who used the traditional method of mattresses and cushions rarely entertained less than ten, and often entertained twenty to thirty individuals at any one time. Notwithstanding, as of 1977 all the house owners in the village still had the traditional sheep-wool stuffed mattresses and would use them when more visitors than the Western-style arrangement allowed for were present.

The absence of a clear-cut bi-sexual spatial division (which was coded in the older floor plan) and the preferential location of the habitational space on the house's second level (usually with only one external staircase to serve as entrance/exit) did not greatly affect the male-female dynamics in the household because, as previously mentioned, the Ḥğerāt did not practice intra-tribal sexual segregation to any measurable extent. Nonetheless, these architectural details promoted even further the traditionally relaxed attitudes regarding the inter-sexual use of space.

During the first half of the 1970s several items of furniture became popular as part of the *mahr*, notably a wooden frame double bed and a wardrobe that, together, left only a little free floor space in the 16 m^2 bedroom, particularly after a baby crib was added. The replacement of the traditional mattresses with beds was more widespread than just for newlyweds and could be observed among some of the more Western-oriented individuals in the 30–40 years age bracket as well. For a while, however, only a single room was used as the family's sleeping quarters because people with more children (that is, older families) did not possess double beds, and the younger families did not have many children. In fact, most middle-aged individuals, who grew up in the tents of the Ẓahara, did not view the number of children as a causal factor to be dealt with by dividing the sleeping quarters. For example, in 1977 one family with five children (ages 3 to 10) and a baby slept in six beds and a crib (the baby slept with her mother), which left very little floor space in the middle of the room. At that time, the household had the *dīwān*, a Western-style living room, and a third room between the latter and the veranda, which was used to increase the area of either of these two public spaces through a pair of double doors as the need arose. The household head (age 40) did not see his sleeping quarters as congested nor had he any plans to change the arrangement of his family's habitational space.

Nevertheless, the availability of electricity; the expanding knowledge and assimilation of Western habitational standards through observing neighboring settlements, workplaces, and television programs; and the increased residential experience in similarly designed houses combined to promote a shift in the traditional use of habitational space by dividing the familial sleeping quarters along predominantly generational rather than sexual lines. Thus, some people in their 30s who already lived in the traditionally designed house moved their children to the smaller third room while talking of redesigning the inner division of their houses to utilize the underused space of the *dīwān*. Others of this group who were in the process of building designed their house with a master bedroom, children's rooms, and so on. Another innovation in these houses was the separation of the kitchen, bathroom, and toilet into three separate units, each with an independent entrance.

Like the livingrooms and bedrooms in the village, the kitchens became increasingly more formal and task-oriented (that is, specific) than the cooking corner in the women's quarters ever was. Prior to the availability of electricity, the kitchen in the standard designed house was a large (approximately 16 m^2) empty room furnished with a sink flanked by two slabs of polished stone tops along part or all of one of its outer walls. In most houses these stone work surfaces topped cupboards or shelves used for storing dried foodstuffs, preserves, and cooking utensils. Cooking was mostly done on a kerosene burner on the floor because placing the burner on the working surface positioned the pot too high for comfortable stirring and watching. In the few households where bottled gas was used for cooking, the gas range was placed on the stone slabs, leaving the floor space open for other activities, be they food preparation, neighborly chats, or sometimes laundry.

Shortly after electricity became available, the Ḥğerāt began to add electrical appliances to their homes and rapidly furnished their kitchens with refrigerators, electric range/ovens, and washing machines. The total range of effects of these appliances can only be guessed. Three, however, could already be observed in 1977—or would be expected within a short time period. First, the physical size of these appliances diminished the general purpose space in the kitchen, turning it into an even more special purpose unit. Consequently, the level of social interaction, which was formerly permitted by the available free space, was reduced markedly. While as of July 1977 cross-visiting among women did not diminish to any degree I could observe, change was observed in the location of the gathering, which moved outside the kitchen and did not always allow for help in food preparation and related tasks. With increased use of timesaving appliances, the amount of help in performing chores could be expected to diminish even further and the quality, if not volume, of the level of female social interaction to change correspondingly. Second, like all timesaving devices, kitchen appliances could be expected to increase the women's leisure time, which, combined with education and employment, would most likely add to the slowly mounting pressures on the realignment of male-female dynamics in the village. It should be further remembered that timesaving appliances enabled single men to make their own meals, if they so chose, thereby adding to the complexity of these dynamics. Finally, the ownership of refrigerators and range/ovens could be expected to change some of the traditional dietary habits in accordance to what was available in their regional milieu.

The changes in the village's appearance, house floor plan, and use of living space primarily impacted the early life experiences of the infants and children of Bīr al-Maksūr, and through them the Ḥğeri cultural system of the not-so-distant future. Although the village was only one of the tribe's three settlements, it was the largest (and still growing), and was the vanguard of the tribe in terms of sedentarization and change, with the Mikmān following suit as best it could. More important is the oft neglected question of the impact of the change in immediate physical settings on infant development and its influence on culture change. Studies of infant development indicate that—far more than was thought possible—infants are cognitively competent and profoundly affected by the spatial organization and the quality of personal relations that form the environment of their early development (e.g., Brazelton 1969, 1974). They, thus, could readily become the vectors of culture change and "modernization" as they matured—especially when combined with formal education, which more than any other facet of culture has brought into focus the growing disparity in the lifestyles of successive Ḥğeri generations.

Formal Education in Bīr al-Maksūr

Formal education and the disposition of the tribesmembers toward it were much like other changes in the Ḥğerāt's lifestyles. The Mandate Period *ḫaṭīb* was replaced by a primary school under the MG, which tried to establish the government's Law of Compulsory Education, 1949 (Isr. Laws 3:125–31). Notwithstanding, the lack of trained personnel, buildings, and equipment and the policies and practices of the MG itself did not promote a modern educational system and the, then, new schools in the Ẓahara, the Mikmān, and later in Bīr al-Maksūr were mainly an expansion of the *ḫaṭīb* instructional method. Nor was there an attempt to enforce the law and send all children of both sexes to school. Consequently, the personal attitudes of the parents and the unopposed rebelliousness of the children to school discipline underwrote how much exposure to school a child received.

With the passage of time and as the average parent became younger, increasingly greater numbers of both sexes gained elementary education and completed the eighth grade.[15] Similarly, a growing fraction of those who graduated acquired secondary education in neighboring high schools in Shfar'am, I'billin, and other nearby institutions and in the vocational school in Nazareth. By 1977 two of these students were in a teacher college, two were registered in the University of Haifa, and one was studying medicine in Germany (see Table 21).

The acceptance of formal education into Ḥğeri lifeways, however, brought to the fore stresses that were extra-tribal in character and that affected intra-tribal dynamics. Extra-tribal stress resulted from the growing exposure of the youth to the regional educational institutions—first the high schools within the Arab sector and later the post-secondary educational institutions in the Jewish sector—each with its specialized set of effects. In general, the high school in Shfar'am and other *fellāḥīn* villages provided exposure to a different political ideology than that of the tribe, whereas the academic institutions of the Jewish sector belonged to a different educational approach with which the Ḥğeri students had little, if any, experience.

The views and political sentiments of the general student body and instructors of the high schools were quite unlike those of the incoming Ḥğeri students. Whereas the Ḥğerāt placed the bedouin/*fellāḥīn* rivalry in the foreground and were involved with the dominant Jewish political parties that enabled them to maintain an upper hand in that competition, the majority of high school and university students from the Arab sector were interested in questions relating to the future of the Palestinian people (cf. Rekhes 1981:186–95). As a result, young Ḥğeris in the ripe age for radical political views and susceptibility to peer pressure were suddenly exposed to an ideology that argued that the differences in

Table 21. The educational level reached by Ḥğeris born 1940–1964 in academic year 1976/1977 (by sex).*

Year of Birth	**Sex**	**Total Number in Age Bracket**	**Elementary Education**				**Secondary Education** (8th Grade = 100%)						**Post-Secondary Education**	
			Total N of Students		Graduated		Total N of Students		Vocational School		Graduated		In Teacher College	In University
		(100%)	N	%	N	%	N	%	N	%	N	%	N	N
	M	96	51	53.1	25	26	5	20			3	12		
1940–1944	F	90	2	2.2	1	1.1								
	T	*186*	*53*	*28.5*	*26*	*14*	*5*	*19.2*			*3*	*11.5*		
	M	60	42	70	18	30	9	50			5	27.8		2
1945–1949	F	81	9	11.1										
	T	*141*	*51*	*36.2*	*18*	*12.8*	*9*	*50*			*5*	*27.8*		*2*
	M	130	107	82.3	72	55.4	20	27.8	1	1.4	11	15.3		1
1950–1954	F	114	49	43	11	9.6								
	T	*244*	*156*	*63.9*	*83*	*34*	*20*	*24.1*	*1*	*1.2*	*11*	*13.3*		*1*
	M	174	165	94.8	117	67.2	63	53.8	3	2.6	33	28.2	2	
1955–1959	F	135	92	68.1	30	22.2	4	13.3						
	T	*309*	*257*	*83.2*	*147*	*47.6*	*67*	*45.6*	*3*	*2*	*33*	*22.4*	2	
	M	201	201	100	112	55.7	57	50.9			1	0.9		
1960–1964	F	198	160	80.8	43	26.9	7	16.3						
	T	*399*	*361*	*90.5*	*155*	*38.8*	*64*	*41.3*			*1*	*0.6*		
	M	661	566	85.6	344	52	154	44.8	4	1.2	53	15.4	2	3
Totals	F	618	312	50.5	85	13.8	11	12.9						
	T	*1279*	*878*	*68.6*	*429*	*33.5*	*165*	*38.5*	*4*	*0.9*	*53*	*12.4*	2	*3*

Key: M = male; F = female; T = total; N = number

*Those born after 1962/1963 would still be in elementary school, and before graduation. This is the reason for the decline in the number of graduates between 1955–1959 and 1960–1964.

interests between a *fellāḥ* and a bedouin were insignificant compared to those between an Arab and a Jew in Israel. Although as of 1977 the adoption of Palestinian Arab ideology seemed limited to a handful of individuals, it could be expected to combine with the disappointments that were generated by exposure to post-secondary academic institutions to increase the identification of the youth with the Palestinian cause and away from the traditional Ḥğeri ideology of separatism. Such a shift would tend to increase the tensions between older and younger generations in the tribe.

As Arab high school graduates successfully passed the state administered matriculation examinations[16] and tried to acquire post-secondary education, they suddenly discovered that the boundary between their high school and the university was not merely one of scope and intensity but a matter of a different educational approach altogether. In fact, the transition between secondary and post-secondary education could be said to be a transition between the Israeli Moslem educational system and its Jewish counterpart. Two major characteristics distinguished the two systems. First was the instructional language—Arabic versus Hebrew. Although Arab students studied Hebrew from grade four, it was taught and treated as a second language (not as a bilingual situation). Second was the difference (mentioned above) in instructional emphasis between recitation and memorization in the rural Arab schools and reading and other individualized learning skills in the Jewish system (cf. Rekhes 1981:183). The combination of these two characteristics made it very difficult for many Arab students to succeed. Moreover, the superposition of language over learning techniques glossed over the more important substantive issue of the latter while concurrently polarizing the issue along a lingual and ethnopolitical axis rather than an academic one. Thus, a failure to be accepted or to survive in a university or the Technion (Israel Institute of Technology) could easily become a sense of political rejection. The situation was aggravated when the universities attempted to confront and solve the problem of the unequal educational backgrounds of their applicants (both urban vs. rural and native vs. immigrant) by offering preparatory classes in which borderline applicants could enroll. If completed successfully, applicants could proceed to the freshman level. If, however, a student failed the preparatory class, the disappointment was greatly increased because not only did the student—who was very good in high school—fail, but she/he had to pay (tuition and other expenses) for a painful lesson. Moreover, since it was the family who financed the effort and since the student often boasted, overtly or covertly, that he/she "studies at the university," the shame was no longer a private matter and was amplified as parents stood by their children.

Similar to the rest of the Arab sector (e.g., *Al Hamishmar*, July 6, 1976) and despite the progress its educational system had undergone since 1949 (e.g., Winter 1981), among the Ḥğerāt the desired results of early exposure to formal education—which instilled basic learning techniques—were further deficient due to the same problems that prevailed during the early 1950s. The most important of these was *low quality teaching* for not only were the teachers untrained or undertrained (because until 1976 they could teach without having any specialized training or certifications), but their motivation to become more committed through updating and upgrading their own training was very low. Moreover, in academic year 1975/76, only four of the Bīr al-Maksūr school's sixteen teachers (nine males and seven females) were Ḥğeris and under some form of kinship responsibility. More generally, since the school was located in four different places (see below), the teachers would chat with passersby who would come in to say "hello" or to visit one another and chat while their respective classes were still in session. Similarly, if a teacher did not feel like teaching some ten minutes before the end of a session, he/she would simply stop teaching and just keep the children quiet in the classroom.

The second deficiency was the *inadequate facilities*. For example, as of academic year 1975/76 the school of Bīr al-Maksūr was still located in four different places in the village. The first was the original four small rooms built in 1958. The other places were located in the enclosed first levels of private houses, which were built for storage rather than as classrooms. In general, all the rooms were small, dark, sometimes windowless, and often dripped water during the winter. The Mikmān had a better single facility that, nevertheless, was in a neglected condition. Finally, there were the *lack of teaching aids* and an *antiquated teaching program* (prepared during the MG era).

No less important than the unqualified teachers was the lack of family encouragement and interest in the children's school experience. This parental disinterest could be passive (for instance, when a father of eleven [born 1933] was asked when he last inquired about his children's schooling, he answered "never, it does not interest me") or active (for example, pulling girls out of class sessions or school in general to help their mothers, and pulling out boys to help in herding or agriculture). School absenteeism, however, points to the reciprocal character of the phenomenon. Often the children themselves preferred to leave the school and, in fact, instigated the withdrawal because when the attitude at home was one of "schooling is not important to one's life career" (especially to that of females), and without adult support, encouragement, and urging, the child saw very little reason to suffer through the boredom and constrictive discipline of the school.

By 1976/77 all these deficiencies in the Ḥğeri educational system were in different stages of amelioration. The new school building in the village was inaugurated and was provided with modern teaching aids while the teaching program was revised. The Ministry of Education's reform effort to "academize" its teaching corps of the seventh through twelfth grades was reaching the Ḥğerāt. In the Arab sector this change meant that all teachers would have to complete at least two years of teachers' college training, an investment of time and money that would select for individuals with a greater commitment to teaching than that of most of those already employed. Unfortunately, the relationship of the Arab sector with the administration and the latter's own style of operation were such that the "academization" of teachers in that sector would be a lengthy and tedious process because teachers who had a patron (that is, a "contact" with the authorities) asked him to intervene on their behalf. For example, the *muḫtār* intervened on behalf of the Ḥğeri teachers in Bīr al-Maksūr, thereby delaying the amelioration of the quality of teaching in the village. Not surprisingly, the two individuals who attended a teachers' college in 1976/77 were members of minor branches of two of the tribe's smaller sublineages.

More importantly, as the average age of Ḥğeri parents declined, they were more likely to have had some education themselves and to have experienced the effects of its lack (for instance, to become an officer in the army or the police one needed a matriculation certificate). Similarly, older brothers who had secondary education or who experienced the effects of not having one were more supportive and encouraging to their younger siblings and often intervened on their behalf with their parents and teachers. In general, the younger parental generation was increasingly more concerned about the quality of education in the tribe's schools and the success and advance of their children and younger siblings.

Nevertheless, the time lag between elementary school age and the attendance of post-secondary institutions would delay the ability of Ḥğeri students to compete successfully with their Jewish counterparts. Since such equality would not be achieved easily or rapidly, the discrepancies between the two sectors could be expected to generate their political and social effects much sooner, for the problems would not stop at the level of successfully acquiring university education but would continue into the academic job market that was already so flooded with qualified personnel that many university graduates looked for jobs abroad upon graduation. For an Arab this situation was even graver for two reasons. First, because Arab students tended to specialize in humanities, law, medicine, and pharmacology, they were less adaptable to job opportunities in the general market, which emphasized engineering. Second, due to the strained relations with the neighboring Arab states, they were barred from finding a job in any security sensitive economic or administrative position (cf. Rekhes 1981:183–84). Moreover, being enmeshed in a kinship network and reciprocal relations, an Arab graduate was less likely to look for a job abroad and more likely to return to his village or town where the only academic job opportunity he had was to be a teacher for the Ministry of Education or the municipal high schools, a job for which he was probably not specifically trained and generally over-qualified (a situation somewhat reminiscent of Eric Wolf's analysis of peasant wars [1969: esp. 287–89]). Although as of 1977 the relations of the Ḥğerāt with the authorities placed them in a position—unlike most of the Arab sector—that would probably enable them to find jobs if and when they achieved university degrees, the process just described was already affecting them through the regional educational system and could be expected to affect them even more so in the future.

Education and Other Change Promoters

The extra-tribal effects of formal education were only beginning to be felt during the fieldwork period and had not yet been articulated by the tribesmembers in any great detail. Thus, for example, only three of about a dozen applicants of those graduating from high school in 1975/76 were accepted to a preparatory class of the University of Haifa in academic year 1976/77. All three failed the class and withdrew from the university during the first semester. None of the three talked of their failure in terms of the Jewish-Arab educational dichotomy, but instead as resulting from their personal academic shortcomings. In fact, two fathers did not want their sons to go to the university—due to the added economic burden and their wish to see them in uniforms (both joined the IDA later)—and were happy when the sons decided on their own not to continue. The third father, however, was very upset and asked me to explain to him: "What was wrong with his son?," "Why did he fail after being so good in high school?" and whether "they do not want them [Arabs, bedouin, Ḥğeris] in the university."

The intra-tribal effects of education were both noticeable and complained about. In the succinct words of a prominent middle level leader: "the youth are not worth a thing and while they think very highly of themselves because they have finished twelve years and think of themselves [as] intelligentsia, they do not know how to talk with other people or how to maneuver in the world [life]." Thus, in combination with a range of other agencies, education predominately promoted the growing disparity between the life experiences and expectations of successive Ḥğeri generations. Apart from its traditional role of exposing the individual to a greater variety of experiences, formal education affected young Ḥĝeris in two subtler and interrelated ways. First, the educational process included removing children from the outdoors (where their elders had most, it not all, of their life experiences in a stimuli-rich context, be it in dealing with nature or with other people as representatives of other sociopolitical groups) and enclosing them in small, relatively stimuli-poor rooms, which were explicitly or implicitly argued to be superior to the outdoors (after all, why otherwise should they be sent there?). Second, the experiential immediacy and intimacy of an outdoors life was replaced by increasingly more abstract representations, which are neither immediate nor intimate, but which were presented to the children as a more powerful method of understanding and manipulating the world/life around them than that of their parents, who lacked formal education. The validity of the arguments in favor of formal education (and through them self-esteem, and to some degree righteousness, of the youngsters themselves) was further "(self-) proven" to the children by their parents' inability to help (and often even to understand) their class material. Consequently, it was not only that the early life experiences of successively younger generations were increasingly foreign to their elders, but the attitude of the youth was beginning to disregard and deprecate their elders' knowledge and attitudes. Needless to emphasize, their elders' knowledge and attitudes were, to a major extent, the traditional Ḥĝeri culture.

Less visibly, formal education provided an outlet for the aspirations of small and/or out-of-power sublineages who invested in this long-term project more than the powerful sublineages, with the implicit hope of achieving greater success in the extra-tribal milieu and through it some realignment of the inter-lineage power positions in the future (see Table 22). A telling incident in this regard occurred during the 1977 parliamentary elections when an educated member of a small sublineage angrily complained that the other candidates of the UAL (the United Arab List, of which the *muḫtār* was a candidate) "always have some educated youth around them but you never see . . . [the *muḫtār*] with educated young men around him." He was angry at being deprived of his "rightful status" to which his education would entitle him because, as of 1977, family affiliation and personal character were still more important than education in determining access to political power in the tribe.

Much like the exposure to Palestinian ideology and politics, the direct effects of education often transcended its curricular boundaries and exposed Ḥĝeri youth to other novel situations that were incorporated under the legitimating cloak of education into their early experiences and later expectations. (I use "legitimating" here because these effects are not generally accepted on their own merits but in toto with education and on *its* merits.) Thus, school trips introduced the children to inter-sexual sharing of nonacademic experiences while incorporating travel into the youth's leisure activities, neither of which was experienced by their elders. After graduating from high school and with some private income, young men took one-day excursions as far south as the Negev. They also went swimming in the Sea of Galilee and other public beaches. These excursions exposed them to the greater diversity of a state environment and brought them into contact with, and raised questions about, the relative differences among different groups. The new experiences

Table 22. The differences among Ḥğeri sublineages in educational levels reached by their members born 1940–1964 in academic year 1976/1977.[a]

Unit	1977 Membership (100%)	Education Completed 8 Years N	%	Completed 12 Years N	%	In Post-Secondary N	%
Ġadāyreh	1348	189	14	24	1.8	3	0.2
Ramlāt	378	62	16.4	4	1.1		
ulād Ġadīr[b]	353	52	14.7	9	2.5	1	1.3
'Afafṭeh	100	11	11	2	2		
the rest[c]	290	34	11.7	2	0.7		
Samrat	227	30	13.2	7	3.1	2	0.9
Ḍiyabāt	706	57	8.1	12	1.7	1	0.1
Ṭa'awāneh	342	31	9.1	9	2.6	1	0.3
D'eyfeh	366	26	7.1	3	0.8		
Ṣawālḥah	1286	183	14.2	17	1.3	1	0.08
Ḥassan al-Ṣāleḥ	126	22	17.5	1	0.8		
Maḥāmīd	455	67	14.7	5	1.1	1	0.2
Ğawāsreh[b]	136	12	8.8	2	1.5		
Sama'neh	208	26	12.5	1	0.5		
Masa'īd	171	29	17	4	2.3		
'Awābdeh	190	27	14.2	4	2.1		
Ḥğerāt	3340	429	12.8	53	1.6	5	0.1

[a]Those born after 1962–1963 would still be in elementary school and, hence, before graduation.
[b]Sublineages providing the current *maḫatīr*.
[c]Includes: *ulād* Sleymān, *ulād* 'Ahmed, and Dabas/Ḫalāyleh.

they encountered included being exposed in their brief swimming trunks to bikini-clad young women, and although many of them were still oriented toward the precepts of traditional honor, their parents would have been very unsettled to find themselves in a similar situation. In 1975 a young soldier (born 1944) organized a trip to Jerusalem, the Dead Sea, and other sites in that area. He generated interest in about ten elderly couples and some eighty young individuals in couples and singles. Consequently he rented an extra bus to separate the two groups because "the young ones like to bathe in the Dead Sea while the older ones want to go to Jerusalem and Hêbron and don't like to see the young bathe." He added that in the future he would organize a trip either for older or for younger people but not for both at the same time because "it is too much of a headache." Such enterprises served to settle some of the worries of the older people about the trips of the younger ones. Nonetheless, the former did not have the same experiences as the youth as they tended to stay and move as a group and did not mingle with the locals.

Similarly, a 1976 school-sponsored theatrical performance by a mixed group of students and graduates, directed by one of the young Ḥğeri teachers (born 1952), introduced the tribe en mass to a new variant of secular entertainment. The performance, which started about 9:45 A.M. and ended at almost 1:00 P.M., began with singing by little boys and girls accompanied by a hired violin player. They sang either solo or as a chorus that was sometimes composed of both sexes. The songs ranged from the traditional to modern popular "hits." This was followed by a one-act play (see below), after which the audience dispersed. Although occasionally someone would shout encouragement to the performers, and once or twice another shot in the air out of excitement and in spirited support, the general listening atmosphere was one of passive rapture, best attested to by the negative public response to the shouts and shots. Similarly, the applause at the end of each act was restrained and arrhythmical, which was very unlike the hand clapping in response to the rhymesters (*ḥadaya*) in weddings. In fact, the only circumstance during which I observed similar raptured listening was on the few occasions when a *sha'er* sang old epics while playing a *rabābah*. The differences between the school show and the *sha'er*, however, ranged from the respective age of the performers and the expected reverence to their state of knowledge and to the actual contents of the performances. While not a totally new form of entertainment, the school performance was a new variant that emphasized passive participation rather than the more common active participatory behavior, and the acceptance of the entertaining act on its own merits, free of other values such as age, traditional knowledge, and history. In other words, the school play engendered the acceptance of the entertaining act in a much simplified and discontinuous context—the characteristic behavioral mode during television watching.

The performance, moreover, included a topical one-act play (written by two of the young actors helped by the teacher), which brought to the fore the growing intergenerational tensions and tried to reassure the audience that the differences in intergenerational behavioral patterns were superficial and temporary and did not affect filial loyalty. In short, in the play an engagement agreement was made between two fathers, after which the groom's father left the house for the *muḫtār*'s to ask for help in arranging his tax bills. The would-be groom stayed in the house reading when three friends who were on the "wrong path" and a young teacher came to visit him. The four youngsters played cards at a table while smoking. Then the three produced a bottle of liquor and coaxed the groom and the teacher to drink with them. Later all left and the groom fell asleep and did not wake until the next day. His father did not press the case but the groom's younger brother pitted him against the father and they quarreled. The groom left home and joined his three friends in a coffee shop, drinking arrack and whiskey, playing cards, and being rude toward the coffee shop keeper. Later the three quarreled and the groom was left alone. He went to a grove and wept over his misfortune while the teacher stood behind a tree.

The three friends came to get him to join them in drinking again but the teacher came out and preached to them and they all decided to mend their ways. The groom returned home while his father was with his friends (the *muḫtār* and the father of the would-be bride) weeping over his misfortune that his firstborn took to the "wrong path," and so on. The groom and his three friends came in and all asked for his forgiveness. The father fainted. The doctor was summoned, who said that the father needed blood, which the son gave without any hesitation, thus bringing his father back to life. Last, they made the wedding and all were happy. (Although the play was planned as a single performance, the troupe was invited to perform it several times in other bedouin communities in the general area of Bīr al-Maksūr.)

Education thus combined with the workplace, the IDA, and the rest of the agencies in the extra-tribal milieu to reduce the differences between the youth of the Ḥğerāt and the population at large, while continuously increasing the gulf between older and younger generations and causing the communication between them to slowly fade. One major area in which intergenerational communication almost completely faded out was in the daily instrumental tasks and experiences, especially those concerning the regional economic milieu. The older individuals often could not help the youth cope with problems simply because they did not have comparable experiences. The youth, therefore, increasingly relied on peer advice and opinions, thereby promoting the importance and influence of peer groups whose formation was facilitated by the rapid increase in the tribe's population and the year-round residence in the settlement. As a result, whereas in the herding camps people usually gathered for a social evening without any age differentiation, in the village people tended to gather as groups within the major age categories (that is, young, middle-aged, and so on).

When such groups met, their members usually chatted, had a discussion, played cards, or watched television. When, however, those present belonged to several age categories, they invariably watched television unless there was a need to discuss a specific matter of general concern to the sublineage, lineage, or the tribe. Television, thus, became an ideal instrument to promote some sense of solidarity in the multigenerational group. It allowed for a sense of subdued togetherness (because there was no need for conversation while the television was on) and the television provided entertainment or information that was usually general enough to provide topics for a detached discussion later. It was not surprising, therefore, that the first appliances the Ḥğerāt acquired, even before the villages had electricity, were television sets. In fact, sets operated by car batteries and accompanied by high antennas could be found in quite a number of tents as well.

Although the growing disparity included all facets of their respective lifestyles, its most striking manifestation was in the gradually shifting sexual mores of the younger generations. It is hard to overemphasize the importance and repercussions of such a shift due to the nature of male-female dynamics in Islam in general (cf. Mernissi 1975) and the connection between female sexuality and family honor and between honor and politics in bedouin society in particular (cf. Abou-Zeid 1965). Whereas middle-aged individuals were conservative, high school-age males could be found in the market of Nazareth or Shfar'am trying to court local and tourist young women, and somewhat older individuals sometimes dated their Ḥğeri fiancées and went to the movies in safe places like Haifa and Acre (see also Shmueli 1973:214).

Similarly, Ḥğeri soldiers often had Jewish women friends with whom they consorted while away from the village. The most committed individual in this respect was a soldier who together with a colleague rented an apartment in a nearby city, which they used alternately for overnight entertainment of female friends when off duty. On the other extreme were those who upheld the traditional ethic of extramarital chastity, although often at a price. One of them, for example, remembered that he was "angry [unhappy] with the bedouin custom [ethic]" about women because when he was in an army educational course in one of the cities, other soldiers would invite him to join them when going to "the girls." He, however, could not join them, and they would ask him why he would "always read and drink coffee alone and would never come with them to have some fun." Nevertheless, it is important to realize that the actual sexual forays of the youth away from the village, especially when in the army, served to diffuse a potentially highly destructive intergenerational tension. This was particularly observable in the behavior of the soldiers when they returned to the village after a period of active duty. During their stay they behaved in accordance with the traditional demeanor and served as examples of model behavior for village youth. In fact, I often heard from both soldiers and former soldiers that when a problem concerning inter-sexual behavior arose in the tribe, it invariably was perpetrated by someone who was not in the army and who did not have a similar outlet for socio-sexual tensions. These tensions arose from the discrepancy between what they saw around them and what they could afford doing within the tribal boundaries. In other words, the state environment not only generated the contradictions underlying some of the intergenerational tensions in the tribe but also, and by so doing, provided for some form for the release of these tensions, albeit according to the state's own values, customs, and organizational formats.

While female seduction was not in and of itself an innovation, the sexual permissiveness of the Jewish and tourist milieu in which the youth reveled was in striking opposition to the self-restraint advocated by tradition and the older tribesmembers. For them, self-restraint did not mean monogamy but how one conducted oneself in inter-sexual matters. Thus, in a chat about one of the major *šiyuḫ* of the Negev, who had a series of wives and who had once remarked that he did not know all his children, a polygynous elder and several middle-aged individuals who were present concurred that although the *šeyḫ* was rich and powerful, he was not "great" because he dishonored himself repeatedly and badly by "running after women." More practically, one young married man was banished from the tribe for having an affair with a young woman from another local tribe. He later eloped with a young woman from a West Bank village. When her relatives came with a leading person from Nazareth to ask for her, the Ḥğeri elders waived any responsibility for the man or his actions and told the villagers to go ahead and take her without fear because if the culprit gave them troubles the Ḥğerāt would protect them. The significance of this anecdote is that under normal circumstance no bedouin tribe would permit outsiders to invade a member's residence, especially not encourage or condone it.

Thus, although the youth were not lewd by any means, the difference between the generations seemed to reach deeper than acts alone and to touch on such basic issues as male-female dynamics and honor. For example, after a locally well publicized "honor execution" (that is, the killing, often publicly, of a woman for elopement and pre/extra-marital sexual liaison) in a *fellāḥīn* village in the region, most Ḥğeri male youth I asked thought it was an immoral anachronism because, as a general rule, elopement was the fault of the parents and not of the eloping couple. As for its anachronistic character, they said that even in that same village they knew of at least three recent elopements where in each case the parents of the woman said "let her go" and what was surprising to them was that the fourth was actually killed. Moreover, they said that in many villages and tribes there were even pregnant unwed young women who were kept at their parents' houses, were helped by them to get an abortion, and were not killed. Similarly, they knew of wives who were not virgins on their nuptial night and whose husbands knew of it and let it pass quietly (in the past, the husband would have returned her to her family and demanded the return of the *mahr* and expenses he had had). Nonetheless, asked if they themselves would elope, the answer invariably was "no, it would dishonor my family." By way of contrast, the middle-aged older individuals I asked about the case either evaded the question or said, shortly, that "her family regained its honor." (The Ḥğerāt, incidentally, have not had any "honor executions" since 1957.)

Intergenerational Tensions as Agents of Culture Change

The combined effect of formal education and the expanding interaction of young adults with their peers in the rest of the country on intergenerational relations proceeded on two levels: the peer group and the individual. As a peer group they tried to edge their way into the tribe's political and decision-making positions. This process became increasingly less latent as the sources of political power became progressively more externalized and diversified. Nonetheless, such competition for power was within the range of traditional generational roles and both parties had some sense of the limits and dangers in relation to the trophies. On the level of the individual, however, no similar traditional roles were available. The youths found themselves torn in their inability to reconcile the intensifying need to make their own personal decisions, in what they came to conceive as their own private affairs, with the traditional values of familialism, honor, and unity—the cornerstones of the tribe's ideology. Thus, of the two levels, the peer and the individuals, it was the latter that posed the greater pressure on Ḥğeri culture to change. In the following paragraphs I address each of these two levels in greater detail.

Until the elections of 1977 the major source of political power (and through it economic benefits) in Israel was the Labor Party and through it the successive coalition governments that it formed and headed between 1948 and 1977. (It is access to this source of power that the *muḫtār* monopolized to maintain leadership in his hands.) Until the late 1950s, the identification of two issues—that of state security and the state's survival—in the mind of the Jewish sector prompted the country's competing political parties to agree in their security-oriented policies, including those relating to the MG and the Arab sector (which was viewed as a possible menace to the state's survival). Consequently, from the Arab sector viewpoint, there was a monolithic power source—the Labor Party as the government and its executive representative, the MG, a model still looming large in the minds of many middle-aged Arabs.

Meanwhile, however, following the 1956 Sinai Campaign and the beginning of the relaxation of MG controls over the Arab sector in 1957, many political parties moved the Arab sector from the conceptual domain of survival (which was non-negotiable) to that of security (which was negotiable) and intensified their quest for potential Arab votes. Nevertheless, so long as the MG was in power, these parties lacked the ability to dispense whatever economic and administrative resources they had in order to attract a following. The dissolution of the MG ended this obstacle and freed all the political parties in Israel to compete for Arab voters while dispensing administrative resources that were formerly in the hands of the MG. Notwithstanding, since the government of Israel was always a coalition government, a few small parties wielded excessive amounts of power relative to their voting support through the governmental ministries that they controlled by coalitionary agreements (for example, the National Religious Party [the *MafDaL*], which represented less than 10.0% of the voting population, traditionally controlled, among other ministries, the Ministry of the Interior, which managed the country's Civil Administration). In the Arab sector this turn of events resulted in partial disintegration of the monolithic power model of the Labor Party and the realization among the younger adults that the resulting fragments also generated power. By 1977 young power entrepreneurs were tapping these smaller sources, which were free from the control of the Labor Party and its Arab representatives (such as the *muḫtār* in the case of the Ḥğerāt).

These newly available power sources were actively kept viable as patron-client interactions between the party and the power entrepreneur and were structurally identical to the relationship of the *muḫtār* with the Labor Party. Parallel to these resources, however, the younger generation slowly realized the existence of a passive yet more accessible source of power in state law. (This source of power was the one the young men tried to tap in their attempt to gain control over the functioning of the executive committee of the village Water Co-Operative Society cited earlier.) Thus, over the years the Arab sector realized that, first, the Jewish sector was not a unified power monolith and that power was more widely distributed and, second, that even the administration abided by the law, thus providing the citizenry with other, albeit much weaker, sources of power that could be effective in intra-community and/or intergenerational conflict.

In and of themselves, these new sources of power did not overly threaten the Ḥğeri cultural system because intergenerational competition for power was endemic to any gerontocracy and each society has developed means and strategies to dissipate enough of the tensions generated in order to keep the society united. These means were usually encoded in the traditional roles of the society (for instance, son-father/warrior-elder) and provided a general sense of what was appropriate and/or permissible to do in the competition and what was not, and how far one could proceed without cutting off "the branch on which one sat." Thus, for example, during the early 1970s there was an attempt to dethrone the *muḫtār* by converting the administration of Bīr al-Maksūr from mukhtarship to local council by the district commissioner of the Ministry of the Interior with the tacit support of the *muḫtār* of the Mikmān. The young adults (ages 25–35 years) supported Muḥammad al-Ḥsēn in defeating the move because although they would have liked a local council into which they could be voted, they did not want "to split the tribe," which would have resulted from a local council where "each family backs up its man."

The aspiring individual did not have access to these traditional roles available to the peer group because it was precisely his individual choices that were at odds with the tribe's traditions. Nowhere was this process more clearly observed than with the shift in the meaning of the concept of love. Among its other attributes, romantic love is the discrimination of interpersonal differences and the exercise of choice among a given cluster of these. Alternately, when "A" loves "B" he/she practices his/her sense of choice, thereby emphasizing the differences that characterize "B" and set her/him apart from the rest of her/his sex. Conversely, it can be argued that passionate love requires the presence and perception of personal differences among members of the opposite sex and is thus influenced by the increased diversity that is generated by modern industrial state milieu.

In traditional society where behavior is highly patterned and social roles stable, individual differences are relatively free of the social roles these individuals perform. Moreover, the familial concerns of the members of such societies prohibit the exercise of romantic love because such a personal and personalizing choice is both largely unpredictable and self-interested. Consequently, romantic love does not play any major role in marriage for two reasons. First, since everyone including the husband and wife knows what is expected of him/her in these and related roles, and there is very little room for deviation, the importance of individual differences or their perception is drastically reduced. Second, although the society sings ballads about and sighs over passionate love, it prohibits its exercise and combats it whenever possible and with whatever tools are available (for example, elopements and their punishments). In fact, among the Ḥğerāt one can place the pair "marriage–love" on the list of culture-nature contrasts.

With the intensifying exposure of the society's younger members to education, the media, industrial milieu, and the like, there was, first, a growing awareness that there were important differences among people, jobs, and so on, and, second, that these differences were legitimate (that is, valid and justified). Hence, it was proper to choose those characteristics that fit the chooser's fancy and capabilities. Furthermore, by legitimating differences these agencies promoted their expression; that is, individuals began to emphasize their respective personal characteristics independently of the social roles they performed. This process resulted in a greater sense of choice in work, leisure, companionship, and so on, followed by a sense that one had the need or right to choose, be it among jobs, types of education, friends, residences, or mates, thus forming a self-reinforcing loop.

Among young Galilean bedouin in general and Ḥğeri in particular, the tensions generated in the youth group by this evolving sense of choice gradually mounted and were converted into latent pressures on the older generations to realign marriage decisions from their traditional familial and public concerns toward increasingly more personal aspirations as expressed by marriage decisions. Thus, in fewer and fewer cases did young women enter marriages against their wish and increasingly their fathers solicited their consent before agreeing to give them to prospective suitors. Among the Ḥğerāt the reasons for this emerging pattern ranged from one father (who had entered a major conflict with his FBS on behalf of his daughter who refused the latter) who said that he loved his daughters as much as he loved his sons and that he wanted to see them all happy in their marriages, to another father who reasoned that if the daughter was satisfied in her marriage there would be no elopements, dishonor, and troubles later on. Not surprisingly, if a woman had no formal education she would be less likely to be discriminate in her taste or aware of options other than to abide by her parents' wishes and, conversely, the more education she had acquired, the greater the investment (economic, emotional, and so on) her parents put in her future and the more important her own opinion became.

Similarly, the young men extended their sense of choice from abandoning herding (because they were ashamed of being called "shepherds") to personal choice of marital partners. Among the young men, however, the obligation to pay the *mahr* and other wedding expenses often created financial dependence on their parents, which was often weightier than education in their process of reasoning. For example, a young high school graduate temporarily followed his father's opinion and went through an engagement to a young woman he did not love. When asked for his reasons he said that if the marriage went sour and he divorced her, he would always be able to tell his parents "it was your fault" whereas if he chose, it would be his own private problem (that is, he would have to provide the *mahr* for the second marriage). The variety, however, spanned from uneducated and economically dependent sons who, like their female counterparts, were more likely to abide by their parents' decisions through some intermediate cases similar to the one just quoted to young men who were economically independent of their parents (for instance, soldiers, members of small or poorer families, and orphans). This latter category, incidentally, by setting the example of (relatively speaking) freely contracted marriages increased the observable discrepancy between what was possible and what was permissible with its major destabilizing effects on those who could not choose their wives due to their familial and/or economic status.

For Ḥğeri youth the realignment of the relations between personal choices and familial concerns was full of pain and uncertainties as the following rendition of a talk with a young man, "X," in the form of a monologue, attests. At the time of the conversation he was 27 years old, newly married, and his wife was expecting a child:

> He said he would not be spending his nights away from home were it not for his lack of love for his wife and that he is always with "A" because "A" had the same problem but was worse off because of the children, otherwise "A" would have divorced his wife long ago "but every time he sees the children he forgets divorce and when he sees his wife he forgets about the children." ["A"'s brother, incidentally, is in the same predicament.] As for himself he said that he was still in love with "1" and had lost many job opportunities because instead of making proposals [he is an independent contractor] he would go to look at her. She loved him too but her father objected because she was promised in marriage to "B." Now, "1" is married to "B" who does not love her but loves "2," who was recently married to "C" although she loves "B," and "C" does not care for her too much. He ("X") then fell in love with the daughter of "D," who objected but the girl asked him to elope. He went to ask the advice of "E" who knew about the affair and who was a friend of "D" and his family and knew them well. "E" told him that neither she nor her family were for him, and that if they eloped he would lose his own family's honor for good and that while "girls come and girls go, honor stays and is more important than anything." He decided to forget

all about her because he figured that if "E," who knew the family better than himself, said that she and her family were not for him then they were not for him. [He commented that even to date, after she was married, if they would meet and he would ask her to make love she would come with him and then go to her husband, but that was not honorable so every time he would see her he would say a cool "hello" and would hurry away.] After his talk with "E" he was distressed "like being drunk." At that time his father told him to go and see "3" [his *bint 'amm*; actually FFFBSD] because "she is a good girl and hasn't meddled with men and is honorable." He went to talk with her and consented to marry her because he was distressed and did not care one way or the other and he wanted "to shut up the mouths of the people in the village" because they had started to say that he doesn't marry "because he is a *manyak* [fucker] and has affairs outside the village." Now he was stuck with her although he did not love her and could not even kiss her. He said he had gone to prostitutes before he got married and he could not kiss them and now he could not kiss his wife as if she were a prostitute while "she is a good girl and does not deserve it" but he simply could not bring himself to kiss her. He told her he did not love her and she told him "if you didn't love me why did you marry me and ruin my life?" and that "kills" him because she was right. Now she was pregnant and when she delivered it would make things even worse. He said he wanted to run away and work in Eilat [the southern sea port of Israel] or abroad, leave the village and her and then telephone her and divorce her so that she would be able to find another man who would love her. But he hesitated about going away because the people in the village would talk and he would lose both personal and family honor. He blamed the restraining life in the village for the problems because "people don't leave you alone but talk all the time" so that "honor is not a private matter like among the Jews but a village affair" and "without honor a man is not a man." He said he was not afraid of leaving the village because of work [economic reasons] for he had a good well-paying profession which was needed everywhere and he had his tools so that he could work as an employee or as an independent contractor, but that it was the loss of honor which kept him in the village. He finally said that he told his two older nieces [ages 16 and 15 years] "who are beautiful and good girls" not to agree to marry anyone they did not love but whom their father [his eldest brother] wanted them to. He said he promised them to support them all the way so that they marry whom they loved and who loved them because it was their lives and no one had the right to ruin their lives by marrying them off to someone who did not love them or they did not love. He concluded by commenting that his own life was ruined but he would not let the girls' lives be ruined too.

A more readily observable symptom of these tensions was the phenomenon of pen pal correspondence abroad by many young Ḥğeris between the ages of 15 and 25 years who either were in high school or were graduates. The youth corresponded, invariably, with young female respondents from all corners of the world (but predominately from Europe and the Americas) with whom they established contact by listing their names and addresses in the pen pal section of an international youth paper published in Finland. The problems they encountered in expressing themselves in English and the rapid turnover of pen pals, which implies a lack of the stamina necessary for maintaining the correspondence, suggest that this activity served some function other than to increase their proficiency in English or a genuine interest in life in other parts of the world. It seemed to be a mechanism to reduce some of the frustrations that resulted from their inability to reconcile their traditions with their aspirations by promoting a fantasy of openness and freedom. The need for such a release arose from their need to cope with the reality of life in the village and "the elders who do not understand," which they continually criticized, and their emotional inability to leave the village and settle elsewhere because, as a result of their socialization in a segmentary (lineage) milieu, they were very dependent on their relatives and the tribe for their sense of security.

Interestingly, one young man in his mid-20s tried to dissipate some of these tensions by organizing an informal forum to air complaints and grievances (in T-group style). The participants were a small group of friends between 17 and 20 years old and the topics ranged from intra-village affairs to extra-tribal encounters. His main emphases were on rising above lineage factionalism and on dealing with people as individuals, be they lineal members, Ḥğeris, Arabs, or Jews. He also tried to explain the behavior of the older generations and to clarify the dynamics of the problems they all faced in order to promote compassion in his group members.

It is important to realize that as of 1977 the issue was not the overthrow of the traditional familial concerns and their replacement by personal choices. What the youth wanted was the addition of another level to the marital decision making process. As mentioned before, the arrival at a marriage decision in the traditional manner was a process of tacit consent. In other words, the groom's parents would decide on a prospective bride, and if she and her family were acceptable to the lineage, the lineal elders made no attempt to block the marriage. Then, if there were no objection to the marriage on the level of the tribe, the parents were allowed to proceed with their plans. However, if any level above the parental level decided that the proposed marriage was against that level's interests, the leaders of that level would try to convince the would-be groom's parents to abandon that specific union, a measure that generally was sufficient. If, on the other hand, the groom or his parents decided to pursue the marriage, their lineal relatives would avoid the engagement ceremony, thus making their displeasure public—a measure that usually succeeded in stopping the marriage from taking place. Thus, for example, a young fatherless member of the Ġadāyreh wanted to marry a young woman from the Ḏiyabāt. His mother and paternal uncles supported him but his mother's relatives—who headed the sublineage to which all belonged—objected to the marriage. Being a soldier, he was financially independent and he decided to proceed with the engagement ceremony, partly because his maternal relatives did not press their disagreement. Nonetheless, the avoidance of the ceremony by the latter relatives made their discontent public, which brought about the cancellation of the marriage by the would-be bride's family.

The youth thus wanted to become the first level in this decision-making process; that is, they would choose the bride and the choice would be subjected to the tacit approval of the various levels of interests: the familial, the sublineal, the lineal, and the tribal. While as a class they had not yet succeeded in establishing this innovation, some individuals, as mentioned above, had already set the example and had chosen their own wives. The majority, however, tried to manipulate the process as best they could. Thus, for example, a young man who did not like his parents' choice pointed to the miserly behavior of his future in-laws during his parents' visit to their tent and brought some gossip about his fiancée (who was reported to have said that his family was stingy and he was moody/crazy), thereby convincing them to cancel the marriage negotiations. In another example, a young man fell in love with a peasant woman but his father objected to the union. The youth went to his grandfather (a lineal elder), who later invited his son (the father) for a talk, during which he said that the girl's family was honorable and had been friends of the Ḥǧerāt for a long time and that from his point of view there was no reason to object to the marriage. The father accepted the elder's opinion and proceeded to marry the son to his choice.

For their part, the elder generations perceived and accepted the change in their surroundings and lifestyle with relative calm, reasoning that "one has to follow the flow of life." That general sense of c'est la vie was quite widespread among the Galilean bedouin in general and more than once I heard an individual, Ḥǧeri and non-Ḥǧeri alike, remark that bedouin traditions were being lost and that in another twenty to thirty years the bedouin of the Galilee would be no more because they would all become *fellāḥīn* for "that's progress." Asked "How does it happen?" some shrugged their shoulders, some suggested that "if enough people do something new it becomes a habit and replaces the tradition," and one said that "progress advances by itself and demands more progress; it is not dependent on intelligence or education because even the greatest backwoods idiot can switch on electricity, turn on a water faucet, or drive a car." Yet "progress" was, among its many facets, the tragedy of the elderly for they were damned if they did follow the flow of life and forfeit the traditional rewards and satisfactions that awaited old age—honor, respect, leadership, and so on—and damned if they did not follow it and were left behind, losing their sense of being members of the community.

At the level of the individual, similar to the younger generations, their level of conservatism seemed to be a function of their age and personal histories. While the elderly submitted to the present but would rather have had "the old ways," the middle-aged, who had led the settlement of Bīr al-Maksūr, were more prone to actively look for change. They, however, sought innovations in material culture and not a change in social ethics and ideals. One man, for example, gave an example of short pants that he would like to wear but would not because people would talk about him and he would lose their respect/his honor.

As a group, however, they were seeing the growing differences between themselves and the tribe's youth but seemed to think that the mounting tension among the latter was the traditional adolescence fever (or, the "hot-bloodedness" of the youth), which would pass with time, and interpreted the latter's grab for power in light of traditional dynamics and tactics. In part, this assessment of the youth was influenced by the practical absence of economic competition among the various generations due to the tribe's involvement in the regional cash economy, which absorbed its excess labor force. Furthermore, the lack of strong agrarian ideology among the Ḥǧerāt meant that, unlike the situation in *fellāḥīn* villages, given free choice most youth would not opt for agriculture as their livelihood. In fact, most wanted to join the IDA. Consequently, not having the traditional explanation for generational conflict—political rivalry (which was not exercised on the individual level) and economic competition—they chose adolescence as the apparent cause for the widening gulf between them. Consequently, they tended to respond to the dilemmas facing the youth in ways that were progressively less effective as the youth became ever younger and, hence, increasingly more distant from the traditions that organized their elders' universe.

It is important to realize that the aforementioned abandonment of "honor executions" and the greater freedom in choosing mates or consenting to a proposed marriage that were being practiced at this time were not an attempt to solve the dilemmas that faced the youth but were collateral allowances that resulted from adhering to the state's law and an attempt to maintain obedience without the need to resort to coercion. In other words, the strong linkage of the Ḥǧerāt to the police and the importance of this link to their regional leadership made "honor executions" very disruptive to the continuance of these relations. Since it was inadvisable to use such drastic measures to ensure the preservation of familial and tribal honor, the solution was to remove the offense, thereby voiding the need to punish. By asking the consent of prospective mates and by letting more independent individuals choose their own mates, the reasons for elopement and, hence, its punishment were reduced to a minor problem. A similar consideration governed the issue of pre- and extramarital sex. Thus, although benefiting the youth, these were solutions to a more efficiently enforced state law rather than an answer to the structural changes the youth required.

On a more general level, this process of adjustment between the youth and their elders could be formulated as the transition from an emphasis on societal future and personal present to an emphasis on personal future and societal present. Alternatively, it is a question of the temporal orientation of the individual: who is more important, he/she or their descendants? The older generations, as in other traditional societies, emphasized the future of the society (that is, their children and grandchildren), and derived their societal rewards through them. Consequently, the individual lived in the present and invested most of his/her actions toward making the future of his/her descendants possible and better if he/she could. (This is exemplified by a local folk tale about an old man who planted an almond tree that would begin to bear fruit after his death. Asked by a passerby "why plant it if you will not be able to enjoy its fruits," he answered, "like my grandfather who planted for me to enjoy I plant for my grandchildren's enjoyment.") Thus, cultivating his/her individual self for his/her own ends was of a lower priority compared to preparing the future for his/her descendants, and was usually subdued if it endangered this end.

By contrast, the younger generations progressively approached the model of the industrial cultural complex, which celebrates the individual and her/his personal future while reducing societal concerns to a subservient level to her/his interest. The individual, thus, strives for self-attainment, personal development, and so on, while continuously reducing her/his concerns of and input toward the maintenance of the social milieu, not to mention that of her/his descendants. For example, in 1976 a major figure in the tribe's sociopolitical hierarchy and an extremely crucial linkage to the police suddenly died of a cardiac arrest. His police profession was a tracker that, although low on the police hierarchy, allowed him ample free time, which he used to manage the tribe's relations with the police and other local groups. Although he was repeatedly offered the opportunity to study in preparation for police officers' course, he had refused the offers. In the havoc and reorganization that followed his death another policeman, a young patrilateral second cousin, was asked to accept the vacant position because he was the most competent choice to fill it. He refused because he had no knowledge of the workings of the Arab sector where the deceased had been stationed, nor did he think that he could "fill his shoes." His other reason, however, was that he had previously transferred from tracking to investigations, had successfully completed detective sergeants' course, and was on his way to police officers' course as soon as he had completed his matriculation examinations and similar prerequisites. To accept the former position of the deceased (which would have given him much more power within the tribe) would have arrested his personal career in the interests of the tribe, which he was not about to do, although he realized that the other individuals who were proposed for the job would not perform it as well and, therefore, this crucial linkage would be greatly weakened.

Although potentially very disruptive to the perpetuation of tribal unity among the Ḥğerāt, the occasional surfacing of these undercurrents were perceived by almost all tribesmembers as aberrations rather than as trend markers. Thus, during the campaign and parliamentary election of 1977 (which will be dealt with in greater detail as part of the discussion of Ḥğeri politics later) practically all the male population of the tribe saw the competition among the different political parties and parliamentary lists as unrelated to the traditional power concerns of the tribe and, hence, to its identity. In other words, the dissident leaders were viewed as competing with the *muḫtār* in an extra-tribal and not in the intra-tribal or even the intra-regional arena where the immediate power lay in his sublineage and in his personal network respectively. The contest was perceived as individuals competing for the link of clientage to the administration and not as a possible reorganization of the internal constitution of power relations within the tribe or their demise altogether—that is, the decline of the tribe from regional leadership.

Furthermore, the traditional rivalries with other tribes and villages in the area and the maintenance of regional leadership in Ḥğeri control provided ample external impetus for the preservation of traditional unity, which endowed individual Ḥğeris with security and pride at being able to say "I am a Ḥğeri" for a century or so. Consequently, as of 1977 the Ḥğerāt were somewhat more conservative than most other local tribes in inter-sexual and intergenerational interactions, both of which were, to a large degree, controlled by the Council of the Elders, which regularly emphasized the need and importance of unity and the role of tradition in its maintenance. Among several other local tribes, in 1976/77 one could observe girls and young women wearing tight slacks and other Western-style clothing, and weddings featuring a live band that played pop dance music to which young males and females danced together after, or parallel to, the more traditional ceremony (that is, food and *ḥadaya*). By contrast, such clothing was not seen among the Ḥğerāt and in the one wedding in Bīr al-Maksūr during which a live pop band did replace the traditional *ḥadaya*, no one danced at all. Similarly, premarital young male-female interactions within Ḥğeri settlements, while somewhat freer than traditional demeanor, were still within customary bounds—for example, no single male/single female interaction in private regardless of reason unless they were married, or in some cases, about to be married. Similarly, among the Ḥğerāt, obedience was still a highly valued response of younger toward older and female toward male. It was common to observe an elder brother (not to mention one's father) lecturing a younger brother on how to behave properly while the latter listened, even in cases where he would conveniently forget it later. Generally speaking, sisters obeyed their brothers, wives their husbands and their husbands' parents, and younger obeyed older. Contingent upon the specific dynamics of the relationship and the situation, disobedience may become a major issue punishable by beating and similar measures. Similarly, the dicta of the Council of the Elders were still accepted as customary law and, in general, the elderly and their advice were respected and listened to even if not followed or actively sought after.

The Marriage Pattern of Generations VII and VIII[17]

It is with this background in mind that the marriage patterns of the seventh and eighth generations that span the Israeli Period have to be approached. Moreover, changing intergenerational relations was only one component in the complex of novel circumstances that affected Ḥğeri marriage strategies during the Israeli Period. To reiterate, the mass departure of the Arab population during and immediately following the 1948 War directly disrupted all patterns of alliances (marital included) either by the disappearance of an ally or that of a foe who provided an alliance with its raison d'etre, as well as generally reducing the pool of prospective marriage mates in the country. As a result, remnant families from formerly competing opponent populations who were previously maritally inaccessible became exempted from the political strategies that governed their inaccessibility in the past and began marrying with the Ḥğerāt—for example, Ṣafūriyeh.

Then, post-1967, a new source for novel marital arrangements was added. The opening of the West Bank to Israeli Arabs provided the smaller, poorer, and powerless families with a new pool of marriageable females that were sought after, owing to the lower *mahr* demanded by their parents. Finally, the rest of the changes—political, economic, demographic, educational, and so on—that accumulated throughout this period only added to the deviation from older motives. Consequently, although the marriage pattern of Generations VII and VIII was similar to those of their predecessors (see Table 23), many of the causes and reasons that were important to the tribe during the Mandate Period gradually lost their former validity to the explanation of the marriage patterns of these two generations.

As Table 23 suggests, the 424 marriages[18] of Generation VII, which span the period from 1940 to 1977, and the 42 marriages of Generation VIII, which were contracted between 1960 and 1977, resemble the pattern set by the preceding two generations in their general distribution between the intra- and extra-tribal marriage categories (subtotals in Table 23). It is interesting to note that regardless of the political and demographic changes that characterized the twentieth century, the general division between these two categories maintained its consistency at a ratio of approximately two-thirds intra- to one-third extra-tribal marriages. Notwithstanding, as the table indicates, the internal constitution of each of these changed, most noticeably in the "endogamous" subcategory, which increased by almost 10% over the past. Second, there seems to be a general trend of a slow increase in marriages with the settled population over those with other bedouin tribes.

Table 23. A comparison of the marriage patterns of Generations IV–VIII of the *'arab* al-Ḥğerāt.

Type of Marriage	Generation IV				Generation V		Generation VI		Generation VII		Generation VIII	
	Recorded		Corrected*									
	N	%	N	%	N	%	N	%	N	%	N	%
endogamous	1	2.9	1	2.1	32	23.9	104	35.6	192	45.3	19	45.2
intra-Ḥğerāt but not endogamous	14	41.2	14	29.2	51	38.1	85	29.1	72	17.0	7	16.7
subtotal	*15*	*44.1*	*15*	*31.2*	*83*	*61.9*	*189*	*64.7*	*264*	*62.3*	*26*	*61.9*
inter-tribal	19	55.9	33	68.8	46	34.3	71	24.3	106	25.0	10	23.8
with villages					5	3.7	29	9.9	41	9.7	3	7.1
with towns							3	1.0	13	3.1	3	7.1
subtotal	*19*	55.9	*33*	*68.8*	*51*	*38.1*	*103*	*35.2*	*160*	*37.8*	*16*	*38.1*
total	*34*	*100.0*	*48*	*100.0*	*134*	*100.0*	*292*	*100.0*	*424*	*100.0*	*42*	*100.0*

*Corrected for sex ratios (see above).

Of these two changes, the increase in endogamy seems to result from the continuous preservation of public security and the shift in sources of political power from lateral alliances to the state administration, which underwrote a milieu within which the tribe was able to invest more of its marital potential in intra-tribal unions. It is important to realize in this context that the higher order segmentary level of the tribe left decisions regarding endogamous unions to the discretion of the involved sublineage and did not meddle in them. Since the purpose of this monograph is to describe the Ḥğerāt at the level of the tribe, previous mentions of any specific sublineage and inquiries into its actions were limited to the items that directly bore on the tribe as a whole. To analyze the specific reasons that promoted the increase in the endogamy rate among the Ḥğerāt would require a detailed diachronic analysis of the marriage strategies of each sublineage against its fortunes and relation to the other Ḥğeri sublineages, similar to Aswad's procedures for the marriages of the Al Shiukh (1971: ch. 4). Such a task would be a major diversion from the course of this project and will not, therefore, be done at present.

One issue, however, needs to be clarified. My use of demographic variables as a "major factor" should not be interpreted to mean a "unicausal force" such as Kressel's use of ideology to explain endogamy among the Jawarish in Israel (1970, 1976). Rather, I use them as a substrate or a limiting factor without which the phenomenon would not exist yet not necessarily define its appearance, similar to their use by Goldberg (1967) in his analysis of village endogamy among Mauritanian Jews in Israel, and like Rosenfeld who lists them as his first "possible reason" (1976:120) for a similar rise in the endogamy of a *fellāḥīn* village in the Lower Galilee. Moreover, since the term *bint 'amm* (Father's Brother's Daughter) includes, in addition to the real FBDs, an assortment of classificatory FBDs (which in the case of Ḥğerāt embrace practically all the females of Ego's generation within his sublineage), increased generational depth is concomitant with an enlargement of the pool of classified FBDs even though the population of real FBDs did not increase. Finally, inasmuch as there was a more intense need to bridge segmentary lineage opposition, such population increase in a society employing segmentary lineage organization had direct political implications, as was noticed by Barth (1954). Unlike Barth, however, I do not think that politics, and especially those at the family level, are the only reason for either the practice or its increase over time. These political and demographic factors worked in combination with Ḥğeri population increase, which reduced the need to rely on alliances to provide for security while intensifying the need to unite the burgeoning and diverging sublineages and concurrently providing the individuals required to answer this need. Unexpectedly, however, the attempt to unite the tribe through marriages did not continue at a rate proportional to the successive segmentary levels through which the various sublineages were linked. On the contrary, the marital decisions behaved as if there was a consistent cut-off point—the aforementioned two-thirds value—that intratribal marriages would not exceed. Since they thus behaved, it is not surprising that the increase in the number of sublineal endogamous marriages was commensurate with a decrease in marriages with other units of the tribe. Two general observations are warranted here. The first is that it seems unlikely that the consistency of this two-thirds value over a four-generation span is an artifact of the data. Therefore, I propose that such a ratio between intra- and extra-tribal marriages might prove helpful in analyzing the political status of, at least, bedouin tribes. In other words, it seems that this ratio identifies the political "steady state" (that is, the balance between unifying the tribe and preventing its isolation) at least in the case of a relatively small bedouin tribe, located in an area of approximately equally matched sociopolitical entities, and where no land ownership was actively involved. Unfortunately, I have not been able to find in the ethnographic literature comparative marriage statistics for whole tribes (not to mention in matching circumstances). Hence, the utility of this measure remains tentative.

The second observation is that the decrease in interlineal marriages suggests that the organizational level of the lineage did not exercise much influence over marital decisions, or, conversely, that the two levels that did exert influence were the familial/sublineal and the tribal. The first level actually made the marriage decision because it managed the affairs of its members while the tribe, being the outward boundary of the maximal unit, served as a filter that may or may not let the decision be implemented should it rise to its level of concerns. Since the familial/sublineal level was the basic self-perpetuating (that is, self-interested) unit in the tribe, it is hardly surprising that faced with the growing social divergence of its members and the weakening of their primary loyalties (which endangered its own survival through its ability to self-perpetuate), it underwrote its survival concerns by reuniting its membership through increasing endogamous unions. But in so doing it also promoted its own interests over the need to preserve the tribe's cohesiveness through the unification of its constituent lineages (that is, interlineal unions). This, incidentally, seems to be the dynamic mechanism that generated the proliferation of tribal segments and the rise of new tribal units and tribes, which have been described and discussed by most students of tribal societies (e.g., Evans-Prichard 1940:247; Lienhardt 1958:114; Peters 1960, to mention but a few).

The second change of interest—the slow general increase in the relative number of marriages with the settled population—had begun, as might be remembered, as a means to promote the cooperation against Ṣafūriyeh. With time that reason was amplified by the gradual settlement of the tribe and its growing involvement in agricultural and industrial cash economy, which slowly eradicated the more prominent differences between the Ḥğerāt and their settled neighbors. Thus, the growing similarity in lifestyles not only facilitated the exchange of women with villagers but with townspeople as well. Similarly, as the daily skills of the sex roles became more general to the region as a whole, other attributes (such as education) became the important criteria that distinguished one person from another in the eyes of the chooser. Free marital choice, incidentally, is the end of a continuum whose other end is prearranged infants' promised marriages. In the case of the Ḥğerāt this continuum is parallel to a sociogeographical continuum at one end of which lies the sublineage while at the other end the town. Thus, all of the mates from the nearby towns were chosen by the marrying males and consented to by their parents while most of the marriages within the sublineage were prearranged by the parents with the consents or compliance of the marrying individuals.

The shift in the sources of political power, made more intense by the growing divergence in vested interests between the Mikmān and Bīr al-Maksūr as a result of their competition for state resources, and the subsequent decline in the direct political role of marriage promoted a tendency to avoid intervention in extra-tribal marriages contracted by the familial/sublineal level provided these did not jeopardize the honor of the tribe as a whole. For example, in 1970 a 17-year-old woman from a small subunit of the D'eyfeh eloped with a man from the village of Saḫnīn. The issue was taken by the tribe as a whole and negotiated by the *muḫtār* and the chairman of the village council of Saḫnīn. The Ḥğerāt demanded the custody of the woman as a precondition for the talks instead of acting against the village immediately. After some maneuvering by the village the Ḥğerāt received her and by the next morning she was made the wife of a son of a leading member of the D'eyfeh, an act that ended the issue. In comparison, in 1974 a teenage female of the Ṣawālḥah eloped with a 20-year-old Ġadāyri male. The negotiations between the elders of the two respective maximal lineages were conducted with the declared intent of preserving tribal unity. The Council's verdict was to allow the two to marry but had them leave the village for one of the herding camps "for seven years"; to have the male's family pay I£20,000 in damages to the girl's father (the average intra-Ḥğerāt *mahr* in 1970–1974 prices was I£5158 [N = 41; range I£2500 to I£10,000]; this sum was not considered to be, even partially, a *mahr*); and had the girl's father renounce his daughter. Thus, when a year later the girl's brother made an attempt on her life, it was not considered to be an inter-lineal affair but a criminal case to be handled by the state's judicial system.

By default, such a tendency of minimal intervention in extra-tribal marriages promoted an extensive rather than intensive marital strategy, adding nine new tribes and ten new villages to the Ḥğeri network, and which, aside from allowing the sublineages to develop the information and assistance network that they required for economic survival, was also in accord with the political aspirations of representing the regional Arab population that had been entertained by the Ḥğeri leadership for the past decade. Thus these extra-tribal ties served as Ḥğeri points of entry into the community with which the marriage was contracted. This political function was very visible during the 1977 election campaign when these households usually provided information on the political mood of the community and its leaders and its male members served as activists for the *muḫtār*'s United Arab List.

The two changes discussed above were not the result of collapsing the data in order to present the tribe as a whole but, as Table 24 indicates, were noticeable in the marriage strategies of each of the three lineages, albeit with some familiar differences. Thus the Ġadāyreh still led in extra-lineal and extra-tribal marriages while the Ṭa'awāneh maintained its primacy in inter-sublineal (or, intra-lineage) marriages, although the relative variance of the three lineages grew much smaller. A more interesting observation is the behavior of the two sublineages of the Ḍiyabāt—the Ṭa'awāneh and the D'eyfeh—who together led the tribe in endogamous unions and separately, respectively, rated fourth and second among the fifteen sublineages of the tribe (the first five in 1977 were: Ġadāyreh, 50.0%; D'eyfeh, 49.1%; Masa'īd, 41.9%; Ṭa'awāneh, 40.5%; and Maḥāmīd, 40.0%). No less interesting is the low level of marital interaction between these two sublineages, which may suggest a probable organizational separation and the assumption of independent status by the Ṭa'awāneh.

Thus, as of 1977 Generation VII of the Ṭa'awāneh took 1 wife and gave 1 daughter (or, 5.4% of the marriages the generation contracted) to the D'eyfeh, who gave the former 4 daughters (7.3% of its marriages). If this pattern and rate are meaningful then not only was there a reduction in the number of women exchanged between them but for the first time the Ṭa'awāneh took more wives than provided daughters in this intra-lineal exchange. Thus, Generation VI of the Ṭa'awāneh took 4 wives and gave 3 daughters (17.5% of that generation's total marriages) while the D'eyfeh took 5 and gave 1 (15.0% of the total), and the respective figures for Generation V were, for the Ṭa'awāneh, 1 taken to 2 given (13.6%) and, for the D'eyfeh, 3 taken to 2 given (20.8%). In addition to the pattern and rate of wife exchange, two other factors and one event make this suggestion feasible. First was the absence of an influential D'eyfi elder and the presence of a Ṭa'awāni one on the tribal level and, second, the residence of the D'eyfi core in the Ḍmeydeh whereas the Ṭa'awāneh resided in Bīr al-Maksūr. Confounding the issue of the absence of a prominent D'eyfi elder (the last of whom died on January 5, 1977) was that sublineage's traditional independence from the *ulād* Ġadīr and their resentment of the latter over the neglect of the Ḍmeydeh by the authorities, which promoted the Ġadāyreh to favor the Ṭa'awāneh, who had traditionally been their closest non-Ġadāyri allies. Similarly, the residence in Bīr al-Maksūr did not only make the Ṭa'awāneh's elder ipso facto the representative of all the Ḍiyabāt who resided there (including those D'eyfi families who relocated to the

Table 24. The marriage pattern of Generation VII and Generation VIII by lineage affiliation.

Lineage	**Membership**			**Endog-amous**		**Intra-Lineage**		**With Ġadāyreh**				**With Ḍiyabāt**				**With Ṣawālḥah**				**With Other Tribes**				**With Villages**				**With Towns**				**Total*** N = 100%
	M	F	Total	N	%	N	%	K	G	T	%	K	G	T	%	K	G	T	%	K	G	T	%	K	G	T	%	K	G	T	%	
Ġadāyreh																																
G. VII	328	314	642	75	38.9	18	9.3	93		93	48.2	3	3	6	3.1	10	9	19	9.8	19	29	48	24.9	13	12	25	13.0	2		2	1.0	193
G. VIII	288	294	582	8	38.1	1	4.8	9		9	42.9	1	1	2	9.5	1		1	4.8		4	4	19.0	2		2	9.5	2	1	3	14.3	21
Ṭa'awāneh																																
G. VII	83	92	175	15	41.7	1	2.8	1	2	3	8.3	16		16	44.4	1	3	4	11.1	4	7	11	30.5	1	1	2	5.5					36
G. VIII	62	64	126																													
D'eyfeh																																
G. VII	84	70	154	27	52.9			3	2	5	9.8	27		27	52.9	3	1	4	7.8	2	4	6	11.8	2	1	3	5.9	4	2	6	11.8	51
G. VIII	84	93	177																													
Ḍiyabāt																																
G. VII	167	162	329	42	48.3	1	1.1	4	4	8	9.2	43		43	49.4	4	4	8	9.2	6	11	17	19.5	3	2	5	5.7	4	2	6	6.9	87
G. VIII	146	157	303																													
Ṣawālḥah																																
G. VII	306	283	589	75	41.4	22	12.2	8	13	21	11.6	2	4	6	3.3	97		97	53.6	14	27	41	22.7	7	4	11	6.1	3	2	5	2.8	181
G. VIII	315	245	560	11	52.4	4	19.0		2	2	9.5					15		15	71.4	3	3	6	28.6	1		1	4.3					23

Key: M = male; F = female; N = number; K = wife taken from the above; G = daughter given to the above; T = total marriages

*These totals include females who were exchanged among the lineages and who were not included in Table 23 in order to avoid duplication in counting the marriages of the tribe as a whole.

village) but also permitted him to be immediately available whenever there was a need for the Council of the Elders to convene. Thus, "real time" calculations also favored his prominence. Finally, there were some tensions between the two sublineages over conduct in a blood case in 1975. During that event, a member of the Masa'īd allegedly killed a man of the Ṭa'awāneh (he died of heart failure). The D'eyfeh's first reaction was to follow blood revenge while the Ṭa'awāneh, under the influence of the Elder of the Ġadāyreh, independently accepted a settlement of blood-payment and the alleged killer's expulsion for seven years. The D'eyfeh interpreted the Ṭa'awāneh's settlement as a compromise of the lineage's honor and a strike for independence in decision making in cases that concerned the lineage as a whole.

The independent behavior of the Ṭa'awāneh and the D'eyfeh, as well as the other two trends discussed before, stand out even clearer when the marriage patterns of the fifth through seventh generations are compared by lineage (see Table 25). Thus, the Ṭa'awāneh's seventh generation seemed to maintain that sublineage's emphasis on marriages with other tribes and avoidance of marriages with townspeople while the D'eyfeh's Generation VII led the tribe with its ties to the settled population that included a major component of marriages with townspeople. This latter development seems the result of the decline of Ḍmeydeh and the gradual dispersal of its population in the aftermath of the rise of Bīr al-Maksūr.[19] Another novelty was the establishment of marital ties between the Ṭa'awāneh and the Ṣawālḥah. Although the immediate significance of these four marriages was unclear, they point to the possible appearance of a new factor in intra-tribal marriages—the development of settlement identity that facilitated inter-lineage marriages between village residents. Thus, of these four marriages, two (involving a male and a female) were a daughter-sister exchange between two married men in an arrangement of second marriages for both. The Ṭa'awāni in this case was a member of a minor and isolated family of that sublineage while the Sama'ni, although in his mid-60s during the fieldwork period and though a brother to the Elder of the Sama'neh, was not considered to be an elder by his sublineage mates. The other two marriages, involving Ṭa'awāni women and a member each of the Sama'neh and the Masa'īd, were first marriages but were contracted during the early 1960s. Since no new first marriages were contracted after this date, while the former two were second marriages, it is hard to assess the significance of these marital ties.

Two major themes thus pervade the marriage patterns of the seventh and eighth generations. The first is the growing range of variations similar to other facets of Ḥĝeri lifestyle while the second is the political import of aggregate marital decisions of particular tribal segments. Of the two the former seems to command more importance because the increase is a directional process; that is, it ranges from traditional, arranged marriages contracted by parents for their own political ends and familial aspirations to "modern" marriages governed by personal choice, which increasingly emphasized the individual and his/her personal needs and tastes. As such they tended to further erode the political importance of marital decisions even when these represented a direction taken by a whole sublineage because the sources of real power no longer lay in the brute force commanded by the elders of a tribal segment nor were yet invested in the number of voters that they could mobilize for the elections for a village council.

To a major degree, the individuals responsible for the slow shift in this direction (epitomizing the general process of culture change that the Ḥğerāt were undergoing) were those members of the tribe who were "unimportant" in traditional terms—the orphans and the sons of weak fathers from small families—for they were allowed to follow their idiosyncrasies more freely. They introduced change to fringe patterns that were previously forbidden in the behavioral repertoire of the group, thereby legitimating these changed patterns. The extent to which the majority of the group will adopt the changed behavior and slowly shift direction as more people perform the new instead of the traditional pattern will largely depend on the degree to which the leading representatives of the traditional order adopt some of the innovations, thus legitimating them for the less daring members of the community. In the case of Ḥğeri marriage choices the growing practice of asking the consent of prospective brides performs precisely that service to the growing demand of the young men to choose their brides.

Although sublineal endogamy might be argued to emphasize the political importance of marriages, at least five factors tended to maintain the political aspect of marriage at a low profile in comparison with the Mandate Period. First was the absence of an arena—that is, a village council—for the acting out of local politics that emphasized marital ties. Second was the aforementioned process of individualization, which had affected the younger generations as individuals and as peer-groups. Third was the pattern of regional ethnicity, which maintained both the process and intra-tribal competition in check as regards political issues. Fourth was the

Table 25. Marriage pattern summary: a comparison of Generation V to Generation VII by lineage (percent).

Lineage	**Endogamous**			**Intra-Lineage**			**With Ġadāyreh**			**With Ḍiyabāt**			**With Ṣawālḥah**			**With Other Tribes**			**With Villages**			**With Towns**		
	V	VI	VII	V	VI	VII	V	VI	VII	V	VI	VII	V	VI	VII	V	VI	VII	V	VI	VII	V	VI	VII
Ġadāyreh	8.0	29.3	38.9	24.0	14.6	9.3	32.0	43.9	48.2	12.0	6.5	3.1	14.0	7.3	9.8	36.0	27.6	24.9	6.0	13.8	13.0		0.8	1.0
Ṭa'awāneh	30.0	35.1	41.8	5.0	10.8	2.8	10.0	18.9	8.3	35.0	45.9	44.4			11.1	55.0	27.0	30.5		8.1	5.5			
D'eyfeh	36.4	30.8	52.9	13.6	12.8		9.1	5.6	9.8	54.5	43.6	52.9	31.6	5.1	7.8	22.7	33.3	11.8	4.5	10.3	5.9		2.6	11.8
Ḍiyabāt	33.3	32.9	48.3	9.5	11.8	1.1	9.5	11.8	9.2	42.9	44.7	49.4	7.1	2.6	9.2	38.1	30.3	19.5	2.4	9.2	5.7		1.3	6.9
Ṣawālḥah	25.9	38.1	41.4	40.7	27.7	12.2	5.6	11.5	11.6	3.7	7.1	3.3	66.7	63.7	53.6	22.2	12.4	22.7	1.8	4.4	6.1		0.9	2.8

residential division between the Ṣawālḥah and the rest of the tribe and the competition for the available sedentarization funds, which it entailed. And, fifth were the patterns of political and economic resource distribution in the country as of 1977 that, at least in the Arab sector, assumed the form of traditional patronage. Should the balance among these factors change, sublineal endogamy might yet assume a greater political importance.

Notes

1. Yodfāt was first established as a forest fire watch in 1958 while its future settlers resided in nearby Segev and worked in reforestation of that mountain range with the Ḥğerāt for the JNF. During 1959/60 they began to build their houses there and, as one of them remarked, "settled with the help of the Settlement department of the Ḥğerāt" headed by the *muḫtār* and under the active leadership of Muḥammad Sleyman al-'Abed, the firstborn son of the former *muḫtār*. In 1961 the settlement was recognized as an official settlement site. The Ḥğerāt in those days guarded and protected the settlement's property and helped in field work sporadically, and Ḥğeri women baked bread for the settlers (flour was provided by Yodfāt). The relationships remained warm and most of the families that still resided in the Ẓahara in 1976/77 had a member or two working in the settlement's flower bulb shop or guarding its fields.
2. The law in question is section 93 of the 1858 Ottoman Land Code, which prohibits obstructing public thoroughfare, including open country, by construction or planting, and is punishable by the destruction of the constructed structure or the uprooting of the plants (cf. Ben Shemesh 1953:142).
3. To what extent his plans would materialize was hard to assess at the end of the fieldwork period because he seemed to have mobilized *Kupāt Ḫolim* without the knowledge of the *muḫtār*. Such a move was interpreted by the latter to mean that apart from the economic rewards of the rent fees and the salary, the former was trying to accumulate power through his position as a branch secretary, which he very likely might use to compete with the *muḫtār*. As a result, when the *muḫtār* received a letter from *Kupāt Ḫolim* informing him of the negotiations, he replied that he "does not know anything about the subject," "was surprised to hear about," and "would they please enlighten him about the matter."
4. The 1961 population statistics of the CBS for Bīr al-Maksūr seem to include the Ḍmeydeh, the Mikmān, and Bīr al-Maksūr. For example, the bureau's 1961 Census provided a total figure of 1929 individuals residing in 226 households (Isr. CBS 1963b:32). This official definition of Bīr al-Maksūr by the bureau had been established in the first census of the area in 1949 (cf. Isr. CBS 1963a:44–45 for 1951, 1954, and 1957 figures) and was used until the 1972 Census (cf. Isr. CBS 1965:15, 1968:5, 1971:33, and 1972c:33 for 1964, 1967, 1970, and 1971 respectively) when a more restrictive definition of the settlement was adopted and the 1961 figures fell to 869 individuals residing in 137 households (Isr. CBS 1974b:12–13). Consequently, the first source of population statistics for Bīr al-Maksūr per se are those collected by Golani (1961) during his survey of the, then, hamlet.

   It should be noted, however, that Golani's figures seem to underrepresent the frequency of females in the lower age categories and especially in the 0–4 years age bracket (45 males:24 females) than might be expected when considering the Ḥğeri sex ratio for this age bracket in 1972 and 1977 (98:112 and 155:152 respectively). The reason for this discrepancy seems to lie in the method of data collection used by Golani, who copied the birth dates of the children from their fathers' ID cards (1961:6), whereas the latter often did not register the birth of their daughter(s) until a male progeny was born. This inaccuracy, in fact, seems to be inherent in the method of relying on official records when the tribesmen do not fully cooperate with (i.e., legitimate) the authorities, and had plagued the CBS 1961 Census returns for the whole tribe as well—218 males:179 females in the 0–4 years age bracket (1963b:164–65). Only with the establishment of the practice of giving births in hospitals have the official sex-ratio birth statistics gained credible accuracy.

5. Although the statistics provided by Golani for the female population should be taken as the lowest value for their frequency in the 0–14 years age bracket, his male statistics are most probably accurate and can serve as a base point for assessing the general development of the village's population. The small difference between the median age of the hamlet's male residents (13.9 years) and that of the males of the tribe at large (14.1) seem to confirm this evaluation of Golani's figures because in 1961 Bīr al-Maksūr's population lived very much like the rest of the tribe—that is, giving birth at home, no easily reached medical facilities, similar diet, only somewhat better protection from the elements, and so on.
6. It should be noted that the 1972 statistics provided by the CBS for females may be somewhat inflated in the 0–14 years age bracket, thus depressing their median age to 9.9 years, which is below what would be expected considering the rest of the table. The reason seems to be the reciprocal of Golani's under-count—that is, those females who were alive but not registered in 1961 were later categorized according to their belated registered age rather than their actual birth date.
7. Birth control or "family planning" is a touchy subject, which many Ḥğeri males would not discuss openly even in cases where their families used it, and hence the absence of information about its spread. In general if a young or early middle-aged woman had a history of birth spacing of 18–24 months and then had stopped for three or more years at the time of my taking the census of the household, when I felt comfortable I would ask the husband if "they are done" (i.e., employed "family planning") and often received an affirmative answer.
8. Most Ḥğeris I asked about the increase in endogamous marriage claimed that FBS-right is no longer an issue and rarely would a young Ḥğeri mention that "her FBS stepped in" and, therefore, he had to look elsewhere. Nonetheless, 45.3% of Generation VII (born 1920–1944) marriages and 45.2% of Generation VIII (born 1945–1969) marriages were endogamous while only 35.7% of Generation VI were marriages of this type. The multiplicity of factors (e.g., political, economic, ideological, etc.), compounded further by the organizational levels through which a marriage decision passes before realization (i.e., individual, family, sublineage, etc.), make the discussion of the increase in endogamous unions on the village level an inherently incomplete topic. For the present, however, it should be remembered that culturally modified sexual disparity is also involved in this phenomenon.
9. There seems to be a disagreement in Golani's figures (1961), which may mean that either there were 55 families or that two "additional individuals" (i.e., a single older parent or a sibling) were lost in the list of family sizes he provided. In short, the list on page 10 ("The average size of the biological family") mistakenly summarized the table on pages 10–11 ("The structure of the biological families") by listing 3 families of 2.0 P/F and 8 of 6.0 P/F whereas the table provides 2 families of the former size and 9 of the latter. Moreover, when either of these lists is tallied the product is 341 individuals and does not match the table on page 5 ("The structure of the population of Bīr al-Maksūr"), which provides a total of 343 individuals.
10. Although Golani (1961) does not mention whether any of the three pairs of co-resident families was composed of older parents and their last son's family (i.e., a case of "tail end of anticipatory inheritance" rather than an inability to build), only one possible case of this sort might be present. (The problem lies in the gender of one "unmarried sons/daughters above 18" in the older family on p. 11). If indeed this is a case of "the tail end of anticipatory inheritance," then the deviance of the reality from the ideal is only 2 of 54 families or 3.7% rather than the figure quoted above.
11. The terms used to denote the males' and females' spaces in the tent seem to vary among the bedouin tribes in the general area. Musil, for example, reports that the Rawala call the male's space "*mak'ad al regāl* (or *rab'a*)" and the female's "*mak'ad al Ḥarīm*" (1929:64). Randolph, who worked among the bedouin of the Central Negev, calls the former "*šiqq*" and the latter "*muḥarram*" (1963:81). Marx, who studied the same area, also calls the former "*shiq*" (1967:82). Shmueli uses

"*shiq*" for the Judean Desert bedouin guest tent (1970:62) but "*maẓafah*" when it is the guest room in the house of the tribe's *muḫtār* (1970:91, 97) after the traditional terminology of the *fellāḥīn* (Bergheim 1894:196). Finally, Ashkenazi (1938:117) reports "*ruba'*" and "*mahallat al ḥarīm*" respectively for the tribes of northern Palestine and elsewhere (1957:125) but adds that sometimes the central guest tent in a camp is also called "*shiq maq'ad al rijâl*." Kressel (1976:82), incidentally, writes that "*shiq*" is the bedouin term while "*maq'ad*" and "*dīwān*" are the terms of the *fellāḥīn* and town dwellers.

The Ḥğerāt did not have a clear answer why they use *dīwān*, which connotes formality, and not *ruba'*. Nonetheless, they used it both as a noun to refer to so-and-so's guest space and as a verb, which they conjugated to connote the action of gathering (e.g., "*'end min ndāwen?*", lit. "at whose place shall we gather?"). I also heard some youth use the descriptive noun *diwānīn* to refer to youth who were courting a girl under the pretext of frequently visiting and spending evenings with her brother or a male neighbor.

12. By 1975/77 renovations and additions made it hard to determine the original core structure of a house. Nonetheless, using windows as indicators of a once outer wall it was possible to establish that two-room structures were the dominant form and that a few triple-room structures were built as well.
13. The architect in question was the person who prepared the master plans for the private lands of the village "almost for no money . . . so that I [will] start to make the building plans for them." This type of continuous relation, while having economic aspects (especially for the architect), was viewed by the village residents primarily as guidance and a buffer from the incoherence of the state's bureaucratic tangle. By 1975 he was planning to extend his services to include the phase of making the request for a construction permit from the Ministry of the Interior on behalf of the applicant "because they don't know . . . so [when they] go to the Ministry by themselves [they] sometimes do not know what to say." See Chapter 11 (Conclusions) for a discussion of the architect's importance as a "cultural broker."
14. This composite unit was the result of the freedom the house owner and the contractor exercised in altering the architect's plans and from attempts to reduce construction related expenses by concentrating all the plumbing elements in a single room. This room was secondarily divided into a kitchen from which one entered the toilet and the shower, which may or may not be located within a single enclosure. A guest, thus, had to walk through the kitchen, which previously was in the *private* domain, to wash his/her hands or reach the toilet.
15. Until 1969 the formal organization of education in Israel was divided into: elementary (grades first through eighth), which was compulsory; secondary (grades ninth through twelfth); and post-secondary. Secondary education could be acquired through an academically, vocationally, or agriculturally oriented high school. After the passage of Amendment No. 5 to the law in 1969, compulsory education was extended to encompass eleven years: kindergarten through tenth grade (Isr. Laws 23:192–94). As a result, a six-year reform program of the educational system was initiated in academic year 1969/70, dividing the old organizational structure into four levels: elementary (kindergarten through sixth grade) and intermediate (seventh through tenth), both compulsory; secondary (eleventh through twelfth); and post-secondary.
16. According to the procedures of the Israeli educational system, upon reaching the age of 18 years one is permitted to take the examinations and if passed, one is qualified by the Ministry of Education to continue in institutions of post-secondary education. There are several batteries of these examinations, the use of which depends on whether one graduated from a high school or whether one has prepared privately or through special courses, as well as language specialization (Hebrew or Arabic). Institutions of higher education, however, considered the "Matrics" as a general official requirement rather than an unequivocal directive and relied more heavily on their own admission examinations in order to maintain their academic quality. Thus, if applicants without a matriculation certificate did well on the admission examinations, they were usually accepted with the condition that they complete their Matrics before graduation, and were not otherwise hampered in any way.

17. Aside from the difficulties in assessing the significance of these marriages as a result of the growing freedom that was exercised by the younger members of both these generations in choosing their mates, there was an additional compounded statistical problem. First, both these generations were still in the process of accretion as new members were being born, so that the marrying population was not as stable as the earlier generations had been. Second, less than half of G. VII and only 5% of G. VIII were married in 1977. Since, as I have tacitly argued throughout this work, this population and its behavior were continuously changing, there was little use in subjecting these data to statistical tests that compare them to the parameters of an infinite population—whose underlying assumption is that it does not change—to find out if the behavior of these samples predicts the behavior of the two generations in toto. While it is possible to describe a changing scenario and use it as a model for the behavior of that infinite population, such a scenario will be as useful (i.e., deficient) as the assumptions and educated guesses used in its construction. As such, I see very little advantage in employing statistical tests in the present cases instead of directly applying educated guesses in attempting to explain the subsequent marriage data. Finally, and to forewarn again, it should be kept in mind that unlike the case of the previous generations, the marriage data of G. VII and G. VII are far from complete, that the behavior of these generations was changing, and that both the period during which these marriages had been and would be contracted and the environment in which they took place was changing relatively rapidly.
18. Two caveats regarding these data. The first is that the starting dates of the two generations denote the first marriage involving a G. VII or G. VIII male. There were three earlier marriages—in 1931, 1938, and 1939—involving G. VII females and one—in 1959—involving a G. VIII female that were omitted when deciding on the lower limit for the time span of these generations' marriages, owing to the patrilineal model employed by the Ḥğerāt. The second caveat involves the marital data of G. VIII, which is all too scant for anything more profound than a suggestion of a probable general trend. Moreover, as Table 24 indicates, none of the members of G. VIII of the Ḏiyabāt were married before or during 1977, hence the data for the tribe as a whole are incomplete (presenting only the Ġadāyreh and Ṣawālḥah) and cannot be combined with the data of G. VII under an assumption of identical temporal conditions. The small amount of the data makes them also seem prone to such biases as brother-sister exchange—the *badl*— (e.g., the two marriages of the Ġadāyreh with the Ḏiyabāt) which, as is the present case, can be a mixture of a choice and a surrender to a counterdemand (i.e., "we will give you our daughter provided you give us one of yours") and not an original (seeking a bride) or reciprocal (providing a bride) free choice. These data are included in Table 24 to provide as complete information as possible although the following discussion centers only on the marriages of G. VII.
19. In two of these marriages a man residing in the Ḏmeydeh and working in Acre and another residing and working in Acre took wives from that town. In the case of the next two, one man residing in I'billin and the other in Bīr al-Maksūr took wives from Nazareth. The last two cases were women who were married in Nazareth and Ramleh respectively.

— 9 —

Ḥğeri Politics

The Segmentary Foundation of the Ḥğeri Judicial and Political Structure

The slow erosion in the importance of marriage in the articulation of intra-tribal politics during the Israeli Period was not followed by a comparable decline in the degree of politicization of the Ḥğerāt, whose segmentary lineage organization promoted politicized behavior. Like similarly organized societies, each Ḥğeri male (teenage and older) perceived himself and was usually perceived by others to be in some sense his own "sovereign," always ready to defend his "domains" be they honor, person, dependents, kin-group, home/possessions, and so on. At the same time he was embedded in larger configurations. Through successive levels of aggregation and inclusion—the nuclear family, the extended family, sublineage, and so on—the amount of relative political power (that is, acumen plus force) that each of these social bodies could muster and the variability, scope, and complexity of the issues involved increased proportionately. Finally, the whole tribe articulated in regional and state politics either as a single entity, as the leader of the tri-tribe alliance it led, or as a subunit within the larger entity of Israeli bedouin.

In the ensuing discussion I follow M.G. Smith's observation that "in a lineage system, relations between superordinate and subordinate lineages are normally administrative and based on authority . . . whereas relations between co-ordinate units are normally political and express relative power" (1956:52). Thus I use "politics" to denote the relations between/among like entities (whether individuals, families, sublineages, and so on) in contradistinction to "administration," which refers to the management of the internal affairs of such entities. Although this usage of the term "politics" is rather unorthodox, I hope that its advantages and those of the model it represents will become evident in the ensuing description and analysis of Ḥğeri politics. (It can be viewed as a rewording—albeit with significance—of the more common usage: for example, the relations between/

among human social bodies and/or their representatives, for in kin-based societies each member represents his/her kin-group at all times.)

It is important to realize that the differences between "political" and "administrative" acts are not inherent in either category but, rather, are the result of the level at which they are encountered (that is, their context). Thus, a political act on one level is an administrative act at the next ascending level. In the ensuing discussion, therefore, whenever presenting a segmentary level, I will treat it as a political actor—that is, as if presenting it through a lens and, hence, showing all those sub-levels that are embedded in it and that it administers while obscuring its more inclusive (that is, ascending) levels. In this way conflicts are presented as competition among equals while their resolution requires the intervention of the first ascending level within which the adversaries are but administrative subunits. Such an approach has the advantage of following very closely the propagation of political and administrative actions in segmentary lineage systems in general and the Ḥğerāt in particular and, hence, provides a good model for such processes.

Similarly, by "politicized behavior" I mean the high degree of sensitivity with which the members of the society register the behavior of other individuals due to their awareness of the possible effects of such behavior (others' and their own) on their welfare as well as of its inter-group implications and probable political outcomes. Such politicized behavior is expressed by an ever-present alertness and continuous monitoring of the behavior of others for possible infringements. It is inherent in segmentary lineage systems, although not particular to them (e.g., cf. Klima 1970:58), not only because it is encoded in Sahlins' principle of "structural relativity" (1961:333–34) but because it in fact ensures that principle's smooth functioning.

It is not surprising, therefore, that while the political importance of marriage declined during the Israeli Period, the general level of politicization remained relatively intact. Although marriage is a major mechanism for the promotion of social cohesion over political antagonism, it is by itself neither the former nor the latter. Nor is it their raison d'etre. Since political antagonism underwrites complementary opposition, which is the basic organizing principle of the tribal form of sociopolitical integration (cf. Sahlins 1961, 1968:14–27), it can be expected to survive longer than any mechanism directed at its reinforcement.

Finally the ability (as well as behavior) of most individuals to perceive the concern of higher levels—for example, sublineal, lineal, tribal, and so on—and hence to refrain from hasty action even where they have the traditional right to it does not void this model because it is the social acceptance accorded the hot-headed individuals that underwrites its validity. In other words, the obligation felt by a cool-headed individual to support a quarrelsome relative even against his own inclination or better judgment means that he accepts the right of the latter to react the way he does (although usually the former will try to dissipate the latter's rage or anger).

Two opposing dynamics permeate this hierarchy: the centrifugal force generated by segmentary opposition and politicization counterbalanced and/or contained by the centripetal effect of conflict mediation and segmentary sociability. Thus, although a high degree of politicization on the level of the individual can easily breed violence, violence in the present context is in fact complementary to politicization for it is the answer, albeit the crudest one, to the information gained through the continuous monitoring mentioned earlier. The sequence proceeds from awareness of actual or assumed transgression, to a flare-up of temper (which serves to demarcate one's "space" or "domains"), to further escalation through verbal abuse, to actual violence, which almost invariably follows. The time lapse between one phase and another may be very short, thus emphasizing action rather than the slower buildup that led to it. It is of little surprise, then, that many characterological descriptions of tribesmen, especially (although not exclusively) pastoralists, mention their quick temper and readiness to fight (e.g., Evans-Prichard 1940:51 for the Nuer; Deng 1972:6 for the Dinka; Klima 1970:58 for the Barabaig).

As a general rule the Ḥğerāt tried to control this propensity so that when uncontrolled violence did erupt, it was contained as fast as possible. More specifically, when two individuals began to exchange blows, bystanders were expected to intervene immediately, separate the combatants, and try to talk them into reason and self-control. As Hall points out, the expectation that bystanders will become involved in and try to stop the conflict is common to the Arab world. He further remarks that "*to fail to intervene* when trouble is brewing is to take sides" (1966:162). Conflict mediation is, thus, an a priori assertion by the adversaries themselves, who perceive it as a behavioral boundary setting mechanism and therefore allow themselves to be reconciled and the conflict resolved. The Ḥğerāt were very aware of this policy and in discussions about this issue often pointed out that "among us, every quarrel ends before it can involve a whole *ḥama'il*," as one of them summarized it.

Not surprisingly, then, that self-control and containing one's temper were idealized adult characteristics, for they enabled their possessor to subjugate his personal concern and follies to kin-group interest,[1] thereby proving himself to be a responsible representative of family, lineage, and tribe.[2] Most outbreaks of violence, therefore, were in the form of fistfights and occurred between teenagers or young men who were not yet expected to behave as fully mature adults. More commonly, and especially when the conflict had substance other than real or assumed insult, the expected course of behavior was to accept or seek the mediation of a third party. Thus, if violence was the individual's fact, mediation was the social fact. While the Ḥğerāt did not try to analyze their violent outbreaks but simply attributed them to their "hot blood," they were very analytical in regard to conflict mediation and its role in underwriting social life. For example, on one occasion when the Council of the Elders had succeeded in settling a "case of honor" in another tribe before violence had erupted, the Ḥğerāt were very proud because their Elders had mended the interfamilial relations in that tribe even before the split had fully formed.

Conflict mediation is one of the "administrative" actions referred to above for regardless of the mediator's social standing, the ideological items he employed to convince the adversaries to resolve their differences and that legitimated his efforts were those of kin-group solidarity and tribal unity. The closer genealogically the kinship linkage between the adversaries, the greater their propensity to abide by these ideological items. Consequently, mediation permitted the identification of the conflict's organizational level—that is, the level below which it was resolved—and, hence, its possible intensity—that is, the number of people who saw themselves involved in it.

Dynamically, a conflict's mediation was an event on a continuum that began with an informal apology by a relative and relatives' pressure on the adversaries to reconcile, moved up through mediation by a sublineal or lineal elder, and finally to formal arbitration, whether by an Elder or by the Council of the Elders. There were no sharp divisions along this continuum and attempts at mediating commonly occurring conflicts often started somewhere at the informal side and slowly made their way toward the formal end until the conflict was resolved. To a large measure a case's entry point onto this continuum was determined by the number of people that it affected (that is, by its intensity) or the organizational entities that it pitted against each other. Thus, economic issues, being private concerns, usually started informally whereas matters of blood and honor were always arbitrated by the Council formally for they immediately caused the aggregation of the largest possible segmentary units. "Cases of honor" (a local euphemism for female seduction) were formally arbitrated because they rapidly escalated into matters of blood. Unlike the latter, however, they involved the family and relatives of the woman on the "aggrieved" side but only the seducer and his immediate family—if any at all—on the "perpetrator" side because even when the seduction provided his kin group with political gain, bedouin ethics categorically condemned seduction, thus forcing his relatives to remain uninvolved as long as no blood was spilled.

Formal arbitration by the Council of the Elders was a subclass of "mediation." Thus, while all activities along this continuum were oriented toward resolving differences between adversaries (i.e., mediation), in its formal end the adversaries surrendered their right to act and promised to abide by the mediator's ruling (i.e., arbitration). I will return to this subject later. Meanwhile, although arbitration may seem somewhat formally similar in form to the Western court system, the respective philosophies, functions, and dynamics of the two systems are quite different (see below).

Below are examples of this continuum:

Low-level resolution: individual level. "A"'s cows ate "B"'s young olive grove, causing I£1100 damage. When "B" (age 61) tried to negotiate a settlement with "A" (age 40), the latter was uncooperative and rude. Consequently, "B" contacted a lawyer with the intention of suing "A" in a civil court. A few days later "A"'s father, "C" (age 66), visited "B" (a gesture that culturally connotes "B"'s righteousness and "A"'s fault), apologized, and explained the circumstances that caused the trespass. He again asked "B"'s forgiveness and offered to pay in damages whatever "B" desired. "B" answered that the appraiser he had engaged to estimate the damage cost him I£250 and if "C" reimbursed him this cash outlay all would be forgiven and forgotten. Thus, in return for an apology, which had restored his "sovereignty," "B" forewent the value of the damage itself and asked only for the immediate cash expenditures caused by the trespass.

Low-level resolution: bystander level. "A" (age 26) sent his daughter to buy cigarettes at "C"'s store. "C"'s daughter told her they were out of cigarettes. Later, "B," a FFBSS of "A" and a bachelor (age 23), arrived at the store and "C"'s daughter sold him some packs. When "A" heard about it he became very angry, went to the store, cursed, and told "C" that "B" was courting his daughter and that was the reason she sold him the cigarettes. "C" went to "B"'s father to complain about "B"'s illicit behavior and when

"B" came home and heard the allegation he went to the store carrying a copy of the Koran on which he swore "he never lain an eye on 'C''s daughter." He then cursed "A," calling him a liar, etc. "A," hearing "B" was at "C"'s, arrived and heated words were exchanged, leading to a fistfight. The two were quickly separated at which point "A" pulled a pistol and twice fired in the air to emphasize his parting words. From that moment on, the immediate respective relatives present, helped by other bystanders, tried to talk "A" into making peace with "B" and "B" into forgiving "A" (not only was "A" libelous but in a quarrel, shooting—even in the air—constituted an assault with intent to kill according to local customary law). By the next afternoon, less than 24 hours after the fight, the two shook hands and the matter was laid to rest. The meeting was held at "B"'s father's *dīwān* because "A" was the one to apologize.

Mid-level resolution: lineal Elder level. At an evening gathering (*dīwān*) in "A"'s (Ramlāt, age 65) tent, "B" (*ulād* Ġadīr, age 43) criticized the way in which the steering committee of the Electricity Co-Op Society was managing the provision of the village with electricity. While he was talking, "C," the committee's chairman (Ramlāt, age 38), arrived and after a short while accused the gathering of creating and spreading dissent in the village, calling it "a *dīwān* of lies." "B" lost his temper and hit "C" with the sole of a shoe (a major insult). He then left for his home. A couple of hours later some four men from both sublineages came and told him that "D"—his father and the Ġadāyreh's lineal Elder—wanted his company on the way to "C"'s house in order to make peace. "B" went to "D"'s house and quoted to him "C"'s insult to the *dīwān* and those present corroborated his report. "D" concluded that both were at fault—"C," because he had insulted the gathering, and "B," because in his violent response he had insulted "A"'s hospitality. "B" then suggested that since he would not go to "C"'s house ("since when does the righteous go to the house of the guilty?") and "C" would not come to his (because that would declare him guilty), they should make peace at "A"'s, where he would apologize to "A" and "C" would apologize to the gathering. "D" agreed and the next day the peace was made although relations remained strained due to previous quarrels.

Structurally, as previously mentioned, each level in the tribe's segmentary hierarchy had the freedom to administer its constituting segments and mediate conflicts among them. Nevertheless, the freedom allowed the individuals concerned—adversaries and mediator—as well as the specifics of the instance itself may cause a case to bypass a level or levels instead of proceeding sequentially. Thus, a quarrelsome individual in conflict with a sublineal mate may prefer to have the case mediated by an elder of another lineage, thereby positing the conflict as an inter-lineal affair. For example, a member of the Ṭa'awāneh (age 40) loathed his sublineal kinsmen because they had accepted blood restitution (*diyah*) instead of avenging their member who was allegedly killed by a member of the Masa'īd. Consequently, whenever he had a conflict with another village member he accepted mediation only by the Ġadāyreh's lineal Elder.

Alternatively, a lineal Elder may reach an impasse and decide to shift from the informality of mediating as an Elder to the formality of arbitrating as a member of the Council of the Elders and in that forum. Also, the leading members of the Council had legal specialties such as land, horses, herd animals, and so on, and topical cases were usually mediated directly by the respective specialist Elder regardless of his or the adversaries' exact kin-linkage and distance. To complicate matters further, in promoting village identity, sedentarization was gradually erasing some of the segmentary distinctions that were previously operative. Consequently, daily cases in Bīr al-Maksūr were often mediated by the elders of the Ġadāyreh or Ṭa'awāneh even when one or both adversaries were members of the D'eyfeh or Ṣawālḥah, and in the Mikmān, the D'eyfi residents often accepted mediation by Ṣawālḥi elders.

This high degree of responsiveness to each case's merits and peculiarities was not the result of the absence of procedural rules to determine the case's development. Rather, it arose from the understanding that the function of conflict mediation was to preserve social cohesion and tribal unity rather than referee between right and wrong in order to realize some abstract legal concept of justice. The Ḥğerāt were by no means a singular case; they represented the rest of the Israeli Arab population in this respect. In fact, the difference between the Western legal model, which seeks to divine right from wrong, and the Ḥğeri—that is, traditional—model, with its emphasis on unity and social harmony, seems to be quite widespread and to conform to Hall's distinction between low- and high-context cultures respectively (1976:106–13). It is of little surprise, then, that for the Ḥğerāt and the rest of the Arab groups in the country the verdicts of the state legal system, which tried all homicide cases, never concluded a case in which an Arab was involved because although ideally establishing right and incarcerating wrong, such court rulings did not restore even a semblance of harmony to the community. This social deficiency was usually recognized by the local police force, which found it an expensive venture to maintain peace in such highly politicized, breached communities. As a result, and as is often the case, the two legal approaches were made complementary in Israel, with the state's courts trying the killers and the respective local Arab dignitaries mediating the differences in order to restore peace to the community with the tacit approval and blessing of the police. Post-homicide peace arbitration—or *ṣulḥa*—also had political overtones, as discussed in greater detail below.

Since tribal unity underwrote the welfare of all Ḥğeris, right/wrong were very relative terms because both sides to a conflict were a priori wrong inasmuch as they threatened to disrupt this necessary unity. Nowhere was this precept clearer than in the aforementioned case of the Masa'īd/Ṭa'awāneh homicide. Although the "killer" was acquitted by the Court of Justice after the cause of death was established as heart failure and because the "killer" had acted in self-defense, the Council of Elders fined him twice the value of the customary *diyah* (blood restitution) and exiled him from the tribe's judicial-political territory for seven years. The reason for the severity of the Council's verdict was to impress upon all tribesmembers that if any of them ever found himself in a similar predicament "he would think five times before he picks up a stick . . . [for homicide] . . . splits the tribe."

The preservation of unity was, thus, the major theme of the Ḥğeri legal ideology and administrative structure, a theme that permeated the hierarchy from family to sublineage to lineage to tribe, for without unity the *'arab* al-Ḥğerāt would not have fared well in the past nor become a regional leader in the second half of the 1970s. It was the elders representing the interests of their respective kin-groups who as the *ḫatyariyyeh*, or the Council of the Elders,[3] were the guardians of this unity.

The Traditional Leadership: The *ḫatyariyyeh*

The Council of the Elders, then, was the apex of the traditional indigenous authority structure and leadership of the Ḥğerāt. Together with its administrative concerns—preserving unity in face of its membership's centrifugal tendencies—it managed the tribe's political strategies and represented it in its dealings with the sociopolitical bodies around it. These two primary functions were inherent in its own segmentary structure and dynamics. Thus, its administrative success depended on its members reaching agreements between and among themselves as individual *Elders* representing their respective kin-groups while its political function demanded the pooling of these elders' talents and experiences to form the single front with which the *Council* met the outside world.

Generally speaking, the Council of the Elders is best understood as a forum for the discussion of administrative and political issues and their formulation into decisions, rather than as a permanent formal body. Neither the Council nor its mode of operation was in any way formal—not all the sublineages or lineages were always represented nor was their representation necessary; it met often but ad hoc; there was no necessary quorum during meetings nor formal procedures to govern these; and there was no set location where its meetings took place.

In theory the membership of the Council included all the sublineal elders of the tribe, thus ensuring a broad base legitimation for the Council, and the resultant cooperation of the tribe's membership with its decisions, which such legitimation implies. In reality, however, only a handful of elders actually managed the affairs reaching this body. As a result, the structural blueprint of the Council included two tiers: (1) the "full" Council, composed of all the sublineal elders, and which convened in toto only on ceremonial occasions, and (2) the "select" or "core" Council, which included only four sublineal Elders: that of *ulād* Ġadīr, who was also the lineal Elder of the Ġadāyreh; that of *ulād* ‘abd al-Sleymān; that of the Samrāt; and that of the Ṭa‘awāneh (see Figure 7).

The difference between these two tiers was readily observable when following the Council's functions and comparing observations to informants' statements. Thus, the invariable answer to "who is in the *ḫatyariyyeh*?" was "all the elders" and, in fact, at the rare ceremonial functions that involved the whole tribe (such as important receptions and funerals), all the elders were present in their traditional formal dress (cloak and head-dress) and their presence was dully observed. On the other hand, in cases of arbitration in Bīr al-Maksūr, it was the "core" Council that sat in on cases and passed verdicts, and although any elder was free to be present and speak his opinion, rarely did the other elders, if present, actually participate in the deliberations. These differences were even more pronounced when political issues were involved.

The concentration of real power in the hands of the "core" Council, and especially those of the tribal Elder, seems to be a result of the shift in the sources of power from

Ḥsēn D̲iyab al-Ibrāhīm
(Ġadāyreh)

Muḥammad Sleymān al-ʻAbed
(Ġadāyreh)

Muḥammad al-Ḥreb
(Samrāt)

Ḥsēn D̲iyab al-Ḥassan
(Ṭaʻawāneh)

Figure 7. The "core" Council.

kin-group membership to state agencies. The description of the Council of the Elders presented for this time period, therefore, portrays a greater amount of centralization than would likely have been the case during the Mandate Period when the Council actually was the only apex of Ḥğeri leadership and power (as measured in wealth and male membership) was more equally distributed among the various sublineages. The discrepancy between the membership of the two tiers, and especially the absence of the representatives of the Ṣawālḥah and D'eyfeh from the higher level, results from two sets of factors working in concert.

The first set of factors is general in character and has been in operation throughout the tribe's history: viz., the way in which the Elders were recruited in combination with the segmentary ideology that legitimated the resultant selective representation. Traditionally, in each sublineage there was usually one elder who outshone his kin-group peers in character, wisdom, acumen, legal experience, and—to a lesser extent by the mid-twentieth century—wealth. It was to him that the members of the sublineage came for mediation and help. He thus became his sublineage's leading figure, and through reciprocal exchanges of services and goods he could convince his sublineal mates to accept tribal policies that were even somewhat restrictive (for example, not pursuing an intra-tribal feud). His position in the lineage and the tribe, however, was also dependent on the power and position occupied by his sublineage relative to other sublineages in the tribe, on the extent of his own personal network of friends and marriage alliances among the other sublineal Elders, and on the younger following he had in the tribe at large.

Traditionally, the various sublineages were graded according to the force (i.e., men) that they could muster to back up demands or promises of their respective representatives because the real test to the strength of a demand and the validity of a promise had always been the ability to keep these in the face of opposition. As a result, the sublineages in each lineage were ranked according to their relative power; the highest-ranking sublineage provided the highest-ranking Elder who became the Elder of the lineage and whose opinions carried the greatest weight in intra-lineage discourse. (Needless to emphasize, the rise of a sublineage was interwoven with that of its Elder, for the efficacy of sheer force depended on the one who deployed it.) Moreover, since segmentary ideology dictates that the scale of units of cooperation are defined in opposition to genealogically like units, if a lineal Elder decided on an extra-lineal policy or a course of action, his decision, ideally, bound all the sublineages of that lineage. It follows, therefore, that in theory the Elders of the sublineages needed not be present when such a decision was reached because they were a priori bound to accept it. The same case applied to the tribe as a whole, where the Ġadāyreh ranked higher than the other two lineages and its Elder—being the highest-ranking Elder in the tribe—de facto decided tribal policies.

In reality, however, rank intervals were not uniform and the differences between some sublineages were close enough that the highest-ranking Elder either had to share decision-making with the Elders of a few close competitors or had to bring in closer and rely on the Elders of the smaller sublineages in order to build a coalition that would provide him with a decisive power base while removing his closest competitors from the management of this base. It is the latter tactic that was almost universally preferred, and among the Ḥğerāt it dictated the alliance of the *ulād* Ġadīr with the Samrāt and *ulād* ‘abd al-Sleymān to outnumber the Ramlāt and the ‘Afafṭeh, and with the Ṭa‘awāneh and (on major issues) the D‘eyfeh to outbalance the Ṣawālḥah.

Finally, this hierarchical model fits closely the Ḥğeri model of representation. As I was instructed, the lineal Elder of the Ġadāyreh could represent any of the other Elders in their absence, but if he was unavailable it must be another Elder of the Ġadāyreh (that is, from *ulād* ‘abd al-Sleymān: *ulād* ’Aḥmed, Ramlāt, or ‘Afafṭeh) who would represent him (but not the lineal Elder from the Samrāt or Ṭa‘awāneh). If the whole tribe had to be represented, then the Elders of the Ġadāyreh (including the lineal Elders from the Samrāt and the Ṭa‘awāneh in this case), Ṣawālḥah, Ka‘abīyeh, and Ḥelf would be present although the latter three could ask the lineal Elder of the Ġadāyreh to represent them. As a matter of fact, any person or elder could be represented by a proxy whose word was accepted as binding for the one represented.

The second set of factors accounting for the discrepancy between the two tiers was particular to the Ḥğerāt in their adaptation during the 1947–1977 period and included three subsets: the two *maḫatīr*, sedentarization, and the low level of unity among the Ṣawālḥah. The most important of these was the senior position of the *muḫtār* of Bīr al-Maksūr and his extensive ties to the administration whose public resources he could mobilize to support Ġadāyri leadership of the tribal Council. The second was the heterogeneous composition of the Maksurean population, which included a sizable portion of the Ṣawālḥah, thus de facto supporting the "core" Council, which administered and represented that settlement. Finally, the loose genealogical ties of the Ṣawālḥah interfered with the ability of its sublineages to promote a lineal Elder to represent them as a unit, especially when three of these already followed Ġadāyri leadership in matters of daily arbitration. This lack of unity was exacerbated by the junior position of the sublineage of the *muḫtār* of the Mikmān within the Ṣawālḥah.

Thus, although the Elders of the Mikmān and Ḏmeydeh mediated daily cases between the residents of these settlements, they did not arbitrate independently cases of blood and honor, which—being the most threatening to the survival of tribal unity—were adjudicated by the "core" Council. Nor did they represent or mediate cases extra-tribally without the latter's tacit authorization. For example, a 1973 quarrel between two members of *ulād* Ḥassan al-Ṣāleḥ, who resided in the Mikmān, climaxed with the non-fatal knife stabbing of one adversary by the other. Had the case not involved blood it would have ended with mediation by the three Elders of that sublineage or, if they were too involved and divided, by the Elders of the Mikmān (that is, those of the Maḥāmīd and the Ğawāsreh). Since it was a blood case, the "core" Council headed by Ḥsēn al-Ḏiyab and assisted by Muḥammad al-Ḥsēn, the tribe's *muḫtār,* arbitrated the case with the Elders of the Ṣawālḥah. (The verdict: I£10,000 to reimburse medical expenses but no payment of blood money "because they were *ulād ‘amm*" [FFFBSSs in fact].)

The "core" Council was thus the focus of the traditional leadership of the Ḥğerāt and as such it also led the tri-tribe alliance with the Ka‘abīyeh and the Ḥelf. For like the Ṣawālḥah—whose leaders were bound by segmentary ideology to accept the authority of the lineal Elder of the Ġadāyreh who thereby became the tribal Elder of the Ḥğerāt—the Elders of these tribes accepted his authority in his latter capacity, thereby promoting him to the traditional leading role of the alliance. And as in the case of the Ṣawālḥah and for all of the same reasons, while the respective Elders of the two tribes mediated daily conflicts that arose among their kinsmen, the Ḥğeri "core" Council and its *muḫtār* arbitrated cases of blood and honor. For example, in 1975 there was a quarrel between two groups in the Ka'abīyeh village. In the heat of fighting one man went home, brought out a gun, and shot and wounded four men of the other group. While the Elders of the Ka'abīyeh, who were not members of either group, were present and participated during the public discussion of the case, the actual verdict was reached by the Ḥğeri "core" Council and the *muḫtār*, both of whom vouched for the continuous compliance of both sides with the conditions of the peace agreement (*ṣulḥa*).

It may seem, therefore, that the "core" Council actively monopolized the arbitration of blood and honor cases due to the major threat they posed to the tribal and alliance unity and, hence, to the Council's own power base. Nonetheless, these cases reached the Council also because its four members—and especially Ḥsēn al-Ḏiyab—represented both the ideal of kin solidarity and the concrete force that this ideal could mobilize, as the 1975 Masa'īd/Ṭa'awāneh homicide case (mentioned above) indicates. In that case, after the death became known, the elders of the Ṭa'awāneh asked Ḥsēn al-Ḏiyab for guidance. He said, "I can send four of my men and they will wipe out the Masa'īd, but," he continued, "what will that do to the tribe? We all live in Bīr al-Maksūr. . . ." He thereby considered and eliminated the option of the use of force and directed the Ṭa'awāneh toward a peaceful settlement.

In addition to the command of force, the four Elders were esteemed arbitrators, a characteristic that, apart from the power they represented, drew to them both less dramatic cases (such as land, movable property, animals) and cases from other tribes and neighboring villages. Thus, in 1976 the "core" Council arbitrated in I'billin a case of a young girl who was run over by a car; a seduction case in Saḫnīn; a divorce case between a member of the *'arab* al-Ḥamdūn and his wife from the *'arab* al-Ğanādi (both members of remnants of pre-1948 local tribes) in Shfar'am's bedouin subdivision; and a youth love/pregnancy affair in Tuba (at the request of the police).

The demand for the arbitration of such diverse cases was further augmented by the Elders' juridical specialization. Case diversity was also amplified by the hierarchy of roles that each of these Elders performed (that is, extended family head, sublineal Elder, and so on) combined with the absence of any established boundaries between these roles, Council matters, and personal juridical specializations. As a result, the topics that reached the members of the "core" Council were quite varied and emphasized the case orientation and informal character of this body.

The beginning of the arbitration process ranged from the informal to the formal. Intratribally, the phase of accepting arbitration was completely informal as the *ḫatyariyyeh* had the authority to step in and arbitrate, although they usually waited for the adversaries to approach them and ask for arbitration. When the Elders arbitrated extra-tribally, some formality gradually seeped in when they asked for the a priori compliance of the adversaries with their authority. If the adversaries came to the Ḥğerāt for arbitration, the Elder asked if they accepted him as arbitrator and would abide by his verdict regardless of its outcome; only after both sides accepted this condition did he take on the case. In this instance the amount of formality was minimal. If, on the other hand, the Elders stepped in to arbitrate—as in the aforementioned case in Tuba—they visited the house of each leading adversary (if it was a sublineage or lineage) and asked if the group the leader represented would accept them as arbitrators and abide by the Council's rulings. In this latter case the amount of formality increased measurably due to the more elaborate social dynamics involved.

The "core" Council in session, or its constituent members at work individually, represented informal occasions open to anyone present and as such served as a training course for aspiring young leaders. Sessions could develop practically anywhere: the home of a member Elder, or the *dīwān* of another tribesmember where two visiting Elders began to discuss a case or where some other guest asked a question about a case and a visiting Elder answered and a discussion evolved, and so on. During such sessions the membership of the Council ranged from one to all four members plus an audience that could include several members of the "full" Council, relatives of the adversaries, and some younger people who were interested in the case or in the event's social aspects. Often the number and relative status of the Elders present indicated the complexity of the issue under discussion. Thus, blood and honor cases always involved at least the Elders of the Ġadāyreh, Samrāt, or Ṭa'awāneh, while breaches of marriage contract (the *'aged*) involved any number of Elders in any composition. Also, during these informal discussions the adversaries themselves could not argue their case once they accepted arbitration. At that time they were asked to tell their full story and thereafter could not participate in the ensuing elaboration process that helped form the Elders' opinion. Consequently, if they happened to be present and had chosen not to leave the room, they remained silent and let their friends or relatives draw attention to aspects of the case that were favorable to their claim.

No ruling was given during these sessions, which served rather to dissect and analyze the case in as many of its human and legal aspects as possible; anyone present could voice his opinion. Nevertheless, people tended to be very measured and thoughtful, for a hasty opinion would draw a gentle rebuttal in the form of a critical appraisal of the argument's faults, and such replies had a shaming quality for the hasty individual. Each speaker tried to point to an aspect of the case and his observation was discussed in relation to other aspects of that case and other precedents, legal and behavioral. When the subject was exhausted and the audience grew tired or had other functions to attend to, the session slowly wound down and broke up, and the Elders were left to think the elaborated case over. Once they felt they understood the case, they decided on the verdict, either individually or as a body, and then made their ruling public.

One of these informal sessions in 1975, for example, dealt with an elopement case. Following a request by the police, the tribal Elders became involved in the case involving the Ka'abīyeh and the Sawā'ed. A *fellāḥa* married to a "crazy" husband of the *'arab* al-Ka'abīyeh eloped with a man from the *'arab* al-Sawā'ed, who deserted her after three days of sexual liaison. The case as such was uncommon, first because it was referred to Ḥsēn al-Ḏiyab by the police and as such was not a strictly Council matter, and second because of the three groups involved. In one of the preliminary sessions, when the woman's father and his relatives were present, one of the Ḥğeri audience remarked that he thought that one detail had been overlooked. Namely, what if she, having become "notorious" and therefore unable to remarry, would want to marry the Sw'edī she had eloped with (a development prohibited by custom). The Elder and the woman's relatives responded with: "*mish mumkin!*" ("No way!" or "It will not be possible!"). After the visitors left, the speaker apologized to the Elder for making this remark in front of strangers but added he did so for the woman's relatives' benefit because the woman's father was a "liar and an SOB." He said that he thought the latter, expecting damages to be less than a *mahr*, would go to the Sawā'ed without the Elder's knowledge and offer them the woman for a *mahr* of I£10,000 and the dismissal of the whole affair—that is, forgetting the damage to his family's honor (an unacceptable deal because by tradition by paying the damages the Sw'edī had acknowledged his misconduct and he was not supposed to enjoy the outcome). Now, after his relatives said "No!" in public, he would not be able to do so. (The verdict: the Ka'abī was told to divorce the woman because he mistreated her; the Sw'edī paid I£5000 to her father as recognition of his wrongdoing in taking advantage of her distress; and the woman was returned to her father's guardianship.) Although this example was somewhat uncommon inasmuch as an audience member actually acted while elaborating a point, his doing so and the acceptance of his intervention by all present emphasizes the collective aspect of the elaboration process.

The announcement of case rulings was by far the most formal part of the arbitration process and was always made a day or more after the ruling had been made public informally. Although to my knowledge there was never a rejection of a ruling made by the Council or its individual members (partly, no doubt, because the preconditions of arbitration precluded such behavior), this time lapse suggests the greater interest in the reestablishment of cohesion and social harmony that dictated this period to express displeasure in the ruling as an extra measure of safety to prevent disagreement and disobedience at the last minute. Here again the variety was great and depended on the scope of the case. In general, intra-tribal cases that did not include the annulment of an *'aged* ended with the two adversaries or their representatives listening to one of the Elders deliver the verdict, the transfer of funds as a financial settlement of fines (used to signify the wrongdoer's recognition of his guilt), and an optional handshake to signify that "all is forgiven and forgotten," and the case was closed. Fines were the arbitrator's prerogative, although not when mediating informally (and as such this difference helped distinguish between mediation and arbitration). Cases of annulment and honor cases were more elaborate and public because the *'aged*, although signed at the engagement ceremony, was an official document of marriage issued by the *Šarī'a* Court and hence had to be annulled by its representative. Consequently, a *qāḍi* (or *šeyḫ*) had to be present to issue a divorce decree. Finally, blood cases were the most formal and included two phases. First, both sides signed a *ṣulḥa* agreement, which at this time was often drawn up by a lawyer with one copy kept by the police. Second was a formal *ṣulḥa* ceremony that included speeches and an obligatory handshake, followed by a feast to which the police were invited as an official witness. These ceremonies could be a major affair attended by neighboring Elders and dignitaries, bedouin and villagers, all of whom served as witnesses to the agreement that was guaranteed by the arbitrator and his followers.

The administrative activities of the Council focused on conflict arbitration and through it the preservation of the tribe's unity and the alliance that it led. As a result, although over time each of the three tribes expanded in membership and grew in generational depth beyond the traditional five generations that marked the "*khams*" (see Aref 1937:37–38), they all belonged to a single "co-liable group," to use Marx's term (1967:64).[4] Thus, all the members of the alliance shared in the protection of their combined membership, pursued their killers, and divided the blood restitution funds. Moreover, the Council's firm stance against intra-tribal violence not only served to preserve its unity but also kept down the number of fatalities from such violence so that in 1976 one Ḥğeri informant could boast that, not counting honor executions, only two intra-tribal homicides occurred in the previous fifty years: one in 1936 and the other in 1975. Both cases were accidental homicides and in both cases the killers were exiled for seven years (to prevent rekindling of the conflict) from what I called the "judicial-political territory" of the Ḥğerāt. The boundaries of this territory followed major roads in the district (see Map 1) and delineated the area to which the tribe could forbid entry to one of its members and within which it saw itself responsible for its guests' safety.

Finally, the Council limited its activities to arbitration and passed on to the younger generations the new administrative functions that grew as a result of sedentarization. Nonetheless, the Council occasionally became involved in these functions and managed the administrators when the need to mediate or arbitrate their internal conflicts arose. Moreover, since these younger administrators were perceived as representatives of their kin-groups, they were under the influence and responsibility of their respective Elders in spite of their managerial independence. Also, the rise to power and importance of the mukhtarship and the family link between the tribal Elder and the *muḫtār* promoted a unity of interests resulting in a division of responsibilities with the *muḫtār* supervising the personnel and working of the new administration and the tribal Elder preserving the tribe's unity as the basis for their family's power base.

The Council of the Elders was as informal in performing its political functions as in its administrative working. Discussions of political strategies had always been done in the lineal or tribal public, thus permitting a free expression of opinions, which ensured the acceptance and legitimation of a strategy as well as its clear understanding by the executors who were often the youth led by the middle-aged. The Council's political public workings did not warrant the conclusion that the decision-making process itself was public. In reality, many political strategies started out as private maneuvers to strengthen one's own position intra- or extra-tribally and only when these reached the level of involving a whole lineage or tribe did they appear as public topics for debate. Such debate served both to amend and to legitimate them.

While these strategies were the core of the tribe's traditional welfare and power, the greater portion of the Council's political activities centered on ceremonial representation of the Ḥğerāt in its neighboring communities during weddings, funerals, and the like. Such representation was not merely an act of courtesy. It was a symbolic gesture of concern and an expression of humane identity between visitor and host, an expression very important for maintaining relations among the Arabs in the area. Although much had changed in the dynamics of power relations in the country and while the greater emphasis in Ḥğeri political adaptation had shifted from these inter-community horizontal relations to vertical relations with state authorities, the importance of these representational functions had not withered. And so, while the *muḫtār* managed the ties with the authorities, the Council maintained the tribe's ties with the Arab communities that made up the region. Failure to do so, as the following example shows, could have dire consequences: "A," a son of the tribal Elder, had asked me to assist him in helping his friend "B," a *fellāḥ* from a village in the Valley of Jezreel. While we were working on the case, a brother of "A" suddenly died and "B" appeared neither at the funeral nor during the *sab'ah* (the seven days of mourning that follow the funeral). After the fortieth day (the last day of immediate mortuary restrictions) I told "A" I had completed my task in order to help "B" and asked when we could visit him. The answer was a flat negative. "A" did not want to hear of "B" again because "B" conveyed as much by not showing for the funeral or sending a proxy.

The ability of the *ḫatyariyyeh* to preserve its range of functions and style of operation in the face of the major political, economic, and social changes in the tribe's environment was the outcome of the division of spheres of activities between father and son, the tribal Elder and the *muḫtār*, the traditional indigenous leadership and the newer, government-induced one, and of the relative protective isolation that the latter provided. The result was a composite leadership made of two interlocking and complementary units: the *ḫatyariyyeh*, made of the Elders and dealing predominantly with conflict resolution and ceremonial representation, and the mukhtarship, made of the tribal *muḫtār* (and, informally, one of his brothers and a FBS) dealing with the authorities, regional politics, sedentarization-related administration, and major cases of conflict resolution.

Although the mukhtarship rose to dominate the Ḥğeri leadership, cooperation between the two units remained harmonious and the Council did not see the rise of the former as usurpation of its own powers for several reasons. Aside from the fact that both institutions were in the hands of the *ulād* Ġadīr sublineage, their respective membership shared the same set of values of kinship and tribal unity, which both perceived as underwriting the welfare of the *'arab* al-Ḥğerāt. They all saw this welfare, its preservation, and amplification as their responsibility and vested interest if they wished to remain in leadership. In other words, the same kinship ideology that legitimated their leadership limited and conditioned their occupancy of these positions to their responsiveness to their kinsmen's needs. Also, the process was very gradual, and if the Elders who were in power during the 1950s did not like to hear too much from a *muḫtār* in his twenties, by the 1970s the Elders were in their 70s as the *muḫtār* approached 50 years of age. Similarly, the Elders of the 1970s were much more attuned than their predecessors to the intricacies of the tribe's involvement with the state and to the importance of talented mediation between the two, a task that they would rather not perform themselves, especially since they were the apex of their respective groups and the Council the apex of the tribe (thus, conceptually, they had no one above them). The *muḫtār*, on the other hand, was a two-way relay midway between the tribe and the authorities. He may have led the tribe, but there was always some national leader or high administrator who could tell him what to do. In addition, the rise of the *muḫtār* to regional power propelled the Ḥǧerāt to regional prominence with the *ḫatyariyyeh* as its representatives. Consequently, the scope of the Council's political functions, even if mostly ceremonial, expanded as well. And finally, not only did the *muḫtār* treat them with all due deference but he also backed up their decisions with his power in order to foster their ability to preserve his own power base—the tribe—united. Then, the decline in the power-related aspects of the Council's political functions was not caused by the *muḫtār* at all. It was the incorporation of all the local communities within the State of Israel and the efficient enforcement of its law that converted much of the previous political activity into administrative actions as the police and courts readily reminded all concerned.

The New Leadership: The Mukhtarship

The muḫtār's Rise to Intra-Ḥǧerāt Prominence

Whereas the Council of Elders was an institution that developed out of the tribe's inherent structure and was, therefore, as resistant to change as segmentary lineage organization itself, the mukhtarship was introduced from the outside by a recent colonial power for its own purposes and was as unstable as the political milieu within which it operated. To wit, the *ḫatyariyyeh* hardly changed in terms of form, style, functions, and dynamics since the tribe reached a size beyond which full participant decision making was too cumbersome, because "the time consumed in making a decision . . . [seems likely to] . . . be the factorial of the number of group participants" (Wright 1969:3). The Ḥǧeri mukhtarship, conversely, changed, and was changing in response to changes in the authorities, the tribe, and its own personnel.

In short, during the Mandate Period (1917–1947), there was a relative match between the wishes of the Mandate authorities and the traditional isolationist policy—at least in regard to the government—of the Ḥǧerāt, and the tribal Elder could be (and was) the *muḫtār*. With no inherent contradictions between the two roles, he tended to see the interaction between the state and the tribe if not altogether avoidable then to be kept as minimal and passive as possible while maintaining the power of the Ḥǧerāt in his hands as the tribal Elder. This approach was in accord with the policies of the authorities as long as the tribe paid its taxes and did not threaten the public order.

Ḥsēn al-Ḏiyab's 1949 career calculations and the resultant assignment of his seventeen-year-old son Muḥammad to the, until then, titular mukhtarship inadvertently separated the two roles, thus freeing them to change (or not) somewhat independently of each other (see Chapter 6). Then, when the MG altered its predecessor's policy of minimal involvement to one of active intervention, it found the incumbent *muḫtār* young, capable, and willing to cooperate for two reasons. First, Muḥammad al-Ḥsēn wished to establish the leadership of the tribe in his family and similarly his own office in face of intra-tribal opposition, for although influential because of his personal contacts with the Israeli authorities, Ḥsēn al-Ḏiyab—about 40 years old in 1950—was not yet an Elder and could not help him to secure his position as *muḫtār*. In fact, their joint rise to power as tribal Elder and *muḫtār* was a mutually reinforcing process within the major cycle of the rise of the *muḫtār* to his 1977 status.

Muḥammad al-Ḥsēn's second reason for cooperation was based on the recognition that, like his father, he believed that the desirable future of the Ḥğerāt was in Israel and not as refugees in a diaspora. As a result, the mukhtarship shifted from a passive to an active mode of operation in its role as the communication relay between the authorities and the tribe, and in the process accumulated increasingly larger amounts of political power that was legitimated by the Ḥğerāt itself while aligning the interests of the tribe with those of the State of Israel as of 1977. Intra-tribally, in becoming the dominant component of the legitimate leadership of the *'arab* al-Ḥğerāt, not only did the mukhtarship shield the *ḫatyariyyeh* from undue pressures to change but it provided the tribe with a more centralized leadership. Such leadership could make better use of the tribe's power both to gain more economic and political support from the authorities and to make it a major factor in regional politics.

These changes, which resulted from the successful articulation of the state's interests with those of the tribe and the tribesmembers without overly compromising either, gradually accumulated, feeding back into the process and accelerating over time. In their center was Muḥammad Ḥsēn al-Ḏiyab, who had set them in motion when he was nominated *muḫtār* (or *ne'emān* in Hebrew)[5] of the *'arab* al-Ḥğerāt in 1949.

The crucial period in this process was the MG era. The insistence of the MG on working with local communities through their respective *maḫatīr* and the over-regulation of daily activities promoted a system of patronage that enabled the young *muḫtār* to nurture a following, rout his competitors, and entrench himself in his office. No less significant, however, and important reasons for his success—unlike most Galilean *maḫatīr*—in surviving the abrogation of the MG were his age, the fact that he was not traumatized by the 1948 Arab defeat, his ambition, and other characteristics one finds among Ḥğeri youth (inquisitiveness, good memory, pride, a strong sense of etiquette and courtesy, and the like), which he employed in learning from the new circumstance as much as he could. Consequently, he learned the workings of the local MG and the bureaucratic administration it represented: its structural hierarchies of specialized units, logic and style of operation, limitations, concern with *time* and *security*, ties to the ruling *MaPaI* party, and so on. He did not substitute this new model for the earlier tribal model he already had nor did he compromise the latter in any way. He simply added the necessary repertoire of logical behavioral items needed when dealing with the administration to his behavioral kit while keeping both sets apart. For example, he avoided joking with Arab women in public but would do so with the Jewish secretaries of his contacts because it was acceptable and created working relations that were important for "she is often more important than him [the official] because she organizes matters for him," as he once commented.

This learning process was tacitly encouraged by the officers at the MG because it attuned him to their style of operation, as was soon apparent in the way he conducted his official business there, and which saved them both time and labor. The following accolades by Israeli officials in 1975–1977 are telling:

- To quote an official of the ILA who helped the *muḫtār* whenever he could "because he is good for the state." Asked to explain, he said "in 1948 most natural [i.e., indigenous, legitimate] leadership of the Arabs escaped from the country so that now the Arab sector lacks natural leaders. The policies of the military government did not allow the growth of natural leadership after 1948 to fill in the void because it favored lick-spits who gained the power instead of the natural leaders. . . . [The *muḫtār*] . . . is a natural leader and not a lick-spit and I help him because the state needs leaders like him who do not sway their followers like ["X"] to oppose the state but lead them to find their place within the Jewish state."

- An official of the Bureau of the Advisor on Arab Affairs (BAAA) commented on the behavior of the *muḫtār* during sessions of the NSBC, saying that "he sits quietly, listening to each speaker in his turn and only after all have finished he asks civilly for attention and when he speaks he speaks in a measured way and to the point." He later added that the *muḫtār* "has a very high sense of judgment."

- Another official (Ministry of Agriculture) said that he preferred to work with and through the *muḫtār* "because he is very intelligent and realistic and he wants to find solutions and therefore [one] can discuss matters over until [one] finds an acceptable solution for both sides which he [then] convinces his men to accept." This official also commented that if he "had to work with twenty people instead of, just, the *muḫtār* it would have taken forever [to get anything accomplished] and often would end unsuccessfully because each would want his private case resolved to his advantage."

- Or, during the 1977 election campaign period, a former *muḫtār* of a *fellāḥīn* village near Nazareth came to ask for some help. The *muḫtār* called the official concerned and was told by his secretary that the man was in a meeting and that she would have him call the *muḫtār* as soon as he came out. Several hours passed, during which the *fellāḥ* tried to convince the *muḫtār* to call again. The *muḫtār* refused, saying "no use, when they finish she will call me." Which she did.

Also, as of 1977 the *muḫtār* viewed himself as an Israeli first and an Arab second for "the Jews did not do the Ḥğerāt any wrong, on the contrary they had helped . . . [him] . . . as an individual and the bedouin as a group." Thus, according to his story, when he visited Jordan in the company of thirty other Arab notables from Israel to pay their condolences to King Husein of Jordan after the death of Queen ʿAlyah and one of the notables told the MC to present them as "Arabs from Palestine," he interjected and demanded to be presented as "Muḥammad Ḥsēn al-Ġadīr of the *'arab* al-Ḥğerāt, Israel." (During that audience he petitioned King Husein to permit Israeli Arabs to travel through Jordan to perform the *ḥağğ* [pilgrimage] to Mecca.) Similarly, while driving in his car one night he responded to a discourse by another bedouin on Arab-Jew relations in Israel, saying that in twenty years or so it would not matter any more to which family, group, or generation a person belonged nor would there be an Arab-Jew distinction—only personal abilities and education would be important in job-hunting and promotions.

It was during the MG period that he also developed the basic network of his connections in the administration and the Arab department of *MaPaI*, and while in and of itself the department was not especially powerful in the organization of the party, it provided him both with a glimpse of the real power in the country (when every four years laws and regulations would be bent for the sake of votes) and with his initial ties in the Israeli labor movement. While this network of connections had a supra-individual logic—viz. the respective wishes of the Jewish state to have expressively loyal Arab groups and of the tribe to ascend the second-class minority status of Arabs in Israel—its workings and performance seemed to be largely dependent on the personal relations of the individuals who had formed it. This personal quality of the network emerged practically every time a high-ranking officer in the police or Border Guard and some government personnel visited him in the village or were visited by him in their offices. And it was here that the payoff for the *muḫtār* was greatest for, like his learning experience, the benefits from this network extended and amplified. During the MG era it enabled him to better nurture his following. Later, as time passed, his individual contacts continued to rise in their respective bureaucratic hierarchies, becoming ever more powerful and influential both horizontally and vertically, thereby increasing their ability to help. The result was an ever-expanding network that the *muḫtār* was always keen on further developing, independently of his old connections.

For example, in the second half of the 1950s, while the *muḫtār* was herding in the Valley of Beisan, three members of a local kibbutz stole three of his cows that had wandered into the kibbutz's fields. He went to the local police and registered a complaint that three of his cows had disappeared. While talking with the station's commander "A" (from whom I heard this story) about it, he suggested that "A" call in Ibrāhīm al-Ḥsēn, his brother, who served as the local police tracker at the station of 'Afulah. "A" called Ibrāhīm al-Ḥsēn and joined the search party in order to see him at work. Ibrāhīm al-Ḥsēn tracked down the animals to a deserted Mandate police fort near the kibbutz, where the party found one cow alive and the skins of the other two, and provided "A" with some information on the three who stole them. "A" became very angry at the three for taking the law into their hands instead of abiding by it and registering a complaint with the police. Consequently, he arrested and charged them with as many violations of the law as he could. The kibbutz tried to pressure him to release the three without trial by having MKs from the kibbutz movement and some of his police superiors call to ask (or threaten) him to let them loose. His answer to all was: "there will not be one law for Jews and one law for Arabs in this country." The three went to court and were released on fines. After the case was closed the *muḫtār* came to thank "A" for his fairness in handling the case and remarked that there were not many fair people around for whom there was only one law. After that a personal friendship developed between the two and as "A" rose in the ranks and became assured of the *muḫtār*'s loyalty to the state, he supported the latter whenever he could. Thus, among other things he began to engage him in arbitrating *ṣulḥa* cases in the region, an activity that markedly increased the *muḫtār*'s political profile. Later "A" became the police commander of the region of Nablus in the West Bank and the *muḫtār* stopped to visit him on his way to Jerusalem one day. "A" introduced him to his subordinates and told them that if the *muḫtār* asked for any help they should comply with his request as if he had "okayed" it in advance. After that, the *muḫtār* visited the subordinates on various occasions and strengthened his friendship with them so that the latter became his friends on their own account. Later, for example, when Jenin (which had been a subdistrict of Nablus) became an independent district, the process repeated itself there. And, while preparing the guest lists for his firstborn's wedding, he gave a directive to invite all the commanders of army units in which Ḥğeri soldiers served. This shotgun approach enabled him to develop a new personal contact with at least one commander of a region where several Ḥğeris were serving as trackers at the time.

The network of connections Muḥammad al-Ḥsēn cultivated with the authorities had its reciprocal network of obligations among the people he served, for the greater his ability to help people through his connections, the greater his following. In this way, a self-reinforcing cycle developed: the more services he could provide the tribesmembers, the more they became bound to him for reasons of both reciprocal obligations and self-interest for more services, the more he was of service to the MG and *MaPal*, the more help he received from these agencies, the more services he could provide his followers, and so on. At first he used this cycle to convert the Ḥğerāt into a following and thereby consolidate the leadership in his hands. With time, however, and especially with the increased presence of the civilian government ministries that accompanied the gradual disappearance of the MG and the subsequent decline in the power of the *maḫatīr*, his favored status with the authorities became public knowledge and increasingly non-Ḥğeris would ask him to intervene with the authorities on their behalf. This cycle gradually expanded and became regional in scope.

The differences between these two complementary networks of connections and of obligations are all the more apparent when considering the *muḫtār*'s mode of operation in each of the two contexts. In his network of connections he was in a negotiating mode. He first listened to the opinions of those present and then quietly and civilly expressed his own conclusions. He was ready to accept others' ideas and change his own, and the mood was one of cooperation in order to solve the problem at hand. This mode he used when among the authorities and when among his siblings, including *ulād* Ḏiyab al-Ibrāhīm as a unit, where family unity meant the control of the tribe's leadership, as was succinctly summarized by a leading member of the family who commented that "the Ġadāyreh [*ulād* Ġadīr] are the strongest family in the tribe but they have to keep their eyes open all the time so that no one tries to play them down or double-cross them. If they even once give in to another family they will be demoted and no longer will lead the tribe. The other families try all the time to double-cross them and even within the Ġadāyreh there are people who would like to replace the *muḫtār* if they only could."

The family's recognition of the need to maintain this unity was also one of the reasons that kept Muḥammad al-Mūsā away from the village. By living on the other side of the Galilee, he would not provide a rallying post for likely opposition to the *muḫtār*. It was not love for the *muḫtār* that kept him there, but the realization that if they competed, the sublineage would split and they would all lose their lead.

The *muḫtār* used a similar style when among the Council of the Elders, although there he was less amenable to negotiation, as one of his brothers commented: "[he] is very talented in speaking; he can change the opinion of the *ḫatyariyyeh* after they have reached an opinion. If he thinks that their ruling is not a good one he talks them around and around until they reach his opinion by themselves and unanimously."

For example, he used the negotiating mode in the aforementioned anecdote about accepting presents on his firstborn's wedding. Similarly, it was the opinion of *ulād* Ḏiyab and his FBSs (*ulād* Mūsā al-Ḏiyab in particular) that convinced him to send his firstborn to serve in the police. Another example occurred after the sudden death of Ibrāhīm al-Ḥsēn, his brother and right-hand man. He became depressed, went into partial seclusion in his tent, and when the time came refused to be present in the village during the *'īd al-fiṭr* (the holiday that concludes the fast of Ramadan, when visitation and hospitality are very popular) because he was in mourning. The night before the *'īd* he was visited by a group from the village led by Muḥammad al-Mūsā, his eldest FBS, who argued that if the Ḥğerāt did not extend proper hospitality people would say that Ibrāhīm al-Ḥsēn's death crushed their spirit and that they could not withstand crises. After a couple of hours of persuasion he finally consented and the next day he was present in the village.

Within the network of obligations the *muḫtār* was in a patron mode. In this mode he did not try to reach a consensus, and negotiating agreements was not an issue. The help-seeker wanted help in settling a specific problem and either the *muḫtār* could or could not help him. Here the approach was very personal and the *muḫtār* was always ready to help, thereby creating "dependency [on himself]; he makes other peoples' problems his own and even if someone comes only for an advice he tells him 'leave it with me,'" as one Jewish official who helped and observed him for a long time commented. If he thought he could help—and he rarely took a chance on this score—he told the person to rest assured he would take care of it. If he was not sure or if he knew he could not help, he accompanied the person to the authorities and had the official concerned deliver the negative answer. He thus always came across as being ready to help to the best of his ability.

During the 1950s and early 1960s when the *muḫtār* was building his following, his personal approach was even more pronounced. In those days, when he was sought out by his tribesmembers or an occasional non-Ḥğeri, he would receive them in his tent in accordance with the rules of hospitality. Thus, apart from the spatial and tactile differences between tents, houses, and government offices, and with the ever-present coffee symbolizing welcome, a younger brother of the *muḫtār* remembered two to three lambs butchered for food each week in those days. He said his brother would butcher "according to their honor" (that is, a fowl, a lamb, or a kid) and then drive them in his car and help them. The ambiance, therefore, was one of familiarity and relative warmth, which stood in sharp contrast to the dehumanizing anonymity of the bureaucracy, and which dimmed the harsher reality of the reciprocal debt relationship that asking for such assistance entailed. As more people looked for help, the time that could be allocated to each shrank proportionately, and slowly the etiquette of hospitality began to diminish. In and of itself the reduced situational sociability and the resultant baring of the event's contractual element did not have adverse effects and was accepted by all as part of the reality of political ascendancy and importance. The *muḫtār* was careful to allocate to all their proper time[6] and honorifics according to their relative social standings, as a *fellāḥ* from a nearby village summarized: "[he] . . . is always very considerate of the honor of people big or small." Finally, he approached all cases as if they were his own.

As his time grew limited the *muḫtār* relied increasingly on the cooperation of Ibrāhīm al-Ḥsēn, his youngest uterine brother, who by the early 1960s lived in Bīr al-Maksūr and worked as a police tracker in Nazareth. Ibrāhīm al-Ḥsēn, who was eighteen when he joined the service in 1955, was in fact groomed by the *muḫtār* long before he became the latter's partner in leadership. Thus, for example, when he wanted to resign from the force in 1957 (as well as several other times) because he was paid too little and spent too much, it was the *muḫtār* who convinced him to stay and who lent him the extra money he needed. Later, when he was stationed in Nazareth and a divorcée, the *muḫtār* arranged for help to construct his house and for a second marriage to a FBSD in 1965. A few years later he helped him buy a car, and saw to it that his work schedule remained flexible. Thus, for example, in 1976 when a new station commander arrived in the Nazareth station and wanted Ibrāhīm al-Ḥsēn to perform "shifts" and all other routine duties according to his rank, Ibrāhīm al-Ḥsēn told him "fine, but then I do no tracking." Since he was the senior tracker of the Police Northern Command, the issue reached his regional commander (the aforementioned "A"), who transferred him to a special tasks unit where he was no longer under the new station commander and where he dealt only with tracking, which preserved his flexible schedule.

The two brothers had complementary characters. The *muḫtār* was intuitive, ambitious, driven, and at times haughty, and although he had good control of his temper, he lost it occasionally. In contrast, Ibrāhīm al-Ḥsēn was logical, unambitious, honest, humane, cool-headed, and unquestionably loyal to his brother. Additionally, both his profession and service location were strategically very important to the *muḫtār*. Professionally, Ibrāhīm al-Ḥsēn had an unregimented daily routine with ample free time because a police tracker's work was sporadic—that is, when there was a case requiring his services. His station was located in the downtown government center of the Old City of Nazareth and next to the courthouse. Moreover, the police maintained only one tracker in each of only a few of the region's main stations, and it was a romanticized occupation because it emphasized human native capacities unencumbered by gadgets and operating manuals. Thus, a good police tracker was a star and was accorded the latitude he wanted, hence the unregimented routine. Ibrāhīm al-Ḥsēn could, thus, serve as a link between the *muḫtār* and the lower and middle ranks of the local police and administration as well as help fellow Ḥğeris clear up minor legal problems, so that after his death a fellow Ḥğeri policeman described him as the clearing post for traffic violation tickets, minor troubles with the authorities, licenses (primarily for guns), and so on.

In line with the *muḫtār*'s personal approach, Ibrāhīm al-Ḥsēn also accompanied the help-seeker through the alien administrative tangle of the police and the court, explaining to them what to expect and at times actually talking for them when the *muḫtār* was unavailable to do so himself. Then, after work he represented the *muḫtār* in Bīr al-Maksūr. His role in the village was so important that following his death, a number of Ḥğeris repeatedly remarked that the *muḫtār* had alienated people (i.e., Ḥğeris) and Ibrāhīm al-Ḥsēn had mended the relations, and that he was the *muḫtār*'s "'back' as far as the support of the people [Ḥğeris] was concerned." He also took care of the day-to-day administrative problems in the village and was referred to by one informant as the "Minister of the Interior" of the mukhtarship and the tribe.

This cooperation crystallized throughout the 1960s and as the *muḫtār* became increasingly more occupied with regional affairs and national politics during the 1970s, increasingly more of the tribesmembers' immediate personal needs were channeled through Ibrāhīm al-Ḥsēn.

* * *

While nurturing a following by extending assistance to individuals was a primary mechanism in ensuring that the leadership remained in his hands during the MG era, the *muḫtār*'s success at remaining the unchallenged leader of the Ḥğerāt until 1977 was no less the result of the acceptance and legitimation of his office by the tribe as a whole. This is not to say that his continuing and expanding network of connections with the civilian authorities that replaced the MG had lost its importance in underwriting his success, for as several authors have observed, Israel was a grand system of party patronage (e.g., Medding 1972; Aronoff 1977; Zohar 1974; Evron et al. 1975). It does say, however, that from the tribesmembers' point of view, alongside the economic and administrative services he provided, Muḥammad al-Ḥsēn became their legitimate representative leader.

The various reasons that combined with economic help to legitimate his office ranged from the ideal to the material. The least concrete among these was the oft-mentioned ideal of Ḥğeri unity that bound the *muḫtār* like any other member of the tribe. In other words, although he tried to ensure his family's hold on the leadership, he did not promote this interest beyond the limits of tribal cohesion. This attitude was very clear during the 1977 election campaign. Unlike the behavior in some other tribes in the area, which bordered on violence, competition among the factions in the Ḥğerāt was relatively subdued and restrained so as not to force confrontations that would seriously split the tribe. Thus, for example, when asked by one of his brothers to censure the dissident factions because "they divide the tribe," the *muḫtār* refused on the grounds that elections come and go but censure would force issues that would not disappear after Election Day. It was interesting, in this regard, to listen to the complaints of individuals and of the opposition factions during the election campaign. The most serious charge against the *muḫtār* was that he did not take good care of the tribesmembers and that he was haughty; the second was familial (i.e., "it is time to replace the *ulād* Ġadīr"); and the third was generational (i.e., "it is time to give more power to the younger people"). In short, he saw himself responsive and responsible to the tribe and—although what he meant by that was questioned by some tribesmembers—he did not abuse his power as *muḫtār* once established in office. Thus, the ideal of Ḥğeri unity limited the freedom of the *muḫtār* to diverge from the accepted norms (beyond which he would lose the tribe's support) and in doing so made himself acceptable to the tribesmembers.

While being ultimately limited by it himself, the *muḫtār* also used the ideal of Ḥğeri unity to his own advantage, for once established in his office he perpetuated the momentum of support for his leadership by promoting the ideal. It is of little surprise, then, that he cooperated with and supported the Council of the Elders from the beginning of his career, for there was an identity of interest there. Not only did he support the *ḫatyariyyeh* as a general principle, and in cases of blood actually sit among their number to lend his weight to the ruling, but he ensured that they upheld the unity they represented. Thus, for example, in 1977 there was a case of an annulled engagement; the Elder approached by the adversaries ruled damages (that is, reimbursement of expenses) plus a fine. Later another Elder commented that the verdict should have been only damages. Consequently, the defendant demanded the fine he had already paid and the two Elders aired their differences in public. The *muḫtār* stepped in, and on the basis of the categorical case supported the second Elder but on the basis of the specifics of the case agreed with the first Elder's verdict. He then commented that the real issue did not lie in the case itself but in the publicity of the disagreement between the two Elders. He continued saying: "you are the Elders and known as the *ḫatyariyyeh*, you should be united in your opinion if you are to lead and if people are to listen to your words, because if one says so and the other says thus people will start to go from one to the other playing one against the other. . . . Your word should be united and final and do not erode that word once it has been made public even if one Elder delivers his own opinion without consulting the others and the others have differing opinions as was in this case. If you do not form a united front to the people they will not heed your verdicts and then, where will your words be?"

Moreover, by promoting the ideal he also redirected public attention to a biased issue—unity—in order to keep tribesmembers from demanding to discuss the real issues—the distribution of power and control.[7]

A somewhat more concrete factor in his legitimization by the tribesmembers was his youth when nominated, for he provided a focus for the tribe's young men in the 1950s when the elder generations lacked the experiences and skills needed to cope with the new administrative environment. Not surprisingly, his initial followers were his peers, who identified with his leadership because of their intergenerational tensions on the one hand and aspirations on the other. By the time his policy of active interaction with the authorities had started to bear fruit during the 1960s and members of the older generations were joining his supporters, his own age group had become parents, thus helping to perpetuate his support.

Third and most concrete were changes in the tribe's regional political climate, which created a need for a leadership that could react more continuously and faster than the consensual methods of the Council of the Elders could handle. From 1949 on, the tribe's adaptive needs shifted the Ḥğeri mode of political operation from a sporadic and reactive mode, in which the Ḥğerāt tried not to initiate new events but only respond after these had occurred, to an active mode in which information was gathered and a course of action was decided and followed in a continuous fashion.

The policies and practices of the MG notwithstanding, on the regional scene the triggering events for this shift were the aforementioned incident with the *muḫtār* of Saḫnīn and, more importantly, the special relations that the Druze and the *'arab* al-Heīb had been developing with the authorities in general and the IDA in particular. As previously mentioned, both groups had cooperated with the IDA during the 1948 War in the Galilee and volunteers from both had joined the army after the war and been assigned (with the Circassians and bedouin from other tribes such as the *'arab* al-Mazarib) to a special unit—the Minorities' Unit (MU)—which was located at the time near Haifa.

The specter of their traditional rivals in uniforms and Bren guns was most alarming, for the ability to carry weapons in public was not only symbolic of their rival's superior contacts with the authorities but, in those early years when the future of the new state was in doubt, was a very real reminder of a community's ability to protect itself if the need arose. In other words, the importance of the weapons lay more in their real potential and the readiness to deploy them than in their symbolic meaning.

One enlightening incident in this regard occurred in the village of Abū Snān near Acre whose population included Druze (about one half), Christians, and non-Druze Moslem Arabs. One night in December of 1975, as retaliation for several dead some three years earlier in a long-standing feud between two Druze lineages, the relatives of the dead shelled their opponents' houses with shoulder-mounted anti-tank rockets, hand grenades, and bullets that they had "borrowed" from their IDA unit. Three people were lightly wounded. A more serious incident occurred in April 1981 following the stabbing death of a Druze in a clash between the respective fans of the D-league soccer teams of Ğūlis (a Druze village) and of Kafr Yāsīf (mixed population, Christian majority) during a Saturday match in the latter village. Until Tuesday noon the Druze refused overtures to make peace (*ṣulḥa*) and that afternoon stormed Kafr Yāsīf, armed with (among other implements) IDA-issued automatic rifles and hand grenades. After one hour and a half of rioting the toll was two dead, seven gun-shot wounded (three critical), thirteen houses in shambles, and ten burnt cars (Hareuveni 1981:1, 3). A less dramatic episode occurred five days before *yūm al-'arḍ* (the "Day of the Land," March 30, 1976), which was organized by Arab activists as a general strike and demonstration to protest the expropriation of state and privately owned lands (most of which were Arab) in the Galilee. On that day the *muḫtār* was in Shfar'am trying to convince some Arab mayors and notables not to support the strike when a crowd of militant Moslem youth began to stone the building. This information was phoned to Bīr al-Maksūr and when the meeting ended and the *muḫtār* called Ibrāhīm al-Ḥsēn to tell him all was well and that he was returning to the village, the latter told him to wait in Shfar'am so that they could come for him. Ibrāhīm al-Ḥsēn and four others, all armed with automatic rifles (mostly M-16s), drove to Shfar'am and, shouldering their rifles, knocked on the town's mayor's door where the meeting was held. They were greeted and served coffee after which they accompanied the *muḫtār* to his car, entered theirs, and the two cars drove off together. The message to the Shfar'ameans was loud, clear, and simple: "if you get violent so will we . . . and we have automatic rifles."

The formation of the MU thus acutely alarmed the Ḥğerāt because although they had a few members in the police, that institution proved to be much less weighty than the MG and the IDA. Not only were they outnumbered in personnel by their rivals but the police were neither as powerful as the MG nor as glamorous and influential as the IDA. From a Ḥğeri viewpoint this alarm was no act of chasing ghosts for all three groups had been doing their best to use the Israeli security complex to elevate themselves out of the second-class status of the Arab minority in Israel (and in 1976 were joined by Christian Arabs [*New York Times* Nov. 1, 1976:1]; see also Oppenheimer [e.g., 1977:237 et passim] for the Druze in the area).

To make matters worse, Ḥassan Ṣāleḥ al-Ḫnefes, their old-time Druze enemy, was elected a member of the Knesset (MK) in 1951 with the help of Ḥğeri votes. More than any other it was this early experience that convinced the young *muḫtār* of the power of *MaPaI* as represented by its Arab department, for it forced the Ḥğerāt to cast their vote in favor of the very person who had vowed to eliminate them. Later, in 1977, he was still convinced of this power even though he knew that the policies of the Labor Party in the Arab sector were completely bankrupt. That a Druze MK had very little power, if any, in the Knesset in general and in directing and noticeably influencing the welfare of another minority community other than his own in particular had very little influence on how the Ḥğerāt viewed their sociopolitical milieu in those days. It was this reality—of the Druze connections at the national seat of power, and the Heīb cared for by a few top ranking IDA officers, while they themselves had to hide their rifles, in addition to the power struggle between the young *muḫtār* and Ibrāhīm al-Nimr—that had convinced Muḥammad al-Mūsā to abandon smuggling and enlist in the police in 1952 (see Chapter 6). Similarly, with this information in mind, the events during the 1951 wedding when Ibrāhīm al-Nimr slapped the Ṣawālḥi father of the groom for inviting the Druze become clearer (see Chapter 6).

Matters got worse in 1953 when a fight broke out between the Druze and the bedouin in the MU camp and in its wake the bedouin left the unit and the army. Although a few bedouin remained as individuals in the IDA and were transferred to serve as trackers with Jewish units, thus setting the pattern for future bedouin recruits, the MU remained effectively Druze in its composition, with no bedouin contingent to counterbalance them politically. The significance of this event was underlined by a Ḥğeri informant: "when a fight with the Druze begins the Ḥğerāt and the Heīb are first of all bedouin and so are the Negev bedouin." Thus, on the more inclusive order of the Arab minority in Israel the bedouin are in opposition to both the Druze and the *fellāḥīn*, including city dwellers, and so on. On the next level down—the bedouin order—it is the northern tribes in opposition to the southern ones (see below, parliamentary politics). Finally, in the north, it is the Ḥğerāt versus the Heīb. The organizational separation between Druze and bedouin following the 1953 fight and especially after 1956 (see below) brought the level of competition down to the regional order, thereby intensifying both inter-group competition and intra-group cohesion within the bedouin ethnic category while relatively disengaging the more intense competition between the "Bedouin" and the "Druze" ethnic groups.

The Ḥğerāt could do nothing about this scenario because—although by then they had monopolized the tracking profession in the police—they had only three men in service and the prospects for more were practically nonexistent. Their first chance to remedy some of this strategic imbalance came in 1955 when the Border Guard, which was formed by the police in 1953, opened a few new tracking positions. As the Ḥğerāt tell it, the opportunity came during a social evening in the *muḫtār*'s tent, which was pitched at the time near Rosh Pinah in the northeastern Galilee. Among those present was the regional commander of the newly formed Border Guard who told the *muḫtār* that they were looking for trackers. The *muḫtār* immediately summoned one of his FBSs, a very cool-headed person who was working as a cattle herder for kibbutz Hasolelim. To what extent the authorities were aware of the Ḥğerāt-Druze animosity and were trying to bring them together in a highly controlled setting is hard to assess. Nonetheless, the *muḫtār*'s choice of the candidate was clearly done with this issue in mind for he had chosen him over a hot-headed uterine brother. Thus, although the personnel for this unit came primarily from Druze and Circassians veterans of the MU, its Jewish commanders, police discipline, and the operational needs of a unit in the field lowered the traditional animosities between Druze and bedouin. While this traditional animosity was kept in check within the Border Guard—because through time bedouin personnel joining the force were not necessarily as cool-headed as were the early recruits—it nonetheless surfaced occasionally outside the force, thereby perpetuating a state of alert preparedness. For example, in March 1977 the remnants of the *'arab* al-Muwāsa went to the town of Mağdal Šams in the Golan Height to communicate (across the wire fence that marked the cease-fire line between Israel and Syria) with their relatives who had fled the country in 1948. While there, a quarrel developed with Druze personnel of the Border Guard and they were chased "half across the town" (as one of them described) by the Druze. When called by the BAAA, the Border Guard regional commander said that the Muwāsa were insolent and had started the fight with his men. It was only after the BAAA insisted that the Druze were armed while the Muwāsa were not and that "maybe it started because the Druze don't like Bedouin" that the Border Guard commander agreed to investigate the event.

In 1956 events took another turn for the worse when Druze and Circassians notables signed a covenant with the State of Israel that, among other items, instituted compulsory military service for the male youth of these groups on the same basis as their Jewish counterparts. This event provided the final touch to the state's drive to have minority servicemen as part of the image of social democracy that it tried to project to the world. It seems that once the pattern of cooperation was established and assured, the real issues of manpower (the difference between a few hundred volunteers and several thousand conscripts) and finance (the difference between the salaries of career civilian personnel and the pay of conscripts) came to the fore and conscription was the obvious solution. When, in the mid-1970s, the state tried to apply the same solution to the bedouin (see below), it failed because the bedouin MK withstood the pressure and refused to sign a similar covenant that was objected to by bedouin leaders across the country. Their objection was not to the military service in itself—on the contrary, they encouraged their men to enlist—but to the compulsory character of conscription (which, they argued, was against the grain of "bedouin character") and to the significant drop in pay that would result. Less publicly there were two additional issues: first, the loss of their role as mediators between the draft officers and the enlistees, and, second, their tribes' status vis-à-vis the rest of the Arab world, for when choosing to work in the army, individual volunteers did not commit the tribe as a whole. This latter issue, by the way, brought the 1972 formation of the Druze Initiative Committee, one of whose major aims was to end Druze conscription as a means to amend relations with the rest of the Arab sector (Oppenheimer 1978:36). Finally, from a bedouin point of view, they had the better deal and they derided the Druze for getting the short end of the stick. Not surprisingly, when the Christian community approached the authorities in regard to service in the army, they asked for the same service conditions of the bedouin (*New York Times* 1976:1).

Although in concrete terms the covenant between the Druze and the state did not pose any real threat to Ḥğeri welfare, especially since their own intra-tribal power struggles had concluded by then, it served to emphasize the "we/they" issue. Thus, according to a Ḥğeri informant, it was the behavior of the Druze during the 1956 Sinai Campaign rather than strictly the issue of conscription that had the greater effect on the Ḥğerāt. To quote: "the Druze moved all over the Galilee and the Valleys, in the villages and on the roads, all armed and boasting." It was immaterial that the Druze were assigned to ensure that the Arab sector would not seize the opportunity to revolt; the Ḥğerāt became worried even though they had men in the police because "the police is not the army. . . . the army is much freer" and therefore formulated the policy that "anyone who wants to go to the army is free and encouraged to do so."

By 1967 the Ḥğerāt were entrenched as trackers in the police and the Border Guard, and several Heībis served as trackers attached to Jewish units in the IDA, while the Druze, who set on a separate course, were in the IDA's Minorities' Brigade and in the police's Border Guard together with the Circassians. As Oppenheimer observed, the service of the Druze in the IDA (especially after the 1956 covenant) and their intensifying ethnicity (1978:30–39; 1977:232–38) set them on a course of "separation . . . from the rest of the Arab national minority" (1978:32). From the bedouin perspective this development was to their own advantage because once the Druze had their brigade, they lost all their maneuverability as individuals and could not compete for tracking positions attached to Jewish units, which were then left exclusively to the bedouin.

Politically, this distribution among the state armed forces meant that the Ḥğerāt were primarily confined to regional ties whereas the Druze and the Heīb had their ties at the national level—the former through their MKs and the latter through their "adopting" Jewish officers. Offsetting this strategic imbalance was the *muḫtār*'s basic network of connections, which was by then well established.

The 1967 War opened a new phase in this competition.[8] Directly, it created an increased demand for trackers. Indirectly, it created a need for a large contingent of people to administer and guard the newly conquered territories. The resultant massive increase in manpower demands of the security complex was answered by an increase in the service duration of conscripts (from 26 to 36 months), reenlistment and hiring of new personnel, and quick promotions for veteran personnel to train and lead the newcomers. It was among the veterans that the *muḫtār* had many of his connections, and their rise in the ranks spelled an accelerated expansion of his network. Through his connections in the security complex, the Ḥǧerāt finally succeeded in entering the IDA as trackers. Then, as previously mentioned, they established their presence in the army alongside the *'arab* al-Heīb and other bedouin trackers (mostly from the Negev), and several of them became noncommissioned officers (NCO).

During the mid-1970s, however, the Ḥǧeris encountered two obstacles in their advance to officers' rank that would ensure their continuous presence in the army independently of the Heīb. The first obstacle was the control the *'arab* al-Heīb exercised over the necessary recommendation for the officers' course to which trackers could apply. This control was possible because although functionally the bedouin served as trackers attached to Jewish units, administratively they belonged to the trackers' unit, whose senior officers were those individuals who had made the army their career between the 1953 fight in the MU camp and the 1967 War. According to the Ḥǧerāt these officers were mostly Heīb, who intentionally blocked the professional advancement of Ḥǧeri personnel while promoting Heībi candidates over Ḥǧeri heads. As a result, advancement on grounds of purely professional merit was closed. This impasse was recognized by at least one Jewish official who said that the Heīb had five officers, one of whom was the commanding officer of the trackers' unit who made sure that any recommendation for officers' course "would go to a Heībi and only to a Heībi." He then commented that this state of affairs "drove the Ḥǧerāt up the wall" because they had no officers at all. Similarly, the one Ḥǧeri who was finally accepted to officers' course in 1977 had remarked a full year earlier that "I don't need . . . [the commanding officer's] . . . help [to get into the course], all I need is that he won't interfere and will stay out of it." When I asked the *muḫtār*'s aide (in charge of contacts with the IDA draft officers in general and the officers' course issue in particular), who had been socializing extensively with that Heībi officer, if the latter would recommend a Ḥǧeri, the aide answered "not a chance."

The issue of the Heībi blockade is another example of the local style of inter-group competitive relations. For example, the Heībi commander of the unit often visited Bīr al-Maksūr, and hunted, partied, joked, and laughed with Ḥǧeris at their homes, thereby projecting common interests—if not actual friendship—and support. At the same time, he systematically rejected Ḥǧeri applications for the course and when Ḥǧeri soldiers invited their Jewish comrades and officers for *ḥaflāt* (sing., *ḥaflah*, a festive feast or party), he came accompanied by other Heībis whenever he could and took over the evening (a major breach of bedouin etiquette) in order to prevent Ḥǧeris from developing off-the-job personal ties with their Jewish officers. The Ḥǧerāt, for their part, retorted by twice, as a joke, stealing the spare tire from his parked car during visits to Bīr al-Maksūr—a major breach of hospitality even as a joke and all the more so when one of the tires was never returned.

The second obstacle was the simple fact that as of 1976 none of the Ḥǧeri NCO possessed a matriculation certificate, one of the formal requirements for entry into the course. As a result, they could not use recommendations by their Jewish commanding officers in lieu of their Heībi officers because these requests were processed through the more formal channels of military bureaucracy, which required the certificate. Serving with Jewish units, however, provided a potential source of the necessary recommendations, and it was just a question of time when the Ḥǧerāt would bypass the Heībi blockade by using it.[9]

Bypassing the Heībi blockade was finally achieved with the confluence of two approaches: the personal and the public. The personal approach was driven by the individual soldiers and hinged on the high professionalism of Ḥğeri trackers. Most, if not all, Ḥğeri trackers were very proud of their skill and of the tribe's reputation. As a result they were usually professionally self-critical and made sure that other Ḥğeri trackers met the tribe's tracking standards by coaching, assisting, and supporting the newcomers so that they did not blunder. To function well a Ḥğeri tracker spontaneously tried to create a familiar and personalized environment within which to work, because in its absence he quickly became alienated and worked poorly. Thus, when a Ḥğeri tracker failed at his job, it was usually not a result of professional mediocrity but of emotional alienation. This point was realized by one regional commander who developed personal relations with his Ḥğeri trackers, and through them with the tribe. When asked, he said the personal contact helped make the Ḥğeri contingent in his region more dedicated and able to outperform his other trackers. Being in field units and close to danger, an already particularizing milieu, and being attached rather than integral elements of their units, Ḥğeris rapidly developed a personalized network of relations in the headquarters of the units to which they were assigned. As attached personnel in these units they stood outside the dynamics and problems of the indigenous authority structure inherent to military organization and did not threaten it by a more personal demeanor. Hence they were allowed more behavioral freedom than the integral elements of the unit provided they maintained a high professional level. The presence of attached personnel, moreover, allowed a commander to be more relaxed when interacting with them precisely because they were outsiders who could not threaten his authority, thus facilitating the development of a familiar milieu from his direction as well. Consequently, when they requested a recommendation, they could often secure one. The fruit of one such personal network was the establishment of a Ḥğeri stronghold in the trackers' section of one command, which later served as the training post for young Ḥğeri recruits with matriculation certificates who could expect a recommendation from their Jewish commander when the time came to apply to officers' course.

Concurrently, through the networks of the *muḫtār* and Maḥmūd al-Mūsā, his aide, the Ḥğerāt repeatedly presented their case—"why no Ḥğeri officers?"—to high-level personnel in the security complex, who kept pointing to the lack of matriculation certificates as the reason for their inability to help. Finally, in the summer of 1976 several youths of the *ulād* Ġadīr successfully completed their examinations and received the coveted certificates so that when in December one of the tribe's recruiting connections asked for more trackers, a few of these youths enlisted. At issue was not that the Ḥğerāt did not have individuals with matriculation certificates before but that these individuals did not belong to the leading family itself or to its close relatives within the *ulād* Ġadīr, and if they did belong, their fathers refused to let them join the IDA. As long as the Ḥğerāt thought that they could graduate their NCO to officers' course sans certificate, the leading family did not pressure its matriculated sons to join the army. Once, however, it became unequivocally clear that the certificate *was* the obstacle, their next crop of matriculated youth were talked into enlisting. Independently of this effort, as previously mentioned, in July 1977 a Ḥğeri NCO who had made use of the educational opportunities provided by the IDA was finally accepted to officers' course. Using this dual approach to bypass the Heībi blockade, the *'arab* al-Ḥğerāt finally established itself in the IDA on an equal footing with the *'arab* al-Heīb.

The perceived danger from the Druze during the 1950s and early 1960s and the later competition with the *'arab* al-Heīb were thus important factors in the *muḫtār*'s ability to legitimate his leadership and unite the tribe around it. In the process of the competition, however, individual Ḥğeri soldiers were able to develop private networks of their own, which they could use independently of the *muḫtār* and against him. The *muḫtār*, aware of this danger, tried to send only his supporters to the recruiting centers and, whenever possible, to control the social occasions that helped cement the personalized character of the network. Nonetheless, at least one individual utilized a previous army connection as a basis for leading one of the four opposition factions that competed with the *muḫtār* during the 1977 parliamentary election campaign.

These social occasions were the aforementioned *ḥaflāt* or dinner parties. In the course of such parties the food served was different from that usually served during *ḥaflāt* for bedouin or *fellāḥīn*. (In the former the food usually included grilled mutton, tahini, cut fresh vegetables, olives, and if the Jews were not religious, yogurt and *labne* accompanied by alcoholic beverages. In the latter the food included meat [often kid or goat] cooked in yogurt sauce and rice [although in informal, spontaneous small *ḥaflāt* for Ḥğeris and personal guests the grilled meat menu in toto was more commonly served].) During these parties any Ḥğeri who wished to be present could come but as long as the guests were present, only they ate while the Ḥğeris served food, made certain everyone was cared for, and maintained the conversation (cf. Aref 1937:127). By the mid-1970s, the Ḥğeris drank alcohol with their guests and the atmosphere was jovial and carefree.

In each of these *ḥaflāt*, for security personnel Ibrāhīm (and after his death a senior FBS), Maḥmūd al-Mūsā, and occasionally the *muḫtār* himself were present and if the guests' importance warranted they themselves would coordinate the service—that is, ensure that everyone was cared for and satisfied—and would dominate the conversation by reason of their seniority (see Figure 8). In this way they made the acquaintance of the people the host had invited and turned the evening from a private affair into a reception by the tribe. The presence of Ibrāhīm al-Ḥsēn and the *muḫtār*, incidentally, was usually sought after by the soldier or policeman giving the party, who would invite them as soon as the invitation to the guests had been accepted and often before it had been extended. Two reasons governed this behavior: first the wish to involve the tribe as a whole in the event, thereby receiving its approval and, second, not to raise suspicion that the party-giver might be trying to "go independent."

The muḫtār's Rise to Regional Prominence

Reinforcing the impetus generated by the competition with the Druze and the *'arab* al-Heīb was a second source of legitimation to the mukhtarship: the extra-Ḥğeri section of the network, which the *muḫtār* had been developing concurrently. Unlike the intra-Ḥğerāt section, which benefited individuals and only occasionally larger units within

Muḥammad Ḥsēn al-Ḏiyab, *muḫtār*

Ibrāhīm Ḥsēn al-Ḏiyab

Maḥmūd Mūsā al-Ḏiyab

Figure 8. The mukhtarship.

the tribe, the extra-Ḥğeri section elevated the tribe's status as a whole, and its benefits were enjoyed by all. Thus, since they were the *muḫtār*'s tribesmembers, being a Ḥğeri in most places meant deference, influence, and security. Security in this sense did not refer strictly to the sense of being free of danger, for accidents and quarrels did occur. Security for the Ḥğerāt meant that had events occurred, the non-Ḥğeri offender would come to Bīr al-Maksūr, apologize, and offer to pay indemnity, thereby establishing their guilt and Ḥğeri innocence. In other words, for the Ḥğerāt, more than its physical attributes, security was a matter of honor, personal and tribal.

This secure status was the outcome of three factors. First, it resulted from help the *muḫtār* could extend and the easier access to him enjoyed by most Ḥğeris, who could thus become mediators between a help-seeker and the *muḫtār*.

Second was the fact that the Ḥğerāt did not abuse their status and in general were helpful, generous, civil, and respectful toward others. To ensure civil behavior was not abused, it was monitored, guided, or enforced among the young, who were most likely to abuse it. For example, after a young brother of the *muḫtār* had hit a young female (*fellāḥīn*) coworker who had antagonized him in the Nazarene factory where they worked, he was severely reprimanded by his eldest uterine brother and Ibrāhīm al-Ḥsēn (his paternal brother), both of whom threatened the youth with the withdrawal of the tribe's support if he got himself into such troubles in the future.

Third, and not least, was the deterrence provided by the latent fighting force of any bedouin tribe, whose edge in the Ḥğeri case was sharpened by the security complex, which also allowed Ḥğeris to carry firearms in public, as post-1967 soldiers had been required to do in response to the increase in PLO activities that followed the 1967 War. This edge, which was kept well sheathed by the *muḫtār*,[10] was both a result and a generator of Ḥğeri unity as well as the source of their pride and their sense of security. For example, during the *yūm al-'arḍ* demonstrations, a Ḥğeri policeman on patrol was stoned by a mob in Saḫnīn, which also threatened to kill him because "the bedouin are traitors" (the *fellāḥīn*, incidentally, accused the bedouin and the Druze for the several deaths that resulted from that day's demonstrations). The Ḥğeri told them that if they killed him, law or no law, the Ḥğerāt would level Saḫnīn. At that point some of the people began attempting to cool the mob, which now demanded the Ḥğeri leave the police jeep he was driving so they could burn it in protest. The Ḥğeri answered that if they wanted to burn the jeep they would have to burn it with him inside because the jeep was given to him in trust, which he was not going to forfeit. By then the mob was divided between those who wanted him to leave and avoid a feud with the Ḥğerāt and those who wanted him and the jeep burnt, and as they started fighting among themselves he left the scene.

Then, in addition to providing the Ḥğerāt with a sense of security, through the careful deployment of this latent fighting force, clients could be helped and opponents discouraged or intimidated. For example, following the 1973 municipal election in Shfar'am, during which the mayoralty moved from Christian Arab control to the Moslem quarter, the former group began rioting against the latter. The new mayor—finding that due to the election the police were short on personnel (as two policemen guarded each polling station in the country)—asked the Ḥğerāt for help. The *muḫtār* responded by sending ten jeeps mounted with some forty armed Ḥğeris to patrol the streets until tempers cooled off.

ṣulḥa Mediation

By the beginning of the 1970s the availability of this force and the *muḫtār*'s ability to see both sides in a conflict of interest and his talents at mediating them were realized at the regional police headquarters. Consequently the police began to use him in arbitrating blood-feud-generating-conflicts—or, *ṣulḥa* arbitration (the assault and battery, elopement/

homicide end of the previously discussed mediation continuum)—at first just within the Nazareth District and then anywhere in the Northern Region. The reasons for police employing the traditional means of conflict resolution were simple. First, as a police commander commented about the *muḫtār*, "he saves me 20–30 men when he goes to arbitrate a *ṣulḥa* immediately." Second, by approaching conflict resolution in the traditional way, the police could soften their image in the Arab sector where their force was well known, while inducing the cooperation of both adversaries in reestablishing public order. The problem for the police, of course, was the need to impose a Western state legal standard on a non-Western kin-based population for which there was no sharp division between legal (i.e., administrative) matters and political (i.e., inter-group) matters. Consequently, when a homicide was a political event the police must separate two kin-groups, each of which might be several hundred or more strong and likely to decimate each other if allowed to pursue the conflict.

The problem was much more acute during the Mandate Period when the police force was smaller and the local population not yet controlled. Muḥammad Mūsā al-Ḏiyab, for example, recounted that in 1935 the two largest lineages in the village of 'Eylūṭ refused to make peace and the police could not keep them from inflicting death and destruction on one another. In an attempt to stop them the police commander of Nazareth established a temporary police station in the village, but to no avail. Finally, Mūsā al-Ḏiyab, who was working for him at the time, suggested that the commander allow him to enlist the help of some nine Ḥğeri friends to replace the policemen in the village and disregard what he heard from the 'Eylūteans for a while. The ten Ḥğeris forced the villagers to feed them, arrested any suspicious character, disrupted the daily routines of the *fellāḥīn*, and in general roughed out the life of the 'Eylūteans. Within two weeks the villagers began to request the commander to make a *ṣulḥa*. Duff tells of a similar case in 1931 when he was the police commander in Nablus. His solution (based on "a hint from the native officer [who] had served in the Turkish police") was to visit the village, Šweīkeh (some 2 km north of Tulkarem), accompanied by "fifty-odd horsemen" and "to take literal [sic. liberal] advantage of the extravagant expression of Arabic courtesy [i.e., hospitality]"; it took two and a half days for the villagers to cooperate (Duff 1953:295–99).

Benefits to the police notwithstanding, *ṣulḥa* arbitration was also a powerful tool in promoting the arbitrator to sociopolitical prominence for two reasons. First, it entailed reciprocation for the arbitrator's services in having the police drop case-related secondary charges against members of either side, because homicide usually induced retaliatory destruction. Consequently, a case may include—aside from homicide—charges ranging from arson, wanton destruction, and assault and battery to disturbance of public order and gathering for unlawful purpose. While personal litigations were waived as part of the *ṣulḥa* agreement, public claims remained in force unless the police waived them as a sign of goodwill and encouragement to end the conflict. Such waivers, incidentally, also reduced police work in terms of collecting evidence and court work.

The second, and more important, reason was that it was the arbitrator who had to vouch to each side for the compliance of its adversary with the peace agreement's articles for as long as necessary. This requirement was embedded in the anatomy of *ṣulḥa* cases. In order to have a *ṣulḥa*, both sides had to want to resolve the conflict for there was no way to coerce them to do so save for incarcerating *all* their respective membership. The problem, however, was that neither side perceived the issues simply in terms of casualties and damages but also, and more importantly, in terms of its honor, which was a generalized concept connoting the group's integrity and "sovereignty," that is, its right of self-defense. Consequently, although dealing with concrete events, the arbitrator tried to bridge the differences without compromising the honor of either side for such compromise would be interpreted as a statement about its future ability to defend itself. As I said before, to ensure his success, an experienced arbitrator demanded that both sides surrender their respective cases to his discretion and agree a priori to abide by his decision. If he failed to take this step he would quickly discover that one of the sides reneged, because ideally there could be no compromise in questions of honor for it reflected on the group's readiness to protect its membership. The same problem existed after the ceremony of the *ṣulḥa*, especially if the stronger side was the one to pay the restitution. The arbitrator, therefore, needed a force at his disposal to serve as a deterrent, for without it his decisions would be disobeyed and he laughed at.

For example, in March 1977 a newly married woman from the village of Dabūrīyeh (*fellāḥīn*) eloped with her lover from the village of ʻArrabeh and with police consent they became *duḫāl* (pl., wards, protégés) of "A," a rich restaurant owner from the village of Ṭurʻān who was trying to add political status to his wealth. The woman's lineal relatives convinced her to return to the village after promising she would not be harmed. "A" agreed to her return but conditioned it on police consent. On his recommendation and after the Elder of her lineage deposited with them an affidavit guaranteeing her safety, the police consented. That night she was executed (knifed) by at least two killers and her husband (a FBS) confessed to the murder. In analyzing the case an informant commented that had "A" had force, Dabūrīyeh would not have ridiculed him because whereas the police would have the husband jailed for life (i.e., twenty years or less), a real *kafīl* (a guarantor, guardian, etc.) would have had to avenge her death from her lineage because it had become an issue of his honor versus her relatives' honor. "A," he said, became rich and thought that money was power, only to discover he could not give his *kafālah* (guarantee) without having a sword to back it up for money without force was no power. He concluded with the saying "*al ḥagg mā lo sayf yibrī mā hū ḥagg*" ("Justice [legal right, claim, etc.] with no sharp scimitar is no justice").

Having both links to the police and a latent fighting force, the emergence of Muḥammad al-Ḥsēn as a leader of a regional measure received a major boost, for alongside his patronage network he rapidly cultivated his image as an indigenous leader who was versed in both the new and the traditional means of leadership.

The Anatomy of a ṣulḥa

The best illustration of Muḥammad al-Ḥsēn's mode of operation as a *ṣulḥa* arbitrator is the October 1976 peace he mediated between the Masarwah and the Yūnis, two large lineages in the villages of ʻĀra and ʻArʻara in the "Little Triangle" (a narrow three- to six-mile-wide strip along the northern bulge of the West Bank including twenty-six Arab villages from Kafr Qāsim in the south to Umm al-Faḥem in the north). The case, which occurred three months earlier, began as tension over the local council chairmanship and the manipulation of teaching posts in the local school escalated through a children's brawl into an adults' fight and resulted in two dead Masarwah men and close to twenty Yūnis houses burnt down in retaliation. A voluntary *ṣulḥa* committee composed of some forty notables from the "Little Triangle" and the West Bank headed by a *qāḍi* convened in an attempt to reinstate peace but deadlocked in its deliberations when it failed to establish commensurate values on the two claims. The Masarwah wanted their two men back and refused to accept the *diyah* (blood restitution), which was generally accepted at the time as I£50,000 per death. The Yūnis, for their part, demanded I£8.5 million, the sum quoted by an official appraiser for the damage to their houses. Consequently, some two and a half months passed with the adversaries still refusing to agree on the terms, let alone willing to surrender their cases. Finally, a delegation of the Masarwah who did not trust the committee (because it was applying economic logic to a non-economic reality) came to Nazareth and sought Muḥammad al-Ḥsēn's arbitration.

The *muḫtār*'s first step was to demand that the Masarwah unconditionally surrender their case into his hands. He sent the delegates to their villages to ensure the rest of their lineage members would accept his condition. Second, he arranged to access the police case files; he read and discussed them with the case officers before going to the village because "you know, they may tell lies." Then he met with the committee and together they drove to the Masarwah where he made his demand formally. After some maneuvers that lineage accepted and the committee moved to the Yūnis to make the same demand. The Yūnis, by custom, were obliged to accept once the relatives of the dead surrendered their case. Following the agreement the committee listened formally to the cases of the two lineages and then retired elsewhere (Kafr Qara') to deliberate the case as customary.

The committee's deadlock was its attempt to equate the sum of the *diyah* with that of the property damage, which was obviously in favor of the Yūnis and hence the reason for the Masarwah mistrust. Allowing for some talk of "eight and a half million here and eight and a half million there" the *muḫtār* then politely requested attention and after appropriate apologies for his rudeness in speaking so rashly and early for he was new to the case he said that "in the Galilee blood is blood and it comes first for the damage was the result of blood." He therefore suggested the committee annul the demand for I£8.5 million. The committee was dumbfounded and objected vehemently. He answered with a saying: "*la mā nazel al-shitā mā sarā al-waḥil*" ("if it did not rain there would be no mud"), meaning that if the Yūnis did not kill, the Masarwah would not burn. (This precept, incidentally, is a bedouin rather than Galilean formulation in which, as 'Araf reports, the relatives of the killed are permitted by custom to rob and destroy the property of the killer's group [although not take their land or dishonor their women] while in their rage over the death, and the damage is not considered as part of—i.e., deductible from—the *diyah* [Aref 1937:39].)

Following some deliberations the committee consented to annul the damages, at which point the *muḫtār* argued that the next step was to determine the sum of the *diyah* and suggested a total of I£100,000 for the two deaths. The committee was again in uproar but after he threatened to leave, its members consented and the *ṣulḥa* document (see Appendix J) was drawn, although the *diyah* was reduced by 10% because the committee argued that the full sum was too severe. When the Yūnis heard the verdict they objected "that it was unfair and impossible but they could do nothing [but accept it] because they had signed to accept the ruling whatever it might be." (And, one might add, because the police supported the committee, and the Ḥğerāt supported their *muḫtār*.)

Relations with the BAAA

Muḥammad al-Ḥsēn's favored position with the BAAA was also strengthened at about the same time. The reasons for this development were exogenous to the *muḫtār*'s career and the Ḥğerāt but their effects not only increased significantly the capabilities of the former as a regional patron but opened his way into national politics. In short, the BAAA's reasons were underlain by two related sets of causes. The first of these involved the strong identity that existed between party politics and the executive agencies in the State of Israel. The second set included developments within the Arab sector, which responded to its second-class minority status by promoting *RaQaH* (the New Communist List), which had split from *MaQI* (the Israeli Communist Party) in August of 1965.

The strong identity between party politics and the state was grounded in the fact that there was no executive branch that functioned autonomously of the legislature in Israel. Not only were the Cabinet members MKs (Members of Knesset), but due to traditional coalitionary agreements certain ministries "belonged" to certain parties, which used them as a grand network of party patronage. This characteristic had its roots in the pre-state history of the politics of the Zionist movement when "*party pre-existed pioneering* [in Palestine] *and all subsequent institutions*" (Medding 1972:9) and, hence, "Israeli political parties have been characterized as 'movements' having provided a wide range of services not normally associated with political parties in Anglo-American tradition" (Aronoff 1977:18). The result was the use of executive favors in exchange for parliamentary votes, which made it easy to assess the returns for executive investments, especially in the Arab sector where the trade-off was most direct (see below). Consequently, it became very clear that *MaPaI*/Alignment/Labor (as the party was called at different times) was gradually losing its Arab support when its following declined almost continuously from a high of 66.5% of the Arab vote in 1951 (see Table 26). This decline worried the civilian heir of the MG—the BAAA—which coordinated government activities in the Arab sector as best it could. It was thus interested in promoting new leaders who could attract voters during election years.

The replacement of *MaQI* by *RaQaH* as the representative of Arab sector interests caused alarm because whereas *MaQI* was a Jewish party with Arab support (see Table 27), *RaQaH* was an Arab party with Jewish support (see Table 28). (*RaQaH*'s political platform advocated the bi-state solution of the 1947 U.N. Partition Plan before June 1967 and a bi-state solution in the post-1967 situation [see Bailey 1970 for a more complete discussion of the Communist movement in Palestine and Israel].) It was also a successful party, which increased its following in the Arab sector markedly, as Table 29 indicates.

Table 26. Arab sector support for *MaPal* and its successors.

1951	1955	1959	1961	1965	1969*	1973
66.50%	62.40%	52.00%	50.08%	50.10%	56.90%	41.70%

(Source: Isr. MI 1977:447)
*The temporary rise in 1969 was caused by its alignment with *MaPaM*.

Table 27. Israeli Arab membership in *MaQI*.*

1955	1959	1961
27.80%	29.60%	41.10%

*Calculated from Isr. IGE 1956:10–11 for 1955, and 1964:20–25 for 1959 and 1961.

Table 28. Israeli Arab membership in *RaQaH*.*

1965	1969	1973	1977
75.50%	76.90%	79.90%	81.40%

*Calculated from Isr. IGE 1970:60–62 for 1965 and 1969, and 1978:49–51 for 1973 and 1977.

Table 29. Votes for *RaQaH* in the Arab sector.*

1965	1969	1973	1977
22.40%	28.20%	35.60%	49.20%

*Calculated from Isr. IGE 1970:60–62 for 1965 and 1969, and 1978:49–51 for 1973 and 1977.

More specifically, it was *RaQaH*'s success in the September 1969 elections to the congress of the *Histadrut* (from 19.8% of the 1965 Arab vote to 33% in 1969 [Bailey 1970:54]) that triggered a hectic campaign by the Labor Party (including its appendages in the executive branch of government) to re-attract the slipping Arab vote to its allied minorities lists for the parliamentary election in October (Bailey 1970:55). Although the campaign was partially successful, *RaQaH* increased its following by about 26% over its 1965 performance including some 1000 votes from the Druze (Bailey 1970:55), who were considered the group most impervious to that party. The Labor replied with a series of measures that included having Sayf al-Dīn al-Zu'abī of Nazareth (one of its allied lists' MKs) elected Deputy Speaker of the Seventh Knesset, and appointed Ǧabr Mu'addī, a Druze from Yirka and another list's MK, Deputy Minister of Communications. These appointments, however, were deemed insufficient by the BAAA because both leaders were seen as "yes-men" of the Labor Party in the Arab sector.

These two sets of causes resulted in an attempt to establish local Arab leaders who were not against Israel and who represented the Arab sector to counterbalance the local pro-Palestine leaders supported by *RaQaH*. Since the *muḫtār* was emerging as a leader in the first category, he found it increasingly easier to secure the BAAA's help and through that agency that of the whole government, excluding the Ministry of the Interior, a fiefdom of the *MafDaL*. His bad relations with the Ministry of the Interior were the result of the person of the district commissioner, who disliked Arabs in general and "the Gadir" in particular. The conflict, in fact, transcended the Arab population and lay between the district commissioner and the BAAA because the former promoted his party—the *MafDaL*—and its election needs over state policies, which, as previously mentioned, messed up the government's sedentarization drive. Thus, when I wanted to set up an interview with him a BAAA official advised me not to mention I had good relations with them if I wanted him to grant the interview.

Thus, by the beginning of 1973 the leadership of the *'arab* al-Ḥğerāt was legitimated and well secured in the hands of the *muḫtār*, who had by then both his administrative organization and his networks of connections and obligations well established on a regional scale and expanding beyond the region.

The Bedouin List and the muḫtār's Rise to National Politics

The year 1973 was both an election year in Israel and a marker year for Muḥammad al-Ḥsēn, who broke into the national scene as the recognized leader of the northern bedouin tribes. The causes for this development—the establishment of the Arabic Bedouin List (ABL) for the Knesset—were the interplay between the events discussed above and the personal actions of the *muḫtār* supported by the majority of his tribesmembers.

The measures (see above) taken by the Labor Party to counteract the growing success of *RaQaH* were considered at best insufficient by some BAAA officials because they served largely to placate a few Arab politicians without changing the general approach of the party or of these politicians to the voters themselves. For example, both Sayf al-Dīn al-Zu'abī and Ğabr Mu'addī were in the Knesset from its early days (the I [1949], II [1951], III [1955], VI [1965], VII [1969], and VIII [1973] and the II, III, V [1963], VI, VII, and VIII Knesset respectively, to be precise). Neither, however, had a good track record with his voters and during the 1977 campaign one often heard complaints and declarations such as "for Sayf and Ğabr we will not vote" from both Arabs and Druze. The basic charge was that they appeared before the elections promising anything under the sun only to disappear thereafter and then "won't even come for a coffee," as one informant succinctly summarized. While the behavior of these representatives was the norm among all the larger parties, its effects were most noticeable in the more kin-oriented segments of this population, both Arab and Oriental Jew. Mu'addī, moreover, had voted in the Fifth Knesset for the continuation of the MG. This 1963 vote brought several Druze notables to demand his replacement in 1965 (Landau 1969:138).

More specifically, these BAAA officials were concerned with the effects of the measures on the bedouin, who constituted the most loyal element in the Arab sector, though lacking parliamentary or administrative representation, for the Druze, the other most loyal group, had had several MKs since Ḫnefes and Mu'addī were elected to the Second Knesset (see Landau 1969:193). Such neglect was assumed to enable *RaQaH* to make headway with the bedouin voter, who was gradually becoming more alienated as a result of the discrepancy between his loyalty to the state and his neglect by politicians during the off-election years. The remedy, as one of these officials commented, was "to give the bedouin their own Knesset representation so they will not be game for the various parties as they were before, when each party would promise them the Garden of Eden for their votes and forget them the day after the election." Not to mention in the North the added reason of trying to keep the *MafDaL* and its active district commissioners in Nazareth at bay.

The alienation became even more acute in the Negev, where the land ownership settlement program stalled while the government expropriated land with legally unsettled claims for public use (see Appendix K). This set of problems arose to a large extent from the coalescence of the government's land policy and the absence of influential enough bedouin leaders who could bargain for a collective settlement that would be acceptable to their own people. The answer to the impasse, then, was to encourage the various bedouin tribes to overcome their differences via the medium of a parliamentary election campaign that would promote a legitimate leader—the MK—who would be able to negotiate for the bedouin as a group. In this way it would be easier for those in government wanting to solve the problem equitably to do so while protecting bedouin rights against those factions in the government that wanted to dispossess them.

Finally, it was assumed that a legitimate bedouin leader—their MK—would be able to convince his followers to agree to conscription and could himself be convinced to sign a covenant to that effect, like the Druze and Circassians seventeen years earlier. As in the former case, such a move would have saved the IDA millions of *lirôt* in the difference between trackers' salaries and draftees' allowances and increased its manpower pool while, one may add, binding the bedouin closer to the Jewish state and promoting their separation from the rest of the Arab sector. Such a covenant would have also facilitated the settlement of the land problem, for if the bedouin could secure the support of the security complex in that issue or at least remove the Complex from the opposition by providing it with conscripts, they would have made major headway toward a more cooperative governmental attitude. Consequently, the BAAA officials conceived the idea to form a bedouin parliamentary list[11] for the 1973 election to the Eighth Knesset.

Subsequently, these officials approached bedouin leaders in the Galilee and the Negev in an attempt to attract them to the idea. In the Galilee, these leaders were Ḥassan al-Falāḥ, the Elder of the influential Falḥāt lineage of the *'arab* al-Heīb, who was enthusiastic about the idea, and Muḥammad al-Ḥsēn of the *'arab* al-Ḥğerāt, who was skeptical about its chances to survive the Labor Party's reaction. Later however, after sampling opinions among other local leaders in the Galilee and the "Little Triangle," the *muḫtār* took over the leadership of the movement to form a list in the north, which had originally fallen into Ḥassan al-Falāḥ's hands by default. When Ḥassan al-Falāḥ realized he was ousted from his leading role, he left the campaign altogether, leaving Muḥammad al-Ḥsēn as sole leader in the North with Ḥamzah Sa'ad al-Zaḥālgah of Kafr Qara' in the "Little Triangle" as his second in charge of that area and the West Bank.

The Labor Party, as the *muḫtār* had suspected, tried to block the establishment of the ABL for at least three reasons. First, it refused to accept the independence demanded by the bedouin and argued that "the bedouin should go where they are sent and not where they want to go," to quote one official who was involved in the idea and its realization. Second, there were the interpersonal rivalries among party leaders, each with his/her own Arab protégé "to push into the Knesset." These rivalries—which were pursued in the wake of the 1973 War and its resultant popular protest demanding the replacement of those very leaders—dominated the scene to the extent that "they no longer saw the state's good as the central issue but only their own personal status," to continue the commentary of that official. Finally, it was feared that splitting the Arab sector's votes among too many lists would reduce the chances of each of them to survive the "qualifying percent" requirement, that is, the minimum votes needed to gain the first Knesset seat of each party or list (see below), a scenario that would have helped *RaQaH*'s dominance in that sector.

The problems of multiple Arab lists had surfaced at least as early as the 1965 election campaign. At that time there was a debate in the Alignment that had started with a proposal by the *Ahdut ha'Avodah* faction in the party and supported by the, then, Advisor to the prime minister on Arab Affairs to do away with the allied lists concept and place Arab candidates directly on the Alignment ballot. In short, they cited the Arab voters' realization of the political powerlessness of the lists and their MKs—some of whom were also mistrusted due to their personal conduct—and the inter-list competition over votes, which split the strength of the Alignment's effort in the Arab sector and which, perforce, supported the Communists. The opposing view, championed by the Alignment's Arab department and its, then, director Amnon Lin, advocated preserving the old approach due to partisan reasons, not the least of which was intra-party bickering over relative positions on the party's ballot (for a fuller summary of the two positions see Lin's report in Landau 1969:243–45). Although, as might have been predicted, the latter view prevailed at the time (Landau 1969:137), the validity of the arguments of the first faction—which had been acknowledged by Lin—remained intact when the Labor's ballot was not threatened, as was the case of the ABL in 1973.

About that time one of the Negev *šiyuḫ* who was attracted to the idea of a bedouin list in the south, *šeyḫ* 'Aūdah Manṣūr Abu Mu'ammer of the 'Azāzmeh tribal confederation, gave a *ḥaflah* for Reserve General Ariel Sharon—the hero of the 1973 War—who was canvassing at the time for an alignment of the right-wing parties and factions in Israel. *Šeyḫ* 'Aūdah had been involved in politics and was the only bedouin to be on a ballot of a list before. He was second on the ballot of the "List of Peace" sponsored by *RaFI* (a splinter group from the Alignment) in the 1965 election campaign. He was also "the only Bedouin decorated for valor by Israel after the 1948 war" (Landau 1969:139) and thus a bedouin leader for the Labor to watch. Three days later *šeyḫ* 'Aūdah gave another *ḥaflah*, this time for Shmuel Toledano—the prime minister's advisor on Arab affairs and the director of the BAAA—to which he invited the Elders and leaders of the northern, central, and southern tribes. During that event the leaders told the advisor that they were tired of being represented by *fellāḥīn* who did not understand an iota of the bedouin's problems, who showed up once every four years, and so on, and that they wanted to form a separate list for the bedouin. The message to the Labor Party was loud and clear: "either we get our list or we look for friends elsewhere," and the Labor grudgingly consented. Thus was born the Arabic Bedouin List to the Knesset with *šeyḫ* Ḥamād Abū Rabī'a in the first slot of the ballot, Muḥammad Ḥsēn al-Ġadīr in second, Ḥamzah Sa'ad al-Zaḥālgah in third, and *šeyḫ* 'Aūdah Manṣūr Abu Mu'ammer in fourth (Eyal 1973:18).

In the election the ABL succeeded in attracting enough votes to surpass the "qualifying percent" requirement[12] and *šeyḫ* Ḥamād Abū Rabī'a became the first bedouin representative to the Knesset. In the north, when the new fiscal year began on April 1, 1974, the *muḫtār* moved to an office at the rundown Labor Party regional branch in Nazareth where he now received those who came to ask for his help. About the same time, the government's sedentarization policy entered its coordinated phase and enhanced budget and the *muḫtār*, being the representative of the northern bedouin, became a member of the executive board of the NSBC (see Appendix G).

1973–1977: At the Pinnacle of Power

Muḥammad al-Ḥsēn's position of leadership in the north thus seemed assured. First, he was the rising Israeli Arab leader on a regional scale who had, as the election proved, popular support that helped expand his network of connections in the Labor Party, which, when combined with his older network of friends in the administration, meant that practically any reasonable request of his was granted. Second, the election had extended his network of obligations, for now he had to reciprocate and help all those who voted for ABL—many of whom were *fellāḥīn*—in addition to his uncontested representation of—hence obligation to—the northern bedouin, many of whom had enthusiastically dedicated their time, vehicles, and so on to ensure the success of "their" list (except for the *'arab* al-Heīb, who protested by voting for other parties/lists). His patronage organization had thus formally expanded from the confines of the district to the expanses of the Northern Region with ties in Tel Aviv (the Party) and Jerusalem (the Government).

Good as they might have seemed, these changes gradually introduced a measure of alienation into the relations of the Ḥğerāt with their *muḫtār* over the following years. Ḥğeris who wanted to see him had to travel to Nazareth and visit the office where the old familiar ambiance was nonexistent and where they had to vie for time with non-Ḥğeris on almost equal footing or wait until he was visiting Bīr al-Maksūr, as he was increasingly less available in his tent. In this latter case the interaction was usually brief because such visits were rather rare and much had to be accomplished. As pressure on him increased, he tried to develop means of coping with the continuous presence of help-seekers who could appear any time of day or night and anywhere he was, be it the office or his tent. One tactic was to not make public ahead of time where he would sleep at any given night. Thus, he could decide in the last minute to have some peace of mind in the tent of a partner near Tiberias or at a friend's in Umm al-Zīnāt. Finally, in September 1976, he began to accept help-seekers only in his office, leaving his tent for privacy and social evenings with friends. Even so, occasionally people from afar (e.g., the Negev) would appear in his tent and he would have to accept them. Similarly, visits to Bīr al-Maksūr before the 1977 election campaign were either to get his children from the village, where they went to school, to take them to the tent for the weekend, or for occasions when BAAA, ILA, or other officials were due for a visit. In the former case he would just drive in, collect the children, who would be waiting for him, and drive away, while in the latter he had more time but also much more on his mind. The result of his declining availability, although somewhat offset by the general elevation in the status and prestige of the tribe as a whole, fed the frustrations of individuals who could not secure his help, slowly accumulating discontent.

At the same time, his position at the NSBC began to influence his relations with the tribe. Aside from the demand it made on his already limited time, the position enabled him to direct some of the available funds to the development of Bīr al-Maksūr—that is, into improvements for the benefit of all village residents rather than for specific individuals. Because they were in the public domain, however, these improvements were often not considered by the individuals who enjoyed them as part of their responsibility to reciprocate in the network of obligations. Moreover, these public works were often considered too slow, too late, and/or insufficient while further polarizing the differences between Bīr al-Maksūr and the Mikmān. Consequently, if the *muḫtār* had ever thought that since general public projects reached more individuals they would efficiently maintain the Ḥğeri section of his patronage network intact in the face of his shrinking time, he was mistaken because it was not so interpreted by many of his tribesmembers.[13]

More specifically, whereas the *muḫtār* "grew up" with his position—or, as he once commented "when I was the *muḫtār* of the *'arab* al-Ḥğerāt I took care of all the Ḥğerāt and not only the Ġadāyreh and when I became the representative of the bedouin in the committee [the NSBC] I represented all the tribes and not only the Ḥğerāt"—a growing number of Ḥğeris felt deserted and interpreted his growth as if he were no longer accessible nor cared about them, regardless of the comforting honor of being members of his tribe. This interpretation found some confirmation when, as he increasingly felt more harried, he gradually began to make distinctions between more and less powerful people and budget his time accordingly. This was a development that, needless to emphasize, intensified the sense of alienation felt by individual Ḥğeris.

It was here that Ibrāhīm al-Ḥsēn, his uterine brother, became ever more indispensable for he took up the slack between the *muḫtār* and the tribe. He maintained the old familiar style of extending help. He cleared those issues he could by himself, passing on to the *muḫtār* only those he could not clear but thought the latter should attend to. He monitored Bīr al-Maksūr, cooling off grudges before they turned into conflicts, and represented the *muḫtār* at some social functions, freeing him for others. In short, he was considered to be the representative of the mukhtarship in Bīr al-Maksūr and the tribe, thus allowing the *muḫtār* to become more involved in regional affairs.

Ibrāhīm's help, however, did not solve all the personnel needs of the mukhtarship and the *muḫtār* began to depend on one of his FBSs, Maḥmūd al-Mūsā, who became a permanent aide for dealing with the lower echelons of the authorities, especially with the new network in the IDA. Maḥmūd al-Mūsā became involved with the mukhtarship before the elections but it was his performance during the 1973 election campaign that proved him to be an asset to the *muḫtār*. Notwithstanding, being an ambitious man himself, he was an a priori suspect and the *muḫtār*, therefore, tried to keep him from independently helping other Ḥğeris too much lest he nurtured too large a following. Moreover, being a cousin he had his first loyalties to his siblings, a loyalty that pitted him against the *muḫtār*, Ibrāhīm, and their siblings several times.

With the addition of Maḥmūd al-Mūsā, the mukhtarship grew to include three people, none of whom was a full-time political functionary: the *muḫtār* (a herdsman), who was expanding more and more into regional administration and national politics while maintaining his old networks; Ibrāhīm al-Ḥsēn (a policeman with a small herd), who administered the tribe, together with the *ḫatyariyyeh*, ensuring the power base of the *muḫtār* and the family as well as providing a link to the police; and Maḥmūd al-Mūsā (a cab owner/operator), a more general purpose aide, primarily dealing with lower echelon ties with the security complex in general and the IDA in particular, and odd projects like bringing electricity to Bīr al-Maksūr. This division of responsibilities among them stabilized that institution, helped keep its opponents in check, and enabled it to continue thriving.

Meanwhile, the support of the authorities spread from the BAAA to more central loci of power in a concerted effort to establish the *muḫtār* as the government-backed leader in the north in order to counterbalance the rising popularity of Tawfīq Ziyād (*RaQaH*'s leader in Nazareth), while tightening the ABL's ties to the Labor Party. This effort had three prongs. First was the older pattern of granting the *muḫtār*'s requests whenever possible to enable him to expand his patronage network ever wider. Second, Bīr al-Maksūr was placed in the political center of the Galilee so that when a major dignitary visited, all pro-government notables were invited by the authorities or the *muḫtār* who, together with the tribe, served as the host, which was an honorific status in itself. Bīr al-Maksūr was put on the tour map of high-ranking officials such as the president of the State of Israel, the secretary general of the Labor Party, and a multitude of lower-ranking government functionaries. Third, the *muḫtār* was placed on the authorities' list of loyal Arab leaders. It was this position that, for example, enabled him to join the aforementioned delegation to Jordan whose successful mission, aside from offering its condolences to King Hussein, was to ask the king to allow passage through Jordan and to intercede with the Saudis to allow Israeli Arabs to make the *ḥağğ* (pilgrimage) to Mecca, which they had been barred from doing since 1948.

It was of no surprise, then, that the July 1976 wedding of the *muḫtār*'s firstborn son was a show of power done in style to emphasize his leadership of the tribe, his prominence in the region, and his favored status with the authorities. The host was the Ġadāyreh, supported by the whole tribe, which gathered many of its members from the herding camps and solitary tents and, in a show of unity, dedicated time to work together for about a week to prepare the event. The Arab guest list included all the bedouin tribes in the Galilee and the Negev through their *šiyuḫ* and Elders, non-bedouin ABL activists, pro-government notables and their factions in the Galilee and the "Little Triangle" who were friendly with the Ḥğerāt or with various individual Ḥğeris, and many other important personae. Its Jewish counterpart included practically every commander in the police and Border Guard, IDA generals, the BAAA, government ministers, MKs, and the president, as well as every major official in the north and all those with whom the Ḥğerāt had daily business. The number of actual guests was estimated at over 5000[14] people. They were all fed, and were entertained by two pairs of rhymesters and a bard accompanying himself on the one-stringed *rabābah*, while the whole event was photographed for the Israeli television network.

The construction of the two guest lists provides insight into both the dynamic aspect of the *muḫtār*'s expanding networks and the more general issue of the tribe's political adaptability, to which I have occasionally referred before. The bulk of the list was compiled during four successive evenings in the varying company of fifty to a hundred tribesmembers as well as occasional non-Ḥğeri allies. It started with the *muḫtār* calling off one name after another. These were registered by the school principal, who would add an occasional name. This section included important civilian state functionaries, major leaders, and so on. Then others joined in and in an orderly fashion they went from one settlement to the next from the environs of Bīr al-Maksūr to the farthest outlying areas. For each settlement there was a "specialist" who knew its population better than the others and who called off most of the names. Meanwhile, during the days, various Ḥğeris who were in contact with members of other groups compiled with the latter's help additional lists of these groups while updating their own political maps of the groups—that is, which subgroup was beginning to rise in power and influence, which was declining, and so on. To these were added the lists provided by the allies. In general there was active participation by most of those present each evening, especially by the faction of the *muḫtār*. Each of those present who wanted to do so could add his friends and acquaintances to the list, provided they were not objected to by others in the assembly. Then, while delivering the invitations, the *muḫtār* or his proxy would ask the one who accepted the batch for each lineage or settlement if the Ḥğerāt had forgotten anyone, and new invitations would be addressed and extra, unaddressed ones would be left just in case. Thus, unless there was an actual objection that was accepted by the Elders and the *muḫtār*, every person in the Galilee or elsewhere that they could think of, including rivals and opponents of this or that subunit of the Ḥğerāt, was invited. The Jewish sector invitations were sent out so that "no one could say later 'why didn't you invite me'" and the *muḫtār* did not expect their recipients to do any more than send a congratulatory telegram, which many of them, in fact, did. In general, the Jewish guest list—save for its police section—was compiled by the *muḫtār* and was greatly augmented by other Ḥğeris working with Jews, who added their names under the general directive that was formulated apropos the IDA: "wherever we have our men, invite them." Nonetheless, this shotgun approach was controlled by the *muḫtār*, who would occasionally reject a name because "he is no longer a friend."

Then, some two and a half months later, Ibrāhīm Ḥsēn al-Ḏiyab died of a heart attack while hunting partridges in the West Bank. The emotional shock of the tribe was deep and general among supporters and opponents of the mukhtarship alike, for he was much loved and respected as an individual. His funeral was a measure of both his personal extra-Ḥğerāt popularity and the prominence of the *muḫtār* and the Ḥğerāt as his tribe. Some 4000 mourners were estimated by the police—which directed the traffic—to have reached the cemetery hill by cars, a figure that did not include most of the Ḥğerāt, who reached it on foot. The eulogies were delivered first by his district commander in the police followed by Ṣāleḥ al-Ḫnefes for the Druze of Shfar'am; Sayf al-Dīn al-Zu'abī for the Zu'bīyeh lineage and for his supporters in Nazareth and the eastern lower Galilee; a community Elder for the Christians of Shfar'am; the mayor of that town for its Moslem population; and then one chairman of local council after another for the major settlements in the Galilee and the "Little Triangle." Later, during the *sab'ah* (the "seven" days of intensive mourning), practically every bedouin tribe in the country sent a delegation to offer their condolences, and there were many leaders and delegations of *fellāḥīn*. Similarly, most senior government officials in the Galilee, many security complex personnel including the military advisor to the prime minister representing the latter, and personal friends among the Jews arrived, while the police published his death with a short eulogy in the two major daily newspapers in the country and donated funds for his tomb.

Ibrāhīm's death was a major blow to the administrative and political layout of the tribe in general and the mukhtarship in particular, both for their extra-Ḥğerāt contacts and for the relations between the tribe and the *muḫtār*. The shock to the extra-Ḥğeri ties in Nazareth was so serious that already during the *sab'ah* people began talking of the urgent need to find another to replace him and began looking around for likely candidates.

The 1977 National Elections

Less than three months later, while both tribe and *muḫtār* were still adjusting to the new circumstance, the *muḫtār* was drawn into the 1977 election campaign, and by March the tribe was drafted into it as well. The campaign was imbued with difficulties caused by incompetent administrators at the Labor Party and its Arab department (see below). In addition, the *muḫtār*, set in his previous course with neither time or patience to reestablish his personal hold over the Ḥğerāt; old grudges; intra- and inter-lineal rivalries; and personal aspirations of younger competitors all fed into the appearance of two vociferous opposition factions in addition to the previous two quiet ones. And, all four factions used the *muḫtār*'s growing distance from the tribesmembers as their opposition platforms, while the election returns indicated an even greater latent opposition.

Opposition to the Leadership

Opposition is inherent in segmentary organization, the dynamic aspect of which *is* "complementary opposition" (Sahlins 1961:332–33). As such, it served as the background theme for intra-Ḥğerāt inter-group relations throughout the tribe's history. Thus the Ġadāyreh took control of the leadership from the Ṣawālḥah at the turn of the century and the *ulād* Ġadīr competed for it until 1949 when they finally took it from the Ramlāt who held it before. This type of opposition, however, is not a behavior in itself but a predisposition to act. It underlies the behavior of individuals and channels it in a genealogical and political way that can be tapped by tribesmembers who contend for the leadership.

Since 1949, superimposed on this predisposition was a behavioral continuum that outlined the intensity of opposition forces to the *muḫtār* and his administration. This continuum began with "free-floating" individuals who had specific grudges or general discontent with the *muḫtār*'s conduct but who did not act on the basis of their frustrations. Such individuals may aggregate with the addition of kin and friends who shared their grievances to form what might be called a "resentment group." Such groups often tried to make their feelings anonymously known by voting during the parliamentary election to a party/list not endorsed by the agency they opposed, although they did not try to compete directly for the leadership. Hence their actions might be called attempts at "passive control" of the leadership. Finally, there were aspiring individuals who tried to mobilize these groups as a source of public power in order to compete actively for the leadership. These individuals were usually members of such a resentment group themselves, and they tried to aggregate several such groups to cultivate a patron in the administration who could provide them with benefits to enable them to nurture a following in return for votes. Or, vice versa, they would make a contact with a possible patron and then try to mobilize votes for his party. In both cases they operated primarily through kinship links so that the sublineal or lineal element of such opposition was very prominent.

Two sets of reasons underlay the phenomenon of votes coming to serve as the units symbolizing dissension from the mukhtarship, thus causing intra-tribal dynamics to find their expression in the medium of national politics. The first was the simple fact that, as for all minorities, power in the Arab sector emanated from the administration. Consequently, any contender for the tribe's leadership and its power had perforce to find a way to tap this source of power, whose currency was electoral votes. This quest for administrative support neither negated nor belittled the importance of public support that legitimated the claim for status of the contender if he was to lead a following. Moreover, public support grounded only in economic benefits was much weaker and more expensive to maintain than support that was accompanied by ideological items such as kinship, for it was wide open to the vagaries of the market place.

The second set of reasons was that just as the *muḫtār* operated according to two separate models—the tribal and the administrative—so did most of the tribesmen, making a distinction between events in the Arab sector and events in the Jewish sector, state administration included. Within the Arab sector the rules of the game were acquired as part of the process of socialization and were well embedded in the individual and his behavior. For the Ḥğerāt this meant a segmentary kinship model that posited the Ġadāyreh versus the Ṣawālḥah but united them against extra-Ḥğeri entities such as the *'arab* al-Heīb in accord with the aforementioned principle of "complementary opposition." Consequently, in daily life in the Arab sector, the rule was that Ḥğeri unity took precedence over interpersonal antagonisms and/or resentment toward the *muḫtār*. This rule applied both because any Ḥğeri, the *muḫtār* included, was a closer agnate than any member of an extra-Ḥğeri group and because disunity and opposition would rapidly undermine the status of the whole tribe in the Arab sector.

Elections, conversely, were a Jewish affair because from 1949 to 1977 all the switching of parliamentary seats in the Knesset did not produce any noticeable change in the continuity of the policy of the administration in the Arab sector. It was not surprising, therefore, to hear the common substitution of *ḥukūmah* (government) for *hazb al-'amal* (the Labor Party) by young Ḥğeris during conversation, and until the 1977 election proved it, it was generally inconceivable to think of replacing the oligarchy of the Labor Party by parliamentary means. As a result, if the repercussions of an action in the tribe or of the tribe in the Arab sector were felt within a short period of time, the repercussions of their behavior in the election had not made a single difference in thirty years. Consequently, elections were viewed as a matter between the *muḫtār* and the administration and not necessarily as a matter of the tribe as a whole. It follows then that voting for another party was viewed as a way to censure the *muḫtār* by making his dealing with the authorities somewhat more difficult but without endangering either his ties to the administration or the tribe's status.

Finally, there were not many occasions on which the *muḫtār* asked for help, and among these the only recurrent ones—hence pattern-producing—that did not happen in the context of the Arab sector were the parliamentary elections. It is not that the tribe had not had the opportunity to refuse to help on other occasions involving the relations of the *muḫtār* to the administration, such as the visit of the President of Israel in October 1975 or the March 1976 visit of some 160 kibbutz youngsters who were hosted in Bīr al-Maksūr in a private effort of a BAAA official to help bridge the gulf between Jews and Arabs in Israel and correct the image of Arabs (especially bedouin) that the youth held. Not only did the tribe come through in these instances, but its members were proud of the opportunity to be hosts. In these cases and in other events like them, however, there was a mixture of elements from both Jewish and Arab sectors and noncooperative behavior of the tribe would have reflected directly on its "Arab sector image" in regard to hospitality, as much as if a guest at the *muḫtār*'s firstborn's wedding had left the village insatiated.

Thus, parliamentary elections provided opportunity to censure the *muḫtār*. In other words, since the resentment against him was formulated as desertion of his people because "he has grown too big and no longer recognizes his own tribe," as one Ḥğeri said, the logical conclusion was "since he did not help me in matter X when I needed him I will not help him in the election when he needs me." This direct exchange approach became all the more poignant in the 1973 and 1977 elections when the old advice that the *muḫtār* gave in the 1950s and 1960s—"vote for X because it is better for us"—was replaced by a direct appeal to the voters. Significantly, he did not use the term "vote for me" but "help me" (*sā'adunī*) in order to distinguish himself, the responsible and responsive leader, from the jaded politicians who usually headed the Arab lists of the Labor Party. Nonetheless, the term helped emphasize the exchange aspect of the relationship and of the elections. The parliamentary elections' voting record of the Ḥğerāt was therefore a record of the expression of opposition to the *muḫtār* since 1951 when they began to vote (see Table 30).

Two phenomena are apparent in Table 30. First is the relative unanimity of the Ḥğeri voter until the election of 1961 and the growing diversity thereafter. Second, there are differences between the Ṣawālḥah and the Ġadāyreh, both in terms of participation rate and in the greater dispersion of Ṣawālḥi votes among possible voting options. Three

Table 30. The parliamentary election results of the *'arab* al-Ḥğerāt, 1951–1977, by lineage (percent).[a]

Knesset Number	Election Year	Lineage	Partici-pation	Minorities			Labor				DaSh	Religious			Communist		H[b]	I[b]	Likud		Shlom-tzion	Other Lists[c]
				Minority Lists	ABL	UAL	MaPaI	A[b]	B[b]	C[b]		MafDaL	D[b]	E[b]	F[b]	G[b]			J[b]	K[b]		
II	1951	Ġad.	100	85			8			7												
		Ṣawāl.	99	89			1			6									1			3
III	1955	Ġad.	95	99																		
		Ṣawāl.	94	89			1								8							
IV	1959	Ġad.																				
		Ṣawāl.	84	91						3		2	1		2							1
V	1961	Ġad.	90	83				10		6												
		Ṣawāl.	83	76				10		3		1			9					1		
VI	1965	Ġad.	92	88			1			7		1				1	1	1				
		Ṣawāl.	78	43			30		3	4		1				18			1			
VII	1969	Ġad.	92	87				6				1										5
		Ṣawāl.	78	59				21				15				3						
VIII	1973	Ġad.	97	1	96							1				1						
		Ṣawāl.	83		79			7				7			1	3						2
IX	1977	Ġad.	61			64		2				10				9			7		8	1
		Ṣawāl.	46	4		49		1			2	11		1		18			9		9	

(Sources: 1951: Israel, Ministry of the Interior, Inspector General of Elections, pers. comm.; 1955: Isr. IGE 1956:165, appendix 1; 1959: Isr. IGE 1961:143, tb. 23; 1961: Isr. IGE 1964:156, tb. 24; 1965: Isr. IGE 1967:195, tb. 26; 1969: Isr. IGE 1970:126, tb. 16; 1973: Isr. IGE 1974:142, 122 respectively, tb. 17; 1977: Isr. IGE 1978:155, 136 respectively, tb. 16)

[a]It should be kept in mind that the CBS listings are by settlement and not by lineage and, hence, there is some mixing of voters from the Ġadāyreh in the Ṣawālḥah poll station. This detail, however, does not seem to significantly affect the conclusions discussed in the text because the latter rely primarily on direct observations and interviews.

[b]Party code letters: A = Ahdut ha'Avodah; B = Rafi; C = Mapam; D = Agudat Isra'el; E = Po'alei Agudat Isra'el; F = MaQI; G = RaQaH; H = ha'Olam ha-Zeh; I = Independent Liberals; J = Herut; K = Liberals.

[c]These are lists that had failed to surpass the "qualifying percent" requirement.

factors seem to account for the first phenomenon: the aforementioned control exercised by the MG and its ties to *MaPal*, voting practices that were prevalent at that period (see Appendix L), and the novelty of the voting experience and its remoteness from daily life under the MG, which caused electoral apathy to amplify electoral naiveté. The second phenomenon, on the other hand, is an expression of the opposition discussed above. This opposition, incidentally, was directed in three ways: the Ṣawālḥah toward their own *muḫtār* (Ḥsēn al-Gāsem), the Ġadāyreh toward theirs (Muḥammad al-Ḥsēn), and the Ṣawālḥah toward the tribe's *muḫtār* (Muḥammad al-Ḥsēn).

This opposition expressed itself in two ways: as electoral apathy, which might be called "passive" protest, and a spread of votes among insignificant parties and lists, which might be coined "active" protest. An example of "passive" protest happened in 1977 in the village of ʿAkbarah, south of the Upper Galilean town of Safad. The village notified the UAL headquarters that they always voted for *MaPal*/Labor but that for this election they would abstain because nothing had been done for them. (They had a continuous conflict with Safad and the ILA and were trying to pressure the then mayor of the town, who was on the Labor's ballot of proposed MKs for the Ninth Knesset, to come to terms and end the impasse.) During the election only 15% of the village's eligible voters participated; a very low figure compared with the previous elections: 1955, 92%; 1959, 99%; 1961, 81%; 1965, 89%; 1969, 80%; 1973, 78% (Isr. IGE 1978: tb. 16; 1956: appendix 1; 1961: tb. 23; 1964: tb. 24; 1967: tb. 26; 1970: tb. 16; 1974: tb. 17 respectively). A similar example, albeit much more complex, accounts for the low participation of the Ḥğerāt in 1977 (see below). Finally, abstention in order not to lose a day's pay in the highly politicized milieu of the Ḥğerāt and similarly organized kin-based groups was a nonverbal statement of protest rather than simple economic greed or ignorance because if the group decided to support a party, it would bring out all its eligible voters and those who abstained had to do so against their relatives' consensus.

In addition to the "passive" protest, Arab voters also spread their votes among a plethora of small parties or lists in what I call "active" protest. These votes, which Landau dismisses as "lunatic fringe vote" (1969:112 et passim), are a good indicator of the state of intragroup dynamics. They represent people who are dissatisfied with the government or its promoted leadership (that is, refuse to vote for the Labor movement) as well as with its opposition in the Arab sector (that is, *MaQI* or *RaQaH*), with which they do not want to be identified—yet they want to be noticed and hence vote for the other available options indiscriminately. An illuminating example of this type of political censure on the level of the Arab sector at large was the results of the 1959 election. Due to the crackdown of Gamāl ʿAbd al-Nāṣir on the Egyptian communists earlier that year and his denunciation (following the USSR) by *MaQI*, this party lost 33% of its Arab support (Bailey 1970:46) and fell from 15.6% of the total Arab vote in 1955 to 10.0% in that election (Landau 1969:152, tb.). This 5.6% difference plus another 10.4% from *MaPal* and its allied lists (on a continuous decline since 1951) ended up partly as a boost to *MaPaM* (the left member of the Labor movement), whose share in the Arab vote jumped from 7.3% to 12.5%, a rise of 5.2%, which probably resulted from the infusion of ex-*MaPal* votes. Mostly, however, these defunct votes were dispersed in such "lunatic fringe support" for "election-eve parties," a category that hiked from 14.7% in 1955 to 25.5% in 1959 (Landau 1969:152, tb.). As Bailey (1970:46) commented on this event, "many Arabs made it clear that . . . the party [*MaQI*] was an *Arab* party only when it supported *Arab* causes."

With the "passive" and "active" types of electoral protest clearer in mind we can return to Table 30. The first difference between the two lineages is the lower level of Ṣawālḥi participation throughout the period. This electoral apathy points to the greater dissatisfaction of the Ṣawālḥah with their *muḫtār* than of the Ġadāyreh with theirs. The Ṣawālḥah, incidentally, were somewhat unhappy with Muḥammad al-Ḥsēn as well, because instead of voting for the allied lists that he promoted and that were usually different from that of Ḥsēn al-Gāsem (see below), many opted not to vote at all. This discontent became more explicit with the passage of time and was most clear in the 1969 election. Aside from 22% Ṣawālḥi abstentions, 70 or 15% of the 455 who participated in this election voted for the *MafDaL*, which was promoted by Ḥsēn al-Gāsem; 250 or 59% voted for the minority list allied with the Alignment (the then Labor) promoted by Muḥammad al-Ḥsēn; 97 or 21% voted directly for the Alignment, which was not promoted by either *muḫtār* (therefore a "protest" but a safe one because it was for the government and not against it, that is, for its opponents); while 20 or 3% voted for *RaQaH* (outspoken protest). By comparison, only 8% of the Ġadāyreh abstained and only 41 or 13% of the 315 who voted did not go with their *muḫtār* (source of raw voting data: Division of Social Statistics, Central Bureau of Statistics, Israel: pers. comm., 1976).

These differences in the relative influence of the two *muḫatīr* were even more pronounced in 1973 when only 3% of the Ġadāyreh abstained and 332 of the 345 who voted (96%) chose the ABL. By contrast, 17% of the Ṣawālḥah abstained; only 448 of 569 (or 79%) voters chose the ABL; 40 votes (7%) went to the *MafDaL* (Ḥsēn al-Gāsem's current patron); 42 "protest" votes (7%) went to the Labor; 16 votes (3%) went to *RaQaH*; and the last 23 votes (4%) were divided among thirteen other parties and lists: 1 party had 4 votes; 2 parties had 3 votes each; 3 parties had 2 votes each; and 7 parties had 1 vote each (Division of Social Statistics, Central Bureau of Statistics, Israel: pers. comm., 1976). As these figures indicate, Ḥsēn al-Gāsem had very little influence in his own lineage and settlement, while Muḥammad al-Ḥsēn's influence in that lineage was quite large, even when allowing for the registration of Ġadāyri voters in the poll station of the Ṣawālḥah/Mikmān.

Unlike abstentions, which are "passive protest," votes for other parties are "active" and a loud message to the leadership. They usually indicate some position along the aforementioned continuum—a discontented individual here, two to four persons there, or the larger "resentment groups." Most of these were not contenders for the leadership and did not seek a patron in the administration, for many of these votes went to parties with no ties to the government nor even continuous presence in the Arab sector, for example, "The Women's Party" (2 votes in 1977), which materialized for that election only, or even extremist anti-Arab groups such as that of the militant Jewish Defense League's founder and chieftain Rabbi Kahana (1 vote in 1977).[15] If any of the groups tried to find a patron, there is no trace either of it or of the leader of such a group. Nonetheless, in 1977 four contenders and the factions they mobilized competed with the *muḫtār* and the UAL he reluctantly promoted, thus providing an example of the dynamics of such opposition. Of these, the oldest faction was that led by Ḥsēn al-Gāsem, who had been trying to loosen the dominance of the Ġadāyreh over the Ṣawālḥah since the 1950s. The other three contenders were members of the Ġadāyreh itself: two from the Ramlāt and one from the ʿAfafṭeh.

The Ḥsēn al-Gāsem Faction

Although the faction he led should have fed on inter-lineal rivalry between the Ṣawālḥah and the Ġadāyreh, Ḥsēn al-Gāsem (age about 64 in 1977) commanded little support in his lineage. To reiterate, he was nominated *muḫtār* in 1951 through the influence of Ṣāleḥ al-Ḫnefes, the, then, Druze MK who wanted to weaken if not control the Ḥğerāt (see above). He was, however, a member of the Ğawāsreh, the smallest sublineage of the Ṣawālḥah, and his nomination ousted the previous *muḫtār*, Ḥassan al-Šhāb of *ulād* Ḥassan al-Ṣāleḥ that, together with the Maḥāmīd, formed the Swl.-Ṣawālḥah, the senior sublineage of that lineage. To make matters worse, Muḥammad al-Ḥsēn's mother, Šehedeh, was the eldest daughter of Ṭaʿamīs al-Maḥmūd, the Elder of the Maḥāmīd until his death in the 1920s, and although this tie did not ensure the group's support to the *muḫtār* of the Ġadāyreh it added to its discontent with its own *muḫtār*. And without this sublineage's support, Ḥsēn al-Gāsem could not establish his leadership of the Ṣawālḥah.

Extra-tribally he was not able to function in the administrative milieu with any ease and as a result was never able to develop a network of connections in order to nurture a following and establish his legitimacy among the Ṣawālḥah in this manner. His survival as *muḫtār* was, thus, due to his patrons in the administration. The first of these was Ṣāleḥ al-Ḫnefes, who was MK until 1959 when he was replaced by *MaPaI*.[16] Ḥsēn al-Gāsem continued as *muḫtār* after that date because the MG needed a *muḫtār* in the Mikmān; because of the support Ṣāleḥ al-Ḫnefes could still provide; and because Muḥammad al-Ḥsēn, who was established by then, did not try to oust him precisely because of his weak status in that lineage, which rendered him politically maneuverable, and as long as he occupied this position, he prevented more energetic and talented leaders from taking over. With the withdrawal of the MG and the assumption of control by the civilian ministries, Ḥsēn al-Gāsem shifted his ties to the Ministry of the Interior and became a client of the district commissioner of that ministry. The arrangement was simple: he provided votes for the *MafDaL* (see Table 30), which controlled that ministry (in addition to those of Welfare and Religions), in return for administrative favors and support (for a similar observation about the *MafDaL* among the Druze see Oppenheimer 1978:40).

As part of his arrangement with the district commissioner as well as for his own aspirations he supported an attempt by the latter to oust Muḥammad al-Ḥsēn and gain more votes for the *MafDaL* in Bīr al-Maksūr by establishing a local council for its Civil Administration. When that attempt failed he succeeded in having the commissioner declare the Mikmān, which was originally planned as a subdivision of Bīr al-Maksūr (named Bīr al-Maksūr B), as an independent settlement (Gīvʿat Mikmanim), thereby entitling it to be administratively free of Bīr al-Maksūr with its own civil and social services.[17] While this measure separated the two settlements and was received in favor in the Mikmān, it delayed most, if not all, of the improvements that otherwise would have been its share as a result of the formation of the NSBC, while providing Muḥammad al-Ḥsēn with the ability to waive responsibility for the settlement while laying the blame for the neglect at Ḥsēn al-Gāsem's door (see also Appendix G). As a result, Ḥsēn al-Gāsem could not turn this success into power because he was not able to develop the village after its recognition. Hence he did not become any major threat to Muḥammad al-Ḥsēn's leadership.

Sublineal antagonism and Ḥsēn al-Gāsem's own inability to bring development to the Mikmān while Bīr al-Maksūr was flourishing or to attract to himself free floating resentment against Muḥammad al-Ḥsēn through the medium of personal services severely limited his power as opposition, while generating all the more discontent. The dissatisfaction was only aggravated by Muḥammad al-Ḥsēn's neglect of the settlement, for its residents felt deserted by the tribal *muḫtār* as well. As a result, the Mikmān saw a proliferation of resentment groups that, lacking in indigenous leadership, became receptive to the contenders from Bīr al-Maksūr, who promoted the *Likud* and *Shlomtzion*, as well as to outside influences such as *RaQaH*.

Opposition in Bīr al-Maksūr: The Ramlāti

Meanwhile, opposition and resentment within Bīr al-Maksūr in general and the Ġadāyreh in particular were much weaker and spottier than that in the Mikmān. After all, this was the center of power of the tribe that enjoyed the most from the *muḫtār*'s connections and influence, where the population's unity was best preserved by the Elders, and where Ibrāhīm al-Ḥsēn's watchful eye and warm manner ensured that possible causes for resentment were quickly dissipated. Consequently, the only mark of opposition, which appeared to suggest a persistent contender rather than a temporary election outburst, was another client of the district commissioner, who had joined the commissioner after the aborted local council affair.

This man (age 39 in 1977) was the junior member of the second smallest of the seven Generation IV subunits of the Ramlāt. He was an unlicensed building contractor until 1975 when he passed the Ministry of Labor's licensing examinations in order to compete on the construction of the new school building in Bīr al-Maksūr. While it was unclear that he had brought the *MafDaL* the four votes (1%) it received among the Ġadāyreh in 1973, it was widely assumed in Bīr al-Maksūr that he had his eyes set on the position of the local council chairman should the district commissioner succeed in subduing the *ulād* Ġadīr and ousting the *muḫtār*.

This assumption was grounded in three issues. First was this contender's good relations at the district commissioner's office, under whose jurisdiction were regional planning, issuing of construction permits that endowed a builder with an allocation of subsidized Portland cement, and other red-tape generating bureaucratic duties. Second were his efforts to represent the Ramlāt in the tribe (for example, his canvassing throughout this lineage to represent its members on the steering committee of the Electricity Co-Operative Society, as result of which he was nominated its chairman). Third was his use of this position to actively instigate dissension and conflict in the village. For example, the Israel Electric Corporation (IEC) divided the installation of the village's electrical network and the connection of the houses to it into three stages from north (which was closest to the feeder line) to south. Stage I covered the northern peak of the hill and its flanks; Stage II covered the "saddle" and top of the southern peak; and Stage III covered the eastern, southern and western flanks of that peak. The completion of Stage I proceeded behind schedule due to financial problems, and the rains arrived before work on Stage II commenced. As a result, the company decided to proceed with Stage III and delay work on Stage II due to rain-related ground stability problems in the installment process. When the Sama'neh, who resided in the area covered by Stage II, asked the chairman for the reason for the switch, he told them it was due to maneuvering by Maḥmūd al-Mūsā, the committee's secretary, because the *ulād* Ġadīr resided on the peak's eastern and southern flanks. It seems that when he told this to the Sama'neh, the chairman knew the company's reasons because shortly thereafter, when told by a brother of the *muḫtār* in private of the people's complaints against Maḥmūd al-Mūsā, he laughed and replied that the decision was the company's, and technical, and that no one could change it.

Finally, like Ḥsēn al-Gāsem, he kept his ties with the district commissioner secret, and although his canvassing for votes on behalf of the *MafDaL,* which received 22 Ġadāyri votes in 1977, was known in the village through individuals he had approached, he campaigned very quietly. This style was in sharp contrast to that of the next two contenders.

Opposition in Bīr al-Maksūr: The Young Ones

These two made their appearance during the 1977 election campaign after Ibrāhīm's death, and had it not been for the Labor's escalating mistakes and the resultant victory of the *Likud*,[18] their effect would probably have been like that of previous resentment groups—that is, a transient "bulge" in the Ḥğeri voting record for a given party. Nonetheless, both these men represented new departures in Ḥğeri politics, both in style of operation and, to a lesser degree, in the issues raised and, as a result, they might in fact have planted the seeds of a change in intra-Ḥğerāt power relations. It is hardly surprising, therefore, that both were young men and both had had some exposure to the IDA and the security complex either directly or indirectly. Such exposure was not only important for learning specifics of developing networks of connections and links to military patrons but, as Enloe (1980:78) has observed, in the more general effects of the experience as well. Thus, the exposure to the Jewish majority's political ideologies and instrumental style that, due to the intensity of contacts with their comrades was more acute than the exposure in the civilian labor milieu, taught them to "be more politically assertive and politically skilled than they were . . . before" (Enloe 1980:78).

Of all the underlying factors in the appearance of these two contenders, the most salient was Ibrāhīm al-Ḥsēn's death. As the 'Afafṭi leader acknowledged, it was hardly likely that had Ibrāhīm been alive they would have been able to pursue their respective campaigns as publicly as they did and, therefore, attract as many votes as they did. Nor, one might add, would they seem to have been able to generate the future probable effect of their style of campaigning on intra-Ḥğeri politics, for while the *MafDaL* clients were campaigning cautiously so as to minimize risks and hence minimize gains (or effects), these two were playing a "maximax" game (maximizing risks in order to maximize gains).

The first of these to appear was a 32-year-old member of the 'Afafṭeh, the smallest sublineage of the Ġadāyreh proper. He worked as a foreman of a pneumatic pavement breaker crew for a construction equipment company. Before that he served in the IDA, which he left as a disabled veteran. He campaigned for *Shlomtzion*—a small right-wing party founded by Reserve General Ariel Sharon—because Sharon was his commander in the service and had helped him secure his disabled veteran benefits. According to his story, the Committee for Disability Determination of the Ministry of Defense did not want to recognize his claim and kept dragging his case from month to month. He had approached the *muḫtār* several times but the *muḫtār* did not help. That the *muḫtār* had no connections in the bureaucracy of the ministry—as opposed to that of the IDA—and particularly not in the Disabled Veterans Department had little influence on his alienation. Finally, he had had enough and went to see Sharon, who was the commander of the Southern Command where he was stationed during his service, and enlisted his help. Sharon saw the claim through the bureaucracy and got the 'Afafṭi his benefits. Afterwards, Sharon helped him in other ways.

The second contender was a 30-year-old sixth son of the third smallest Generation IV subunit of the Ramlāt.[19] His two younger brothers were serving in the IDA and he had worked for a major countrywide security guard company until he had an accident, after which he lived from his insurance benefits and the odd guard job. He campaigned for the *Likud* and his patron was 'Amal Naṣir al-Dīn, a Druze who had himself canvassed among the Druze for that party in 1973 under the slogan "'not a step [of the Occupied Territories back to the Arab States]' arguing that moderate [or restrained] policies toward the Arab states are a mistake" (Eyal 1973:18). He thus represented the most extreme form of what Enloe (1980) in general and Oppenheimer (1977, 1978) in particular have described as the ethnicization of the Druze in Israel.

Both contenders canvassed openly and throughout the tribe. The 'Afafṭi and his cousins worked in Bīr al-Maksūr and the Mikmān, and then spread to outlying bedouin settlements and subdivisions in the area. The Ramlāti made a *ḥaflah*, at his home, for 'Amal Naṣir al-Dīn, which was attended by some fifty or sixty people after which they drove to the Mikmān to canvass there and a fortnight later made house visits in Bīr al-Maksūr promising early release of a prisoner here, a permit there, and so on. By canvassing in public, both tried to appeal to followers across kin-group lines with a single message: "the *muḫtār* has grown distant and no longer cares for the tribe; hence it is time to replace him and the way to do it is through changing the government by installing Begin (or Arik) who will care for us better." The 'Afafṭi also tried to appeal to the youth directly by adding that the *muḫtār* had particularly neglected the tribe's young men.

Together the two men attracted 84 Ḥğeri votes (39 for *Shlomtzion* and 45 for the *Likud*) or only 14.1% of the total Ḥğeri vote of 1977. This was more than the 62 votes (10.4%) received by the *MafDaL* but less than the 90 (15.1%) voters in the two lineages who responded to the *RaQaH* canvassers, who did not appear in the village at all. Similarly, they did not appeal beyond the traditional pool of "resentment groups"—that is, they did not get votes from the actual supporters of the *muḫtār*. Aside from the contenders' own kin the only group to join en masse any of them was a small (seven men and their wives) Generation IV subunit of the D'eyfeh who joined the *Shlomtzion* campaign. This group had several complaints against the *muḫtār*, ranging from lack of help in solving a problem with the Committee for Disability Determination and another problem regarding reinstatement in a police job, to unenthusiastic and insufficient support and protection after a fight that two members of the subunit had with the *'arab* al-'Arāmšeh (a bedouin tribe near the Lebanese border). Another person who joined these opposition groups was a Ramlāti who went with the *Likud*. He complained before the election that the *muḫtār* did not help him to transfer from the Border Guard to the police proper but added that he would vote UAL if the *muḫtār* came through. Similarly, the Maḥāmīd votes for the *Likud* in the Mikmān were in retaliation for the neglect of the Mikmān and because, as one of them said, the *muḫtār* had advised the ILA against them in some sedentarization-related issue.

Nevertheless, the importance of these two far outstripped that of the two older contenders for by arguing the real issues of power and its sources in public, they called upon the *muḫtār* to answer in kind and to not evade the debate by mobilizing bias and resorting to issues of tradition, unity, and the old power sources (i.e., kinsmen). This new style of debate, which tended to enhance the cooperation of small kin-groups in order to counterbalance and keep in check the power of a larger group, was characteristic of election campaigns for local councils. The two thus may have, while dealing with extra-Ḥǧeri relations, inadvertently prepared the way for the advent of intensified inter-lineage competition in intra-Ḥǧeri organization with its far-reaching effect on tribal unity, if local councils in the Galilee and the "Little Triangle" can serve as examples. These councils were fraught with the predominance of lineal and sublineal loyalties and inter-unit rivalries—often violent—over village welfare and administrative issues in their political discourse. For example, in February 1976 there was a fight between the two major lineages of Kafr Manda over the local council chairmanship. The conflict ended a few days later with the nomination of a member of a small local lineage for that position after the votes of the representatives of all the lineages ended in a 3:3:3 tie among the two major groups and a coalition of the smaller lineages of the village who had decided they had had enough of the fighting of the first two.

Two factors underlay this phenomenon of inter-kin-group polarization and fighting. The first was the emotional ties to one's kin-group, which governed one's reactions in this context. This issue was raised by a young man from the Ramlāt who supported the move against a local council in Bīr al-Maksūr. He said he would have preferred a local council to the mukhtarship but he was aware that the former would split the village along family lines and not along lines of age or interests and that if he became a council member he would have to support his sublineage against the other sublineages for better or for worse even though personally he did not like to operate in this manner. The second factor was of an econopolitical nature and resulted from the council chairman's ability to repay his supporters and nurture a following by nominating them to administrative posts in the council's jurisdiction. It was precisely such a nomination that triggered the aforementioned feud in the villages of 'Āra and 'Ar'ara.

Finally, although these contenders, in their attempt to oust the *muḫtār*, divided the tribe in a way that might not have been as transient as they originally thought, the adaptive value of this opposition process should not be overlooked. Like the different allies of the contenders for the leadership in 1947–1950—Ibrāhīm al-Nimr (al-Qāwuqği), Ḥsēn al-Gāsem (Ṣāleḥ al-Ḫnefes), and Ḥsēn al-Ḏiyab (the Nahalal Station Jewish policemen)—which enabled the tribe to survive the 1948 War and flourish until 1977, the presence of political diversity during that year's election proved adaptive also. The *Likud/Shlomtzion* coalition, after all, had won the election. Therein lay another distinction between the *MafDaL* clients and the younger contenders who worked for that coalition. Whereas the latter joined, for better or for worse, with the national competitors of the Labor Party in order to oust the *muḫtār* in a flamboyant way, the former, in a much more self-serving approach, worked for a party that had never tried nor would ever be able to replace the Labor or *Likud* on its own and which was only after a few votes here and there.

The United Arab List (UAL)

To a large measure the success of the opposition in attracting 45% of the 595 votes that the tribe cast in 1977 was due to two closely interrelated factors: the unenthusiastic campaign and leadership of Muḥammad al-Ḥsēn and the abstention of 52% of the eligible voters of the Ḥğerāt. Directly, both factors resulted from the Arab department of the Labor Party's decision to unite its allied lists for fear of losing the party's foothold among the Arabs in the face of *RaQaH*'s rising popularity in that sector through its penetration into local politics. For example, in December 1975 it won the mayoralty and eleven of the seventeen seats of Nazareth's municipal council, and in May 1976, in elections for seven local councils (six in the Galilee and one in the "Little Triangle"), it won two council chairmanships as well as seats in all of the locations (notably in Saḫnīn). The significance of these victories was that traditionally *RaQaH* was considered a national party to be voted into the Knesset whereas local and municipal councils were held by pro-government factions that could solicit civil benefits from the administration (cf. Landau 1981:208–10).

Indirectly, the Arab department's concerns resulted from the general worry of the party's leadership that for the first time in its history the Labor Party might lose both the elections and the government—due to the party's jaded oligarchic elite and internal dissent as well as to public disillusionment and the split and departure of "The Democratic Movement for Change" (*DaSh*).[20] Consequently, each vote—Arab included—became crucial, and the links between the vagrancies of the Jewish sector, the administrative elite of the Labor Party, and its followers in the Arab sector became tighter than ever before, generating instability and endangering the lots of pro-government Arab leaders.

From early December 1976 the Arab department began pressuring the ABL to unite with its other allied list, "Progress and Development" (PD)—which had Sayf al-Dīn al-Zu'abī and Ğabr Mu'addī as its MKs—to form the UAL. The party's explicit reasons were simple: it was estimated that the value of the "qualifying percent" would be about

18,000 votes. It was further estimated that Sayf al-Dīn al-Zu'abī would attract about 17,000 votes, Ǧabr Mu'addī about 5000, and the ABL another 17,000, and that Ǧabr Mu'addī would rather go alone than with Sayf al-Dīn al-Zu'abī if only the latter won a seat. Consequently, it was assumed that if the three were to go separately they would all fail to qualify whereas if the two lists united they would get two to three seats in the Knesset. The "qualifying percent" not withstanding, the Arab department seemed to have had other, ulterior motives: the ABL was the product of BAAA efforts that were imposed on the Labor, and in the first week of January 1977, while the talks with the ABL were still at their exploratory stage, Shmuel Toledano, the prime minister's advisor on Arab affairs, resigned his post and joined the *DaSh* campaign. Since the last time a faction (*RaFI*) left the (then) Alignment it sponsored an Arab allied list ("The List of Peace"), it was unlikely that the possible attraction of the ABL to the *DaSh* camp went unnoticed in the Labor Party headquarters.

Moreover, for the 1977 election campaign each MK received some I£650,000 in campaign expenses (2/3 before the election and the last 1/3 pending reelection) from the State Treasury and the Labor worried that if the three MKs went their separate ways they would spend the money on doomed campaigns with the Labor losing both the seats and the money. The Labor Party was especially short of money for the 1977 election after a series of public scandals revealed illegal transfer of funds from *Histadrut* organs such as its health services (*Kupāt Ḫolim*) to the party's coffers. While these practices were not peculiar or particular to the Labor (the *Likud*, for example, had a similar scandal at the same time with funds from its members' retirement fund, *Qeren Tel Ḫai*), legal and public attention made it difficult to overspend the party's Knesset-allotted campaign funds and its own legal monies.

The UAL, argued the Arab department, would be the "insurance" of the two lists. It would not be a merger (to which the ABL would not have agreed at all) but a confederation, or an alignment, for the sole purpose of winning the election, after which each partner would go its own parliamentary way. Hence, each of the lists would retain its own "organization"—viz. funds—independent of the other. The order of the names on the UAL ballot was set by the department to start with Sayf al-Dīn (PD) in slot no. 1, *šeyḫ* Ḥamād Abū Rabī'a (ABL) in no. 2, Ǧabr Mu'addī (PD) no. 3, Muḥammad al-Ḥsēn (ABL) no. 4 and so on. The department's reason for this specific order was that Sayf al-Dīn was senior among the candidates and "honor is honor" while the rest simply followed.

Again other, ulterior motives seemed to be involved in this decision. In 1966 the Alignment withdrew its previous support from Sayf al-Dīn al-Zu'abī's campaign for the municipal election of Nazareth in November. He ran independent and won four of the fifteen seats in the council (by comparison, in 1965, with the Alignment's full support he won five seats). Since he headed the bulk of the seven pro-government seats he was supposed to become the next mayor. *MaPaM* (2 seats), however, made its coalition with the Alignment (which once again represented Sayf al-Dīn) rather than with *RaQaH* (6 seats) conditional upon Sayf al-Dīn not being the next mayor (Landau 1969:172–74). It was "[o]nly with great difficulty . . . [that he was] . . . persuaded to renounce his claim to the mayoralty" (Landau 1969:199). And if, over time, Sayf al-Dīn had proven himself a capable foil with a history of loyalty to the Labor, the ABL, by contrast, had imposed itself on the party, whose power elite was neither forgetful nor forgiving (e.g., cf. Aronoff 1977:26, 52, 69–70, etc.).

Nonetheless, the director of the Arab department promised the ABL that Sayf al-Dīn only wanted to be elected for the last time in order to retire while in power rather than in defeat. Consequently, after reelection and owing to his heart ailment he would resign to a comfortable quasi-government job in Nazareth and *šeyḫ* Ḥamād would automatically become the head of the UAL. Similarly, the director said that all Ğabr Mu'addī wanted was a post of a *qāḍi* (or *šeyḫ*) at the Druze religious court because he knew this was his last election since not many Druze would vote for him again and he wanted the post because as an MK "he is a slave of people but as a *šeyḫ* he will be master of slaves" (cf. Landau 1969:14 for the intra-Druze dynamics for Mu'addī's wish). To placate Muḥammad al-Ḥsēn, he promised that after the election Mu'addī would be nominated *qāḍi*, thereby leaving slot no. 3 free for the *muḫtār*. With two seats in the Knesset and with Sayf al-Dīn al-Zu'abī and Ğabr Mu'addī out of the way, the ABL would have two MKs instead of its previous single seat and if the UAL won more seats even more bedouin representatives could be brought in.

The bedouin were reluctant to lose their independence, arguing that bedouin issues were not *fellāḥīn* issues and that the only reason they had run in 1973 was to look after bedouin concerns. Moreover, the PD's two MKs were jaded politicians who forgot their promises after Election Day and the public knew it. The ABL, conversely, was new, had worked continuously with the people since its establishment, and had emerged as an attractive alternative to the PD. To unite the two lists would be to stain the ABL with the PD's jaded image. Finally, continued the bedouin, the dynamics of the election in the traditional Arab sector were such that in a village with two competing lineages one would vote for one list and the other for a second list for reasons of independence of image and honor. If the Labor were to offer only one list it would lose roughly half of its prospective voters, who would be forced to vote for another party, which in the new Arab sector meant *RaQaH*. The Arab department replied that all these arguments were immaterial because the real issue was the very survival of the lists—a reply that was an ironic reversal of the aforementioned 1965 Toledano-Lin debate with the party adopting the same arguments it had rejected eight years earlier and the ABL arguing the party's previous line (see above).

Although neither believed the Labor's survival argument or its promises, the two bedouin leaders were divided on the UAL idea. *Šeyḫ* Ḥamād, who bore the responsibility for the land settlement issue in the Negev and on advice from a few private Jewish citizens with much influence among Galilean bedouin and other Arab voters, wanted to disengage from the Labor and campaign as an independent list. Privately he argued that an independent ABL could attract the necessary votes for one and very possibly two seats in the Knesset because many lineages who gave them only a few votes in 1973 to see how the ABL would perform were now ready to support it more heavily for it had proven itself the list of the people, bedouin and *fellāḥīn* alike. Similarly, although many of these voters were tired of PD and in no way would they vote for it, they did not want to vote for the *RaQaH* alternative either and the ABL would be able to attract them. For example, a few days before the February 6 meeting, during which the idea of the UAL was discussed, several men from the all-Druze village of Sağūr in the western Lower Galilee invited Muḥammad al-Ḥsēn for a February 4 meeting to speak with their elders about going with the ABL because they were disenchanted with Mu'addī (they ended up by voting 18% for the Labor; 10% for *DaSh*; 20% for UAL; 1% for *RaQaH*; 22% for *Likud*; and 24% for Plato Sharon [a private businessman who ran for the Knesset in order to escape extradition to France]; Isr. IGE 1978: tb. 16). Similarly, on February 5, the *muḫtār* met with the leader of the Fāhūm family (the dominant lineage in the north during the Mandate Period and before the rise of the al-Zu'abī family under Israeli rule), who expressed support for the ABL (but not, one might add, for the UAL with a Zu'abī at its head). Also, when the *muḫtār* visited the village of Naḥf (western Lower Galilee) on May 14, a few villagers inquired why the Labor established the UAL for, after all, "no one likes Sayf, and Ğabr [they like] even less."

To the Arab department *šeyḫ* Ḥamād pointed out the fallacy of its director's assurances regarding Sayf al-Dīn's resignation. By Knesset law, he argued, the position of the head of a list is omnipotent. Hence, if he actually resigned—not any too predictable in itself—he could bypass *šeyḫ* Ḥamād and nominate Ğabr Mu'addī to replace him as head, which would leave bedouin issues politically dead because Mu'addī had not cared for his own people, let alone bedouin. In fact, *šeyḫ* Ḥamād said, he would not trust any promise of either of these MKs even in writing because they had promised someone, in writing, that if he brought the PD 600 votes "he would be in," and after the man brought the votes they reneged on the deal, leaving him with a worthless piece of signed paper that was inadmissible as evidence because of Knesset law. Ğabr Mu'addī, who was deputy minister of agriculture at the time, by the way, seemed to enjoy a measure of disrepute also among Jewish administrative officials. Both in his own ministry and in the BAAA I heard several who said, "for Ğabr I would not move a finger" or "when he calls I am simply not here."

Muḥammad al-Ḥsēn, conversely, argued for accepting the Labor's plan because in light of the director's repeated assurance that "Rabin [the Prime Minister] and Zarmi [the Secretary General of the Party] want it [viz. 'support it']" and that "as the Party see it, it is the only viable solution," he did not think that the Labor would let them "run" independent, and cited the example of several dissidents, including David Ben Gurion and his *RaFI* list, who were made to "serve as a lesson as to what can happen to even powerful politicians who do not play by the rules of the Labor Party game in Israel" (Aronoff 1977:70).

Neither did he think that without the support of the massive party machine and resources of the Labor could an independent list attract enough votes to pass the "qualifying percent" requirement. For—with no exception—every list that had been allied to a party other than the Labor—*MaPaM*'s "Popular Arab Bloc" (1949); General Zionists' "Arab List—the Center" (1955); *Ahdut ha'Avodah*'s "Israeli Arab Labor Party" (1959); the *MafDaL*'s "Progress and Work" (1961); RaFI's "List of Peace" (1965); and the various independent lists throughout the period—had failed to attract enough votes (Landau 1969:110, 121,

128, 133, 147 respectively). Closer to home, there was always the example of Ṣāleḥ al-Ḫnefes and all the attempts of Arabs to launch independent Arab parties that never took off the ground due to government opposition (e.g., Landau 1969:72–74).

Finally, even if the ABL succeeded in winning a seat or two in the Knesset, without the Labor Party it would join the other lists with one or two MKs who "talk a lot but can do nothing" because they did not have access to executive power to implement their demands. Since an Arab MK was not a Jewish MK, if he could not help his supporters, he was wasting their trust and his time in the Knesset.

Consequently, Muḥammad al-Ḥsēn pressured *šeyḫ* Ḥamād to agree to the plan, and after the director had promised other assurances of Sayf al-Dīn al-Zu'abī's resignation and that the UAL would be the only allied list of the Labor, the UAL was declared publicly in the first week of March. All the agreements were vouched for by the party, which was represented by some of its top officials in the government including the prime minister and the secretary general of the party. Nonetheless, Muḥammad al-Ḥsēn was highly disillusioned by this development because even though he had forced *šeyḫ* Ḥamād's hand, he felt coerced into a union against his wishes or better judgment. Positionally, from an almost sure-to-win second slot on the ABL ballot he dropped to the fourth place on the UAL's, which was expected—regardless of the predictions of the Arab department and its director—to win two seats at best. Similarly, from the sole parliamentary leader of the bedouin in the north he became one of the three parliamentary leaders who divided that area now. Nor did he like the idea of working for the reelection of Sayf al-Dīn al-Zu'abī or Ğabr Mu'addī, and he knew that the public resented them as well. Disillusionment bred apathy.

The UAL Campaign

The UAL was launched with television coverage by the Arab division of the state-controlled television network, which maintained an active interest in the news of the list throughout the campaign period. Similarly, every day until the May 17 Election Day, the Jerusalem Arabic daily, *al-'Anbā*, carried large UAL election advertisements on its front page as well as elsewhere in the paper. Organizationally, and in accordance with the principle of confederation, the campaign in the north was divided into three headquarters (HQs): Nazareth, the Eastern Galilee, and the Valleys of Jezreel and Beisan under Sayf al-Dīn al-Zu'abī; Shfar'am, Western Galilee, and the Druze under Ğabr Mu'addī; and the bedouin tribes in addition to a few villages allied with bedouin under Muḥammad al-Ḥsēn. This division introduced maladaptive rigidity into the campaign as, for example, bedouin activists could not canvass in villages of the other two HQs without their permission, which was never given due to the endemic mutual mistrust plaguing the UAL candidates from the beginning. Consequently, voters who would not open the door to the activists of, say, Sayf al-Dīn but who would have listened to an ABL-HQ canvasser could not be reached.

The *muḫtār* was assisted by two private Jewish citizens well versed in the region, its politics, and traditions, and who had many friendships among its Arab citizens, many of which dated from the Mandate Period. The senior of the two, "A"—who became the regional coordinator of the ABL-HQ in the UAL—was asked by "C" (a close friend and one of the BAAA officials to conceive the ABL in 1973) to join the campaign because "A"'s friendships included the *'arab* al-Heīb and other competitors of the Ḥğerāt and/or Muḥammad al-Ḥsēn in the Galilee. "A" consented because in addition to his friendship with "C," he was an old friend of *šeyḫ* Ḥamād Abū Rabī'a. The younger Jew, "B"—who worked independently and was administratively attached to the Labor's Western Galilee HQ in Acre—joined the campaign because he was "A"'s friend. Both had served the state before and although disillusioned with the Labor Party and its conduct they felt that it was the only entity that could keep the Jewish state viable, a view basic to the understanding of pre-1977 Israeli politics. Aside from its objective causes, this identity was promoted by party ideology that "elevated [the] party above the individuals in it, and the state above the party, while simultaneously elevating the . . . party view of what was good for the state over any other view of what was in the state's interest" (Medding 1972:304). Not surprisingly, "[f]or the party to fail, to split, or to lose power would in the view of Mapai and its members create irreparable harm for the state" (Medding 1972:305). This identification of the party and the state, as Aronoff pointed out, led to the norm "that to criticize Government [read: Labor power elite's] policy or to raise controversial issues when the country faced a critical security situation was tantamount to disloyalty to the country [read: the State]" (1977:62–63).

In spite of these impressive beginnings the campaign itself turned into a fiasco. It started with the director of the Arab department's failure to transfer the ABL-HQ campaign funds from the party's Tel Aviv banks to a Nazareth bank until finally "A" had to drive down in person and get the money at the party HQ in Tel Aviv on March 27. The next day the single telephone in the Labor Party regional branch (Eastern Galilee) in Nazareth—where the ABL-HQ was located together with the Labor's own campaign HQ—was disconnected by the Ministry of Communication's telephone service due to unpaid bills. On April 6 it was reconnected after the director of the Arab department—who was responsible for the party's HQs and its finances in the Arab sector—finally paid the outstanding bills. Then the funds for operation, including Election Day, were cut in half—hardly sufficient to cover the expenses of Election Day alone. Thus, for example, the ABL-HQ had to pay I£200 for a jeep and I£300 for a small pickup truck to transport voters to their poll stations, even though in the case of the bedouin the distances involved included the whole north of the country. These sums were insufficient to finance the gasoline (at over I£5 per liter) that the vehicles consumed and many drivers stopped their cars when the money ran out. By comparison, other parties reportedly paid I£500 per vehicle.

To complicate matters further, the director, who had agreed in the first week of April to pay "A" I£25,000 in expenses for the three campaign months, two of which were already past, changed his mind by the second week and claiming he "had made a mistake in calculations" reduced the contract to I£15,000, which "A" interpreted as sheer harassment. To begin with, the I£25,000 did not cover his expenses because aside from his transportation outlay he had to leave his small cattle ranch in the hands of paid untrained help who, by then, had already lost "A"'s Hollander milch cow (worth approximately I£5000) and a calf due to neglect and "A" was expecting to lose more because it was spring and both the cattle and its fodder needed more attention and work.

To antagonize "A" further, the director stalled until the end of April on giving him the right to countersign the checks issued by the ABL-HQ because "A" did not want to promise money, expenses, or wages to activists without the assurance that he would be able to keep his word. Since the finances of the 1973 campaign as well as those at the beginning of this one were somewhat shady and since he did "not want to end up a liar or to have to sell the [cattle] herd to back up [his] promises," as he said, "A" demanded the right as a way to control expenses and ensure that obligations were honored. ("B," by the way, had received this right by mid-April.)

Finally, on May 4, "A" resigned, at which point the administrative coordinator of the Arab department wanted to engage "C" of the BAAA—who, as a government official, could not "campaign publicly on behalf of political parties" (Medding 1972:236)—to replace "A" and when this administrative coordinator was asked "has 'C' agreed [to replace 'A']?" he answered "everyone likes money." This turn of events seems to have been prompted by "A"'s friendship with *šeyḫ* Ḥamād, whom the director of the Arab department mistrusted completely due to the *šeyḫ*'s independence and commitment to the bedouin cause rather than to the Labor Party. More deeply it seems that the director was afraid that "A" would influence Muḥammad al-Ḥsēn to join with *šeyḫ* Ḥamād and leave the UAL on one of the several occasions that presented themselves during the campaign (see below). Such an event would have gotten the director into major discord with his superiors.

In addition to the Arab department's dedication to *RaQaH*'s success in the election,[21] the Labor Party leaders added their share by political in-fights over the promotions of their personal clients. Thus, although the UAL had been guaranteed as the party's one and only allied list, the deputy prime minister was trying to promote his protégé, Maḥmūd 'Abāssī, as head of a second list for Arab intellectuals and white-collar professionals. This effort was finally blocked by the party and 'Abāssī "ran" independent, but in the meanwhile it added to the atmosphere of suspicion and mistrust in the UAL. Then, on April 7 the prime minister and head of the Labor Party resigned for personal reasons and again the ABL-HQ questioned the validity of the agreements vouched for by the Labor. The problem was that no one, and especially not the Jews who supported and/or worked for the ABL-HQ, trusted the promises of the Labor Party as a corporate political entity. Consequently, if the individual whom one trusted left the scene, one was not sure that his successor would respect, whether in part or in full, the party's previous commitments promised by his predecessor.

Similar disarray was experienced at the regional branch (Eastern Galilee) of the Labor Party in Nazareth, which was permanently situated in the shell of a rented second floor of a privately owned house. Plywood dividers partitioned the shell (that is, the stuccoed concrete outer walls) into one small office and three cubicles along one wall, leaving most of the floor space for a public gathering and waiting area plus a small enclosure for the *gahawanği* (the man who made Turkish coffee for the guests and officials of the branch). The space's temporary character was repeated in its "once-in-four-years appearance" mode of operation. There were no current lists of eligible voters in the region (although one could find those from 1973); no files on party activists; no information about previous sympathizers, opponents, and so on; and no updated knowledge of them. (In comparison, the Labor's regional branch in Acre [Western Galilee] was the exact opposite: smoothly run, updated information, and an air of continuity and permanence.) Operationally, the senior of the two officials who staffed the branch was occupied more with intrigues against the Nazareth *Histadrut* officials (who were also Labor members) than with campaigning for the election per se.[22] He was also an alleged supporter of Maḥmūd 'Abāssī.

This "once-in-four-years appearance" had been the approach of the party in general. Thus, Aronoff quoted a local leader in a *Jewish* branch who complained to the secretary general of the party that "[e]very time there is a new leadership they come and listen to our problems, and then we do not hear from them for three and a half years until they are organizing an election" (1977:60). The approach, moreover, became an institutionalized attitude of the party's national leadership who "simply do not need the branches which are 'nudniks' (bothersome), even if justified. But who needs them? . . . We really only need them for elections—between elections it is a game!" (the former head of the Organization Department of the Labor Party quoted by Aronoff 1977:61).

And if the Jewish political parties were organized on a "once-in-four-years appearance" basis in the Arab sector, the sector had adapted to this behavior as to the MG before. Summarily, as a notable from I'billin said in response to "A"'s comment that he was "busy with the election now" in order to raise the subject of votes: "Ah, the election. Good. We have demands. We want electricity."

The items in this grand barter system of votes in exchange for goods and services could be classified into two major categories: communal interests and private interests. The first category was the direct result of the differential investment of government resources in Jewish as compared with Arab settlements. It included, therefore, paved roads, electricity, running water, clinics, schools, and the like. As one of the *maḫatīr* associated with the ABL-HQ commented, "one tries to get the best [most] for oneself and we need a [paved] road and a school and a clinic so we look [shop] around."

The second category became a set response to the solicitation of the various parties. By 1977 it ran the whole gamut from exemption of unqualified teachers from the campaign to "academize" the state educational system; favored admission to universities; land rentals and land settlement deals with the ILA; change of land zoning status; irrigation water from the Ministry of Agriculture; jobs with the police; gun permits; amnesty requests from the president of the state; release of criminals and some security-related convicted and pre-trial prisoners; to *qāḍi* posts in the *Šarī'a* Courts.

Save for a few public speeches and one or two rallies, this type of barter interaction (and predominately of the latter category) *was* the campaign of the UAL in the north. It added, however, apprehension to the previous disillusion and apathy of Muḥammad al-Ḥsēn, for although similar in some respects to his personal style of operation, it was different in two major details. First, it was not tactful and hence endangered the goodwill of his personal contacts in the administration. Second, he rarely, if ever, promised or took it upon himself to solve someone's problem if he was not sure to succeed, and he knew—as he often told his own tribesmembers—that the state's budget was limited, the demands on it were many, and, therefore, promises of public projects would end up as public lies for which he would be held responsible.

A case in point was the aforementioned honor execution in Dabūrīyeh. The day after the killing the police arrested the victim's husband, three others of their immediate kinsmen (according to one version his F, his FB who was also her F, and her MB), and the Elder of their lineage. Following the arrest, lineage members approached Sayf al-Dīn al-Zu'abī to intervene with the police to release all but her husband, who had confessed to the killing. Sayf al-Dīn, however, did not have influence with the police and, hence, came to the ABL-HQ to ask Muḥammad al-Ḥsēn to arrange for their release. After the former had left, the *muḫtār* was angry with him and said: "first they butcher her like a chicken and then come running to me to get them out of prison while the matter is still hot" and added that he "told Sayf [who had pressured him] that even if it were my own brother who had killed [someone] I would have waited at least two weeks before starting to move [to release him]. But no!! Sayf wants them out now because of the election."

Muḥammad al-Ḥsēn consequently occupied himself with personal favors and avoided promising communal projects that had been the major style of PD campaigns and were, therefore, expected of him as well. Thus, when confronted by requests for public projects he would answer "elections come and elections go but I stay [lit. 'present': '*'ana maūğūd*,' i.e., 'I am accountable']" and added that after the rush of the election he would look into the matter and do his best to help. Focusing on personal favors, however, meant that he remained mostly in the office where individual help-seekers could find him, and he only occasionally ventured into the field for settlement and house visits where communal projects were more likely to be requested or demanded. This inactive style of campaigning was reinforced, first, by the occasional intrigues of Ğabr Mu'addī, who had been spending his time intriguing in each and every direction to strengthen his weakening position among the Druze, which made it necessary for the *muḫtār* to be readily accessible in order to monitor and counteract these schemes. For example, when the Labor's prime minister designate—Shim'on Peres, who had replaced Yitzhak Rabin after his resignation—wanted to visit Acre on April 27 to hear the opinions of that city's Arab population, Mu'addī arranged through the director of the Arab department to divert the visit to two Druze villages, one of which was Yirka (his home base), and sent out printed invitations to that effect without the party's knowledge. More specific to the ABL-HQ, about mid-March after Muḥammad al-Ḥsēn had arranged for the release of three prisoners, Mu'addī called the police officer who handled the case and told him he was coming to get the three in order to deliver them to their families. As it happened, Muḥammad al-Ḥsēn reached the officer first and got them himself. Also, a week or so later the *muḫtār* of the *'arab* al-'Amariyeh gave a *ḥaflah* in honor of Mu'addī in order to antagonize Muḥammad al-Ḥsēn and through him the government. Mu'addī accepted the invitation, thus forcing his Alignment partner to be there himself in order to monitor the Druze.

The second reason for this inactive style of campaigning was the heritage of unpaid bills and unhonored checks from the ABL campaign of 1973 that, although not of his own doing, made it unpleasant to meet the list's former activists in the field. According to "A" there were two ABL activists who were in charge of reimbursing the expenses (such as gasoline receipts and similar bills) of the other campaign activists. There was either not enough money or some other problem but many bills were not reimbursed and among those that were, many checks were bounced by the bank. As "A" commented, if after the 1973 election Muḥammad al-Ḥsēn had visited all these activists to thank them and had told them of the ABL's troubled financial state, most, if not all, of these men would have discarded the bills and checks as a donation to *their* list. As it was, in many outlying bedouin settlements one could see the 1973 memoranda and encounter some bitterness that Muḥammad al-Ḥsēn, although available for help in Nazareth, did not come for a visit after the election.

The cumulative effect of these factors was a passive campaign style through which Muḥammad al-Ḥsēn tried to avoid endangering the networks he had so carefully developed in the administration and in the tribe for so long. But whereas the administrative personnel were as aware of the election as the *muḫtār* was and, hence, allowed for the greater pressure, he tried as much as possible to apply in his old tactful way. However, his own tribesmembers were confused and perplexed by the storm around them. As one person of the Ṭa'awāneh said on May 4 (when the turmoil was entering its intensive phase), "it is not good. Everyone is going in a different direction," and that he worried this election would split the tribe. "For thirty years," he continued, "we went as one to the election. Now anyone who is not happy starts a list for himself" and concluded "*kul al-dunyā mağnunīn*" ("all the world crazy").

For the first time in Ḥğeri history there was open and vociferous opposition to the leadership (the *muḫtār*), the list he represented, and the government. Moreover, not only did the *muḫtār* not censure the opposition, but instead of telling his followers "vote for the UAL" he told them "vote for whomever you want." The *muḫtār*'s reason in allowing for so much latitude was a sincere attempt, at all costs, to prevent a showdown with the opposition, thus forcing the tribesmembers to adopt sides and positions that might split the tribe forever. A brother complained on May 4 and again on May 8 that the election split the tribe and that "instead of being together people go to 'Amal [Naṣir al-Dīn], Arik [Sharon], and I don't know what else. . . . This election is trouble and the people behave like the *fellāḥīn* in the villages each to his separate *ḥamūleh*." He, therefore, wanted the *muḫtār* to censure the opposition. On both occasions the *muḫtār* answered that elections come and go but if he took measures against those working for other parties it would become a matter of honor. Moreover, he was not going to bring the tribe under pressure and endanger its unity only to get Sayf or Ğabr into the Knesset. He was doing his work in the election but not jeopardizing anything. The *muḫtār*'s reasons notwithstanding, many Ḥğeris interpreted it either as a test to find out who were his loyal supporters or as the absence of leadership, which was even more baffling. This latter interpretation was made more credible by the opposition, which presented it as a sign of weakness and guilt. It was of little surprise, then, that 51.6% of the eligible voters of the *'arab* al-Ḥğerāt chose not to vote.

The Aftermath

The 1977 parliamentary election and the victory of the right-wing *Likud* Party was another turning point in the life of the Ḥğerāt, as it was in the life of the country as a whole. In the aftermath of the election, however, not much changed, for the previous momentum kept old projects—such as the effort to enter the IDA officers' course or the plans to construct a mosque in Bīr al-Maksūr—rolling. Nevertheless, a few cracks began to develop in the old scenario. Most noticeable was the *muḫtār*'s withdrawal from politics and his decision to look after his private affairs. Thus, when his brother, who represented him in the village after Ibrāhīm's death, and Maḥmūd al-Mūsā asked him to intervene in an intra-tribal affair, he advised them to take a vacation and look after their own interests at least for awhile. In the village, one or two individuals from other sublineages became somewhat more expressive in their resentment toward Maḥmūd al-Mūsā and no action was taken to censure them. Then, barely two months after Election Day, a *dīwān* was held at the house of the Ramlāti supporter of the *MafDaL* during which some of the Elders discussed the need to terminate the *muša'* and divide the lands of Bīr al-Maksūr permanently. Their reason was the growing need of all Ḥğeris for land (even those who did not cultivate it) at a time when a few individuals claiming squatters' rights were cultivating more than their fair share, a practice that would generate conflicts and undermine tribal unity.

Notes

1. Although beyond the scope of the present project it would be rewarding to find out the extent to which such social ideals that set externalized (as opposed to internalized) behavioral boundaries promoted heightened emotional tension and related physiological conditions in adult males, for several Ḥğeri young adults I knew quite often took Valium (5 and 10 mg pills) to relax, and alcohol consumption was quite common among early middle-aged men and youth.
2. The celebration of self-control should not be understood to mean that violence qua violence is rejected but only that its uncritical use is objectionable. This gradual increase in personal self-control and the progressively more critical use of violence, as Sahlins (1968:4–13) has suggested, provide for an evolutionary continuum from the state of nature to the nature of the state.
3. The Ḥğeri term *ḫatyariyyeh* is a collective noun denoting "the Elders." Since, however, it was used to refer only to the group of the few influential elders who led the tribe, I refer to them as "the Council" in order to connote this choice group.
4. The alliance in general and the Ḥğerāt in particular supported Marx's argument (1967:64–65) that it is the actual sharing of full responsibilities rather than a rigid generational count that determines the scope of the co-liable group. The Ḥğerāt, in fact, although they knew it, did not use the term *ḫams* when referring to their co-liable group. Instead, they used *'ašīreh* (tribe) or *ḥamūleh* (lineage). Nor do they use the more elaborate tribal subdivisions such as the *ruba'* (sub-tribe or tribal section) that the Negev bedouin studied by Marx (1967:67–72) use.
5. *Ne'emān* (lit. "Trustee") is a position in the bureaucratic hierarchy of the Ministry of the Interior and includes prescribed duties in assisting the fulfillment of functions that usually fall under the responsibilities of a variety of governmental ministries. For example: maintaining peace in the village and providing the police with information about criminals, strangers, and suspicious individuals; reporting to the police any major offense, accident, or unnatural death

and damage to public property (e.g., railroads, roads, telephone lines, etc.); accompanying the police or army when involved in "security related" activities in the village; registering vital statistics and transferring them to the regional office of the Ministry of the Interior; informing the regional clerk (Ministry of the Interior) of the death of people with landed properties and providing him with a list of these; authenticating all documents requiring authentication; informing the supervisors of the Ministry of Health of any contagious disease and assisting them in maintaining public health; informing the Ministry of Agriculture of animal and plant diseases, locusts, etc.; assisting tax collectors, especially in the case of tax evaders; informing the authorities of the discovery of antiques and preserving them; in short, "to help government officials in performing their duties" (Ashkenazi 1957:63; for a more complete list of the 1951 ministry's job description see Ashkenazi 1957:60–63).

This lengthy list of high-variety duties without authority is a good indication of the position's colonial origins for it testifies to both the absence of government services at the local level and to the disjointed status of the mukhtarship from the sources of governmental power and authority. It was precisely this dual characteristic that made the position attractive to the MG when it inherited the area from the Mandate authorities, for like the latter it was short of personnel and administered an alien population, and what is more, the office was not expensive, as the *ne'emān* was paid only a minimal salary.

6. This feat was not too hard to accomplish because for the Ḥğerāt—like many other traditional societies (cf. Hall 1976:17–24)—events in time are not always sequential. In other words, when several people were present in the *muḫtār*'s *dīwān* to ask for help, each listened and everyone talked—now about this, now about that—without any apparent case sequence. Consequently, the *muḫtār* discussed several cases with several people at the same time without overstepping etiquette. If an individual preferred to keep his matter private, he briefly whispered into the *muḫtār*'s ear and joined the general conversation.
7. For a more complete discussion of the role of "the mobilization of bias" in power and control see Bachrach and Baratz (1962). Here it suffices to mention that "power is also exercised when A devotes his energies to creating or reinforcing social and political values and institutional practices that limit the scope of the political process to public consideration of only those issues which are comparatively innocuous to A" (Bachrach and Baratz 1962:948).
8. For implications of this competition to the understanding of the military-minority relations in Israel see Appendix I.
9. A soldier could become a cadet by submitting a request to be accepted to officers' course. The request had to be recommended by his/her commanding officer and together with the soldier's personal file was reviewed by a selection officer/committee who decided its fate. Usually a request would not be considered if the soldier did not possess a matriculation certificate. If, however, all other characteristics were equal, high competency and excellent recommendations could serve to waive the certificate requirement so the individual could be accepted to the course sans certificate. The same was true if the cadet was destined to become a special-purpose professional officer (in which case criteria equivalent to the certificate were high professional competency and recommendations). Trackers fell under the latter category; i.e., they were professional personnel and could only be commissioned as trackers' officers. Hence, they did not require the certificate if they were highly skilled and recommended by their administrative commanding officer. It was here that the Heībi blockade was placed. The Ḥğeri alternative, then, would be to take the normal route of having all the formal requirements accompanied by the recommendation of their de facto commanding officers—i.e., the Jewish commanders of the Jewish units to which they were attached.
10. During a *ṣulḥa* feast in the *'arab* al-Ka'abīyeh, the *muḫtār* complimented the regional police commander, who was present as a witness, on his tact in employing the traditional mode of conflict resolution by saying that "people need to know that the leader [ruler] has a sharp sword but the wise leader [ruler] does not draw it from its sheath."

11. I have not been able to ascertain the definitional difference between a "party" and a "list" in Israeli politics. In the Arab sector, however, where the successful lists to the Knesset have been invariably sponsored by the *MaPaI*/Alignment/Labor Party, some of the characteristics of such lists and their MKs are somewhat clearer. First, they are "allied" to the party and as such have no independent administration or financial organization but make use of the Labor's party machine, and their finances are managed by its Arab department. Second, as Landau has noted (1969:195–98), the MKs of such allied lists rarely speak off the Knesset floor unless on specific issues regarding the Arab sector—such as the relaxation of MG controls before 1966 and of civil services thereafter—issues that have been raised by other MKs whether from the government or from its opposition. Similarly, in voting they are required to follow the Labor's position on central issues by coalitionary agreements that make "[a]n independent vote in accordance with individual conscience . . . extremely rare" (Landau 1969:197) and promoted Sayf al-Dīn al-Zu'abī to complain "that the Arab allies of the Alignment in the *knesset* were hardly ever consulted, though directed as to how to vote" (Landau 1969:197).
12. The "qualifying percent"—*aḥūz haḥasīmah* (lit. "the blocking/barring percent")—is the number of votes necessary to secure the first Knesset seat for each party or list participating in the election. Its purpose is to block the proliferation of small parties by dividing the number of valid votes in the country by one hundred and not by a hundred and twenty (the total number of seats in the Knesset). Consequently, the first seat is 17% more "expensive" than the second and all subsequent seats. In fact, the rest of the seats are even "cheaper" because the votes of the parties that have failed to pass the blockade are distributed among those that made it. For example, 1,500,000 valid votes provide for 15,000 as the "qualifying percent." Assume that 13 of the 22 parties/lists that participated have passed it while the 9 that have failed attracted a total of 50,000 votes. The second seat, then, will be worth 1,500,000/120 = 12,500 minus the bonus each winning party gets of the defunct 50,000 votes, which are divided according to their relative success in the election.
13. The relation between public projects and private use was not very clear among the Ḥğerāt or the Arab sector. For example, the informant who equated income tax with *ẖawa* (tribute, protection fees) did so even though he was aware of the services provided by the government. He also called the National Insurance's children allowances a *hadiyah* (a present) that spoiled the people because they did not work for it and who therefore saw it as a free gift of which they wanted more. Similarly, during the 1977 election campaign, I heard some people from Saẖnīn say they had received "nothing" from the government, although each month that year this village received over one million *lirôt* in children allowances alone. On a higher level of analysis this muddled view of the relations between taxes and services seems to be the result of the failure of the government that—being busy distributing favors instead of rights and obligations—had left the majority of the Arab sector to interpret modern socialist state ideological items according to its traditional framework and standards.
14. This number does not include some 1000 guests who by mistake appeared the evening before the wedding. These were also fully fed and entertained by a hastily summoned pair of rhymesters before being informed of the mistake at the end of the evening, and were asked to join again the next evening.
15. Although I was not able to detect such a phenomenon among the Ḥğerāt, one should not rule out the possibility of actual purchase of votes for cash. Similarly, one should not disregard the presence of such background noise as ignorance, apathy, etc.
16. The reason for his replacement was the felt need of *MaPaI* to introduce "new faces" (in that party's jargon) in order to attract more votes (cf. Landau 1969:124). Subsequently Ṣāleḥ al-Ḫnefes formed an independent list for the 1959 election but failed to attract enough votes for a Knesset seat (Landau 1969:128). In the following elections of 1961 he ran as an allied list of the *MafDaL* but failed again (Landau 1969:132–33). In 1965 he ran in the third place on the ballot of the "List of Peace" allied to *RaFI*, which also failed (Landau 1969:193, 147

respectively). Since 1965 he retired from parliamentary politics and campaigns. During his repeated attempts to win a Knesset seat he was supported by Ḥsēn al-Gāsem and it is very likely (although not confirmed) that the latter's shift to the *MafDaL* in 1969 was a result of previous contacts through Ṣāleḥ al-Ḫnefes.

17. This recognition of the Mikmān seems to have been directed as a personal vendetta at Muḥammad al-Ḥsēn (on another occasion the commissioner was quoted by a Jewish official to have said "the Gadir will come to me on all fours and beg before I sign [i.e., approve] it [a permit application to build a gas station in Bīr al-Maksūr]"). It was, however, given in return for the 1969 Ṣawālḥi votes for the *MafDaL* and in anticipation of the 1973 votes. As I mentioned before, the recognition angered the planning board of the sedentarization program (the NSBC), which responded by putting the Mikmān on the bottom of its priorities list. One member of the Maḥāmīd who voted *Likud* in 1977 commented that "before 1973 . . . [the District Commissioner] . . . recognized the settlement but instead of voting *MafDaL* they [the Mikmān] got mixed-up and voted 'A' [ABL] so . . . [he] . . . doesn't help them any more."
18. During the 1977 election, in spite of the split caused by Ariel Sharon, the *Likud* increased its following by 110,659 voters compared to the 1973 election, attracting 583,968 votes in all. The Labor, conversely, attracted only 430,023 votes, losing 191,160 of its 1973 supporters, many of whom voted for its splinter group *DaSh*—"The Democratic Movement for Change"—which attracted 202,265 votes. Had the leadership of the Labor tried to prevent the split by reforming the party as was demanded of them before the 1973 election, the party would have been able to preserve most, if not all, of the 621,183 votes it received in 1973, thus maintaining its majority in the Knesset and forming the next government (voting data source: Isr. IGE 1978:51, tb. 7).
19. In the pre-1948 traditional setting, this family of eight adult brothers would have tried to win the leadership similarly to Ibrāhīm al-Nimr and his four brothers. According to some members of the *ulād* Ġadīr, that was precisely what this contender had in mind, although the informants saw it as an anachronism. A few of these brothers, by the way, had an election related fight near the voting station during the election to the congress of the *Histadrut* on June 27, 1977.
20. For a detailed analysis of the Labor Party and development of these problems see Aronoff 1977.
21. *RaQaH*, as was previously mentioned, not only increased its following from 35.6% in 1973 to 49.2% in 1977 but almost doubled its take among the bedouin (6.5% and 12.4% respectively; Isr. IGE 1978: XVI), who were considered loyal followers of the Labor. Or, as *šeyḫ* Ḥamād told "A": "it cannot be an Arab head [which conjured the idea] that gets the Communists stronger by the day; it must be a Jewish head and a plan to drive the Arabs into the hands of the Communists." Naturally, the director himself did not see these results in that light at all (see his post-election comments in Mazori and Rahat 1977:4).
22. The rivalry and intrigues between party branch officials and *Histadrut* branch officials had been endemic to local level politics in Israel (see Aronoff 1977: esp. 124–25; Medding 1972: esp. 93–94 and 97–98).

PART V

Conclusions

— 10 —

Epilogue

Thirty-three years have passed since I left Bīr al-Maksūr and Israel on August 1, 1977. This period has seen many changes in the life of the *'arab* al-Ḥğerāt, as in Israel at large. The decline in the tribe's favored status with the new authorities, which resulted from the rise of the *Likud* to power in 1977, effectively brought the demise of herding, but was also followed by the thoughtful establishment of a local council in 1990, an increase in education, and a much more diversified involvement in Israel's social and economic life.

As the *Likud* became entrenched, Ḥğeri herds, together with other bedouin tribes' herds throughout the country, were subjected to harassment by the "Green Patrol"—the armed paramilitary vigilante unit of the Nature Reserves Authority (NRA)—which used intimidation, violence, and illegal means to, among other things, enforce the 1950 Black Goat Law that had lain dormant since its enactment. Originally the Green Patrol was formed in 1976 to supervise ILA-administered lands and control their use to prevent trespassing and encroachment by squatters. After the 1977 change of government, *Shlomtzion*'s Ariel Sharon became minister of agriculture and encouraged Reserve General Avraham Yofeh, the NRA's director, and Allon Galili, the "commander" of the Green Patrol, to enforce the Black Goat Law ("Protection of Vegetation Law/Goat Damages–1950"). The law limits the number of goats that can be owned by a person in order to curb their effect on the country's feral vegetation. Although not a police unit, the Green Patrol enforced the law by intimidation with fear, physical violence, and the use of firearms, which resulted in at least one accidental death, that of an *'arab* al-Kašḫar baby in the Negev. The Green Patrol has also been involved in house demolition and similar enterprises, while not being empowered to do so by any legal authority (although it has been used as such by the Ministry of the Interior, for example). Although the state comptroller criticized its conduct in 1980, the government took no action to contain it (for a full account see Miron 1982). In 2000, the Green Patrol name was changed to the Green Police (in the Ministry of Environmental Protection), although it is not part of the Ministry of Public Security and its Israel police. By January 1982, a letter from Bīr al-Maksūr read: "all the rest of the Ḥğerāt [who live] out of the village [Bīr al-Maksūr] . . . slowly slowly concentrate inside the village and not one will be left outside [the village]." The resulting demise of the tribe's larger herds invalidate my prediction (see Chapter 8) that these herds would survive and become commercialized.

These economic and demographic changes found clear expression in the 1981 parliamentary election when the *Likud* grossed some 47% of the actual votes of the Ṣawālḥah (*Ma'ariv* July 1, 1981:8).[1] Similarly, the Ġadāyreh "all . . . voted *MaHaL* [*Likud*] in the hope that it will help them to camp in the places [areas] of the *minhal* [ILA] but . . . [it] . . . helped no one," to continue the letter above, which also mentioned that "the *muḫtār* does not deal with politics *at all*!!"

The poor performance of the Labor Party among the bedouin in that election was also caused partly by the abrupt end of bedouin representation in the Knesset. The UAL won only one seat in 1977 and, as agreed, Sayf al-Dīn al-Zu'abī resigned and left his seat for *šeyḫ* Ḥamād Abū Rabī'a. In 1979 Ğabr Mu'addī demanded to replace *šeyḫ* Ḥamād (as he had also demanded in 1956 of Mas'ad Qasīs, a Greek Catholic who ran with both him and Sayf al-Dīn al-Zu'abī in *MaPaI*'s allied Democratic List of Arabs in Israel [Landau 1969:75, note]). *Šeyḫ* Ḥamād refused, arguing that the Druze had two MKs in the *Likud* whereas the bedouin had no representation other than himself. Moreover, the land problem in the Negev was worsening due to the peace agreement with Egypt, as result of which the IDA compressed its bases from the Sinai into the Negev. After a court upheld *šeyḫ* Ḥamād's right to refuse, he was assassinated on January 20, 1981, and that same night Ğabr Mu'addī's three sons were arrested as suspects and on February 10 were indicted for the murder. Although *šeyḫ* Mūsā al-'Aṭaūnah demanded in the name of the Negev *šiyuḫ* that the UAL seat be passed on to Muḥammad al-Ḥsēn, the Labor Party—fearing to lose the seat in court entanglements—followed the normal succession rule and accepted Ğabr Mu'addī's claim to the seat for the remainder of the term of the Ninth Knesset. With that came the end of the Arabic Bedouin List.

In September 1990 Bīr al-Maksūr and the Mikmān were combined and converted into a local council with an appointed head of council (appointed by the Ministry of the Interior), and with this step a new stage in the evolution of the *'arab* al-Ḥğerāt commenced.

The appointed head of council, Uri Borovsky, and his voluntary council (three Jews and one Ḥğeri) established the administrative structures of the council in accordance with the applicable laws and regulations of the Ministry of the Interior, thereby eliminating the problems inherent in the previous cooperative societies, such as those of the water and electricity I mentioned before. Such legal base also separated the elected officials of the council from its administrative employees, making nepotism less likely. It also established the frameworks for efficient public service, primarily with regard to education, village infrastructure and visual aspects. Finally, the appointed council attempted to make Maksūr a regional center by establishing there the Regional Bureau for Welfare for the northern bedouin tribes. In many respects, Borovsky's work accomplished the original intent of the Northern Supreme Bedouin Committee (NSBC) to make Bīr al-Maksūr an example for the other bedouin tribes in the region. He also succeeded in establishing a civil service administration that in combination with the traditional principle of Ḥğeri unity superseded segmentary loyalty and the divisiveness it introduces to *fellāḥīn* local councils. Thus, while the election to head of council is heavily influenced by segmentary loyalty, the actual functionality of the council administration is not. Borovsky's heritage thus allays the concerns I raised regarding local councils in the Arab sector (see Appendix K).

Since the first election to the council in 1994 there have been five elected heads of council: two from the Masa'īd, one from the Ġadāyreh (elected twice), and one from the Ramlāt. The Ġadāyreh commented that in each instance where they lost the elections (1994 and 2006), it was caused by their fielding multiple candidates (that is, they did not unite behind a single candidate). Nevertheless, the incorporation of Maksūr and the Mikmān into a single administrative unit suggests that the two maximal lineages of the Ḥğerāt, the Ġadāyreh and the Ṣawālḥah, reached an approximate balance in terms of population size, which is likely to help preserve Ḥğeri tribal identity and protect it from the all-out competition seen in the *fellāḥīn* villages.

Since my departure in 1977 the population of the Ḥğerāt has almost tripled in size, from about 3400 to over 9000 individuals, with some 8000 of them residing in Bīr al-Maksūr and the Mikmān. In terms of population structure, however, it remains much as it was in 1977—very young, with the 0–9 years age bracket flaring out of the base of the population pyramid. While there are still a few families who limit the number of children, by and large the process of reducing family size I observed during the fieldwork period was reversed due to the rise in religious identity and observance, a process I will return to later.

Like the population, the educational process, which began with the new school in 1976, continued to amplify its impact so that by 2009 there were some 2500 students in the Council's area: 500 students in fourteen nursery schools and kindergartens in both settlements, 900 students in three elementary schools (two in Maksūr and one in the Mikmān), 500 students in one junior high school (*khtivat beiynayim*) in Maksūr, and 450 students in one high school in Maksūr. Of the graduates, eight have become M.D.s (physicians, a geneticist, and a pathologist) and have five Ph.D.s in various fields of study. There are several lawyers and other professionals providing the managerial needs of the council and the tribe. A similar process has occurred in the security complex, so if in 1977 the first Ḥğeri with a matriculation certificate was sent to wrestle control from the *'arab* al-Heīb's monopoly over officers' course, by 2009 the Ḥğerāt had a number of mid-range officers in the IDF, the police, and the prison service.

Herding has become the occupation of some elderly individuals who keep small herds of cattle and some ungulates mostly "for the peace and calm" that herding provides them. These herds are trough-fed and can be found on the hills around the village. Thus, herding, once the primary economic pursuit of the *'arab* al-Ḥğerāt and the source of its identity, has ceased to exist as an economic force. The Ḏmeydeh remains an agricultural village whereas in the council's area (Maksūr and the Mikmān), the picture is more complex. While field crops seem to gradually follow herding into demise, arboriculture in the shape of nuts and similar groves dot the landscape. Nevertheless, as land is converted to buildings while salaries in agriculture (NIS 5269 in 2008) keep lagging behind nearly all

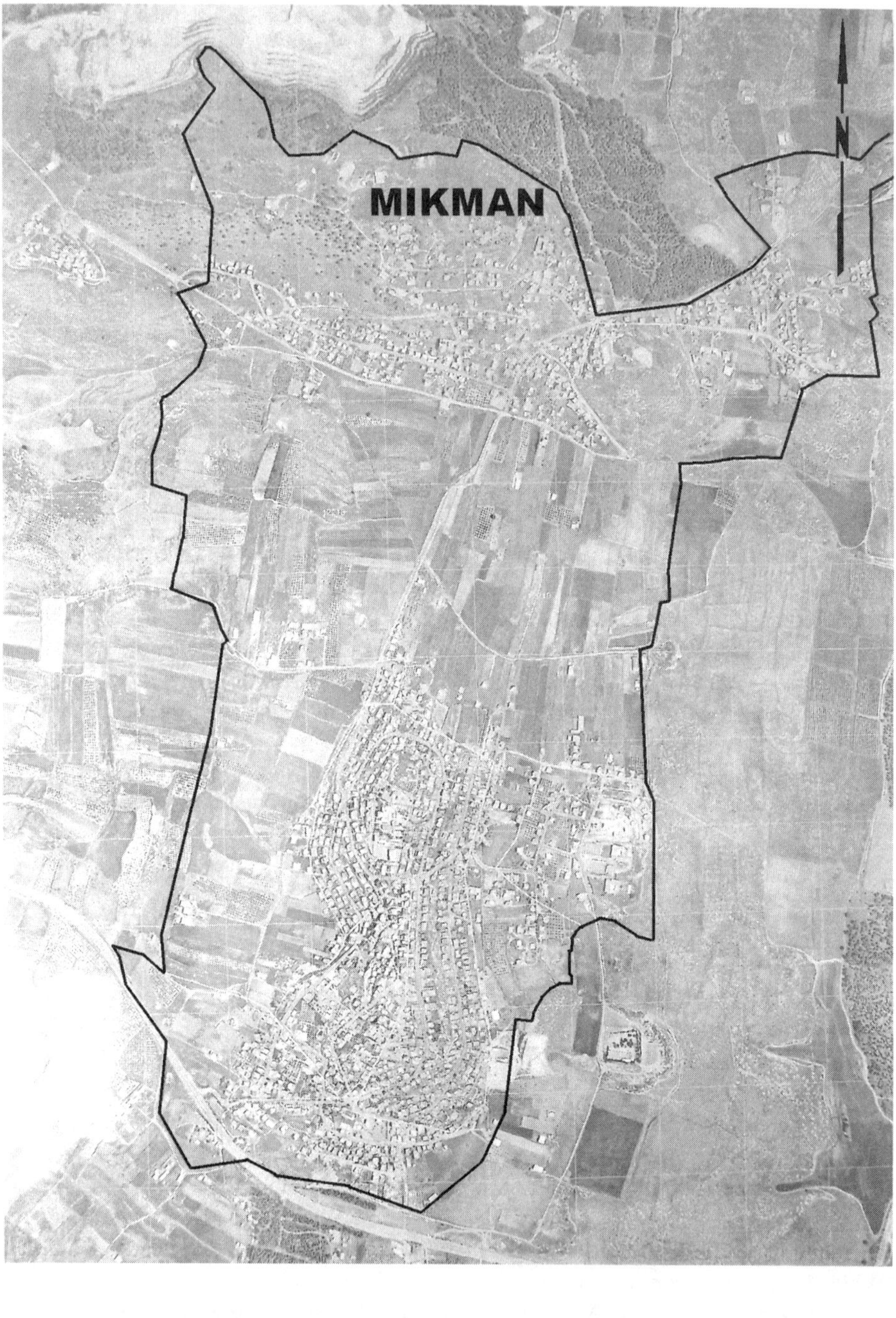

Figure 9. Aerial view of Bīr al-Maksūr council area, 2007 (photo by Ḥetz Hatzafôn, Mipui veHandasa Limited; courtesy of the Bīr al-Maksūr Local Council).

Figure 10. Bīr al-Maksūr in 2009.

other professions (see Isr. CBS Abs. 2009: tb. 12.36), agriculture seems bound to disappear. Most Ḥğeri males are still involved in wage labor, although increasing numbers among the middle-age cohort have become entrepreneurs providing niche services to the various industries in the region (for example, one man started a guard company that now services the entire Northern District and has some 500 employees). Nevertheless, while the successes in education and enterprise are good indications for the longer run economic health of the Ḥğerāt, their enmeshment in Israel's wage market has meant sharing the impact of the recent global recession. This shift has found some expression in a few acts of vandalism, unheard of thirty years ago. The council's plans to develop industrial zones, in partnership with the Jewish settlements that have sprouted around Maksūr, to provide employment to the youth could help alleviate the problem but if, and only if, the general economy is growing.

The susceptibility of the Ḥğerāt to the upheavals of the Israeli and global economic systems, as well as their continued existence in a bi-ethnic state system that was amplified in intensity by the *intifāḍa*, seems to have fueled their growing identity as Moslems in Israel. Whereas in the mid-1970s few Ḥğeris (mostly elderly) prayed and quite a large number drank alcohol, by 2009 most pray, a growing number have undertaken the *ḥağğ*, and alcohol is no longer visible in the village. Three mosques in Maksūr and one in the Mikmān dot the skyline and in a recent wedding the leader of the Islamic Party gave the keynote speech and some 1500 guests prayed before the festivities began. One can only ponder whether this growing Moslem identity of bedouin in Israel is a response to the growing religious observance of the Jews in Israel, coupled by the historical marginalization of Arab settlements (which can only aspire to administrative grade 2 [out of a possible 5 grades], effectively disabling them from competing equally with Jewish settlements [which range all the way to grade 5] for the governmental assistance programs that this scale defines). At the same time, several members of the tribe who served in the IDF have married Jewish wives, which may point to yet another direction in the adaptation of the *'arab* al-Ḥğerāt to its ever-changing environment. Meanwhile, the Bīr al-Maksūr local council is a thriving village, as indicated in Figures 9 and 10.

Note

1. The Labor Party got almost 24%; Moshe Dayan's *Telem* collected 14%; *RaQaH* declined below 7%; Arab lists got 4%; *MafDaL* got 0% (not a single vote); and seven other parties/lists shared the last 4%. Finally, less than half of the eligible Ḥğeri voters participated (*Ma'ariv*, July 1, 1981:8).

— II —

Conclusions

The preceding account has sought to describe the processual development of the *'arab* al-Ḥğerāt from a small familial herding camp to a three-and-a-half-thousand-member tribe of regional importance as a case study of culture change. Although there were no specific theoretical foci toward which the project oriented itself, the general intent was to describe Ḥğeri adaptation with as much detail as seemed pertinent and to let field observations viewed from a processual perspective raise issues of theoretical import to the study of culture and of culture change.

Two theoretical reference points underlay this project. The first is that no human society, hence its culture, is an isolate and should not be described as such, while the second is that in the absence of causes to do otherwise, a society continues in its momentum (that is, its traditional lifeways) indefinitely. Applying these concepts to a viable system such as a human society can delineate and emphasize the nature of the forces that generate change in the lifeways of the society. Two general categories of such forces were identified: an internal set, which included population increase, the developmental phases of individual maturation, the principle of "complementary opposition" in segmentary organization, and so on; and an external set, which included economic incentives, inter-group competition, state control, and the like. These two categories were seen to operate at alternating rates of speed and intensity, were usually in varying degrees of mutually-causal interaction, and their effects have been amplified over time. Similarly, although during different time periods one force might prove more immediate than others to the well-being of the tribe, other factors would nonetheless continue at work and would propagate their effects throughout the system. Therefore, I found it advantageous to adopt a multi-causal model in order to describe and explain the evolution of the Ḥğerāt as a tribal society and its adaptation to its various state environments.

At the starting point of the account the future *'arab* al-Ḥğerāt were a typical herding camp of a small bedouin kin-group. That is to say they had already had—or, were—the segmentary organizational model and ideology that characterize bedouin sociopolitical organization in general. Their economy, although organized around sheep, goat, and cattle herding, seems to have included some agriculture and the collection and hunting of wild species to make ends meet. Apart from its economic importance, herding also served to identify this group as bedouin to others, thus reinforcing their own cultural identity with its concrete sociopolitical concomitants. Throughout this early period, from about 1790 to 1870, the only significant change was the slow internal increase in their membership both through procreation and through adoption, alliance, and an extensive marital strategy. The importance of this increase lay in the establishment of their small population as the independent sociopolitical entity its members claimed it to be, as opposed to their being obliged to join a larger group for their safety and survival as individuals.

The Ḥğerāt at this point was almost identical to the Ḥağarah tribe of the Lağa' from which its founding fathers sprang save for two differences: their more diversified economy and, possibly, their extensive marital strategy, which cannot be verified without comparative marital data on the eighteenth-century Ḥağarah. Both these differences arose from their immediate life circumstances, but whereas their marital strategy seems to have stabilized once population size and general security reached a certain threshold, their economic strategy of multi-resource extraction had deviated further from its traditional bedouin model. The difference in the behavior of the two traits seems to be related to their relative importance in preserving the identity of the culture in question. Thus, although economic pursuits underwrote the available caloric reservoir of the population, the specific resources tapped seem, from the group's perspective, less meaningful for the preservation of its cultural identity than did its marital strategy.

The tribe's move from Tel al-Šummām to the Ẓahara was undertaken to preserve the momentum of the reconstructive process in which they had been involved—viz., the successful preservation of their group and its lifeways—from the threat of increased control by the Ottoman government and its tax collectors. In other words, this move was of conservative rather than innovative intent, for it rendered "possible the maintenance of a traditional way of life in the face of changed circumstance" (Hockett and Ascher 1964:137). Nonetheless, their new location, while out of the authorities' way, was in the midst of a more densely populated mountainous area where old villages could survive the previous decline of law, order, and safety. Consequently, they soon found themselves the catalyst of an informal aggregation of some small villages and tribes in response to the belligerence of the larger tribes (e.g., the *'arab* al-Muwāsa), villages (e.g., Ṣafūriyeh), and the Druze. This closer contact with sedentary life reinforced the earlier deviation from the traditional baseline of bedouin economic resources, technology, and so on. By the turn of the twentieth century, with the purchase of land and the construction of houses, these changes had become established.

The British Mandate Period saw a further innovation in Ḥğeri economics and material culture when wage labor (police) became acceptable, new consumer goods were added to their daily needs (e.g., kerosene), and all previous changes were further reinforced.

Similarly, although originally their conflicts with the Druze and Ṣafūriyeh were the result of an immediate need for self-preservation, the aggressive political and military strategy they employed was so successful that this interaction became established in competition for leadership of the area (for example, during the 1936–1939 Arab Rebellion), which, in turn, helped reinforce their self-identity and unity. Finally, due to British reluctance to intervene in local level activities beyond security, the administrative changes that the authorities instituted were—save for taxes—mostly innocuous (the mukhtarship) if not outright beneficial (economic development and relative public peace). In both cases, therefore, the direct influence of these changes on the Ḥğerāt was minimal (while their peaceful introduction did not create resistance to their acceptance).

The year 1949 marked a turning point in the evolution of the *'arab* al-Ḥğerāt and the events that followed this date have provided at least two insights of a theoretical nature. The first of these insights concerns the organization of their cultural system and its approach to coping with change. During the previous periods, changes in Ḥğeri lifeways had accumulated at a slow enough rate to make possible their assimilation without exposing the tribe to great instability. Diversified economic resources, sedentarized material culture, increasing standard of living, and rising importance on the local political scene were all commensurate with Ḥğeri population size, its needs, its strengths, and its organizational paradigm. The viable cultural system that is the *'arab* al-Ḥğerāt, therefore, could regain its stability after each perturbation, much like the aforementioned realignment of the overall Ḥğeri marital strategy with intra-lineal and intra-tribal preferential endogamy.

After 1949 the rate of these changes increased to a crescendo and their diversity engulfed all aspects of life. As a result, fissures began to form in the coherent continuity that had been Ḥğeri culture. The economic activities of the tribesmembers were no longer commensurate with *Ḥğeri* economy and its resources, for many of the resources were now located in the industrial as well as other sectors of the national economy. Consequently, Ḥğeri labor in excess of what could be supported by *Ḥğeri* resources is now absorbed by the national economy, thus alleviating competition among the tribesmembers over the available *Ḥğeri* resources. Also, a national economic recession triggered by events across the ocean can overwhelm the tribe's resources, which are no longer prepared to handle or absorb the resultant unemployed labor. Similarly, medical services and hospital births have upset the traditional age structure of the population, a perturbation that has been picked up and amplified by the educational complex to increase the gulf between the generations while eroding the old face-to-face familiarity that previously reinforced the recognition of common interests and tribal unity. Next, many of these changes became encoded in the tribesmembers' house design, in its contents, and in the use of its enclosed spaces to amplify the deviance of the immature members from the traditional norms.

The question arises: at what point in this growing distance between old traditions and new behaviors can one establish that the *'arab* al-Ḥğerāt as a tribal cultural system has ceased to exist and became the Ġadāyreh or the Ramlāt of Bīr al-Maksūr like the *fellāḥīn* or, Muḥammad al-Ḥsēn and Ibrāhīm al-Nimr, private citizens of the state? As of 1977 this erosion of tribal identity—both in their own self-perception and in the way their neighbors perceive them—was not discernible. For all the changes the Ḥğerāt have undergone, their organizational model—the oft-mentioned segmentary lineage organization—has remained practically unchanged and so effective that even the opposition to the tribe's leadership has behaved according to its basic rules. This is not to say that segmentary organization is infallible or that other tribes in the Galilee have not begun to show signs of disintegration expressed by the repeated positioning of individual wants prior to the group's needs. It does, however, suggest that many traditionally diagnostic characteristics of the category "bedouin"—such as economic pursuits or endogamous marriage strategy—can be temporarily or permanently changed without changing the organizational paradigm of a bedouin tribe beyond which its membership will not be able to reconstitute itself again as a bedouin tribe. If this is the case, the diagnostic characteristics of any viable cultural system would seem to be hierarchically organized with the system's organizational paradigm at its core, and the more biologically oriented variables further from the core and, hence, more amenable to change with the least adverse effects on the perpetuation of that cultural system.

By "organizational paradigm" I mean a set of a few general principles—"heuristics" to use Beer's term (1972:69)—which together specify the type of that cultural system. For example, Sahlins has identified six such principles to identify segmentary lineage organization: *lineality*, *segmentation*, *local-geneological segmentation*, *segmentary sociability*, *complementary opposition*, and *structural relativity* (1961:330–34). Similarly, Toffler has isolated six for modern industrial cultures: *standardization*, *specialization*, *synchronization*, *concentration*, *maximization,* and *centralization* (1980: ch. 4). Further out one finds the items that individualize the particular cultural system with growing specificity, but which are not strictly essential for its survival and hence are increasingly more expendable.

The organizational paradigm permeates the culture as ideological principles that underwrite very basic behavioral patterns embedded in the members of the society during their earliest life experiences and are, therefore, hard to unlearn or change later in life. The paradigm, thus, attempts to preserve itself against the pressures to change that accumulate in the daily life of the society—that is, the *viable* aspect of the cultural system.

The second insight provided by the post-1949 events regards the articulation of the *'arab* al-Ḥğerāt as an ethnic group within the State of Israel. Throughout the present work I have repeatedly pointed to their competition with other groups and, later, to their membership in the minority sector in Israel as key circumstances that have promoted tribal identity and unity. My emphasis on their minority status does not mean that bedouin tribes elsewhere are not minorities within state organized populations (cf. Awad 1959:26). Rather, it refers to the effects of the fact that in Israel there is one more barrier that *all* members of the Arab sector theoretically have to pass before they may enjoy all the benefits accruing to the members of the majority. And, until 1977, the major effect of minority status has been to promote intense competition among several of the groups that comprise the Arab sector, each in order to gain as many benefits for its membership as possible.

This competition highlights the "ethnic boundary" (to use Barth's 1969 term) of the *'arab* al-Ḥğerāt, which seems to operate in two directions: horizontal and vertical. Horizontally and traditionally among like groups on the local level it serves to delineate their participation in the competition over the available resources (for instance, space, productive means, and so on) that are conceived as *finite* by all the participants. It is a "zero-sum game." Relations among groups are thus political in character—hence the importance of carrying firearms—and each group presents its boundary as a sociopolitical boundary that is thus recognized by its respective competitors. Post-1949 a new dimension, a vertical one, was added, and the group's "ethnic boundary"—that is, *bedouin*—became useful in identifying the Ḥğerāt in its relations to the authorities at the national level. These relations are administrative in character and the tribe presents its boundary to the state as a complex of economic and socio-ideological differences in its quest for the resources of the state that the tribesmembers usually perceive as *infinite*.

The distinction between these two levels—the local and the national—seems to be the underlying cause for the two opposing theoretical models offered by cultural anthropologists like Barth (1969), who seems to be dealing with the horizontal, or *political*, boundary aspect, and by political anthropologists like Vincent (1974), who seems to be dealing with the vertical, or *administrative*, aspect of "ethnic boundary" articulation. In this regard, minority nationalist movements seem to be a composite of the two levels, positioning their "ethnic boundaries" horizontally in competition with the "boundary" of the national authorities when their quest for the resources of the state proves to be repeatedly futile or when they perceive the state itself to be but another ethnic group that had temporarily seized the power within the polity.

The vertical "ethnic boundary" and the "ethnic identity" it helps to generate have been dynamically maintained both by the Ḥğerāt and by the state authorities that have utilized them to attenuate the demands made by individual tribesmembers on its limited time and personnel, for voting purposes, for designating possible pools of prospective army recruits, for an internationally projected image, and so on. While the authorities' use of ethnicity seems often, although not always, to be opportunistic in motive, the preservation of its "ethnic identity" is, for the Ḥğerāt, a complex set of phenomena that together with economic and political consideration includes socialization and subconsciously embedded organizational paradigms and symbols. Thus, the boundaries, in their mutually-causal turn, have promoted the preservation of the Ḥğeri segmentary organization and ideology that have underwritten their tribal or "ethnic" identity in spite of all the changes that have eradicated other aspects of their culture, thereby reinforcing their boundaries and so on.

These two types of "ethnic boundaries" have selected for different mechanisms of communication to bridge them and thereby define the extra-tribal relations of the Ḥğerāt and their degree of susceptibility to change. Until 1949 they had to contend mostly with groups like themselves; consequently, communication proceeded across their horizontal or *political* boundary hence constituting—what I have called after Smith (1956)—their political relations. Two mechanisms have been in use in this case. If peaceful negotiation was desired, it was their legitimate representative body—the *ḫatyariyyeh*—that conducted it; if an aggressive approach was preferred, then raiding, intimidation, or some such activity by the younger men could serve to carry the message across. The same held true for their relations with the Ottoman and Mandate authorities. These relations were negotiated by the Elders because, like the stronger local tribes, neither of the two regimes were interested in managing the life of the Ḥğerāt beyond maintaining public order and exacting taxes (or *ḫawa*) from them and the Ḥğerāt recognized the futility of acting aggressively.

These mechanisms of communication, however, could handle neither much nor complicated nor diversified information. Consequently, they minimized the amounts and intensity of the changes that this information could generate not only because it was filtered though very few channels but also because its frame of reference was the tribe as a unit and not its individual members. As a result, aside from its practical aspects, a prospective innovation often took on "political" meaning inasmuch as it differed from "the Ḥğeri way"—that is, their ethnic identity.

Since 1949 the "political ethnic boundary" of the Ḥğerāt has lost much of its previous importance as a new style of communication was promoted by their *vertical* relations with the authorities. This style was determined by the increasingly more complex interaction between the authorities and the tribe, which not only proceeded between non-equals but, being *administrative* in character, also included all facets of the Ḥğeri lifestyle. As a result, two types of channels for *administrative* communication have developed, each with its particular kind of relays (mechanisms relaying information from one level to another), which have generated increasingly more changes in Ḥğeri culture.

The first type channels information through a variety of special purpose relays that relate limited and specified regulatory information unidirectionally from the authorities to the tribe—such as the aforementioned architect who executes building codes or a tax advisor who ensures compliance with the state tax laws. Since, however, a culture is an integrated system, the variety that these special purpose relays are meant to attenuate—for example, confine the variety of all possible house plans and locations to those specified by the authorities' building regulations—often triggers changes in other aspects of the culture, which affect a much more diverse and a greater area than the relays' original intent, although all these changes lie in the general direction favored by the state for they individualize—that is, simplify—the tribal social fabric. Thus, the architect who remodels a house's habitational space affects the modes of social interaction that are conducted therein and the inhabitants' concept of privacy, while the tax advisor who advises financial investments as tax shelters helps alter his Ḥğeri advisee's perception by emphasizing a future time orientation as well as promoting greater trust in the impersonal ways of banking institutions. It was due to this capacity for diffused effects and their great variety of agents—for example, teachers, architects, agricultural guides, and so on—that I have referred to them in the text as "cultural brokers." The presence of these special purpose relays or middlemen and the influence they exert on the changing local culture provides some additional theoretical insights.

The major one of these insights is that "cultural brokership" is a wider phenomenon than simply "power brokership," "political leadership," "economic mediation," or all of the above combined, as has been commonly implied by the use of the term (e.g., Geertz 1960; Obermeyer 1973). Their possible variety, in fact, seems to be a function of the number of active interfaces that the encapsulated local community has to maintain with its encapsulating universe. In addition, they do not just "stand guard *over* the crucial junctions or synapses of relationships which connect the local system to the larger whole" (Wolf 1956:1075, emphasis added)—they *are* these synapses. For when a local community chooses to maintain its "ethnic boundary" (cf. Barth 1969:15–16), it perpetuates cultural discontinuities that the national administration may strive to abolish in order to prevent the probable formation of competing power enclaves. By using brokers to bridge these gaps selectively the local community can comply with the administration's regulations while only minimally, and in a controlled manner, breaching its own boundaries.

The assimilation of a local ethnic group by a national state culture, therefore, can be viewed as a process of the continuous decrease in the number of interfaces that make up the community's ethnic boundary, through the increase in and localization of the number of these channels in each interface. In other words, the state forces or coaxes the members of the community to deal directly with the national administration (e.g., Vinogradov 1974:215–16 for the Shabak of northern Iraq) or as in the promotion of bank accounts for direct deposit of welfare checks. The end of this process is reached when the only interfaces left are those the administration itself wants to maintain, viz., those relating to power, whether political or economic. Notwithstanding, the state may choose to perpetrate ethnic identities and boundaries rather than erode them with the opposite results to those of the process just described (cf. Enloe 1980: esp. ch. 1).

"Cultural brokers" are thus channels of communication dealing with a variety of aspects of life in the community. The extent to which they can manipulate the information they handle for their own ends seems to be a function of their scarcity, personal aspirations, and individual abilities. The extent to which one of these ends is political and/or economic power seems to be further dependent on the type of information they channel. Finally, they may arise from within the community (e.g., Obermeyer 1973), from another community or minority within the state (e.g., the aforementioned architect is an urban Christian Arab), or from a nationwide supra-community network (e.g., Geertz 1960).

If "cultural brokers" are a variety of unidirectional "special purpose relays," the second type of relays are "general purpose relays"—for example, local leaders such as the *muḫtār*—who do not have built-in specificity that limits them to any particular type of information and who are two-way informational relays. Characteristically, they handle large amounts of diverse information that they simplify while collapsing its variable uses to serve their own limited political ends on the local, regional, or national levels. While they deal with politics—hence my reference to them as "power brokers"—their activities are usually felt more broadly and diversely than originally intended. In fact, since they manipulate large volumes of diversified information, their effects on the changing culture will be more pronounced and will appear more quickly than those of the special purpose kind. Ethnographically, these general purpose relays are a broad category that includes "patrons" and similar types of local leaders who may also try to retard rather than promote culture change in order to preserve economic or political (or both) power in their hands.

The importance of these relays in the adaptation of the Ḥğerāt to the Israeli state environment caused a change in the way the account of their history proceeded. Until 1949 one could approach the Ḥğerāt from a cultural level—that is, disregarding specific individuals' roles in one or another societal action under the assumption that regardless of the individual concerned, an action would have been accomplished due to its adaptive significance. The same could not be assumed during the Israeli Period. From its onset it was but one person who was properly situated, and of the proper disposition to go against the consensus of the tribe, who caused the tribe to remain in Israel and continue its evolutionary growth while most other tribes were traumatized and their development arrested. The same phenomenon was repeated with that man's son, the *muḫtār*, who promoted the tribe to regional prominence while propelling himself to national level politics. Consequently, the Israeli Period was approached from a particularizing historical perspective—that is, emphasizing the conjunctures of space and time through which the more general and culturological was approached.

To summarize, as the foregoing ethnographic history described, the evolution of the *'arab* al-Ḥğerāt proceeded from a self-sufficient stable phase—during the Ottoman Period—through growth and expansion during the Mandate Period to a phase of increased internal centralization of power and leadership, relative economic prosperity, and an overall dependence on the far less stable Israeli state/party complex. As long as the Labor Party was in power the status of the Ḥğerāt and the effects of their prominence on their well-being was ensured through their *muḫtār*. The party's 1977 and 1981 defeat, however, spelled a decline for the Ḥğerāt as well. As the incorporation of traditional societies within unstable modern state organizations increases, the role of individuals such as the *muḫtār* and their prominence in ethnographic analysis increase proportionally. I made, therefore, an effort to analyze the behavior of individuals as well as corporate bodies such as the state or the party as a way to gain understanding of the processes that their decisions formed or reformed.

The emphasis on process and the attempt to explain it resulted in an admittedly complex and at times cumbersome presentation. Yet, as increasingly few of the world's people today remain isolated and unchanging (if they ever were), describing them as a static fiction with simplified separable component parts becomes increasingly divorced from the social reality that such ethnographic accounts report. While the way chosen to present the Ḥğeri data is still literately unwieldy, it is hoped that it represents the Ḥğerāt more accurately. Finally, it is hoped that this approach will contribute to an emphasis on the finer mapping of dynamic processes, thus eventually leading to a working model of culture.

APPENDICES

– Appendix A –

Patrilateral Genealogy of the ʿarab al- Ḥǧerāt

(Generations II–VII)

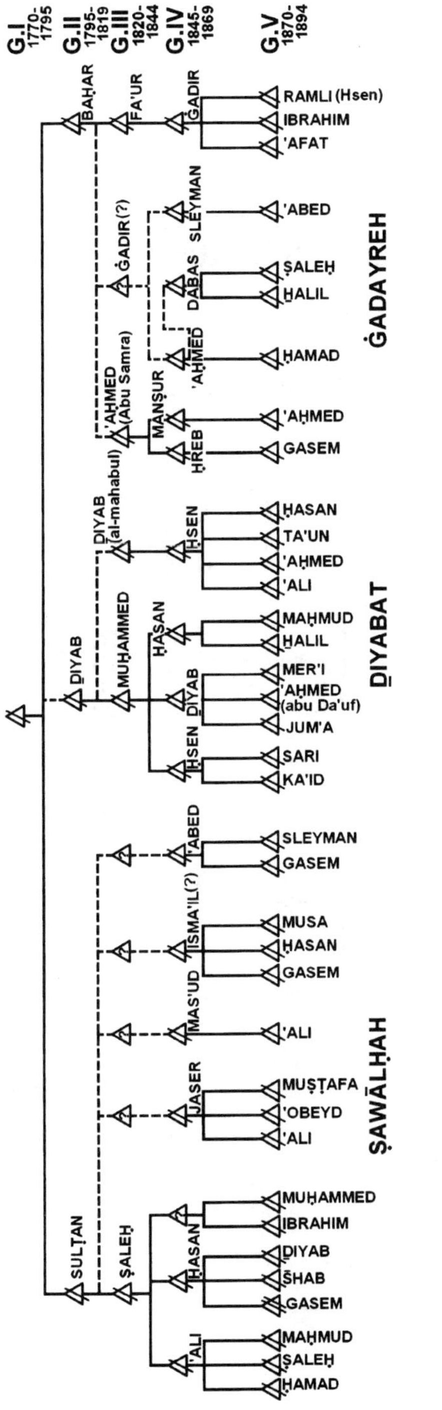
G.I 1770-1795
G.II 1795-1819
G.III 1820-1844
G.IV 1845-1869
G.V 1870-1894
BAHAR
FA'UR
GADIR
RAMLI (Hsen)
IBRAHIM
'AFAT
ĠADIR (?)
SLEYMAN
'ABED
DABAS
ṢALEḤ
ḪALIL
'AḤMED
ḤAMAD
'AḤMED (Abu Samra)
MANṢUR
'AḤMED
ḪREB
GASEM
ĠADAYREH
ḎIYAB (al-mahabul)
ḤSEN
ḤASAN
TA'UN
'AḤMED
'ALI
ḎIYAB
MUḤAMMED
ḤASAN
MAḤMUD
ḪALIL
ḎIYAB
MER'I
'AḤMED (abu Da'uf)
JUM'A
ḤSEN
SARI
KA'ID
ḎIYABAT
'ABED
SLEYMAN
GASEM
ISMA'IL (?)
MUSA
ḤASAN
GASEM
MAS'UD
'ALI
JASER
MUṢṬAFA
'OBEYD
'ALI
ṢAWĀLḤAH
SULṬAN
ṢALEḤ
ḤASAN
MUḤAMMED
IBRAHIM
ḎIYAB
ŠHAB
GASEM
'ALI
MAḤMUD
ṢALEḤ
ḤAMAD

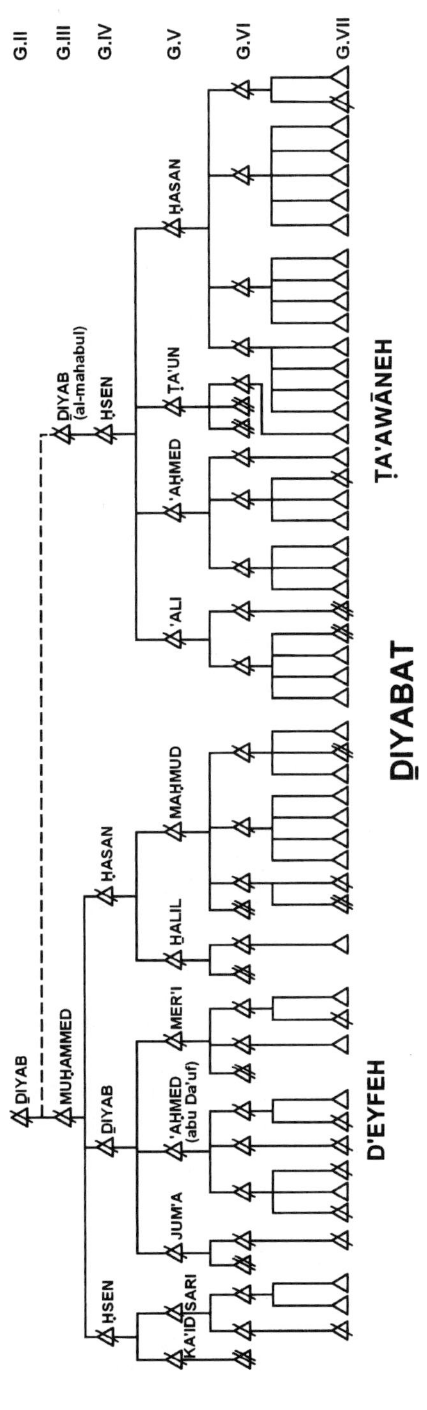
G.II
G.III
G.IV
G.V
G.VI
G.VII
ḤASAN
ḎIYAB (al-mahabul)
ḤSEN
ṬA'UN
'AḤMED
'ALI
ṬA'AWĀNEH
ḎIYABAT
MAḤMUD
ḤASAN
ḪALIL
ḎIYAB
MUḤAMMED
MER'I
ḎIYAB
'AḤMED (abu Da'uf)
JUM'A
ḤSEN
SARI
KA'ID
D'EYFEH

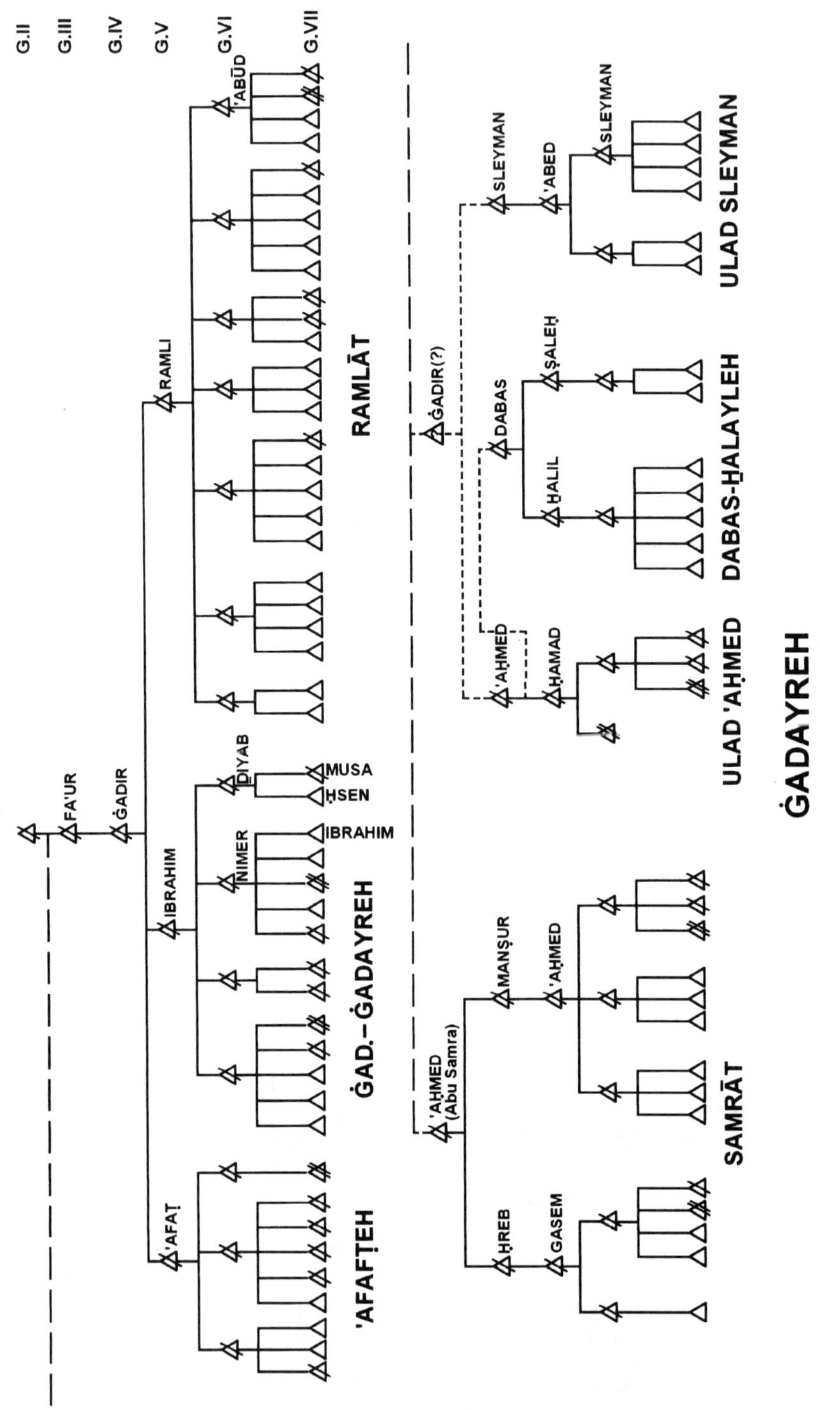
G.II
G.III
G.IV
G.V
G.VI
G.VII
FA'UR
ĠADIR
RAMLI
'ABŪD
IBRAHIM
ḎIYAB
MUSA
ḤSEN
NIMER
IBRAHIM
'AFAṬ
RAMLĀT
ĠAD.-ĠADAYREH
'AFAFṬEH
ĠADIR(?)
SLEYMAN
'ABED
SLEYMAN
DABAS
ṢALEḤ
ḤALIL
'AḤMED
ḤAMAD
'AḤMED
(Abu Samra)
MANṢUR
'AḤMED
ḤREB
GASEM
ULAD SLEYMAN
DABAS-ḤALAYLEH
ULAD 'AḤMED
ĠADAYREH
SAMRĀT

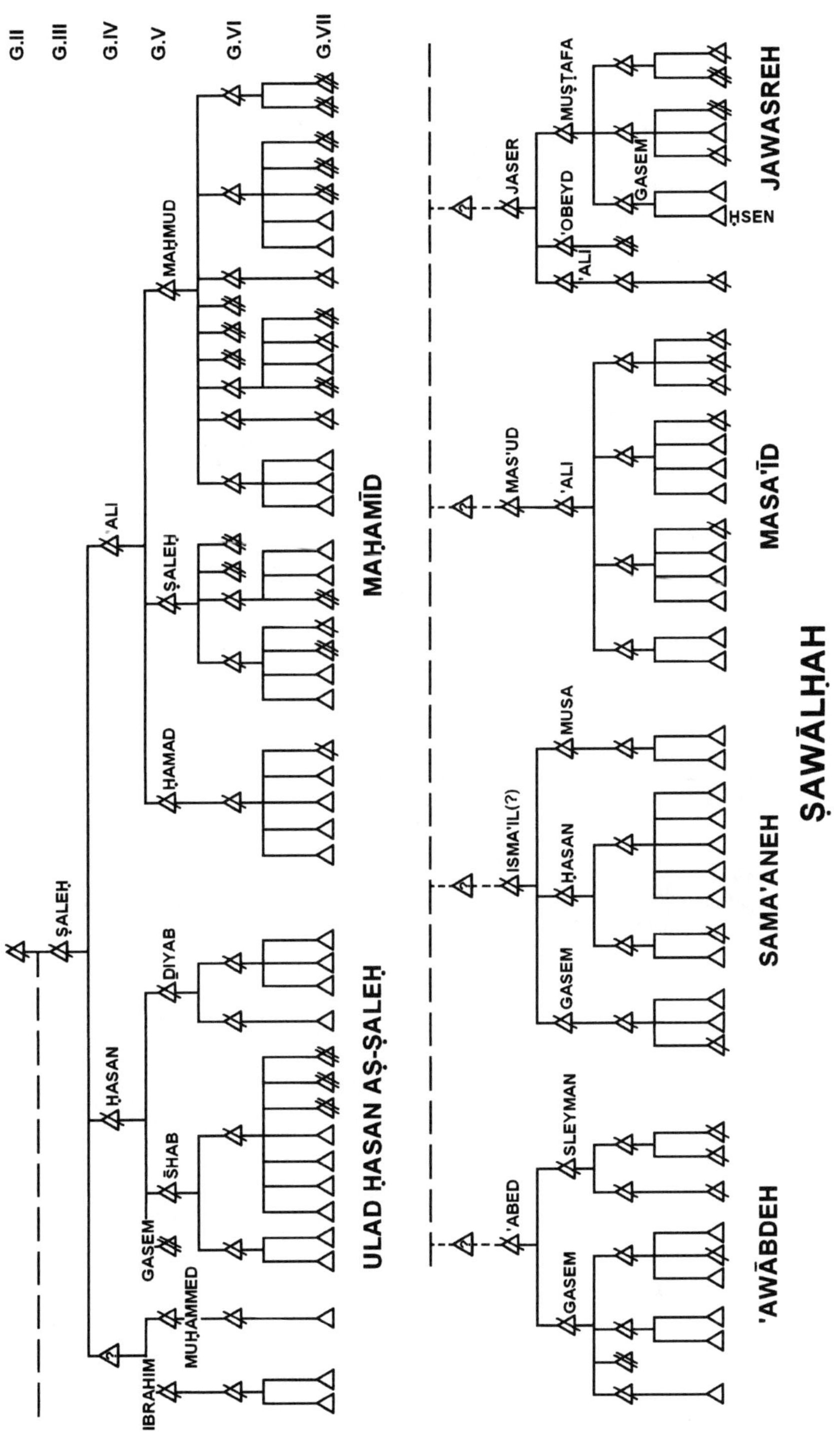
G.II
G.III
G.IV
G.V
G.VI
G.VII
ṢALEḤ
ḤASAN
'ALI
IBRAHIM
MUḤAMMED
GASEM
ŠHAB
ḌIYAB
ḤAMAD
ṢALEḤ
MAḤMUD
ULAD ḤASAN AṢ-ṢALEḤ
MAḤAMĪD
'ABED
GASEM
SLEYMAN
ISMA'IL(?)
GASEM
ḤASAN
MUSA
MAS'UD
'ALI
JASER
'ALI
'OBEYD
MUṢṬAFA
GASEM
ḤSEN
'AWĀBDEH
SAMA'ANEH
MASA'ĪD
JAWASREH
ṢAWĀLḤAH

— Appendix B —

Estimated Land/Population Ratios of Some Neighboring Villages of the ‘arab al-Ḥğerāt[a]

Village	Population	Cultivated Area[b] (in *faddāns*)[c]	Area/Person Ratio	Page Reference
Saḫnīn	1100	100	0.09	286
Ṣafūriyeh	1800	150	0.08	280
Tamrah	1200	80	0.07	273
I‘billin	800	50	0.06	169
Sha‘ab	1500	80	0.05	271
Mya‘ār	1500	30	0.02	271
Karf Manda	200	20	0.1	274

(Source: Conder and Kitchner 1881)

[a]These estimates were made in the nineteenth century, i.e., before the Ḥğerāt arrived in the Ẓahara.

[b]These figures probably refer only to parts of the cultivated areas. The figures may be, therefore, underestimates.

[c]*Faddān* = 1.038 acre, or 4200.833 m^2, or about 4.7 Palestinian *dunum* (1 *dunam* = approximately 900 m^2), or 4.2 Israeli *dunams* (1 *dunam* = 1000 m^2).

– Appendix C –

Israel: Consumer Price Index (CPI)

(1948-1977)

Year	CPI	% Increase over previous year	Year	CPI	% Increase over previous year
1948	38		1963	151	6.6
1949	39	2.2	1964	159	5.2
1950	36	-6.6	1965	171	7.7
1951	42	14.1	1966	185	8
1952	66	57.7	1967	188	1.6
1953	84	28.1	1968	192	2.1
1954	94	12.1	1969	196.3	2.3
1955	100	5.9	1970	208.3	6.1
1956	106	6.4	1971	233.3	12
1957	113	6.5	1972	263.4	12.9
1958	117	3.4	1973	316.1	20
1959	119	1.5	1974	441.5	39.7
1960	122	2.3	1975	615.1	39.3
1961	130	6.7	1976	807.6	31.3
1962	142	9.5	1977	1087	34.6

(Sources: 1948–1966: Halevi 1968:110, tb.; 1967–1977: Isr. CBS Abs. 29:267)

– Appendix D –

The 1975 Inventory of Store No. 1

I: Canned Foods

cucumbers, pickled
eggplants, pickled
hot peppers
jam
mackerel
okra
olives
peas
peas and carrots
sardines
tahini

II: Dried Foods

noodles
peanuts
pretzels
salt
spaghetti
sugar
sunflower seeds

III: Dehydrated Foods

chicken bouillon
package soups

IV: Baby Foods

powdered milk

V: Sweets

almond candy (box)
candy (by weight)
chocolate (bars, box)
wafer cookies

VI: Personal Care

cologne
hand cream
shaving cream
toothpaste

VII: Household Dry Goods

bowls
brooms, short
detergent (liquid, powder)
elastic bands
glasses
hemp washcloth (*lifeh*)
insecticide (spray, liquid)
knives (fruit)
matches
paper towels
plastic pitchers
plastic gallons
scissors
soap paste
sponges
steel wool
strainers
thread
toilet paper
toilet plungers
trays

VIII: School Supplies

notebooks
pens

IX: Miscellaneous

baby outfits
blankets
rings
shirts
sweaters
trousers
watchbands

– Appendix E –

Comparative Inventories of Stores Nos. 2 and 4 in 1975

Category	Store No. 2	Store No. 4
I: Canned Foods	cucumber, pickled	cucumber, pickled
	hot peppers	
	hummus	
	jam	
	okra	okra
	olives	
	peas	peas and carrots
	sardines	
	tomato paste	
	olive oil (5-liter cans)	
II: Dried Foods	black pepper	
	cinnamon	
	coffee	
	flavoring (powder)	
	noodles	noodles
	pretzels	pretzels
	rice (packed and by weight)	
	salt (packed and by weight)	
	sugar (packed and by weight)	
	sunflower seeds	sunflower seeds
	tea (loose)	
III: Dehydrated Foods	milk	
	packaged chicken soup	packaged chicken soup
IV: Baby Food	dried milk (canned)	
	formula (canned)	formula (canned)

Category	Store No. 2	Store No. 4
V: Sweets	almond candy (box)	candy bars
	bubble gum	gum
	Chiclets	
	chocolates (box)	chocolates (box)
	cookies	cookies
	marshmallows (choc. covered)	
	soda pop	soda pop
	wafer cookies	wafer cookies
VI: Personal Care	combs	
	hair pins	
	hand cream	
	shaving cream	
VII: Household Dry Goods	batteries	
	bowls	
	brooms	
	coffee sets (6)	
	detergent (liquid)	detergent (powder)
		hemp washcloth (*lifeh*)
	lantern wicks	
	laundry pins	
	matches	
	plates	
	platters	
	soap, paste	
	soap, powdered	
	soap, laundry	soap, laundry
	soap, toilette	
	steel wool	
		thread
VIII: School Supplies	erasers	
	notebooks	
	pens/pencils	
	rulers	rulers
	sharpeners	
IX: Miscellaneous	cigarettes (2 brands)	

– Appendix F –

The Population of Bīr al-Maksūr in 1961, 1972, and 1977 by Age and Sex

Age	April 1961			May 1972			April 1977		
	M	F	Total	M	F	Total	M	F	Total
80+	2	2	4	2		2	1	1	2
75–79				1	2	3		5	5
70–74	1		1		3	3	5	3	8
65–69	1	2	3	6	1	7	11	10	21
60–64	2	6	8	5	5	10	10	10	20
55–59	8	3	11	4	2	6	6	12	18
50–54	3	4	7	7	10	17	9	8	17
45–49	5	3	8	10	7	17	13	12	25
40–44	5	7	12	9	13	22	21	24	45
35–39	6	4	10	18	12	30	40	25	65
30–34	9	15	24	28	22	50	50	46	96
25–29	14	14	28	37	37	74	51	37	88
20–24	9	7	16	28	19	47	70	72	142
15–19	23	18	41	44	45	89	87	61	148
10–14	23	18	41	56	37	93	101	127	228
5–9	30	30	60	84	105	189	133	153	286
0–4	45	24	69	98	112	210	155	152	307
Total	*186*	*157*	*343*	*437*	*432*	*869*	*780*[a]	*776*[b]	*1556*[c]

(Sources: 1961: Golani 1961:5, tb.; 1972: Isr. CBS 1976:16–17, tb.; 1977: personal notes)

[a]Includes 17 males for whom no age was available.

[b]Includes 18 females for whom no age was available.

[c]Includes 35 individuals for whom no age was available.

– Appendix G –

A Short History of the Sedentarization of the Bedouin in Israel

The sedentarization of bedouin in Israel began, in fact, during the Mandate Period when the government attempted to resettle "landless Arabs" who were displaced due to the development of the land on which they resided (e.g., G.B. Col. 1937:37–38, Memorandum No. 11; Pls. Gov. 1946[1]:298–99). Since the PJCA (Palestine Jewish Colonization Association) and the JNF (Jewish National Fund) purchased and developed most land, it was agreed that the government would provide state land and the two agencies would prepare the site for settling the "landless Arabs" each agency displaced. Thus during the 1920s and 1930s the PJCA built Ǧisr al-Zarqa for the *'arab* al-Ġawārneh and the JNF built Umm al-Ġanam for the *'arab* al-Sa'aydeh. These projects, however, were not part of a coherent policy of the Mandate Government to sedentarize the local bedouin.

After the establishment of the State of Israel and until 1960 the JNF continued to administer the state's lands. As part of this responsibility it made some efforts to convince local tribes in the north to settle in more compact settlements, such as the effort made by Yosef Naḥmani in his aforementioned visit to the Ẓahara. Similar to those made during the Mandate Period, these efforts were only a corollary to other projects and were not part of a bedouin sedentarization policy.

A new period in the sedentarization of the bedouin in Israel can be said to have begun on July 25, 1960, with the creation of the Israel Land Administration (ILA) to manage state lands (Isr. Laws 14:50–52). This was followed by a comprehensive agreement between the JNF and the government on their respective responsibilities, including the transfer of the JNF's dealings with the bedouin to the ILA.

With the gradual transfer of control from the MG to the civilian authorities, the latter began to develop regional master plans in order to direct the development of their respective regions according to their and the state's future needs. Thus, for example, Golani's *Field Survey for the Bedouin Region: Bīr al-Maksūr* was prepared for "the Planning Department of the Ministry of the Interior and according to its guidelines" and "was to serve as a basis for a program to plan the location" (1961:2). In the northern region the plans polarized the problems associated with spontaneous bedouin settlements, primarily the twin problems of the wide scattering of houses and the resultant absence of a settlement center, or core (universal issues among bedouin; for example, cf. Amiran and Ben Arieh 1963:177–78 and Shmueli 1973:92–112 for a general discussion; Golani 1966:22–33 for the Alonim-Shfar'am Hill area; Shmueli 1970:83–92 and 1980:273–76 for the Jerusalem-Judean Desert area; Aswad 1971:44 for the Al Shiukh of the Hatay, Turkey; Montagne 1932:56 for bedouin and Kurds in the Jazireh, Syria; Katakura 1977:143, Fig. 16 for Bushur, a bedouin village near Mecca, Saudi Arabia). The severity of these problems was twofold. First, the dispersal and disorder of house sites interfered with regional planning, invaded state lands, and wasted a very scarce resource in Israel—land—thus hindering the establishment of new Jewish settlements, which, in turn, influenced both intensified economic production and state security. Second, such scattering made the provision of a modern settlement infrastructure (that is, roads, water, sewage, electricity, and so on, as well as services such as health care, postage, telephone, and the like) much more expensive than their costs in a planned settlement.

Consequently, in order to plan the region it became imperative to develop a coherent governmental policy to sedentarize the bedouin in planned settlements that more efficiently used land and permitted the provision of civil services including transportation linkage to the residents' places of work. The first experiment in this regard began in 1962 with the planning of Basmat Ṭab'un for the *'arab* al-Zbeydāt and the *'arab* al-Sa'adiyeh. By 1965/66 these plans were in an advanced stage and when the MG was abrogated in 1966 and the civilian authorities achieved full legal powers in the region they began to realize some of the plans.

Until 1973 three agencies were prominent in dealing with bedouin settlement: the Bureau of the Advisor on Arab Affairs (BAAA) in the prime minister's office as a supervisory body; the Ministry of the Interior as the regional planner, the guardian of the legality of house construction, and responsible for settlements' self-government; and the ILA as the agency in charge of bedouin settlement planning and of providing the settlement with its infrastructure. Other agencies such as the Ministry of Habitation (which provided easy-terms loans for house construction) or the Ministry of Education (which financed the schools in the settlements), while participating to a greater or lesser extent, were much less visible. The budget for the project, however, although predominately going to the ILA, which coordinated its expenditure, was divided among all the agencies, causing duplicated services and wastage. Similarly, the ministries' personnel often were more loyal to their own political party, which held the ministry as part of the government's coalition agreements, than to the bedouin project, causing many mistakes and partisan intrigues to plague the project.

In the parliamentary elections of 1973 the bedouin in the south and the north united to form the Arabic Bedouin List (the ABL) to the Knesset, which won a seat in that institution. This show of unity and voting power and the appearance of regional speakers for the bedouin, combined with the ILA's refusal to deal with sedentarization per se (it lay outside its legal authority) and the government's realization of the need for a coordinated policy in order to avoid waste and loopholes, promoted the formation of two Supreme Bedouin Committees, one for the north (NSBC) and the other for the south (SSBC).

The major function of the committees was to coordinate and control the government's bedouin sedentarization program. For that purpose each committee included representative(s) of each of the governmental agencies dealing with the bedouin in particular and/or administering the region as a whole under the chairmanship of the Advisor on Arab Affairs. Each of the two committees also included a bedouin member who sat on its executive board. During the field study period the bedouin representative in the SSBC was the MK of the Arab Bedouin List, *šeyḫ* Ḥamād Abū Rabī'a, and in the NSBC the list's number two man, Muḥammad al-Ḥsēn, *muḫtār 'arab* al-Ḥ̮ğerāt.

As of 1977 the bedouin policy was de facto controlled by the executive boards of the respective committees through their control of the budget, which was channeled to them via the Ministry of Habitation budget. During fiscal 1975/76 and 1976/77 the budget per committee was I£15 million and during 1977/78 it was I£20 million (or 0.06%, 0.04%, and 0.04%) of the government's total budget respectively (source of government budgets: Isr. CBS Abs. 29:615). In the north, these sums were used to finance the construction of infrastructure in the original fourteen planned settlements and to provide grants for special projects such as connecting a settlement to the regional electrical network.

Although the project became much more efficient, better organized, and more responsive to the needs and wants of the bedouin than ever before, two major problems plagued its smooth functioning. First were partisan politics, which circumvented or outright contradicted the committee's policies in order to win votes for the parliamentary elections. Second was the characteristic of "complementary opposition" (Sahlins 1961:332–33), inherent in bedouin tribal organization (e.g., the aforementioned rivalry over the school in Beit Zarzir), and bedouin use of loopholes created by partisan politics (e.g., to demand recognition of spontaneous settlements as official settlements over and beyond the fourteen planned ones). These problems were severe enough that at least one committee member representing one of the ministries remarked in July 1977 that he thought the policy had lost all credibility with the bedouin, who were making it a laughingstock.

An example of the operation of these two problems was the Ministry of the Interior's move to replace the settlements' *maḫatīr* by appointing local councils. Objectively, the *muḫtār* position had been gradually emptied of its official functions by the post-MG normalization of the operation of the Arab sector. Thus, the Ministries of Health and the Interior kept vital statistics, the Ministry of Agriculture monitored disease and controlled agriculture and animal husbandry, and so on. Consequently, it was within the state's interest to reduce the duplication of agencies and to establish local councils that would only administer the settlement within the confines of the bureaucratic framework of the Ministry of the Interior. Moreover, since local councils were elected bodies and *maḫatīr* were nominated officials, replacing the *maḫatīr* by local councils was a strike for democracy that allowed the state to claim that it did what it could to eliminate the differences between Arab settlements and their Jewish counterparts.

In addition to the state's own reasons for the policy, the Ministry of the Interior, in whose jurisdiction the matter and its execution lay, and the *MafDaL*, which controlled this ministry since the early 1950s, had their own ulterior motives, which contravened the state's interests. Local council budgets—save for the monies derived from local taxes—as well as other administrative benefits were channeled though the ministry's district commissioner, which enabled him to patronize factions in the village and play them against each other in order to gain votes for his party. For example, during the 1973 and 1977 elections the *MafDaL* had received at least 7.2% and 4.2% respectively (calculated from Isr. IGE 1978:47–54, tb. 7) from Arab communities, which had inherently very little in common with this right-wing Jewish religious party that was not pro-Arab or neutral by any means. (For example, one of its MKs was the leader and parliamentary sponsor of Gush Emunim, the militant colonizing movement that had been establishing settlements in the Occupied Territories, while another of its members, a district commissioner, authored the "Koenig Report" or "Document," which recommended that the government "establish a policy of reward or punishment (legally) to leaders and settlements who express hostility to the state and to Zionism in any form," "increase the presence of the various police and security forces in the Arab street [sector]," "find a way to neutralize the giving of Allowances to families with many children [the Institute of National Insurance's Children's Allowance] to the Arab population," and so on [*Yedi'ot Aharonot* Oct. 7, 1976:1; Hameiri 1976; *Ma'ariv* Oct. 8:1; Meizles 1976; etc.].) The motives of the ministry are even clearer when the *MafDaL*'s loss of votes (which went to *RaQaH*) between the two elections is calculated by settlement type. In settlement types where the influence of a district commissioner was relatively small due to the sheer size of the population and the established character of, and services in, the settlement, *MafDaL* lost votes. For example, in Arab cities/towns there was a decline from 4.0% to 2.2% respectively; in urban settlements it fell from 6.0% to 3.0%; and in large villages from 9.8% to 5.2%. By contrast, in those settlement types with a greater need for services or for an officially recognized status in order to force other agencies to provide services, such as small villages and bedouin tribes, the figures went from 6.1% down to 6.0% and from 2.2% up to 2.7% respectively (calculated from Isr. IGE 1978:47–54, tb. 7).

That this process was in operation for quite some time is suggested by a similar scenario that emerges from an analysis of the election to the Seventh Knesset (1969) depicted in diagram form (Isr. IGE 1970:3, diagram no. 1). The figure describes the success in the elections to local authorities that took place in many locations at the same time as a national election. The striking feature of the figure is that whereas, save for the religious parties, all the parties in the diagram that participated in the elections for local authorities lost votes in the parliamentary election, the religious parties experienced an overall increased support for the Knesset in those settlements that elected local authorities (see also Isr. IGE 1970: VIII). Thus although on the surface the move to replace *maḫatīr* with local councils appeared to be a move toward democratic self-rule, in reality it rendered the Arab minority even less competitive for state resources than it had been before, while enabling strategically located political parties to exploit the Arab voter even further, thereby undermining the government's bedouin sedentarization efforts.

– Appendix H –

Letter of Complaint Over the Mismanagement of the Water Co-Operative Society of Bīr al-Maksūr

(translated from Hebrew)

To:

The Registrar of Co-Operative Societies Ministry of Agriculture Jerusalem	The Supervisory Board of Co-Operative Societies [*Histadrut*] Tel Aviv

January 5, 1975
Dear Sirs,

Re: al-Ḥğerāt Society for Drinking Water; a demand to convene a general meeting in order to elect a new [executive] board to the said society

We the undersigned request you to see to it that a general meeting of the membership of the society be convened for the election of a new board to replace the present board. These are the reasons for the request:

Already in the minutes of the August 31, 1974 general meeting of the society it was decided that at the beginning of 1975 there would be held a general election for a new board. Although the appointed date had passed, to the present date neither was a new board elected nor was a general meeting convened.

The present situation in the village is pitiful and general chaos plagues the provision of water. People receive water even though they have no [water] meters and are not members; much water is wasted; negligent fee collection; as well as negligence in accountancy and record keeping. Your intervention in the functioning of our society can suffer no delay, and it is [legally] right and just to convene immediately a general meeting to elect a new board to the said society.

I am [sic] waiting therefore to your positive reply and swift intervention.

Sincerely yours,

The Members of
the al-Ḥğerāt Society
COPY:

Mr. –	Control Board *Histadrut* Nazareth

– Appendix I –

Minority Relations in Israel

Some Aspects of Ethnicity and the Military

The competition between the Druze, the Ḥĝerāt, and the Heīb was about securing a better deal from the authorities than the rest of the Arab minorities in Israel could. The three groups thus used the security complex as a means of rising out of the minority "immutable" (i.e., powerless) category in the power hierarchy of the state (cf. Vincent 1974:377) and the low status of the Arab sector at large not only to gain benefits for their own membership but also to try to monopolize (albeit generally unsuccessfully) the link to the authorities in order to force other groups into clientage to their mediation. Ideally, these competitive relations have two directions: a vertical axis between each group and the authorities, along which the group bargains for as good a deal as it can get and which channels the benefits down, and a horizontal axis among the groups in the field, in which they react, one to the initiatives of the others, and along which the benefits/obligations flow laterally. Interestingly it was the lateral flow and its dynamics that have been neglected in the discussion of the minority-military relations in Israel (e.g., Ben Dor 1973; Oppenheimer 1977, 1978; Enloe 1980: passim).

This neglect seems to be the result of "emic" perspective versus "etic" analyses. Those Ḥĝeri informants I have asked about their involvement with the security complex clearly saw the horizontal intra-sectoral rivalry and were aware of the benefits of monopolizing the vertical access to the authorities. Thus, their drive to get into the IDA was a declared response to Druze soldiering while their attempts to become officers were a response to the virtual monopoly held by the Heīb over the nomination of candidates for the officers' course. The Heīb, as I will presently show, seemed to share the Ḥĝeri view—at least in regard to the interaction between these two tribes.

The Druze, by contrast, were reported by Oppenheimer (1978:32–33) to perceive their conscription as a completely internal development caused by their traditional leaders who "were interested in the establishment of an institutional framework which would provide them with offices, and hence, resources for broadening and legitimization of their leadership and influence, and for the chanelling [sic] of favours to themselves and to their supporters" and who "were pressed into making the request [for a covenant] in exchange for specific favours" (1978:33). In the main this view seems to be corroborated by the perceptions of the authorities as presented by one official who was directly involved in the process and who told me that "after the war 'X' went to their [Druze and Circassians] Elders and told them that this is a democracy and it is their country and that they have to defend it like the Jews . . . and later they [the authorities] got Ṣāleḥ al-Ḫnefes to sign [the document for] their conscription."

Nevertheless, the history of the involvement of Ṣāleḥ al-Ḫnefes with the Ḥĝerāt, as well as the Shfar'amean Druze who were killed because they were Druze and the Druze villages raided during the 1936–1939 Arab Rebellion, suggests that apart from grinding their own axes, as Oppenheimer reports, the Druze leadership was responding to and/or mobilizing fears and sentiments that were present at the time (i.e., the early and mid-1950s) in the Druze community at large. This appears all the more plausible when it is realized that conscription eliminated the role of low and middle leadership as mediators between the authorities and prospective enlistees, a role with the widest distribution of benefits, as in medieval feudalism (see also Enloe 1980:23). Whether, however, the Druze had responded to specific rivals similarly to the Ḥğerāt's responsiveness to the Druze remains unclear, although they clearly responded to the Arab sector in general.

There is little doubt that indirectly, through their vertical interaction with each of the groups, the authorities sustained, revitalized, and deepened the ethnicity of both Druze and bedouin and set them further apart from the rest of the Moslem Arab sector (for a fuller discussion of this issue in general see Enloe 1980). In fact, it seems likely that the authorities consciously fed this division of loyal groups from the rest of the Arab sector by, for example, using the Border Guard instead of police to rid Arab Nazareth of the protection racket, violence, and hoodlums in April 1976, a deployment all the more conspicuous for coming after the aforementioned March 30 *yūm al-'arḍ* (to my knowledge, the Border Guard had not been used for ridding organized and unorganized crime in the Jewish sector). Another example was the late arrival of the police to Kafr Yāsīf (whose local council was in the hands of *RaQaH*), thus allowing the Druze of Ǧūlis ample time to vent their rage on the Yasifeans with no interference (cf. Hareuveni 1981). Needless to emphasize, such tactics revitalized and deepened the ethnic identities of all concerned, including the Arab sector at large, which had been channeling its frustration into national aspirations, a process that was popularly called "the Palistinization of Israeli Arabs."

The authorities had no need of a policy of willfully and systematically playing the Druze and bedouin against each other on the horizontal axis in order to gain a better deal (i.e., conscripts) from either. First, it seems there was enough pre-Israel history to give the rivalry a momentum of its own. Second, although conscription was a concrete benefit, the main use of minorities in the IDA, as I have argued before, was the demonstration of their open support for the Jewish state, permitting Israel to project an image of social democracy and thus—among other items—enabling it to ask for and receive Jewish and non-Jewish world support, without which it could not survive. It should be kept in mind, however, that high-ranking individuals within the state apparatus promoted their personal protégés in competition with the protégés of other high-ranking officials and officers, protégés who might be members of the three groups: Druze, Ḥğerāt, or Heīb. Such personal rivalry, while influencing the regional scene, was not a state policy to promote competition among the three groups.

— Appendix J —

The ṣulḥa Agreement between the Masarwah and the Yūnis of the Villages of ʻĀra and ʻArʻara[a]

(translation from the Hebrew copy of the Police)

IN THE NAME OF GOD THE FORGIVING AND THE MERCIFUL
AGREEMENT OF ṢULḤA (CONCILIATION)

The *ṣulḥa* Committee consisting of the undersigned convened in the house of Mr. Muḥammad Khaled Masarwah on Monday 25/10/76 [October 25, 1976]; and in reference to the authorization given (to the Committee) by the two disputing families Masarwah—and Yūnis in the villages ʻĀra-ʻArʻara and after consideration in the matter (of the conflict) between the said two families which caused the death of Ahmed Ḥsēn Marzuq and Muḥammad ʻAbd al-Hafiz Marzuq, of blessed memory, the Committee has decided the following decisions:—

(1) The *ṣulḥa* [ceremony] between the said two families will be [performed] according to the traditional "*ʻašeyrī*"[b] manner, and it will include all the members of these families and it will bind them all.

(2) To surrender all rights; to cancel all mutual complaints of the two sides in regard to matters of property.

(3) To surrender all personal rights without interfering in the legal procedures of [i.e., regarding] the said two casualties in the matter of the deaths.

(4) The Committee decided that the Yūnis family will pay the sum of 90 thousand *lirôt* "as *diyah*" (as ransom) for the said two slain.

(5) The Committee decides to make general *ṣulḥa* [ceremony] on Saturday 6/11/76 [November 6, 1976], 12 noon[.] After the *ṣulḥa* anyone who wants to return to his house (his habitation) may do so in peace.

(6) The Committee recommends that all complaints regarding matters of property will be canceled by the two sides; without the payment of any damages.

(7) The Committee decides that the two sides are obligated to preserve peace and tranquility [or, security]; and not to damage any property, apartments, etc. As of this date any side which will violate this condition will be solely responsible for its deeds.

This is our decision and God will lead us; the agreement was written and signed on Monday 25/10/76 [October 25, 1976], 2 in the month of *Dhu al-Qa'dah* 1396 according to the Hijra date.

---

[a]This is an English translation of the Hebrew copy of the original document in Arabic. The Hebrew copy was kept at the police station nearest to the two villages, and my deepest gratitude to Police Commander Peri for his help in securing a photocopy of that copy. In its translation I tried to keep as close to the Hebrew text and punctuation as possible and if a few commas are missing, so be it. Finally, the words in parentheses are original Hebrew clarifications to the Arabic text, while those in square parentheses are my own clarifications to the Hebrew text.

[b]Notice the influence of Muḥammad al-Ḥsēn in imposing the bedouin tribal code (*ʻašeyrī* refers to the *ganūn al-'aša'īr* [lit. "Law of the Tribes"]) on a *fellāḥīn ṣulḥa* agreement.

– Appendix K –

The Land Problem in the Negev

The land problem in the Negev stems from two issues: one legal and the other practical. Legally, the 1858 Ottoman Land Code classified the land of the Negev as *mawāt* (lit. "dead" land), "which is occupied by no one and has not been left for the use of the public. . . . (Land Code, Act 6)" (Doukhan 1938:80), and which, therefore, falls under the *miri* category: "state land, the legal ownership of which is vested in the Treasury, . . . the enjoyment of which is granted by the government [Art. 3]" (Doukhan 1938:77; see also Pls. Gov. 1946[I]:233). The Government of Israel, following the Mandate Government's Land Ordinance of 1921—which repealed the provision of Article 103 of the Ottoman Code that allowed for a person cultivating a *mawāt* land without authorization to pay its registration fee and receive a title deed to it at the discretion of the authorities (Doukhan 1938:81)—considers the Negev to be its ultimate property.

The same ordinance, however, provided also for bedouin claims by allowing for "[a]ny person who has already cultivated such waste land [at the time of publication of the ordinance]" to notify the authorities within two months and apply for a title deed for it (Doukhan 1938:81). As late as 1946 the Mandate Government conceded that regarding the area of Beersheba (about 12,552 km^2) "[i]t is possible that there may be private claims to over 2000 square kilometres which are cultivated from time to time" (Pls. Gov. 1946[I]:257) and that "[i]t is frequently difficult to assume that there was in the past no [land] grant and consequently it is not safe to assume that all the empty lands south of Beersheba . . . , for instance, are *mawāt*" (Pls. Gov. 1946[I]:256).

The bedouin, meanwhile, both for reasons of kin-responsibilities—that is, making claims for relatives who are in the diaspora, such as Jordan, under the name of a claim maker in Israel—and for reasons of "negative reciprocity" (Sahlins 1972:195–96), because they mistrust the government and its intentions, have made claims often in excess of the estimated farm size limits under traditional conditions of local bedouin economy. Boneh (1981:31), for example, reports claims of 1000–2000 *dunam* each for extended families in the group he studied and comments that the claims are somewhat "suspicious" due to the rounding-off of claim figures and due to the high correspondence between current kin-unit size to claim size (i.e., units with 8–10 nuclear families claiming 2000 *dunam* while smaller units claim progressively smaller sizes), which do not always correspond to their pre-1949 conditions.

Practically, the problem has been intensified by the sense of mission of the Israeli government, which tries to convert as much as possible the land in Israel to the land *of* Israel (i.e., Jewish people-owned land), a mission well encoded in the term employed: *g'ullat adamah* (lit. the "redemption" or "deliverance" of land). Consequently, the MG and later the ILA tried to gain control of the Negev lands by "a doctrine of expulsion at first, which later turned into a doctrine of land expropriation, using legal means" (Marx and Sela‘ n.d.:4), while dragging out the settlement of the claims in the courts. The result has been bedouin despair at the prospect of an equitable legal settlement (e.g., Boneh 1981:28–30) and intensifying resentment whose echoes could be heard among the Ḥğerāt, who accepted land expropriation for public use as such but resented the differential allocation of such public land between Jews (all) and Arabs (none) once it was expropriated.

– Appendix L –

Election Practices in the Arab Sector

In order to explain these practices—as well as the general voting milieu in the Arab sector—it is necessary to describe the act of voting in Israel in the mid-1970s. Succinctly, a voter approaches the poll box committee, identifies her/himself, and receives from the committee chairperson (who is the all-powerful presence) an official election envelope that she/he takes to the voting booth or enclosure. There the voter finds a latticework tabletop stacked with packs of approximately 3 × 4-inch loose note pages bearing the name and identifying letter code of a party/list. Each party/list is represented by such a pack and the chairperson is responsible for ensuring that there are enough notes of each in the latticework tabletop. The voter puts a single note (with no additional marks on it to ensure the anonymity of the vote) in the envelope, emerges from the booth, inserts the envelope in the poll box located in front of the committee desk, and leaves. At the end of the day, the box is opened by the chairperson in front of the committee members and the votes are counted in their presence as well as in the presence of any other official representative of a party/list not represented on the committee. The results are recorded on tally sheets and signed, and the box, notes, and tally sheets are shipped to the Regional Election Committee, which forwards it to the National Committee.

According to a veteran Labor Party election activist (a non-Ḥğeri bedouin) who has been involved with that party's campaigns in the Arab sector since the 1950s, the earliest and simplest voting practice was "the shopping basket method," as it was sometimes descriptively called. According to this method, one person—usually the *muḫtār*—would come to the poll station with a shopping basket full of his lineage, village, or tribesmembers' ID cards. Provided the chairperson was "ours," he would get a batch of envelopes and vote for the whole group, although he had to remember to cast a few votes for other parties (e.g., those of the other committee members) to avert suspicion in the regional or national checks. This method was easy for all concerned because for the majority of the Arab voters the elections were a meaningless hassle in the face of the reality of the MG and the loss of a working day. It also reinforced the image in the Jewish sector that the Arab sector voted by lineages, thereby perpetuating the doctrine of dealing with lineage heads instead of with voters. Finally, it caused the 99–100% participation rate in quite a number of Arab settlements across the country during the 1950s and was at least a partial cause in the heavier participation rate of Arabs over Jews from the establishment of the MG (1951) and through 1973, as Table 31 shows.

As other parties moved into the Arab sector and competition intensified, the "voting" methods were elaborated and cross-fertilized among the respective party activists, while providing the rest of the explanation for the heavier Arab participation rate as well as a partial explanation for the relative uniformity of the voting patterns. The simplest and basic method was to buy votes for cash or in barter. For example, an informant from the *'arab* al-Ǧawāmīs told me that during the 1977 campaign the *Likud* Party "gave in many houses of the Ǧawāmīs about I£200 for the vote of the family." Another campaigner for the UAL told me that the same party offered I£15,000 to the Elder of a leading lineage of the *'arab* al-Heīb but that "he will go with us for old friendship's sake" and for a symbolic I£2000 (which was all that the Labor Party would give). Aside from cash—which was what the parties outside the administration ladled out—votes could be assured by barter against special favors from the administration, predominantly the Labor and *MafDaL*.

Since both cash purchases and barter deals required a monitoring procedure to ensure proper delivery of the votes, the paying party voting note would be bent or folded in a predetermined way, the chairperson or a "party observer" would scratch the envelope in which the note was placed with his nail, and other similar methods were developed to subvert the anonymity of the vote ("which, of course, is secret" as Landau [1969:152] had commented). It is hardly surprising, then, that the participation of the Arabs was heavier than that of the national average—they had to pay back and usually in advance. (What is surprising, in fact, is that studies of the voting behavior of the Arab sector such as Landau's *The Arabs in Israel: A Political Study* attribute this heavy participation to "a growing appreciation of the democratic process," or to a "wish to react to legislation directly affecting them," and so on [Landau 1969:150].)

The uniformity of votes was ensured by yet another method. Again the bedouin Labor campaigns' veteran provided details: once voting ended and the poll box was opened (sometimes prematurely if particularly troublesome representation of the competition was opportunely out of the room), it was sometimes "switched" or "changed" (i.e., the notes of the competition replaced with those of one's own party) while counting the votes. This method was particularly rewarding in the "small polls" (i.e., settlements) that were, as he said, "the real bread." If a poll box was really "bad" (i.e., contained a solid vote or too many votes for the competition), it "might get lost" on the way to the Regional Committee's headquarters. He himself once "lost" a poll box in this way and, for example, the publication of the 1959 election results (Isr. IGE 1961: tb. 23) contains no entry for the poll box of the Ġadāyreh in Bīr al-Maksūr because "[m]ay be that for now unknown reasons the voting results were not received at the Central Committee" (Schild, Deputy General Inspector of Elections, pers. comm., 1981). Nor is that the only instance of missing data in the 1951–1977 election returns.

To these methods one might add those used by *RaQaH* in the December 1975 municipal election in Nazareth according to a Labor Party Arab department official during briefings for the 1977 "regional campaign headquarters' coordinators" held in Tel Aviv in May 1977. One method was to cover each of the note stacks with a few notes of *RaQaH* so that the next voter would see only these and, not finding his/her choice, would choose to place a *RaQaH* note in the envelope instead of going back to the committee's desk. Or, ink mark the side or back of the notes in the packs of the competition in the enclosure, thus voiding them when found in the poll box for they were no

Table 31. Comparative voting participation of the Ḥğerāt, the Arab sector, and the national average (90% Jewish) 1949-1977 (percent).

	Election Year								
	1949	1951	1955	1959	1961	1965	1969	1973	1977
Ḥğerāt	-	99.5	94.5	84	86.5	85	85	90	53.5
Arab Sector	79.3	85.5	91	88.9	85.6	87.8	82	80	76.2
National Average	86.9	75.1	82.8	81.6	81.6	83	81.7	78.6	79.2

(Sources: Arab participation, 1949–1973: Isr. MI 1977:446, 1977: Isr. IGE 1978: XV; national average 1949–1977: Isr. IGE 1978: IX, tb. 2)

longer anonymous. Or, take away the whole note pack of a major competitor from the voting enclosure so that when the next voter looked for this note and did not find it, he/she would choose a note of someone else (hopefully *RaQaH*), or he/she would tell the chairperson "there are no notes of 'X'," thereby disqualifying him/herself because the vote was no longer anonymous. (He/she should say "there are notes missing here" or some such general phrase and no more.) Or, if one was more actively inclined, one could block the street on which the voting station was located so that no cars of the competition could go through to bring voters to the poll, or hassle pedestrian prospective voters for the competition if the cars dropped them at the end of the blocked street. Or, as unknown activists had done in 'Afulah and Tel Aviv in 1981, puncture the tires of the cars of the competitor's activists (in this case the Labor Party's) on the night before the election (*Ma'ariv* June 30, 1981:1).

This repertoire of methods for enhancing the "democratic process" in the Arab sector was compiled in regard to the Galilee as a whole and has grown in sophistication over time. It is, therefore, not strictly descriptive of Ḥğeri voting practices. Nevertheless, this was the general atmosphere in the sector and, as such, is informative of the probable cause for the reversal between the relative unanimity during the MG era and the growing diversity thereafter. Moreover, although much of this repertoire may no longer be in practice, this information is necessary for understanding the period.

References

Abir, Mordechai

1975 Local leadership and early reforms in Palestine 1800–1834. In *Studies on Palestine during the Ottoman Period*, edited by Moshe Ma'oz, pp. 284–310. Jerusalem: Magness Press.

Abou-Zeid, Ahmed

1965 Honour and shame among the bedouin of Egypt. In *Honour and Shame: The Values of Mediterranean Society*, edited by Jean G. Peristiany, pp. 243–59. London: Weidenfeld and Nicolson.

Abramson, Arieh

1937 'al dmey re'im; 'im hatzon (Of friends' blood; With the flock). In *kovetz hashômêr* (*The Compilation of hashomer*), pp. 211–18. The Archive and Museum of the Labour Movement. Tel Aviv: The Labour Archive.

Al Hamishmar

1976 bamigzar ha'aravi haserîm 3000 hadrey kitah (The Arab sector is short by 3000 classrooms). *Al Hamishmar* (Tel Aviv) July 6, 1976.

Allon, Ygal

1965 *ma'arâchôt Palmah: mgamot vama'as* (*Battles of the Palmach: Orientations and Deeds*). Tel Aviv: Hakibutz Hameuchad.

Amiran, D.H.K.

1953 The pattern of settlement in Palestine—I, II, III. *Israel Exploration Journal* 3:65–78, 192–209, 250–60.

Amiran, D.H.K., and Y. Ben Arieh

1963 Sedentarization of bedouin in Israel. *Israel Exploration Journal* 13:161–81.

Antonius, George
1938 *The Arab Awakening: The Story of the Arab National Movement*. London: Hamish Hamilton.

Antropova, V.V., and V.G. Kuznetzova
1964 The Chukchi. In *The Peoples of Siberia*, edited by M.G. Levin and L.P. Potapov, translation edited by S. Dunn, pp. 799–835. Chicago: University of Chicago Press.

Arad, A.
1975 L'ân n'elâm 'ôtzar hamdînâh (Where disappeared the exchequer). In *hashever* (*The Crisis*), edited by Sh. Everon et al., pp. 74–93. Israel: Hôtzâ'âh Myuhedt.

Aref, 'Aref el
1937 *shivtey habedu'îm bemahôz Be'er sheva* (*The Bedouin Tribes of BeersHêba District*), translated by M. Kapelyuk. Tel Aviv: Bustenaî.

Aronoff, Myron J.
1977 *Power and Ritual in the Israel Labor Party: A Study in Political Anthropology*. Assen/Amsterdam: Van Gorcum.

Arthur, George
1920 *Life of Lord Kitchner*. London: Macmillan and Co.

Ashbel, Dov
1947–50 *ha'aqlîm be'eretz Yisrâ'êl ûshkhênôteyha* (Annual Report of *The Climate of Palestine and Adjacent Countries*, Nos. 26–29). Tel Aviv: Sifriyat haSâdeh.
1957 *Encyclopaedia Hêbraica*, 1st ed., 6:159–78, s.v. "ha'aqlîm" ("climate").

Ashkenazi, Tuvia
1938 *Tribus Semi-Nomades de la Palestine du Nord*. Paris: Paul Geuthner.
1957 *habedvîm hayeyhem ûmînhâgeyhem* (*The Bedouin, Their Lifeways and Customs*). Jerusalem: Rubin Mass.

Assaf, Michael
1967 *toldôt hâ'arâvîm byisrâ'êl* (*History of the Arabs in Palestine*). Vol. 3, *hit'orerut ha'arâvîm ubrîhâtâm* (*Arab Awakening and Flight*), Pt. 1. Tel Aviv: Tarbut VeHinukh.

Aswad, Barbara C.
1971 *Property Control and Social Strategies in Settlers in a Middle Eastern Plain*. Anthropological Papers, no. 44. Ann Arbor: Museum of Anthropology, University of Michigan.

Avitsur, Shmuel
1975 The influence of western technology on the economy of Palestine during the nineteenth century. In *Studies on Palestine during the Ottoman Period*, edited by Moshe Ma'oz, pp. 485–94. Jerusalem: Magness Press.
1976 *âdâm ve'amâlô* (*Man and His Work*). Jerusalem: Carta.

Awad, Mohamed
1959 Settlement of nomadic and semi-nomadic tribal groups in the Middle East. *International Labour Review* 79(1):25–56.

Bachrach, Peter, and Morton Baratz
1962 Two faces of power. *The American Political Science Review* 56:947–52.

Badia y Leblich, Domingo
1816 *The Travels of Ali Bey el Abbassi . . . between the Years 1803–1807*. London: Longman, Hurst, Rees, Orme and Brown.

Baer, Gabriel
1971 *mavô' letôldôt hayahasîm ha'agrâriyim bamizrah-hatikhon 1800–1970* (*Introduction to the History of Agrarian Relations in the Middle East 1800–1970*). Tel Aviv: Hakibutz Hameuchad.
1975 The impact of economic change on traditional society in nineteenth century Palestine. In *Studies on Palestine during the Ottoman Period*, edited by Moshe Ma'oz, pp. 495–98. Jerusalem: Magness Press.

Bailey, Clinton (Yitzhak)
1970 The Communist Party and the Arabs in Israel. *Midstream* (New York) 16(5):38–56.

Bailey, Yitzhak (Clinton), and Rafi Peled
1975 *shivtey habedvîm besinay* (*Bedouin Tribes of the Sinai*). N.p.: Government of Israel, Ministry of Defense, Sinai Region Command.

Barth, Fredrik
1954 Father's brother's daughter marriage in Kurdistan. *Southwestern Journal of Anthropology* 10:164–71.
1961 *Nomads of South Persia: The Basseri Tribe of the Khamseh Confederacy*. Boston: Little, Brown and Co.
1969 Introduction. In *Ethnic Groups and Boundaries*, edited by Fredrik Barth, pp. 9–38. Boston: Little, Brown and Co.

Bates, Daniel G.
1973 *Nomads and Farmers: A Study of the Yörük of Southeastern Turkey*. Anthropological Papers, no. 52. Ann Arbor: Museum of Anthropology, University of Michigan.

Beer, Stafford
1972 *Brain of the Firm: A Development in Management Cybernetics*. New York: Herder and Herder.
1974 *Designing Freedom*. London: John Wiley and Sons.
1975 *Platform for Change: A Message from Stafford Beer*. London: John Wiley and Sons.

Ben Dor, Gavriel
1973 The military in politics of integration and innovation: The case of the Druze minority in Israel. *Journal of Asian and African Studies* (Jerusalem) 9:343–69.

Ben Porath, Yoram
1966 *The Arab Labor Force in Israel*. Jerusalem: Maurice Falk Institute.

Ben Shemesh, A.
1953 *hûqey haqarqa'ôt bmdînât yisrâ'êl* (*Land Laws of the State of Israel*). Tel Aviv: Massada.

Ben Shemesh, A. (translator)
1979 *The Noble Koran*. Tel Aviv: Massada.

Berger, Morroe
1962 *The Arab World Today*. Garden City, N.Y.: Doubleday and Co.

Bergheim, Samuel
1894 Land tenure in Palestine. *Palestine Exploration Fund Quarterly Statement* 1894:191–99.

Boneh, Dan
1981 *mimtzay mehqar beqerev qvûtzâh bedu'it mimfuney 1949, hayoshevet besmikhut l'ayarah tel sheva'* (*Findings of Research among a Bedouin Group of the 1949 Evacuees, Located Near the Town of Tel Sheva*). Beersheba (Israel): Government of Israel, Law of Land Acquisition in the Negev (Peace Treaty with Egypt) 1980, Implementation Authority.
1983 *Facing Uncertainty: The Social Consequences of Forced Sedentarization among the Jaraeen Bedouin, Negev, Israel*. Ann Arbor: UMI.

Bongaarts, John
1980 Does malnutrition affect fecundity? A summary of evidence. *Science* 208:564–69.

Bowden, Tom
1975 Policing Palestine 1920–1936. In *Police Forces in History*, edited by George L. Mosse, pp. 122–30. London/Beverly Hills, CA: Sage Publications.

Brazelton, T. Berry
1969 *Infants and Mothers*. New York: Delacorte Press.
1974 *Toddlers and Parents*. New York: Dell Publishing Co.

Buckingham, James S.
1821 *Travels among the Arab Tribes, including a Journey from Nazareth to the Mountains beyond the Dead Sea*. London: Longman, Hurst, Rees, Orme and Brown.

Burckhardt, J.L.
1822 *Travels in Syria and the Holy Land*. London: J. Murray.

Cohen, Amnon
1973 *Palestine in the 18th Century: Patterns of Government and Administration*. Jerusalem: Magness Press.

Cohen, Amnon, and Bernard Lewis
1978 *Population and Revenue in the Towns of Palestine in the Sixteenth Century*. Princeton: Princeton University Press.

Conder, Claude R.
1878 *Tent Work in Palestine*. London: Richard Bently and Son.
1880 *Map of Western Palestine* . . . London: Palestine Exploration Fund.
1889a *The Survey of Eastern Palestine*. Vol. 1, *The 'Adwan Country*. London: Palestine Exploration Fund.
1889b *Palestine*. New York: Dodd, Mead and Co.

Conder, Claude R., and H.H. Kitchner
1881 *The Survey of Western Palestine*. Vol. 1, *The Galilee*. London: Palestine Exploration Fund.
1882 *The Survey of Western Palestine*. Vol. 2, *Samaria*. London: Palestine Exploration Fund.

Coon, Carleton S.
1958 *Caravan: The Story of the Middle East*. New York: Holt, Rinehart and Winston.

Deng, Francis M.
1972 *The Dinka of the Sudan*. New York: Holt, Rinehart and Winston.

Dickson, Bertram
1910 Journeys in Kurdistan. *The Geographical Journal* (London) 35:357–79.

Diqs, Isaak
1969 *A Bedouin Boyhood*. New York: Praeger.

Donovan, Bernard T.
1979 *The New Encyclopaedia Britannica* (*Macropaedia*), 15th ed., 10:582–84, s.v. "lactation, human."

Doukhan, Moses J.
1938 Land tenure. In *Economic Organization of Palestine*, edited by Sa'id B. Himadeh, pp. 75–106. Beirut: American University.

Duff, Douglas V.
1934 *Sword for Hire*. London: John Murray.
1935 *Galilee Galloper*. London: John Murray.
1953 *Bailing with a Teaspoon*. London: John Long.

Elon, Amos
1971 *The Israelis: Founders and Sons*. New York: Holt, Rinehart and Winston.

Eloul, Rohn
1982 *Culture Change in a Bedouin Tribe: An Ethnographic History of the Arab al-Hjerat, Lower Galilee, Israel*. Ann Arbor: UMI.

Enloe, Cynthia H.
1980 *Ethnic Soldiers: State Security in Divided Societies*. Athens: University of Georgia Press.

Etingen, Shlomo
1957 *Encyclopaedia Hêbraica*, 1st ed., 6:960–66, s.v. "msilôt habârzel" ("railways").

Evans-Prichard, E.E.
1940 *The Nuer*. New York: Oxford University Press.

Evron, Shaul, et al.
1975 *ha-shever* (*The Crisis*). N.p. (Israel): Hotsa'ah Meyuhedet.

Eyal, Eli
1973 Gam habedvim "ratzim" laknesset (The bedouin too "run" for the Knesset). *Ma'ariv* August 17, 1973:18.

Falah, Salman
1975 A history of the Druze settlements in Palestine during the Ottoman period. In *Studies on Palestine during the Ottoman Period*, edited by Moshe Ma'oz, pp. 31–48. Jerusalem: Magness Press.

Finn, James
1878 *Stirring Times*. London: C. Kegan Paul and Co.

Fleisher, G.
1937 bamir'eh (In the pasture). In *kovetz hashômêr* (*The Compilation of hashomer*), pp. 218–23. The Archive and Museum of the Labour Movement. Tel Aviv: The Labour Archive.

Fyzee, Asaf A.A.
1964 *Outlines of Muhammadan Law*, 3rd ed. London: Oxford University Press.

Garthwaite, Gene R.
1972 The Bakhtiyâri Khans, the government of Iran, and the British 1846–1915. *International Journal of Middle East Studies* 3:24–44.

Geertz, Clifford
1960 The Javanese Kijaji: The changing role of a cultural broker. *Comparative Studies in Society and History* 2:228–49.

Gibb, H.A.R.
1971 *Mohammedanism*, 2nd ed. London: Oxford University Press.

Gichon, Mordechai
1969 *âtlas carta letôldôt eretz-yisrâ'êl mbeytar v'âd tel Hay (historya tzva'it)* (*Carta's Atlas of Palestine from Bethther to Tel Hai—Military History*). Jerusalem: Carta.

Golani, Gideon
1961 *seqer sadeh le'ezôr habedvim: bîr al-Maksûr* (*Field Survey for the Bedouin Region: Bir al-Maksur*). Mimeograph. Jerusalem: Government of Israel, Ministry of the Interior, Department of Minorities.
1966 *hitnahalût habedvîm begvâ'ôt alonîm-shfar'âm* (*The Sedentarization of the Bedouin in the Alonim: Shfar'am Hills*). Mimeograph. Jerusalem: Government of Israel, Ministry of the Interior and Hêbrew University.

Goldberg, Harvey
1967 FBD marriage and demography among Tripolitanian Jews in Israel. *Southwestern Journal of Anthropology* 23:176–91.

Great Britain. Army, Egyptian Expeditionary Force
1919 *The Advance of the Egyptian Expeditionary Forces . . . July 1917 to October 1918*. Cairo: Government Press and Survey of Egypt.

Great Britain. Colonial Office
1925 *Report of the High Commissioner on the Administration of Palestine 1920–1925*. Col. 15. London: H.M. Stationary Office.
1925–39 *Report by His Majesty's Government in the United Kingdom of Great Britain and Northern Ireland to the Council of the League of Nations on the Administration of Palestine and Trans-Jordan for the Year* (1924, 1925, 1926, 1927, 1928, 1932, 1935, and 1938). Cols. 12, 20, 26, 31, 40, 82, 112, 166. London: H.M. Stationary Office.
1930 *Palestine. Report on Immigration, Land Settlement and Development*, by Sir John Hope Simpson. Cmnd. 3686. London: H.M. Stationary Office.
1937 *Palestine Royal Commission*. Memoranda prepared by the government of Palestine. Col. 133. London: H.M. Stationary Office.

Great Britain. Commission on Palestine . . .
1930 *Report of the Commission on the Palestine Disturbances of August, 1929*. Cmnd. 3530. London: H.M. Stationary Office.

Great Britain. [Admiralty] Naval Intelligence Division
1920 *A Handbook of Syria (including Palestine)*. London: H.M. Stationary Office.

Great Britain. Palestine Royal Commission
1937 *Report*. Cmnd. 5479. London: H.M. Stationary Office.

Great Britain. Parliament. Parliamentary Papers (Commons)
1921 *An Interim Report on the Civil Administration of Palestine during the Period 1st July, 1920–30th June, 1921*. Cmnd. 1499. London: H.M. Stationary Office.
1922 *Mandate for Palestine* . . . Cmnd. 1785. London: H.M. Stationary Office.

Gunther, Mavis
1968 Diet and milk secretion in women. *Proceeding Nutritional Society* 27:77–82.

Halevi, Nadav
1968 The characteristics of Israel's economic growth. In *Economic Development Issues: Greece, Israel, Taiwan, and Thailand*, pp. 79–120. Committee for Economic Development. New York: Frederick A. Praeger.

Halevi, Nadav, and Ruth Klinov-Malul
1968 *The Economic Development of Israel*. New York: Frederick A. Praeger.

Hall, Edward T.
1959 *The Silent Language*. Garden City, N.J.: Doubleday.
1966 *The Hidden Dimension*. Garden City, N.J.: Doubleday.
1976 *Beyond Culture*. Garden City, N.J.: Doubleday.

Hameiri, Yehezkel
1976 mismakh kenig hores et hayahsīm shnirkemu me'az kum hamedina (The Kenig Document destroys the relationships that have developed since the birth of the state). *Yedi'ot Aharonot* October 9, 1976:9, 10.

Hardin, G.
1968 The tragedy of the commons. *Science* 162:1243–48.

Hareuveni, Meir
1981 'asarōt palshū lekfar yasif, yrū lecol ever hishlīchū rīmonim veholelū heres rav (Scores invaded Kafr Yasif, fired in all directions, threw grenades and caused much damage). *Ma'ariv* April 15, 1981:1, 3.

Harrell, Barbara B.
1981 Lactation and menstruation in cultural perspective. *American Anthropologist* 83:796–823.

Heyd, Uriel
1942 *daher al 'umar: shâlît hagâlîl bamê'âh hayôd-hêt* (*Dhahr al-Umar: Ruler of the Galilee in the 18th Century*). Jerusalem: Rubin Mass.

Himadeh, Sa'id B.
1938 Industry. In *Economic Organization of Palestine*, edited by Sa'id B. Himadeh, pp. 213–99. Beirut: American University.

Hirsch, Siegfried
1933 Sheep and goats in Palestine. *Bulletin of the Palestine Economic Society* (Tel Aviv) 6(2).

Hizki, Moshe
1957 *Encyclopaedia Hêbraica*, 1st ed., 6:980–83, s.v. "hado'ar" ("postal service").

Hockett, Charles F., and Robert Ascher
1964 The human revolution. *Current Anthropology* 5:135–68.

Hopen, C. Edward
1958 *The Pastoral Fulbe Family in Gwandu*. London: Oxford University Press.

Hopkins, Lister G.
1938 Population. In *Economic Organization of Palestine*, edited by Sa'id B. Himadeh, pp. 3–40. Beirut: American University.

Horowitz, Dan, and Moshe Lissak
1978 *Origins of the Israeli Polity*. Chicago: Chicago University Press.

Horwitz, Jacob Kalman
1957 *Encyclopaedia Hêbraica*, 1st ed., 6:498–504, s.vv. "mthîlat hamê'âh ha-19 'ad rêshît hahityâshvût hahadashah (1800–1882). 1. historyah klalit" ("From the beginning of the 19th century until the beginning of the new settlement [1800–1882]. 1. General History").

Horwitz, Shmuel
1967 *Encyclopaedia Hêbraica*, 1st ed., Supplement to Vols. 1–16, pp. 466–67, s.vv. "hahakla'ût byisrâ'êl" ("agriculture in Israel").

Howell, Paul P.
1951 Notes on the Ngork Dinka of western Kordofan. *Sudan Notes and Records* 32:239–93.

Hütteroth, Wolf-Dieter, and Kamal Abdulfatah
1977 *Historical Geography of Palestine, Transjordan and Southern Syria in the Late 16th Century*. Erlanger Geographische Arbeiten 5. Erlangen: Palm and Elke.

Irons, William G.
1975 *The Yomut Turkmen: A Study of Social Organization among a Central Asian Turkic-Speaking Population*. Anthropological Papers, no. 58. Ann Arbor: Museum of Anthropology, University of Michigan.

Israel. Central Bureau of Statistics
1955 *Registration of Population* (8 XI 1948). Pt. A, *Towns, Villages and Regions*. Special Publications Series No. 36. Jerusalem: Central Bureau of Statistics.
1961 *qôvetz statîstî* (*Statistical Compilation*). Jerusalem: Central Bureau of Statistics.
1962–78 *Statistical Abstracts*. Nos. 13 (1962), 17 (1966), 23 (1972), 24 (1973), 25 (1974), 26 (1975), 27 (1976), 28 (1977), 29 (1978), 60 (2009). Jerusalem: Central Bureau of Statistics.
1963a *Census of Population and Housing 1961*. Vol. 10, *The Settlements of Israel*, Pt. 1. Jerusalem: Central Bureau of Statistics.
1963b *Census of Population and Housing 1961*. Vol. 11, *The Settlements of Israel*, Pt. 2. Jerusalem: Central Bureau of Statistics.
1964 *Census of Population and Housing 1961*. Vol. 17, *Moslems, Christians, and Druze in Israel*. Jerusalem: Central Bureau of Statistics.
1965 *reshîmât ha-yeshûvîm, ukhlûsiyatâm, ve-sîmleyhem* (*The Listing of Settlements, Their Population and Emblems*). Technical Publications Series No. 20. Jerusalem: Central Bureau of Statistics.
1968 *reshîmât ha-yeshûvîm, ukhlûsiyatâm, ve-sîmleyhem* (*The Listing of Settlements, Their Population and Emblems*). Technical Publications Series No. 28. Jerusalem: Central Bureau of Statistics.
1970 *Agriculture in Israel 1948/9–1968/9: Statistical Series*. Pt. 2, *Factors of Production, Land Utilization, Marketing and Other Series*. Special Publications Series No. 327. Jerusalem: Central Bureau of Statistics.
1971 *reshîmât ha-yeshûvîm, ukhlûsiyatâm, ve-sîmleyhem* (*The Listing of Settlements, Their Population and Emblems*). Technical Publications Series No. 36. Jerusalem: Central Bureau of Statistics.
1972a *Labour Force Surveys—1970*. Special Publication Series No. 376. Jerusalem: Central Bureau of Statistics.
1972b *Census of Agriculture 1971*. Vol. 1, *Preliminary Data*. Jerusalem: Central Bureau of Statistics.
1972c *reshîmât ha-yeshûvîm, ukhlûsiyatâm, ve-sîmleyhem* (*The Listing of Settlements, Their Population and Emblems*). Technical Publications Series No. 37. Jerusalem: Central Bureau of Statistics.
1973 *Census of Agriculture 1971*. Vol. 3, *Field Crops and Vegetables*. Jerusalem: Central Bureau of Statistics.
1974a *Census of Agriculture 1971*. Vol. 4, *Livestock*. Jerusalem: Central Bureau of Statistics.
1974b *Census of Population and Housing 1972*. Vol. 4, *Population and Households for Localities and Statistical Areas*. Jerusalem: Central Bureau of Statistics.
1975 *Census of Population and Housing 1972*. Vol. 6, *Demographic Characteristics of the Population*, Pt. 1. Jerusalem: Central Bureau of Statistics.
1976 *Census of Population and Housing 1972*. Vol. 11, *Demographic Characteristics of the Population*, Pt. 3. Jerusalem: Central Bureau of Statistics.

Israel. Inspector General of Elections . . .
1956 *totz'ot habhirôt laknesset hashlîshît 'ulerashuyot meqomiyot* (*Results of Elections to the Third Knesset and Local Authorities*) 26 VII 1955. Special Publications Series No. 51. Jerusalem: Central Bureau of Statistics.
1961 *totz'ot habhirôt laknesset harevi'ît 'ulerashuyot meqomiyot* (*Results of Elections to the Fourth Knesset and Local Authorities*) 3 XI 1959. Special Publications Series No. 111. Jerusalem: Central Bureau of Statistics.
1964 *totz'ot habhirôt laknesset hahamîshît 'ulerashuyot meqomiyot* (*Results of Elections to the Fifth Knesset and Local Authorities*) 15 VIII 1961. Special Publications Series No. 166. Jerusalem: Central Bureau of Statistics.
1967 *totz'ot habhirôt laknesset hashîshît 'ulerashuyot meqomiyot* (*Results of Elections to the Sixth Knesset and Local Authorities*) 2 XI 1965. Special Publications Series No. 216, Vol. 1. Jerusalem: Central Bureau of Statistics.
1970 *totz'ot habhirôt laknesset hashvi'it 'ulerashuyot meqomiyot* (*Results of Elections to the Seventh Knesset and Local Authorities*) 28 X 1969. Special Publications Series No. 309. Jerusalem: Central Bureau of Statistics.
1974 *totz'ot habhirôt laknesset hashmînît 'ulerashuyot meqomiyot* (*Results of Elections to the Eighth Knesset and Local Authorities*) 31 XII 1973. Special Publications Series No. 461. Jerusalem: Central Bureau of Statistics.
1978 *totz'ot habhirôt laknesset hatshi'ît 'ulerashuyot meqomiyot* (*Results of Elections to the Nineth Knesset and Local Authorities*) 17 V 1977. Special Publications Series No. 553. Jerusalem: Central Bureau of Statistics.

Israel. Laws, Statutes, etc.
1949–75 *Laws of the State of Israel*. Nos. 3 (1949), 13 (1959), 14 (1960), 19 (1965), 23 (1968/69), 29 (1975). Jerusalem: Government Printer.

Israel. Ministry of Information
1977 *shnâtôn hamemshalâh* (*The Government Yearbook*). Jerusalem: Government Printer.

Israel. Survey
1958 *Map*. Sheet 17-24 (Kafr Manda). 1:20,000 series. N.p.: Survey of Israel, Ministry of Labor.
1970 *Atlas of Israel*. Jerusalem: Survey of Israel, Ministry of Labor; Amsterdam: Elsevier Publishing Co.
1972 *Map of Israel*. Northern Sheet. 1:250,000 series. N.p.: Survey of Israel, Ministry of Labor.
1975 Aerial photo of Bīr al-Maksūr.

Israeli Labour Party
n.d. *rikuz totz'ôt habhîrôt bamigzâr h'arâvî laknesset hatshi'it (17.5.1977)* (*Concentration of Results of the Election to the Ninth Knesset in the Arab Sector, 17.5.1977*). Mimeograph. Tel Aviv: The Israeli Labour Party, the Arab Sector Election Headquarters. Undated (June 1977).

Jakubowska, Longina A.
1985 *Urban Bedouin: Social Change in a Settled Environment*. Ann Arbor: UMI.

Katakura, Motoko
1977 *Bedouin Village: A Study of a Saudi Arabian People in Transition*. Tokyo: University of Tokyo Press.

Klima, George J.
1970 *The Barabaig: East African Cattle-Herders*. New York: Holt, Rinehart and Winston.

Klinov-Malul, Ruth
1966 *The Profitability of Investment in Education in Israel*. Jerusalem: Maurice Falk Institute.

Konner, Melvin, and Carol Worthman
1980 Nursing frequency, gonadal function, and birth spacing among !Kung hunter-gatherers. *Science* 207:788–91.

Kressel, Gideon M.
1970 nisu'ay wâlad 'amm bejwarish: aspectîm shel 'iyûr umasoret (Father's brother's children marriage among the Jawarish: Aspects of urbanization and tradition). *Hamizrah Hahadash* 20:20–51.
1976 *pratiyût le'ûmat shivtiyût* (*Individuality Against Tribalism*). Tel Aviv: Hakibbutz Hameuchad.

Landau, Jacob M.
1969 *The Arabs in Israel: A Political Study*. London: Oxford University Press.
1975 The educational impact of western culture on traditional society in nineteenth century Palestine. In *Studies on Palestine during the Ottoman Period*, edited by Moshe Ma'oz, pp. 499–506. Jerusalem: Magness Press.
1981 nikûr umtâhîm behitnâhaqût politit (Alienation and strains in political behavior). In *ha'arvim byisrâ'êl: retzîfût utmûrôt* (*The Arabs in Israel: Continuity and Change*), edited by Aharon Layish, pp. 197–212. Jerusalem: Magness Press.

Lattimore, Owen
1951 (1940) *Inner Asian Frontiers of China*. Boston: Beacon Press.

Levy, Emanuel
1955 *Israel Economic Survey 1953–1954*. Jerusalem: Jewish Agency, Economic Department.

Levy, Reuben
1957 *The Social Structure of Islam*. Cambridge: Cambridge University Press.

Lewis, Bernard
1954 Studies in the Ottoman archives—1. *Bulletin of the School of Oriental and African Studies* (University of London) 16:469–502.
1970 Egypt and Syria. In *The Cambridge History of Islam*. Vol. 1, edited by P.M. Holt et al., pp. 175–230. London: Cambridge University Press.

Lienhardt, Godfrey
1958 The western Dinka. In *Tribes without Rulers*, edited by John Middleton and David Tait, pp. 97–135. New York: Humanities Press.

Luke, Harry C., and Edward Keith-Roach
1922 *The Handbook of Palestine*. London: Macmillan and Co.

Ma'ariv (staff)
1981 *Ma'ariv* June 30, 1981:1.

1976 sar hapnim: "mismakh kenig"–de'a pratit: hdrisha lehadiḫo–re'aḫ shel hasatah (Minister of the Interior: "The Kenig Document"–A private opinion: The demand to remove him–Smell of incitement). *Ma'ariv* October 8, 1976:1, 15.

Madina, Maan Z. (compiler)
1973 *Arabic-English Dictionary*. New York: Pocket Books.

Ma'oz, Moshe
1968 *Ottoman Reform in Syria and Palestine 1840–1861*. London: Oxford University Press.
1969 *eretz-yisrâ'êl bitqûfat hashiltôn ha'othmâni: hartza'otav shel profesor uri'el hed* (*Palestine during Ottoman Rule: The Lectures of Professor Uriel Heyd*). Jerusalem: Aqademon.

Marx, Emanuel
1967 *Bedouin of the Negev*. New York: Frederick A. Praeger.
1981 pînuy bedvîm me'zôr malhatâ (The eviction of bedouin from the Malhata region). *reshimôt benosê habedvîm* (*Notes on the Bedouin*) 12:36–44.

Marx, Emanuel, and Moshe Sela'
n.d. *matzavam shel beduay haneqev* (*The Conditions of the Bedouin of the Negev*). Mimeograph. N.p.: undated (1979).

Mauss, Marcel
1969 *The Gift*, translated by Ian Cunnison. London: Cohen and West.

Mazori, Dalia, and Menahem Rahat
1977 rogez btzibur ha'aravī 'al she'aliyat RaQaH babhirot hekhnisa mu'amadīm yehudiim laknesset (Anger in the Arab public about RaQaH success in the elections which installed Jewish candidates in the Knesset). *Ma'ariv* May 19, 1977:4.

Medding, Peter Y.
1972 *Mapai in Israel: Political Organization and Government in a New Society*. Cambridge: Cambridge University Press.

Meizles, Moshe
1976 "mismakh kenig" mas'ir et mifleget ha'avoda–ho'alu drishot leganoto bharifut ("The Kenig Document" rages the Labor Party–there were demands to strongly denounce him). *Ma'ariv* October 10, 1976:2.

Mernissi, Fatima
1975 *Beyond the Veil: Male-Female Dynamics in a Modern Moslem Society*. New York: John Wiley and Sons.

Miron, Mikhal
1982 hasayeret hayerôqah: hatzava' hapratî shel Alon Galili (The Green Patrol: The private army of Alon Galili). *shavu'ôn yede'ot ahronôt* (*Yedeot Ahronot Weekly*) January 22, 1982:3–5, 39.

Mohsen, Safia K.
1967 The legal status of women among Awlad 'Ali. *Anthropological Quarterly* 40:153–66.

Montagne, Robert
1932 Quelques Aspects du Peuplement de la Haute-Djezire. *Bulletin d'Etudes Orientales* (Damascus. Institute Francais) 2:53–66.

Morag, Amotz
1967 *mîmûn hamemshalah byisrâ'êl: hitpathût ub'âyôt* (*Public Finance in Israel: Problems and Development*). Jerusalem: Magness Press.

Musil, Alois
1929 *Manners and Customs of the Rawala Bedouin*. Oriental Exploration and Study, No. 6. New York: American Geographical Society.

Nelson, Cynthia
1973 Women and power in nomadic societies of the Middle East. In *The Desert and the Sown*, edited by Cynthia Nelson, pp. 43–59. Research Series, No. 21. Berkeley: University of California, Institute of International Studies.

New York Times
1897 HE HAD NO MONEY TO LEND; Beyroot merchant refused to heed the request of one of the Sultan's advisers. *New York Times* April 18, 1897 (Archive).
1976 Israel says Arabs seek to join army. *New York Times* November 1, 1976:1.

Obermeyer, G.J.
1973 Leadership and transition in bedouin society: A case study. In *The Desert and the Sown*, edited by Cynthia Nelson, pp. 159–73. Research Series, No. 21. Berkeley: University of California, Institute of International Studies.

Oliphant, Laurence
1976 (1887) *Haifa or Life in the Holy Land 1882–1885*. Jerusalem: Canaan Publishing House.

Oppenheim, Max A.S. Freeherr von
1939 *Die Beduinen*. Vol. I. Leipzig: Otto Harrassowitz.
1943 *Die Beduinen*. Vol. II. Leipzig: Otto Harrassowitz.

Oppenheimer, Jonathan W.S.
1977 Culture and politics in Druze ethnicity. *Ethnic Groups* 1:221–40.
1978 The Druze in Israel as Arabs and non-Arabs: An essay on the manipulation of identity in a non-civil state. *Cambridge Anthropology* 4(2):22–44.

Orni, Efraim
1974 *Agrarian Reform and Social Progress in Israel*. Jerusalem: Jewish National Fund.

Palestine. Census Office
1923 *Report and General Abstracts of the Census of 1922*, compiled by J.B. Barron. Jerusalem: Government of Palestine.
1932 *Census of Palestine 1931. Population of Villages, Towns, and Administrative Areas*, compiled by E. Mills. Jerusalem: Government of Palestine.
1933 *Census of Palestine 1931*, by E. Mills. Alexandria: Government of Palestine.

Palestine. Department of Forests
1946 *Empire Forests during the War, 1939–1945*. Jerusalem: Government Printer.

Palestine. Government
1946 *A Survey of Palestine*. Jerusalem: Government Printer.
1947 *Supplement to Survey of Palestine*. Jerusalem: Government Printer.

Palestine. Survey
1941 *Map*. Sheet 17-24 (Kafr Manda). 1:20,000 Series. N.p.: Survey of Palestine 1941.
1942 *Map*. Sheet 2-5. 1:100,000 Series. N.p.: Survey of Palestine 1942.

Peters, Emrys
1960 The proliferation of segments in the lineage of the bedouin of Cyrenaica [Libya]. *Journal of the Royal Anthropological Institute* 90:29–53.

Porath, Yehoshua
1971 *The Emergence of the Palestinian-Arab National Movement 1918–1929*. Jerusalem: Hêbrew University.
1977 *The Palestinian Arab National Movement: From Riots to Rebellion*. Vol. 2, 1929–1939. London: Frank Cass and Co.

Randolph, Richard R.
1963 *Elements in the Social Structure of the Qdiiraat Bedouin*. Manuscript.

Rappaport, Roy A.
1970 Sanctity and adaptation. *Io* 7:46–71.

Rekhes, Elie
1981 hamaskîlîm (The intelligensia). In *ha'arvim byisrâ'êi: retzîfût utmurôt* (*The Arabs in Israel: Continuity and Change*), edited by Aharon Layish, pp. 180–96. Jerusalem: Magness Press.

Rosenfeld, Henry
1958 Process of structural change within the Arab village extended family. *American Anthropologist* 60:1127–39.
1969 tahlîkhêy shinûy veqormey shimûr bamishpâhâh ha'aravît hakafrît byisrâ'êl (Processes of change and factors of preservation in the rural Arab family in Israel). *Hamizrah Hahadash* 19:208–17.
1976 Social and economic factors in explanation of the increased rate of patrilineal endogamy in the Arab village in Israel. In *Mediterranean Family Structure*, edited by Jean G. Peristiany, pp. 115–36. London: Cambridge University Press.

Sahlins, Marshall D.
1961 The segmentary lineage organization: An organization of predatory expansion. *American Anthropologist* 63:322–45.
1965 On the ideology and composition of descent groups. *Man* 65:104–7.
1968 *Tribesmen*. Englewood-Cliffs, N.J.: Prentice-Hall.
1972 *Stone Age Economics*. Chicago: Aldine.

Said, Edward W.
1978 *Orientalism*. New York: Vintage Books.

Sawwaf, Husni

1938 Transportation and communication. In *Economic Organization of Palestine*, edited by Sa'id B. Himadeh, pp. 301–42. Beirut: American University.

Schumacher, G.

1887 Population list of the Liva of 'Akka. *Palestine Exploration Fund Quarterly Statement* 1887:169–91.

Shamir, Shimon

1975 The impact of western ideas on traditional society in Ottoman Palestine. In *Studies on Palestine during the Ottoman Period*, edited by Moshe Ma'oz, pp. 507–14. Jerusalem: Magness Press.

Sharon, Moshe

1964 *habedvîm b'eretz-Yirâ'êl bam'eot hashmoneh-'esreh vehatsha'-'esreh* (*The Bedouin in Palestine during the Eighteenth and Nineteenth Centuries*). Mimeograph. Jerusalem: Hêbrew University, Department of Islamic History.

1975 The political role of the bedouin in Palestine in the sixteenth and seventeenth centuries. In *Studies of Palestine during the Ottoman Period*, edited by Moshe Ma'oz, pp. 11–30. Jerusalem: Magness Press.

1976 tahalikhey hûrbân venomâdizatzyah b'eretz-yisrâ'êl tahat shilton ha'islam 633–1517 (Processes of destruction and nomadization in Palestine under Islamic rule, 633–1517). In *sûqiyôt btôldôt 'eretz-yisrâ'êl tahat shilton ha'islam* (*Problems in the History of Palestine under Islamic Rule*), edited by Moshe Sharon, pp. 7–32. Jerusalem: Yad Yitzhak Ben-Tzvi.

Shim'oni, Ya'aqov

1946 *'arvzyey 'eretz-yisrâ'êl* (*The Arabs of Palestine*). Tel Aviv: 'Am 'Oved.

Shmueli, Avshalom

1970 *hitnâhalût habedvîm shel midbâr Yehûdâh* (*The Sedentarization of the Judean Desert Bedouin*). Tel Aviv: Gomê.

1973 *hitnâhalût navadim bmerhâv yerushalayim bmêah ha'esrîm* (*The Sedentarization of Nomads in the Vicinity of Jerusalem in the 20th Century*). PhD dissertation. Jerusalem: Hêbrew University.

1980 The bedouin of the land of Israel: Settlement and change. *Urban Ecology* 4:253–86.

Smith, C. Gordon

1975 The geography and natural resources of Palestine as seen by British writers in the nineteenth and early twentieth centuries. In *Studies on Palestine during the Ottoman Period*, edited by Moshe Ma'oz, pp. 87–100. Jerusalem: Magness Press.

Smith, M.G.

1956 On segmentary lineage systems. *Journal of the Royal Anthropological Institute* 86:39–80.

Stenning, Derrick J.

1958 Household viability among the pastoral Fulani. In *The Developmental Cycle in Domestic Groups*, edited by John R. Goody, pp. 92–119. Cambridge Papers in Social Anthropology No. 1. Cambridge: Cambridge University Press.

Tadmor, C.
1952 *Israel Economic Survey, January–June, 1952*. Jerusalem: Jewish Agency, Economic Department.
1953 *Israel Economic Survey, July–December 1952*. Jerusalem: Jewish Agency, Economic Department.

Toffler, Alvin
1980 *The Third Wave*. New York: Bantam Books.

Veicmanas, B.
1938 Internal trade. In *Economic Organization of Palestine*, edited by Sa'id B. Himadeh, pp. 343–83. Beirut: American University.

Vincent, Joan
1974 The structuring of ethnicity. *Human Organization* 33:375–79.

Vinogradov, Amal R.
1972 The 1920 revolt in Iraq reconsidered: The role of tribes in national politics. *International Journal of Middle East Studies* 3:123–29.
1974 Ethnicity, cultural discontinuity and power brokers in northern Iraq: The case of the Shabak. *American Ethnologist* 1:207–18.

Volney, Constantin F.C., Comte de
1798 *Travels Through Egypt and Syria in the Years 1783, 1784, and 1785*. New York: John Tiebout.

Warriner, Doreen
1948 *Land and Poverty in the Middle East*. London: Royal Institute of International Affairs.

Watson, William
1973 *British Colonial Policy and Tribal Political Organization*. 9th International Congress of Anthropological and Ethnological Sciences, No. 2356, Chicago.

Winter, Michael
1981 b'ayôt ysôd bema'arakhet; hahînûkh (Basic problems of the educational system). In *ha'arvîm byisrâ'êl: retzîfût utmûrôt* (*The Arabs in Israel: Continuity and Change*), edited by Aharon Layish, pp. 168–79. Jerusalem: Magness Press.

Wolf, Eric R.
1956 Aspects of group relations in a complex society: Mexico. *American Anthropologist* 58:1065–78.
1969 *Peasant Wars of the Twentieth Century*. New York: Harper and Row.

Wright, Henry T.
1969 *The Administration of Rural Production in an Early Mesopotamian Town*. Anthropological Papers, no. 38. Ann Arbor: Museum of Anthropology, University of Michigan.

Yedi'ot Aharonot (staff)
1976 hamemuneh 'al maḥoz atzfon, Israel Kenig, hegish doḥ lerosh hamemshala: "rov 'arvi shel 51 ahuz bagalil ye'ar'er shlitat Israel be 1978" (The North Region Commissioner, Israel Kenig, delivered a report to the Prime Minister: "Arab majority of 51 percent in the Galilee will undermine Israel control in 1978"). *Yedi'ot Aharonot* October 7, 1976:1, 3.

Zohar, Ezra
1974 *bitzvat hamishtar* (*In the Grip of the Regime*). Jerusalem: Shiqmonah.

Zohary, Michael
1957 *Encyclopaedia Hêbraica*, 1st ed., 6:178–97, s.v. "hatzimhiyah vehatzomeh" ("vegetation").
1962 *Plant Life of Palestine: Israel and Jordan*. New York: Ronald Press.

Index

1858 Ottoman Land Code, 15, 27, 46, 196, 303
1948 War (of Independence), 3, 66, 79, 98–99, 188, 225, 242, 257; Operation *deqel*, 76–77; Operation *Ḥirām*, 78
1956 Sinai Campaign, 96, 104, 180, 228
1967 "Six-Day War," 150, 228–29, 233

ʻAbāssī, Maḥmūd, 263–64
Abdulfatah, Kamal, 12, 315
Abir, Mordechai, 13, 307
ABL. *See* Arabic Bedouin List
ABL-HQ, 261–65
Abou-Zeid, Ahmed, 107, 177, 307
Abramson, Arieh, 22–23, 307
Abū Snān, 225
ʻAfafṭeh, 103, 111, 140, 175, 210, 252, 255
'aged (marriage contract), 212–13
'Aḥmed al-Ğazzar, 14, 20, 25
Al Hamishmar, 171, 307
Allon, Ygal, 76, 307
'Amal Naṣir al-Dīn, 255, 266
Amiran, D.H.K., 11, 14–15, 94, 296, 307
al-'Anbā, 261
Antonius, George, 44, 308
Antropova, V.V., 46, 308
ʻarab al-'Adwān, 20
ʻarab al-ʻAmariyeh, 265
ʻarab al-ʻArāmšeh, 69, 256
ʻarab al-Ġawārneh, 107, 296
ʻarab al-Ğanādi, 162, 211
ʻarab al-Ğawāmīs, 304
ʻarab al-Ḥağarah, 19, 26, 278
ʻarab al-Ḥamdūn, 211
ʻarab al-Hanādi, 14, 27, 30–31
ʻarab al-Heīb, 32, 76, 104–5, 225–26, 228–231, 240, 242, 247, 262, 268, 273, 300–301, 304
ʻarab al-Ḥelf, 24, 31, 39–40, 56, 58–59, 67, 69, 162, 210
ʻarab al-Hazaīl, 31
ʻarab al-Kašḫar, 271
ʻarab al-Kaʻabīyeh, 24, 26, 31, 40, 56, 69, 162, 210, 211–12, 268
ʻarab al-Kaʻabneh, 24, 26
ʻarab al-Lağa', 32
ʻarab al-Mazarib, 225
ʻarab al-Mreysāt, 67
ʻarab al-Muwāsa, 32, 56, 98, 227, 278
ʻarab al-Saʻadiyeh, 297
ʻarab al-Saʻaydeh, 296
ʻarab al-Ṣbeyḥ, 56, 58
ʻarab al-Sawāʻed, 143, 212–13
ʻarab al-Sweytāt, 39
ʻarab al-Zbeydāt, 297
Arab Rebellion, 44, 55–57, 279, 300
Arabic Bedouin List (ABL), 239, 241–42, 244, 249, 251, 257–262, 265–66, 270, 272, 297
Arad, A., 132, 308
Ardu of Arabistan, 14
Aref, ʻAref el, 26, 214, 231, 236, 308
Aronoff, Myron J., 139, 223, 237, 259–60, 262, 264, 270, 308
ʻArrabeh, 78, 235
Arthur, George, 79, 308
Ascher, Robert, 278, 314
Ashbel, Dov, 78, 93, 122, 308
Ashkenazi, Tuvia, 22, 24, 26, 30, 32, 46, 51, 60, 67, 69, 107, 138, 198, 268, 308
Assaf, Michael, 15, 34, 43, 308
Aswad, Barbara C., 67, 189, 296, 308
al-ʻAṭaūnah, *šeyḫ* Mūsā, 272
ʻAūdah Manṣūr Abu Muʻammer, *šeyḫ*, 241–42
Avitsur, Shmuel, 15, 43, 54, 308

Awad, Mohamed, 280, 308
'ayūn al-Kawkab, 30
'Azāzmeh Confederation, 241

BAAA. *See* Bureau of the Advisor on Arab Affairs
Bachrach, Peter, 268, 309
badl. *See* brother-sister exchange
Badia y Leblich, Domingo, 13, 22, 309
Baer, Gabriel, 12, 15, 27, 43, 54, 309
Bailey, Clinton/Yitzhak, 24, 237–38, 250–51, 309
Bani 'Amr, 19
Banū Hilāl, 11
Banū Saḫr, 14, 26
Banū Sulaym, 11
Bar Giora, 58
Baratz, Morton, 268, 309
Barth, Fredrik, 34, 36, 40, 190, 280–81, 283, 309
Basmat Ṭab'un, 297
Bates, Daniel G., 40, 309
Beer, Stafford, 5, 280, 309
Ben Arieh, Y., 94, 296, 307
Beirut secret society, 44
Beit Zarzir, 94, 297
Ben Dor, Gavriel, 300, 309
Ben Porath, Yoram, 80, 87–88, 92, 96–97, 99–101, 103–4, 107, 135, 139, 309
Ben Shemesh, A., 114, 196, 309–10
Berger, Morroe, 43, 310
Bergheim, Samuel, 198, 310
B'eyneh, 30
Beyt Ğan, 32
Bīr al-Badawiyyeh, 30, 59
Bīr al-Maksūr, 35, 53–54, 58–59, 69, 76, 82–85, 89–92, 98–99, 103, 107–10, 115–17, 120, 122–23, 133, 136, 141–99, 206–7, 211, 222–23, 225, 229, 232, 242–45, 248, 252–56, 267, 270, 271–76, 279, 295–96, 299, 305
blood restitution (*diyah*), 205–6, 214, 236–37, 302
Boneh, Dan, 104, 303, 310
Bongaarts, John, 70, 310
Border Guard, 96, 103–5, 219, 227–28, 244, 256, 301
Bowden, Tom, 51, 79, 310
Brazelton, T. Berry, 164, 169, 310
brother-sister exchange (B-Z exchange, *badl*), 39, 199
Burckhardt, J.L., 13, 310
Bureau of the Advisor on Arab Affairs (BAAA), 218, 227, 237–41, 243–44, 248, 258, 260, 262–63, 297
Byzantine, 11–12

CBS. *See* Israel Central Bureau of Statistics
Civil Administration, 45, 79, 81, 313
coffee (*gahwa murra* or Turkish), 23–24, 60–61, 82, 163, 166, 178, 221, 225, 239, 263, 293–94
Cohen, Amnon, 12–13, 25, 310
co-liable group (*ḫams*), 24, 214, 267
communal land (*muša'*), 3, 15, 54, 115, 267
Communist Party of Israel (*MaQI*), 237–38, 249–51
complementary opposition, 133, 202, 246–47, 277, 280, 297
Conder, Claude R., 9, 14, 20, 22–23, 27–33, 40, 56, 290, 310–11
Consumer Price Index (CPI), 121, 135, 291
Coon, Carleton S., 44, 311
Council of the Elders (*ḫatyariyyeh*), 46, 84, 187–88, 194, 203–5, 207, 209, 211, 214–17, 221, 224, 267, 281
cultural brokers, 4, 282–83. *See also* relays

Dabas/ Ḫalāyleh, 8, 175
Dabūrīyeh, 235, 265
ḍamān, 122, 140
Day of the Land (March 30, 1976) (*yūm al-'arḍ*), 225, 233, 301
Democratic Movement for Change (*DaSh*), 249, 257–58, 260, 270
Deng, Francis M, 203, 311
D'eyfeh, 8, 20, 23–24, 31, 33, 38–39, 66–68, 70, 78, 110–11, 117, 140, 147, 175, 191–95, 206, 209–10, 256, 287
dīwān, 34, 60, 163–64, 166–67, 198, 205, 212, 267–68
Ḍiyab *al-mahabūl*, 20, 24–25
Ḍiyabāt, 8, 20, 24, 37–40, 66–68, 70, 83, 110–11, 113, 139, 147, 162, 175, 184, 192–93, 195, 199, 287
al-Ḍmeydeh, 8, 59, 61, 67, 69, 76, 78, 83, 100–101, 110, 123, 138, 141–42, 160, 163, 192, 194, 196, 199, 210, 273
Dickson, Bertram, 23, 311
diet, 23, 48, 61, 63, 70, 152, 156–57, 197
dietary laws (*kashrut*), 99, 126
Diqs, Isaak, 60, 311
Domestic Mode of Production (DMP), 120
Donovan, Bernard T., 70–71, 311
Doukhan, Moses J., 303, 311
Duff, Douglas V., 44–46, 50–51, 55–56, 69, 79, 311

education, 87–89, 94, 101, 103, 105, 107, 109, 136–38, 147, 155–57, 168–75, 177–79, 181–82, 185, 188, 191, 198, 219, 230, 264, 272–73, 276, 279, 297
Egyptian Expeditionary Force, 45, 312
electoral protest, 251. *See also* resentment groups
Elon, Amos, 43, 311
Eloul, Rohn, 19, 311
Elyaqim, Moshav, 128
Enloe, Cynthia H., 254–55, 300–301, 311
ethnic boundary, 280–83
ethnicity, 4, 195, 228, 281, 300–301
Etingen, Shlomo, 34, 311
Evans-Prichard, E.E., 6, 191, 203, 311
Evron, Shaul, 139, 223, 311
Eyal, Eli, 242, 255, 312
'Eylūṭ, 234

Faḫr al-Din II, 13
Falah, Salman, 53, 312
fantaziyeh (festivities), 59
Fedayeen, 104
falasṭīn, 44
al-Falāḥ, Ḥassan, 240
Finn, James, 12–14, 312
Fleisher, G., 22–23, 312
Fyzee, Asaf A.A., 114, 312

Ġadāyreh, 8, 19–20, 22–24, 31, 33–34, 36–40, 46, 48–51, 59, 66, 68–70, 76–78, 82–83, 85, 91–92, 98, 103, 105, 109–11, 113, 117, 123, 139, 147, 162, 175, 184, 192–95, 199, 205–10, 212, 220, 243–44, 246–53, 255, 272–73, 279, 305
Ġadīr, 'Abūd al-Ramli, 46, 50
Ġadīr, Ḏiyab al-Ibrāhīm, 31, 33–34, 40, 50
Ġadīr, Ibrāhīm al-Ḥsēn, 219, 221–23, 225, 231–33, 243–45, 253–54
Ġadīr, Ibrāhīm al-Nimr, 76, 78, 81–82, 85, 87, 91–92, 94, 226, 257, 270, 279
Ġadīr, Ḥsēn al-Ḏiyab, 50, 77–79, 81–83, 85, 92, 147, 210–12, 216–17, 245, 257
Ġadīr, Maḥmūd al-Mūsā, 230–32, 243–44, 254, 267
Ġadīr, Muḥammad al-Ḥsēn (al-*muḫtār*), 81–85, 89, 91–92, 98, 105, 142–43, 181, 210, 216–17, 220, 223, 232, 235–37, 239–40, 242, 250–53, 257–66, 270, 272, 279, 297, 302
Ġadīr, Muḥammad al-Mūsā, 76, 82, 221, 226, 234
Ġadīr, Muḥammad al-Sleymān, 77, 208
Ġadīr, Mūsā al-Ḏiyab, 48–50, 69, 77–78, 87, 92, 147, 234
Ġadīr, Sleymān al-'Abed, 33, 50, 76–77
Ġadīr, *ulād* 'abd al-Sleymān, 207, 210
Ġadīr, *ulād* Ḏiyab al-Ibrāhīm, 50, 81, 85, 105, 220
Ġadīr, *ulād* Ġadīr, 69, 111, 162, 175, 192, 205, 207, 210, 215, 220, 223, 230, 246, 253–54, 270
Ġadīr, *ulād* Nimr al-Ibrāhīm, 81
Galilee, 5, 6, 9–11, 13–14, 21–22, 29, 34, 40, 43–44, 47–48, 83, 101, 128, 133, 137, 139–40, 185, 190, 221, 225, 227–28, 236, 240, 244–46, 256–57, 260–64, 280, 306
Garthwaite, Gene R., 46, 79, 312
Geertz, Clifford, 282–83, 312
General Syrian Congress, 44
German Templar Society, 15–16
Gibb, H.A.R., 88, 312
Gichon, Mordechai, 13, 79, 312
Golani, Gideon, 22, 142, 153, 158, 160–61, 196–97, 295–96, 312
Goldberg, Harvey, 189, 312
Government of Palestine, 80, 320
Great Britain. Colonial Office (G.B. Col. or G.B. Col. R.), 27, 43, 45–46, 51–52, 55, 63, 94, 294, 313
Great Britain. Commission on Palestine (G.B. Com.), 44–45, 55, 313
Great Britain. [Admiralty] Naval Intelligence Division (G.B. Naval), 13, 23, 30, 32, 34, 40, 54–55, 313
Great Britain. Palestine Royal Commission (G.B. Pls.), 42, 45–46, 55, 79, 93–94, 313
Great Britain. Parliament. Parliamentary Papers (G.B. Par.), 45–46, 93–94, 313
Green Patrol, 128, 271, 318
g'ullat adamah, 303
Gunther, Mavis, 70, 313

habitational space use, 166
Haderah, 8, 103, 119, 128
ḥaflah, 229, 241, 255, 265
Haganah, 58
ḥaǧǧ, 219, 244, 276
Halevi, Nadav, 51, 55, 80, 89, 93–94, 96, 101, 103, 291, 313
Hall, Edward T., iii, 46, 93, 118, 136, 164, 203, 206, 268, 313
Ḥamād Abū Rabī'a, *šeyḫ*, 242, 258, 262, 272, 297
ḫams. *See* co-liable group
ḥamūleh (*ḥama'il*, pl.), 8, 60, 266–67
Hameiri, Yehezkel, 298, 313
Hardin, G., 120, 313
Hareuveni, Meir, 225, 301, 314
ḥarīm, 34, 60, 163, 197–98
Harrell, Barbara B., 70, 314
Hasolelim, 84, 227
ḫaṭīb (teacher), 87–88, 94, 169
ḫatyariyyeh. *See* Council of the Elders
headman. *See muḫtār*
"Hebrew Labor," 45, 96
ḥenna, 62
herding contracts, 129–30
Heyd, Uriel, 13, 314
Himadeh, Sa'id B., 55, 314
Ḫirbet Ğfāt, 28, 30. *See also* Yodfāt
Ḫirbet Kana, 28, 30
Ḫirbet Qireh, 24
Hirsch, Siegfried, 22, 30, 60, 314
Histadrut, 96, 99, 147, 151, 238, 258, 264, 270, 299
Hizki, Moshe, 34, 314
Ḥğerāt, 'Abdāllah al-Ṣāleḥ, 50
Ḥğerāt, Ḥassan al-Šhāb, 50, 83, 252
Ḥğerāt, Ḥsēn al-Gāsem, 77, 83, 91, 98, 250–54, 257, 270
al-Ḫnefes, Ḥassan, 58
al-Ḫnefes, Ṣāleḥ al-Ḥassan, 58–59, 77–78, 82–83, 91
Hockett, Charles F., 278, 314
Hopen, C. Edward, 40, 314
Hopkins, Lister G., 69, 314
Horowitz, Dan, 96, 314
Horwitz, Jacob Kalman, 13, 34, 314
Horwitz, Shmuel, 102, 314
Howell, Paul P., 46, 314
Ḥūrān, 19–20
al-Ḥusayni clan, 45, 57
al-Ḥusayni, al-Ḥaǧǧ Amīn, 45, 57
Hütteroth, Wolf-Dieter, 12, 315

I'billin, 28, 31, 66–67, 99, 110, 117, 142, 169, 199, 211, 264, 290
Ibrāhīm Pasha, 13–14
'iltizām, 27
intifāḍa, 276
intergenerational relations, 100, 133, 137, 176–80, 187–88, 224
Irons, William G., 40, 315
Israel. Central Bureau of Statistics (Isr. CBS), 87, 93, 99, 101–2, 104–5, 107–8, 111–15, 119, 124, 129, 135, 139–40, 148, 153, 160–61, 196, 251, 276, 291, 295, 297, 315–16
Israel. Inspector General of Elections (Isr. IGE), 238, 249–50, 260, 270, 298, 305, 316
Israel. Laws, Statutes, etc. (Isr. Laws), 104, 137, 140, 169, 198, 296, 316
Israel. Ministry of Information (Isr. MI), 238, 305, 316
Israel Defense Army (IDA), 76–78, 82, 89, 103–6, 110, 112–13, 116, 135, 138–39, 160, 173, 177, 185, 225–26, 228–31, 240, 243–45, 254–55, 267, 272, 300–301
Israel Electric Corporation (IEC), 148, 254
Israel Land Administration (ILA), 110, 119, 122, 124, 128, 140, 143, 147, 149, 160, 162, 218, 243, 250, 256, 264, 271–72, 296–97, 303
Israel Police, 106, 112–13, 222, 302
Israel Survey, 7, 10, 21, 86, 90, 316
Israel Workers List (*RaFI*), 242, 258–59, 269
Israel Workers Party, Israeli Labour Party (*MaPaI*), 81, 84, 217, 219–20, 226, 237–38, 249–50, 252, 269, 272, 316

Ğabr Mu'addī, 238–39, 257–61, 265, 272
Jakubowska, Longina A., 104, 316
Ğawāsreh, 8, 175, 210, 252
Jewish Agency, 128
Jewish National Fund (JNF), 52, 89, 97, 103, 108, 128, 140, 196, 296
ğhāz (dowery), 103
Ğisr al-Zarqa, 296
Ğūlis, 225, 301

Kafr Manda, 30, 32–33, 38, 57, 59, 66–67, 85, 117, 142, 256
Kafr Qara', 236, 240
Kafr Qāsim, 104, 236
Kafr Yāsīf, 225, 301
Katakura, Motoko, 296, 316
Kawkab Abū al-Hejā', 28, 32, 57, 66–67
Kfar Zeytim, 128
Kibbutzim, 126
Kiryat Shmonah, 8, 128
Kishon River (*nahar al muqutta'*), 20, 22
Kitchner, H.H., 9, 20, 22, 27–28, 30–33, 79, 290, 311
Klima, George J., 202–3, 317
Klinov-Malul, Ruth, 51, 55, 80, 87–89, 93–94, 96, 101, 313, 317
Knesset (of Israel), 226, 238–42, 247, 249–50, 257–61, 266, 269–70, 272, 297–98
Konner, Melvin, 70, 317
Kressel, Gideon M., 60, 103, 108, 139–40, 189, 198, 317
Kupāt Ḫolim (HMO), 151, 196, 258
Kuznetzova, V.G., 46, 308

Lağa', 19, 26, 56, 278
land cultivation contracts, 117–18
Land Ordinance of 1921, 303
Land Registry, 51
Landau, Jacob M., 43, 239, 241, 250–51, 257–61, 269, 272, 305, 317
"landless Arabs," 296
Lattimore, Owen, 40, 317
League of Nations, 46
Levy, Emanuel, 80, 93, 317
Levy, Reuben, 87, 115, 317
Lewis, Bernard, 11–12, 310, 317
Lienhardt, Godfrey, 191, 317
Likud, 249, 253–58, 260, 267, 270–72, 304
Little Triangle, 235–36, 240, 244, 246, 256–57
Lissak, Moshe, 96, 314

Ma'ariv, 272, 276, 298, 306, 317
Madina, Maan Z., 40, 87, 318
MafDaL. *See* National Religious Party
Maḥāmīd, 50, 175, 192, 210, 252, 256, 270
mahr (*feḏ*), 36, 40, 100, 103, 139, 167, 179, 182, 188, 191, 213
Mağdal Šams, 227
male-female dynamics, 138, 167–68, 177, 179, 187
Ma'oz, Moshe, 12–15, 25, 318
MaPaI. *See* Israel Workers Party
MaPaM. *See* United Workers Party
MaQI. *See* Communist Party of Israel
marriage, 23–25, 36–40, 48, 64–68, 91, 100, 103, 107, 116, 139, 155–57, 181–82, 184–86, 188–95, 197, 199, 201–2, 209, 212–13, 222, 280
Marx, Emanuel, 40, 60, 80, 115, 127, 197, 214, 267, 303, 318
Masa'īd, 8, 91, 140, 148, 175, 192, 194, 205–6, 211, 273
mawāt, 303
Mauss, Marcel, 84, 318
Mazori, Dalia, 270, 318
Medding, Peter Y., 96, 139, 223, 237, 262–63, 270, 318
Meggido (*lağğūn*), 20
Meizles, Moshe, 298, 318
Member of Knesset (MK), 82, 91, 219, 226–28, 237–41, 244, 250, 252, 257–61, 269, 272, 297–98
Mernissi, Fatima, 107, 177, 318
Mikmān, 6, 31, 34, 37, 53–54, 61, 67, 76–78, 82–83, 89, 91–92, 98–101, 103, 117, 123, 136, 138–39, 141–42, 149, 160, 163, 168–69, 172, 180, 191, 196, 206, 210, 243, 251–53, 255–56, 270, 272–73, 276

Military Government (MG), 75, 80–85, 88, 91–93, 95–98, 100–101, 104, 108, 114, 128, 141–42, 169, 172, 179–80, 216–20, 223, 225–26, 237, 239, 250, 252, 264, 268–69, 296–98, 303–4, 306
Ministry of Agriculture, 94, 101, 121, 123–24, 126–29, 135, 147, 218, 264, 268, 298–99
Minorities' Brigade (MBr), 228
Minorities' Unit (MU), 225–27, 229
miri, 303
Miron, Mikhal, 271, 318
Mohsen, Safia K., 23, 318
Montagne, Robert, 296, 319
Morag, Amotz, 51, 94, 319
Mother and Child Clinic, 142, 148, 155, 166
Mt. 'Atzmon (*ǧabel Daydabe*), 9, 28, 31, 77
Mt. Tabor, 98
Mt. Ṭur'ān, 33
Muḥammad 'Ali, 13
muḫtār (*maḫatīr*, pl.; *ne'emān*), 4, 46, 50, 57, 69, 76–85, 89, 91–92, 96, 98, 110, 175, 210, 217, 220, 264, 267–68, 298
multi-resource extraction, 134, 278
Musil, Alois, 197, 319

naḥal tzipporī (*wādi* al-Malik), 30–31, 53
NaḤaL, 89
Nahalal, 77–78, 257
Naḥf, 260
Nahmani, Yosef, 89, 91, 296
al-Našāšībi clan, 45, 57
al-Nāṣir, Gamāl 'Abd, 250
national insurance, 136, 138, 140, 142, 155, 269, 298
National Religious Party (*MafDaL*), 180, 239–40, 249, 251–55, 257, 260, 267, 269, 270, 276, 298, 305
National Water Company (*Mekorot*), 97, 146
Nature Reserves Authority (NRA), 271
Nazareth, 9, 11, 28, 38, 48, 51, 59, 61, 69–70, 76, 83, 89, 92–93, 99–100, 103, 108, 122, 129, 131, 143, 149, 151–52, 155–56, 162, 169, 177–78, 199, 218, 222, 234, 236, 238, 240, 242, 244, 246, 257–59, 261–64, 266, 299, 301, 305
Nelson, Cynthia, 23, 319
New Communist List (*RaQaH*), 237–39, 241, 244, 249–51, 253, 255, 257–60, 263, 270, 276, 298, 301, 305–6
New York Times, 27, 226, 228, 319
Northern Supreme Bedouin Committee (NSBC), 143, 148, 218, 242–43, 253, 270, 272, 297
nzaleh, 63, 118

Obermeyer, G.J., 282–83, 319
Occupied Enemy Territory Administration (OETA), 45, 94
Oliphant, Laurence, 27–28, 40, 54, 56, 319
Oppenheim, Max A.S. Freeherr von, 19, 26, 30, 32, 51, 70, 319
Oppenheimer, Jonathan W.S., 226, 228, 252, 255, 300, 319

Orni, Efraim, 52, 319
Ottoman, 3, 5, 6, 11–15, 27, 40, 43–44, 46, 51, 54, 61, 69, 94, 278, 281, 284

Palestine. Census Office (Pls. Census), 46, 51–52, 63, 69–71, 114, 319
Palestine. Department of Forests (Pls. Forests), 55, 320
Palestine. Survey of Palestine (Pls. Survey), 47, 67, 69, 320
Palestine, Government of Palestine (Pls. Gov.), 51–52, 79, 93–94, 114–15, 296, 303, 320
Palestine Exploration Fund (PEF), 29
Palestine Jewish Colonization Association (PJCA), 45, 296
Palestine Liberation Organization (PLO), 105, 233
Palestine Police, 34, 44, 48–50, 56, 69
Palestine Rescue Army (PRA), 75–78
PalMaH (*Plugot Maḥatz*), 59
parliamentary elections, 80, 174, 248, 297
patronage, 4, 196, 217, 223, 235, 237, 242–44
peasants (*fellāḥīn*), 6, 12, 14–15, 22–23, 30, 32–34, 38, 43, 45, 51–53, 58, 62, 67, 71, 75, 85, 94, 97, 107, 116, 118–19, 126, 130, 133, 139–40, 146, 169, 179, 185, 190, 198, 218, 226, 231, 233–35, 241–42, 246, 259, 266, 273, 279, 302
peddlers, 150
Peled, Rafi, 24, 309
Peters, Emrys, 191, 320
population dynamics, 152
Porath, Yehoshua, 15, 44–45, 52, 57–58, 76, 320
Progress and Development List (PD), 257

qānūnnāme (Civil Code), 12
al-Qāwuqǧi, Fawzi, 75–77

Rahat, Menahem, 270, 318
Ramlāt, 50, 69, 92, 103, 140, 148, 175, 205, 210, 246, 252–53, 255–56, 267, 273, 279
Randolph, Richard R., 60, 197, 320
Rappaport, Roy A., 132, 320
RaQaH. *See* New Communist List
Rekhes, Elie, 169, 171, 173, 320
relays, 31, 215, 217, 282–83
resentment groups, 247, 251, 253–54, 256
Rosenfeld, Henry, 133, 189, 320
Royal Air Force (RAF), 52
Rummāneh, 30–32, 38, 57, 64, 67

Safad, 75, 98, 250
Ṣafūriyeh, 32, 40, 52–53, 56–57, 59, 63, 66, 70, 76, 78, 84, 94, 188, 191, 278–79, 290. *See also* Tzipori
Sahlins, Marshall D., 24, 120, 133–35, 202, 246, 267, 280, 297, 302, 320
Said, Edward W., 136, 320
Sağūr, 260
Saḫnīn (village), 33, 85, 191, 211, 225, 233, 257, 269, 290

Ṣāleḥ al-Šibl, 53, 58, 69
Sama'neh, 8, 91, 148, 162, 175, 194, 254
Samrāt, 8, 34, 38, 147–48, 162, 175, 207–8, 210, 212
sanğaq of 'Akā (Acre), 14, 20–21
sanğaq of *lağğūn*, 13
Šarī'a, 40, 111, 114, 116, 213, 264
Ṣawālḥah, 8, 19–20, 23, 31, 36–40, 50–51, 53–54, 59, 64, 66–68, 70, 77–78, 82–83, 91–92, 98–99, 110–11, 113, 117, 162, 175, 191, 193–96, 199, 206, 209–11, 246–52, 272–73
Sawwaf, Husni, 11, 34, 321
Schumacher, G., 30, 70, 321
sedentarization, 3–4, 110, 133–34, 141–42, 148, 152, 156, 168, 196, 206, 210, 214–15, 239, 242, 256, 270, 296–98
Segev, 89, 196
segmentary lineage organization, 6, 64, 98, 133, 190, 201–2, 216, 280
Sela', Moshe, 303, 318
senior citizens' and widows' pensions, 136–37
Šfā'amr, 6, 9, 28, 53, 58, 61, 67, 70
Shamir, Shimon, 43, 321
šarikah, 118, 140
Sharon, Ariel, 241, 255, 266, 270–71
Sharon, Moshe, 11–15, 22, 321
Sharon, Plain of, 9, 23, 40
Shfar'am, 6, 9, 77, 91, 93, 98–99, 101, 103, 117, 138–40, 149, 151, 169, 177, 211, 225, 233, 246, 261
Sheikh Abreik, 27, 58
Shim'oni, Ya'aqov, 43–45, 321
Shlomtzion, 249, 253, 255–57, 271
Shmueli, Avshalom, 24, 94, 163, 178, 197, 296, 321
Silat al-Ẓahr, 57
Smith, C. Gordon, 14–15, 321
Smith, M.G., 201, 281, 321
Southern Supreme Bedouin Committee (SSBC), 297
Standard of Living, 69, 135–36, 157, 179
Stenning, Derrick J., 40, 321
ṣulḥa (peace arbitration), 31–32, 58–59, 94, 206, 211, 213, 220, 225, 233–37, 268, 302
Sultan Abdulmajid, 13, 27, 43
Sursuk (or Sursock), 27, 34
Syria, 11–13, 19, 32, 44, 56, 58, 227

Ṭa'awāneh, 66–67, 98, 110–11, 147–48, 162, 175, 192–95, 205–8, 210–12, 266
Ṭababšeh, 24, 31–32, 39, 58
Tadmor, C., 80, 93, 322
Tel al-Šummām (Tel Šem), 6, 19, 20–23, 25–27, 31, 40, 278
tithe, 51, 56
Tnuva, 99, 126, 131, 140
Tobacco Commission, 121–22
Toffler, Alvin, 280, 322
Trans-Jordan Frontier Force, 52
Tribal Code (*ganūn al-'aša'īr*), 19, 40, 302
tribute, protection fee (*ḫawa*), 14, 25, 32, 56, 269, 282
Ṭubās, 55, 70
Ṭur'ān, *ṭur'ān*, 70, 235
Ṭurabāy, 13
Tzipori, 84

ulād 'Aḥmed, 210
ulād 'abd al-Sleymān, 207, 210
Umm al-Ġanam, *umm al-ġanam*, 70, 296
Umm al-Zīnāt, 8, 110, 128–29, 132, 140, 161, 242
United Arab List (UAL), 174, 192, 249, 250, 252, 256–64, 266, 272, 304
United Workers Party (*MaPaM*), 238, 249, 258, 260

Valley of Beit Netofah (*sahel baṭṭūf*), 9, 28, 30, 33, 43, 52–53, 55, 85, 97–98, 117
Valley of Beisan (Beyt She'an), 56, 92, 219, 261
Valley of Jezreel (Izra'el, Marğ ibn 'Amr), 19–20, 22, 33, 40, 53, 215, 261
Valley of Saḫnīn (Sahel Saḫnīn), 28, 30, 33, 52, 60, 85
Veicmanas, B., 55, 322
Veterinary Service, 124–25
Via Maris, 9, 20
vilāyet Bayrūt, 3, 12
vilāyet of Sayda (Sidon), 43
Vincent, Joan, 281, 300, 322
Vinogradov, Amal R., 43, 283, 322
Volney, Constantin F.C., Comte de, 12–13, 22, 322

wādi al-Ḫaldiyeh, 53
wādi al-Malik. *See naḥal tzipporī*
wādi al-Mzagga, 8, 98, 110, 128–29, 132, 161
wādi I'billin, 28, 31, 99
wādi Salāmeh, 78
Warriner, Doreen, 52, 114, 322
Watson, William, 46, 322
weddings, 30, 59, 61, 70, 100, 176, 187, 214
Winter, Michael, 171, 322
Wolf, Eric R., 173, 283, 322
Worthman, Carol, 70, 317
Wright, Henry T., 216, 322

Yedi'ot Aharonot, 298, 323
Yirka, 238, 265
Yodfāt, 5, 28, 142, 196. *See also* Ḫirbet Ğfāt

Ẓahara, 5–6, 8, 24–25, 27–28, 30–34, 36, 38, 40, 46, 54–55, 57–59, 61, 66–67, 69, 76–78, 81–83, 85–87, 89, 91–92, 98–99, 101, 128, 138, 142–43, 147, 161–63, 167, 169, 196, 278, 290, 296
al-Zaḥālgah, Ḥamzah Sa'ad, 240, 242
Ẓāhir al-'Umar, 13
Zaïd, Alexander, 45, 58, 75–77
Zohar, Ezra, 139, 223, 323
Zohary, Michael, 22, 28, 323
al-Zu'abī, Sayf al-Dīn, 238–39, 246, 257–61, 265, 269, 272
Zu'bīyeh, 57, 246